AF550771

JOURNAL OF A CAVALRY OFFICER; INCLUDING THE MEMORABLE SIKH CAMPAIGN OF 1845-1846

First published 1854
This edition published by Lector House in 2023

ISBN: 978-93-5800-739-8
Edition copyright © 2023 by Lector House LLP
All rights reserved under the International Copyright Conventions.

Every possible effort has been made to ensure that the information contained in this book is accurate at the time of going to press and the publisher cannot accept responsibility for any errors or omissions, however caused, in this unabridged, slightly corrected republication of the text of the first edition. No responsibility for loss or damage occasioned to any person, acting or refraining from action, as a result of the material in this publication can be accepted by the publisher. The publisher is not associated with any product or vendor mentioned in the book. The contents of this work are intended to further general scientific research, understanding and discussion, only. Readers should consult with a specialist, where appropriate.

No part of this publication may be reproduced, stored in a retrieval system, or transmitted, in any form, or by any means, electronic, mechanical, photocopying or otherwise, without the prior permission of the publisher.

Lector House LLP
Registered Office: H. No. 96, Block C, Tomar Colony,
Burari, Delhi – 110084, India
info@lectorhouse.com
www.lectorhouse.com

JOURNAL OF A CAVALRY OFFICER; INCLUDING THE MEMORABLE SIKH CAMPAIGN OF 1845-1846

WILLIAM WELLINGTON WATERLOO HUMBLEY

2023

LECTOR HOUSE LLP

JOURNAL OF A CAVALRY OFFICER;

INCLUDING THE MEMORABLE SIKH CAMPAIGN OF 1845-1846.

BY

W.W.W. HUMBLEY, M.A.

TRINITY COLLEGE, CAMBRIDGE;
FELLOW OF THE CAMBRIDGE PHILOSOPHICAL SOCIETY;
CAPTAIN, 9TH QUEEN'S ROYAL LANCERS.

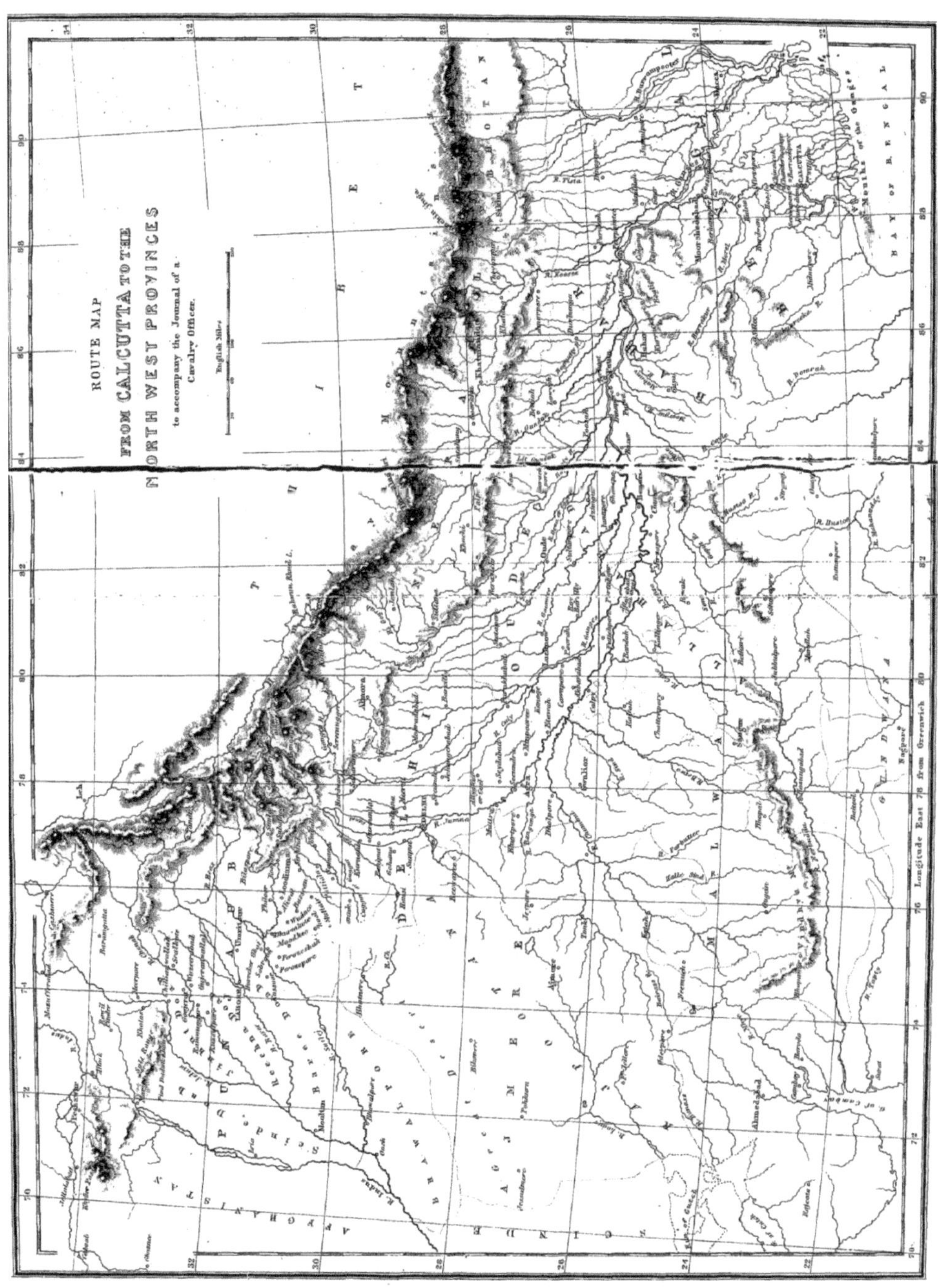

ROUTE MAP FROM CALCUTTA TO THE NORTH WEST PROVINCES TO ACCOMPANY THE JOURNAL OF A CAVALRY OFFICER.

Drawn and Engraved by E. Weller, 27 Duke Str[t] Bloomsbury

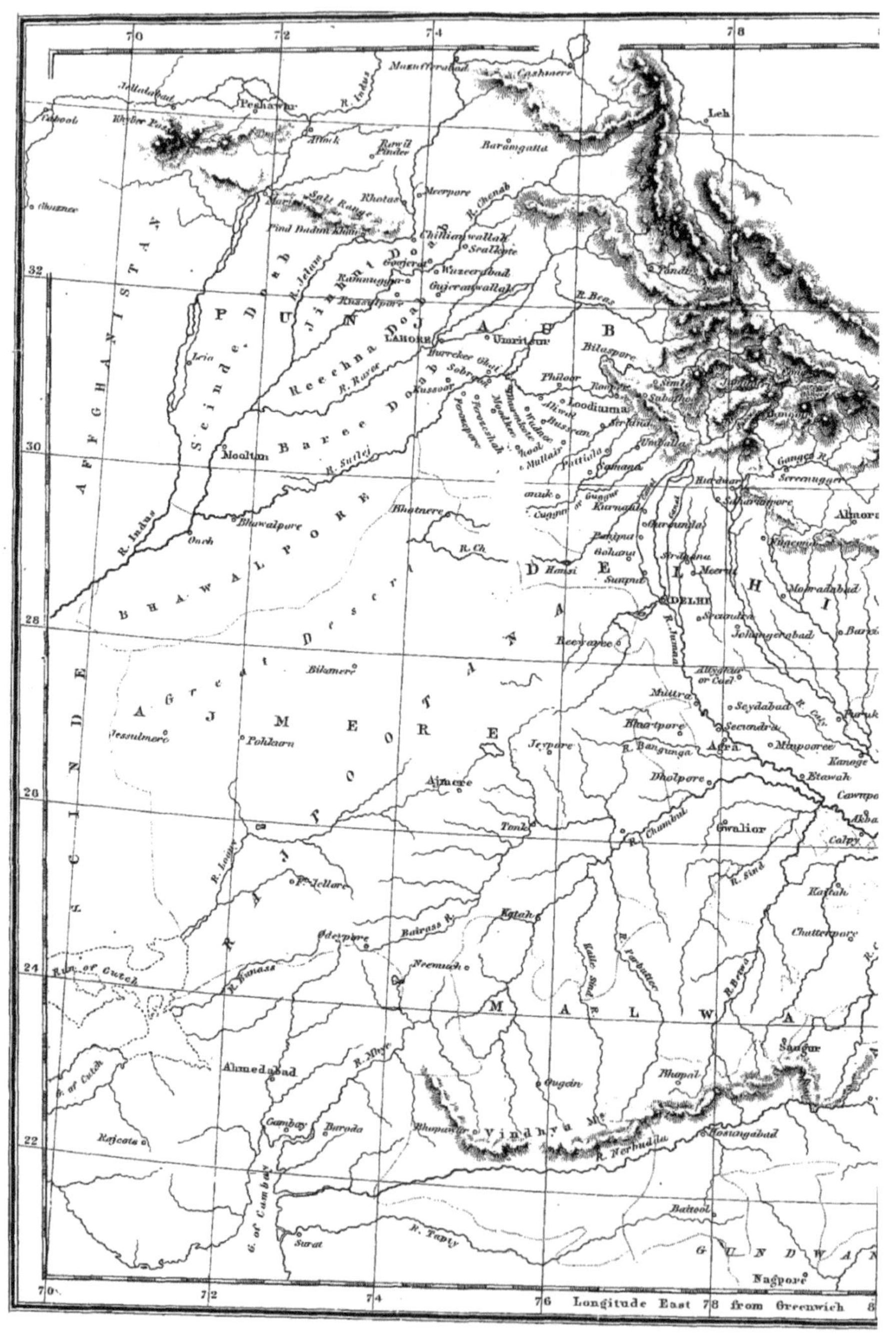

Route Map from Calcutta to the North West Provinces (*Enlarged - Left*)

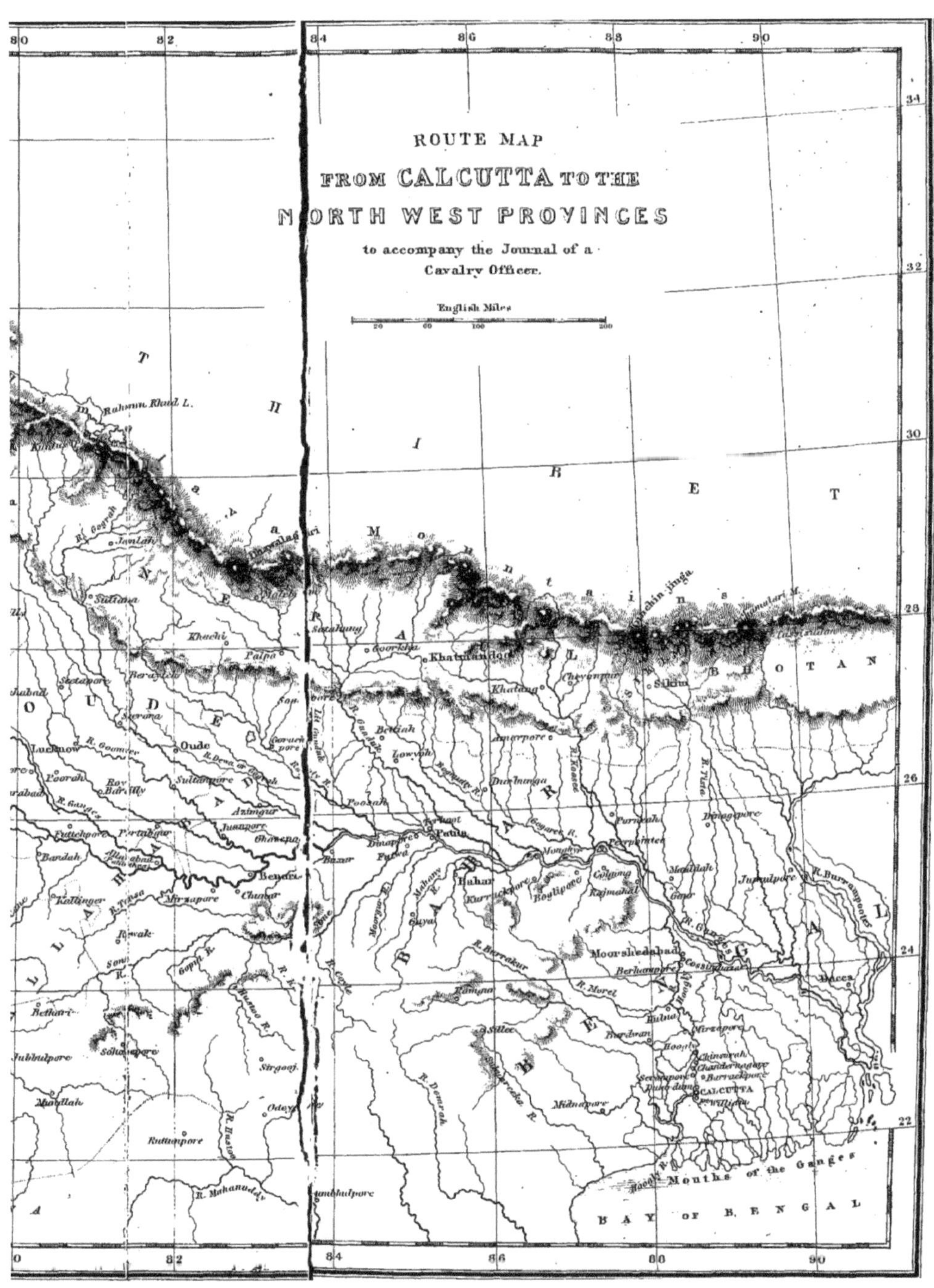

Route Map from Calcutta to the North West Provinces (*Enlarged - Right*)

TO
LORD STANLEY, M.P.

THIS VOLUME
IS
BY PERMISSION DEDICATED
AS A
SMALL TOKEN OF ADMIRATION AND REGARD,
BY HIS
FRIEND AND SERVANT,
THE AUTHOR.

CONTENTS

Page

Introduction. 1

CHAPTER I.

Voyage to India—Advantages of Sailing with Troops on Board—Regulations at Sea—March from Cawnpore to Meerut—Return from Nougawa Ghât to Meerut—March to Ferozepore—Cantonments at Kurnaul—Colonel Campbell's Force—Number of Cattle required on a March—Sunday—Rev. W.J. Whiting, M.A.—Distribution of Prize-Money—Advanced Guard—Governor-General—Major Broadfoot and Captain Nicolson—Suspicions of the Sikhs—Sir David Ochterlony—The Sikh Army—The Battle of Moodkee—Tej Singh. 7

CHAPTER II.

Colonel Campbell's Advance—Provisions required—Camp Followers—Samana—The Doabs—Gooroo Govind—The Akalees, their quoits—Sikhs attack Ahmed Shah—Maha Singh—Maharattas—General Thomas—Runjeet Singh—Holcar—Sir Charles Metcalfe—Ochterlony's Proclamation—The Akalees routed—Generals Allard and Ventura—Treaty with Runjeet—Runjeet's Army—Runjeet's Death—Shere Singh Murdered—Dhuleep Singh—Ajean Khan—Battle of Moodkee.. 20

CHAPTER III.

Nidampore—Christmas-day—Munsorepore—Kotla Mullair—Phurawallee—Bussean—Surrender of Wudnee—Cession of Ferozepore—Bhaga Poorana—False Alarms—Roree Bukkur—Sir John Littler—Sir H.M. Wheeler—Ferozeshah—Aliwal—Sikh Forces—British Forces—Sikh Entrenchment—Returns of Killed and Wounded—Sir H. Hardinge—Battle of Ferozeshah—Sudden Attack by Tej Singh—His Blunder—Appearance of a field of Battle—Fate of the Wounded. 33

CHAPTER IV.

Return to Bussean—Sir John Grey's Detachment—Battle of Assaye—Sindiah's Troops—Generals Allard and Ventura—General Lloyd's Observations on the Art of War—Tactics of the Sikhs—Runjeet Singh's Discipline—Sikh Artillery—Goojerat—Moodkee—Sir Joseph Thackwell—Bootawalla—Pontoons—Their Value to an Army—Great Rise in the Price of Food.. 43

CHAPTER V.

Hurrekee Ghât—Chain Bridles—Sir Thomas Dallas—Victory of Sir Harry Smith at Aliwal—Umballa—Preparations of the Sikhs—Capture of Dhurmkote—Loodianna—Runjoor Singh—Buddiwal—Sirdar Ajeet Singh—Invalids at Loodianna—The Pattiala Rajah—Alarm at Loodianna—Siege-train in Danger—Convoy inadequately protected—Sikh Artillery at Aliwal—Major Lawrenson—Singular Formation of the Sikh Infantry at Aliwal—16th Lancers—Desperation of the Sikhs—Colonel Cureton—Charge of Lancers—Marshal Marmont's Opinion—Sikhs evacuate Buddiwal—Rapid Movements of the Sikhs—Brigadiers Godby and Hicks. . . . 51

CHAPTER VI.

Richard Bond, the Messman—Sikh Grass-cutters—Choice of Camps—General Lloyd's Opinions—Lieut.-Colonel Irvine and Sir H. Maddock—Position at Sobraon—Brigadier E. Smith's Plan—Colonel Irvine's Plan—Goolab Singh's Policy—Sir Robert Dick's Division—Major-General Gilbert's Division—Sir Harry Smith's Division—Brigadier A. Campbell—Sir Joseph Thackwell—Brigadier Scott—British Batteries—Rockets—Sikh Batteries—Assault on the Sikh Entrenchments—Brigadier Stacey—Captain Cunningham's Account—The 10th Foot—Lieut.-Colonel Franks—Sikh Entrenchments stormed—Sirdar Sham Singh destroys the Pontoon—Sikh Retreat cut off—Great Loss of the Sikhs—Peace Principles inapplicable to India—Sikhs driven across the Sutlej—Tej Singh.. 58

CHAPTER VII.

The Advanced-guard cross the Sutlej—Burial of Sir Robert Dick—Bridge of Boats—Kussoor—Surrender of the Sikhs—Dhuleep Singh—Lulleanee—Lahore—Runjeet Singh's Monument—The Summer Palace—The Governor-General's Address. 72

CHAPTER VIII.

Review of the Army—Eastern Mode of Adoption—Cashmere assigned to Goolab Singh—Defeat of Affghan Cavalry—Major John

Cameron Campbell—Security of the North-west Frontier—Fertility of the Punjaub—Infantry introduced into the East—Hyder Ali's Notion of English Power—Runjeet's Craftiness—Improvement in the Punjaub—Dhuleep Singh professes Christianity—Dr. Login—Dhuleep baptized by the Rev. W.J. Jay—Dhuleep Singh's Sincerity. 78

CHAPTER IX.

The Army of the Sutlej broken up—Set out on a Tour—Dhool—Ferozepore—Grandeur of the Himalayas—Misri-Wala—Ferozeshah—Moodkee—Bhaga Poorana—Bussean—Phurewallee—Kotla Mullair—Munsorepore—Samana—Goelah—The River Cuggur—Pehoah—Khol—Kurnaul—Military Stations—Transport of Artillery—Ali Merdan's Canal—English Church—Malaria—Sir David Ochterlony—Gurounda—Minarets—Somalka—Paniput—Battles of Paniput—Baber—Ibrahim Lodi—Ahmed Shah—Defeat of the Maharattas—Nadir Shah—Capture of Delhi—Mahomed Shah—Troops engaged—Native Armies—Sunput—Change in the Weather.. 86

CHAPTER X.

Delhi—Mahmood of Ghuznee—Shah Jehan—Gates of Delhi—Mosques—The Palace—Hall of Audience—Chapel of Aurungzebe—The Gardens—The Jumma Musjeed—Khoonee Durwaza—Protestant Church—The Observatory—Tomb of Zufder Jung—The Cootub Minar—Allah-ud-Deen—Gheias-ud-Deen—Mahomed Togluk—Humayoon—Nizam-ud-Deen—The Cantonments—Mahomedan College—Delhi—Produce of Delhi—Shah Allum II.—Lord Lake—Monsieur Louis Bourgion—Sir David Ochterlony—Holcar—Lieutenant-Colonel W. Burn—Mr. E. Thornton—Allahabad—Marquis Wellesley—Defence of Delhi—Mahomedan Population—Colonel Ochterlony's good Generalship. . 102

CHAPTER XI.

Ghazenuggur—Secundra—Allyghur—The Fort—The Church—Monuments—The Gaol—Akbarabad—Meerun-ke-Serai—Kanoge—Tombs—Ancient Coins—Language of Kanoge—Supposed Site of Palibothra—Population of Benares—Streets of Benares—Singers and Musicians—Productions of Kanoge—Poorah—Cawnpore—Court Etiquette at Lucknow—Nawab of Oude—His Regal Rank—Military Depôt at Cawnpore—Saddlery Sirsole—Dâk Bungalows—Arapore—Lohunga—Allahabad. 110

CHAPTER XII.

Allahabad—Pilgrimages—The River Jumna—Hurdwar—Akbar—Allum II.—Fortifications—Inscriptions on Column—Military Depôt—Lieut.-Colonel A. Abbott, C.B.—Colonel Kyd discovers a Cave—Ancient Palibothra—Arrian's Account—Megasthenes—Dr. Adams—Heeren—Chundragupta—Patna—The Sacred Rivers—Bhaugulpore—The Mandara Hill—The Chundun—Palibothra—Rajmahal—Antiquity of Kanoge—Allahabad—Extent of Asiatic Cities—Mahomedan Invasion—Extent of Hindoostan. 117

CHAPTER XIII.

Steamers on the Ganges—Native Pilots—Course of the River—Mr. Sims proposes Shields to the Banks—Shoals—Tributary Streams—Rapids—The Jumna—Mirzapore—Benares—Trimbuckjee Danglia—Chunar—Sultanpore. 129

CHAPTER XIV.

Benares—Bathing in the Ganges—Water-carrying by Women—Extent and Population of Benares—Attempted Tax—Mosque of Aurungzebe—Observatory of Rajah Jey Singh—Bazaars—Jewellery—Cultivation of Sugar—Secrole—Murder of Mr. Cherry—State Prisoners—The Maharannee of Lahore. 136

CHAPTER XV.

Ghazepore—The Opium Trade—Marquis Cornwallis's Mausoleum—Sand-banks—Buxar—Cossim-Ali-Khan—Sir Hector Munro—Battle of Buxar—Nawab of Oude—Emperor of Delhi—Revelgunge—The Sonus—The Ganges and Jumna—The Indus—The Berhampooter—Arrian—Dr. Alexander Adam—Dinapore—Captain Strachan—Bankipore—H.M. 16th Lancers—Deegah—Grain Golah—Earl of Munster—Patna—Buildings of Patna—Population of Benares—Magistrates—E. I. Company's Charter—Products of Patna—Walter Reinhard—Snowy Mountains—Tirhoot—Juggernauth—Gyah Proper—Cave of Nugur-jenee—Sir Charles Wilkins—Futwa—Phoolbarea—Bar—Beggars. 143

CHAPTER XVI.

Monghyr—Wells of Seetacoond—The Fort of Monghyr—Storms on the Ganges—Cossim Ali Khan—Monghyr the Birmingham of India—Employment of Women—The Gaol—A Sacred Bathing-place—Bhaugulpore—Its Population—Hill Rangers—The Bheels—Mr. Cleveland—Lieut.-Colonel Tod—Colonel Francklin—Colgong—The Jungheera Rocks—The Fakeers—The Rajmahal Hills—Sickreegullee—Boatmen of the Ganges—Rajmahal—Ruins of Gour—The Bhaugurетty—Soottee—The Sunderbunds—Bogwangola—Jungepore. 154

CHAPTER XVII.

Moorshedabad—Cossimbazar—"Eina Mahal"—The Nawab Cowar Krishnath Roy—"Snake-boats"—Population of Moorshedabad—Berhampore—Ivory and Silk Manufactures—Kulna—The Tidal-bore—English Factory at Kulna—Hoogly—Chinsurah—Chandernagore—Ishapore—Barrackpore —Serampore—Dum-Dum—Garden Reach—Calcutta. 164

CHAPTER XVIII.

Project of a Railway to Calcutta—Calcutta, a Six Months' Trip from England—The Strand Road—The Mint—Professor Weidemann—The Strand Mills—The General Post Office—Custom House—Auditor General's Office—Military Board—The Commissariat—The Ice House—Metcalfe Hall—The Public Library—Bank of Bengal—The Oriental Bank—Indian Failures—Chandpaul Ghât—Baboo Ghât—Docks of Howrah—Prinsep's Ghât—Kidderpore Ghât—Fort William—Mir Jaffier—Arsenal—Chowringhee Road—Ochterlony Monument—Government House—Entertainments at Government House—Policy of Marquis Wellesley—Hotels at Calcutta—Theatricals—The Town Hall—Concerts—Fancy Fairs—The Mayor's Court—Newspapers—Merchants—Agency Business—Railways—Asiatic Society—Martinière Charity—College of Fort William—Haileybury College—Military Seminary at Addiscombe—Colleges—Schools—Mesmeric Hospital—Chloroform—Sailors' Home—Alms Houses—Masonic Lodges—Botanical Garden—Charter of 1834—Lunatic Asylums—Law Courts—Police Office—Provident Funds. 171

APPENDIX.

I. The Treaty with Lahore of 1809. 205

II. Sir David Ochterlony's Proclamation of 1809. 206

III. General Thomas's Opinion of Artillery. 206

IV. The Treaty with Lahore of 1806. 207

V. Proclamation of Protection to Cis Sutlej States against Lahore of 1809. 208

VI. Proclamation of Protection to Cis Sutlej States against one another of 1811. 209

VII. Indus Navigation Treaty of 1832. 210
VIII. Declaration of War of 1845.. 214
IX. Services of Captain Humbley, Rifle Brigade.. 215
X. Inscription on Colonel Cureton's Monument. 216
XI. Official Despatches. 217
XII. The late Major-General Sir Robert Henry Dick. 233
XIII. Proclamation of Peace. 234
XIV. First Treaty with Lahore of 1846.. 235
Supplementary Articles to the First Treaty with Lahore of 1846.. . . . 238
XV. Punchees or Punchayets. 239
XVI. Treaty with Goolab Singh of 1846.. 240
XVII. Second Treaty with Lahore of 1846. 241
XVIII. Notification. 244
XIX. Supply of Horses in India. 246
XX. Revenue of the Emperor of Delhi. 246
XXI. Notice of Dr. James, Bishop of Calcutta. 247
XXII. Ancient Scriptural Customs. 247

JOURNAL
OF
A CAVALRY OFFICER IN INDIA.

INTRODUCTION.

The remark has often been made, that India is but little known to persons in England and on the continent of Europe. That there is ample ground for such a remark none can deny. For, whether we consider its vast territorial extent, covering an area of upwards of a million of square miles, with a population of more than 150 millions; its commercial wealth and enterprise, from the remotest ages of antiquity, and its immense natural resources; or, whether we regard India in a more intimate point of view, as forming an integral part of our own dominions, owing allegiance to one sovereign ruler, bound up with us by social relations and family ties, and consider what an El Dorado it has proved to the British empire for upwards of two centuries and a half; it is indeed a matter of no small surprise, that India should be so little, and so imperfectly, known by us.

We can scarcely comprehend how, until recently, the Emperor of China and his subjects should have looked upon the celestial empire as the most important in the world; but it is yet more astonishing that we, to whom the whole world lies open, should be contented to remain in ignorance of what it is so obviously our interest to understand.

Nearly six centuries have elapsed since that enterprising Venetian, Marco Polo, first visited India, and revealed to Europe the treasures of the Eastern Hemisphere; nay, they are familiar to us from the earliest records of the sacred writers; and, in later ages, Herodotus and other Greek authors dwelt upon the wonders of the East, its history, its resources, and its races. It is true that Marco Polo gained little credit for the marvels he related; but, we must bear in mind that he did not always speak from personal observation: he not only noted down what he saw, but eagerly collected all the information which he could obtain respecting those regions which he was unable to visit himself. His "Maraviglie del Mondo da lui descritte" were sneered at and discredited by many, in former times, as the visions of an enthusiast. People, indeed, believed in the existence of such cities as Agra and Delhi, because it was corroborated by the Chinese and Arabic maps which he brought home; while the fact of there being such an individual as the Great Mogul, was demonstrated by the painted representation of his Sublime Majesty on the royal court cards, which are supposed to have been then first introduced. More accurate investigations, however, have proved his veracity; and the researches of Klaproth, and other distinguished travellers, of modern times, have amply verified the truth of his statements.

The discredit at first thrown upon Marco Polo's narratives, may, in a great measure, be attributed to the Jesuit missionaries in India and China, who followed in his track, and who, while they availed themselves of the valuable information which he had supplied, scrupled not to add the most unblushing and incredible falsehoods. These Jesuits, though the most learned men of their time, composed a class of writers whose object it was to appear to surpass all other European travellers in information; and who sought to acquire an ascendancy in Asiatic countries, for the benefit of their master, the Pope, and the sovereigns of the European States.

The maps brought home by Marco Polo, and the information which he communicated, proved invaluable to the Pope's missionaries, and to the Venetian and Portuguese traders and navigators who succeeded him, and aided the gallant Vasco di Gama in discovering the passage to India by the Cape of Good Hope. The Jesuits, however, did not make full use of the advantages which they possessed; for, while employed in constructing their excellent map of the Empire of China, which gained them free access to every part, they lost an opportunity for investigating and describing its natural productions, which might never have occurred again, but for the present movement in China. In the reign of Kang-hi they obtained permission to establish a college for the promotion of Christianity; but his successor regarded the institution with different feelings; and, being jealous of the influence which it was calculated to produce, ordered it to be broken up, and thus deprived us of the means of obtaining much valuable information.

Among the few Oriental works which modern scholars have been able to obtain, the only one that has as yet been translated into English, from the Sanscrit, is, a History of the Kings of Cashmere, down to the Mahomedan conquest, entitled, "Raja Tarengini," published in 1835.

It was not till about seventy years ago, during the war with Hyder Ali, and the subsequent hostilities between the sovereigns of Mysore, from 1792 to 1799, that the English became acquainted with the state of Southern India; when (to our shame be it spoken) the capture at Seringapatam of the Sultan's library, revealed the fact of an extensive political correspondence with Napoleon Bonaparte, the Directory, and the French governor of the Isle of France; also with the Shah of Persia, with Shah Zeman of Affghanistan, the Maharattas, and many other native princes of India.

With so many salient points of tangible danger to defend, it might have been expected that the Government of India would have employed—as Russia does, and as France has ever done—competent officers in their service to travel in Persia, Afghanistan, and, in fact, in all the countries from whence the danger of an invasion was to be apprehended: especially as it was well known that Zeman Shah of Affghanistan had, in 1796, '97, and '98, made attempts to invade India.

Foreigners have asked the question: "How is it that you English, who have so long possessed a considerable portion of India, know so little of that country, that, in our day, Baron Humboldt, a foreigner, should contemplate a visit to India, to explore the Himalaya mountains?" It is true, that nearly forty years ago, Lieutenant Webb and others had ascertained that the highest peak was about 27,000 feet above the level of the sea, and that it was the loftiest in the world; but doubts were expressed as to the amount of scientific knowledge possessed by a Bengal subaltern. Captain Fraser and other Englishmen have since visited those snowy regions; but it still remains to be seen what enterprising nation will equip an expedition to explore the character and resources of India.

That the English, as a commercial nation, have not as yet ascertained all the products of India, is a matter of yet greater astonishment to all foreign travellers. It is a fact, that the existence of that useful article, coal, has only been known within the last few years; and the same may be said in regard to other natural productions. The truth is, that, till the year 1814, the East India Company, who possessed the exclusive right of trade within the limits prescribed by their Charter of 1660, were the chief merchants of India; and their investments were almost wholly confined to the exportation of silk, and the usual cargoes of tea from China. It is to private enterprise that we are indebted for the commerce in indigo, sugar, and other articles of modern exportation; till the free trade with China, since the year 1834, opened up a more extended commerce.

Since that period, both India and China have become better known to us; and the wars in the latter country have naturally made us acquainted with the eastern portions of its vast dominions.

It cannot, however, be expected that persons pursuing commercial speculations should have leisure or inclination to write on Indian subjects, beyond the facts relating to their own traffic. Some men will not even take the pains to learn the language of the people, but trust to such natives as speak English. Though some of these gentlemen have certainly acquired a colloquial knowledge of the language, and made themselves acquainted with the localities in their immediate vicinity—yet, as they have never travelled much in India, their statements are of course imperfect and superficial. It is from the pen of the civil, military, and other servants of the East India Company, and from officers in Her Majesty's service, that we must look for accounts descriptive of different parts of India, and of the various tribes and races of its inhabitants.

The removal of the army from place to place, affords an observant officer not only an opportunity of investigating the geological formation, natural history, and productions of the country, but also gives him great facilities for studying the history, religion, and civilization of the people, from the various monuments and inscriptions, both ancient and modern, which lie on his route.

The rapid extension of our Eastern empire since our first occupation of Hindoostan may, in some measure, account for our imperfect acquaintance with the productions and natural resources of the several great Presidencies under our jurisdiction at the present day. Great Britain, in self-defence, rather than from choice, or from a policy of self-aggrandizement, such as she might reasonably be excused in adopting, has been forced to extend her sway, and to annex numerous native territories; for a long time, indeed, she only assumed a passive military tenure of dominions thus acquired, while her natural reluctance to obtrude or infringe upon the rights and prerogatives of others has not only influenced her general policy, but even led her subjects invariably to observe the same caution in indulging their natural bent for investigation and discovery. This, coupled with an apprehension for personal safety, and a want of confidence in native integrity and honour, has greatly impeded a free and frequent intercourse, and damped the ardour of enterprising and scientific enquiry.

The well-known faithlessness of the native character, and the internal disaffection existing among various tribes, have also tended to interrupt or preclude the possibility of travelling about among the people, for the purpose of investigating their manners and customs, and the general state of the country.

The wars with the Sikhs afforded many opportunities of becoming practically acquainted with the perfidy and duplicity of the natives. The treachery of Tej Singh at the battle of Ferozeshah, the artful and wily conduct of Goolab Singh, in his negotiations with the Maharannee and the British, and the subsequent perfidy of our professed friend and ally, Shere Singh, at the siege of Mooltan, where he caused the defection of the Sikh army from the British to Moolraj, and thereby prevented our taking the fortress, are indisputable proofs of this trait. It is a painful peculiarity in the Oriental character, which will ever stamp it in the eyes of a European with an indelible stigma. This inherent vice, and our cognizance of it, have hitherto checked, and will continue to check, the ardour of all enquiry and enterprise, even where pecuniary gain, and still more, scientific information, are the objects in view.

We may also refer to the history of Moolraj, his confederates, and their diabolical schemes; but, thanks to an over-ruling Providence, the arch-traitor and his base accomplices were defeated; their designs were marred, and fell upon themselves. Truly it is said, "Man proposes, but God disposes." Who could have foreseen or anticipated the results of the deliberations within the walls of Mooltan? Who could have foretold that Moolraj would be dethroned and immured in a British prison, and his rich and extensive territories revert to a British Queen? His treachery, however, led to the wanton murder of two of our officers, and to an immense sacrifice of the lives, both of natives and Europeans.

Our unwillingness to invade, or to annex to the British dominions, even partial portions of frontier countries, virtually in our possession before, has proved, as we have seen, a great barrier to enterprising researches; and our officers, generally speaking, had more work upon their hands, than allowed of much leisure or inclination for scientific expeditions into adjacent, and still less into more distant localities. We feel justified in offering this explanation, in order to do away with the reproaches to which the civil and military officers in India, have been subjected in regard to this question.

With respect to the Punjaub, our Government was perfectly justified in its annexation; and the act was quite consistent with wise policy, and compatible with our previous and general mode of dealing with Indian rulers. No other power except Great Britain would so long have abstained from punishing a local authority, which had so shamefully and recklessly disregarded and violated its own solemn pledges and engagements, upon the faith of which, and which only, the rule of the Sikhs rested and eventually depended. Great Britain ought to have annexed this country long before, even as early as 1845. She relied on the gratitude and fidelity of the Sikh rulers, and was betrayed and disappointed.

What is applicable in one case, as in that of the Punjaub, may apply equally to all or any of our Indian acquisitions, and account, in a great measure, for our still imperfect knowledge of the products and vast resources of India.

We will not conceal from ourselves, nor leave the public in ignorance of the fact, that while all classes at home are unanimous as to the benefit and vast importance of steam communication, the case is far otherwise in India. The imperative necessity for improvement in facilitating the means of communication in the interior of India, by means of roads, bridges, canals, railways and river navigation, has not obtained that fair share of attention and support which the past and future wants of India, her products, resources, and trade demand. These reforms are only in their infancy. India, strange to say, is still as backward as Turkey in these respects. It is extraordinary that in a country like India, and under such a rule as the British, no line of railway should have been laid down till the year 1851, when the attempt was made in the short line from Bombay.

Any contributions, however scanty, respecting India will be better appreciated now that a more judicious system has been adopted with regard to the qualification of candidates for Indian affairs. There are few families who have not friends and relations in some part of India, and these are now beginning to give their attention to subjects bearing upon its history, its people, products, institutions, and religion.

If we have been remiss in the past, and of this there is no question, we must endeavour, in the future, to regain our credit as a nation by progressive reform, and the promotion of civilization. India and her riches, her mountains of light and her hills of gold, must not blind us to our duties, nor cause us to forget the true though trite saying, that, "Property and its possession have their duties as well as their rights." We must not lose sight of the well-being of the country and her people, in the pursuit of personal aggrandizement, and thus expose ourselves to the world's obloquy, our children's detriment, and our disgrace as a nation whose glorious destiny it was to elevate India to a high and proud position, compared with that state in which we found her.

It must not be supposed, from the foregoing remarks, that the author of these pages intends to write a history of India; all he presumes to do is to give information respecting that part of the country in which his regiment was on active service, and which is perhaps the most imperfectly known, namely, the vast district in the north west of India, where the Sikh battles were fought. Moreover they are not written for the scrutinizing eye of the public, but only for the amusement of his friends, and of those who have a personal interest in the war.

The author left England in the year 1836, and served with H.M.'s 4th (Queen's own) Light Dragoons for seven years. He studied both the Oordoo and Maharatta languages, passed his examination, and became Interpreter to the regiment, and was therefore able to converse with the natives. Returning to England in 1842, he joined the 9th Queen's Royal Lancers, and was engaged in the Sikh campaign in 1845-46, which prostrated the power of that people, and exhibits a series of the most triumphant successes ever recorded in the military history of India.

The author has endeavoured to delineate scenes presented in a time of war, which could not be familiar to the general traveller, because the presence of two hostile armies exhibits the people in their native character, calling forth their hopes and fears as to the issue of the combat. In times of peace, the minds of the inhabitants repose upon the prospects of a good harvest and a fruitful season. The grand features of an Indian life are comprehended in the expressive phrase: "āb aur hawa humaree bustee kee achchha huen; mi khoob khata aur khoob sota hon:" *i.e.*; "The climate (air and water) of our village is good; I eat well and sleep well." If the Indian has plenty of good water and food, his family share it with him, and he is content; he is no politician, but when war rages between hostile parties close to his own door, he can be no longer indifferent, and all his energies are aroused in estimating the issue. In losing his old masters, the English, he would fall under the iron rule of the Sikhs; or should the Sikhs suddenly attack his village and carry off his grain, he would have reason to apprehend that this act might be construed into "aiding the enemy," while a refusal to give up his corn to the Sikhs would involve the burning of his village.

In this way I shall, therefore, endeavour to represent the character of these people as I myself observed them in peace and in war, that the reader may judge whether there exists among the natives of her north-western provinces any peculiarity of character, or whether we have any reason to conclude that the actions of human nature there are much the same as in similar countries in the East; for we must not judge them by those of the West.

It is to be hoped that better days are in store for the East; and, in that comprehensive term, I would include China, and countries nearer home, Asiatic Turkey, Persia, etc. I am sanguine that the bright dawning of a happy future is awaiting these interesting countries. If the British people have conquered India, it is their imperative obligation to promote the welfare of their possessions; and we are glad to notice a laudable spirit in recent legislative measures to promote many desirable improvements. India, under an improved system, and with greater facilities of intercourse, will more than recompense any effort, or application of capital, on our part. Its internal resources are beyond our conception, and its people will unquestionably advance and improve in proportion to its elevation as an empire. Schools, industry, and commerce, if based on a solid foundation, will be the quick harbingers of peace, good-will, and prosperity to the people and their rulers, both native and European.

May this happy era be expedited in the good Providence of God!

Eynesbury, St. Neots,
Huntingdonshire,
May, 1, 1854.

CHAPTER I.

Voyage to India—Advantages of Sailing with Troops on Board—Regulations at Sea—March from Cawnpore to Meerut—Return from Nougawa Ghât to Meerut—March to Ferozepore—Cantonments at Kurnaul—Colonel Campbell's Force—Number of Cattle required on a March—Sunday—Rev. W.J. Whiting, M.A.—Distribution of Prize-Money—Advanced Guard—Governor-General—Major Broadfoot and Captain Nicolson—Suspicions of the Sikhs—Sir David Ochterlony—The Sikh Army—The Battle of Moodkee—Tej Singh.

The circumstances of a voyage to or from India are so well known, from their frequent occurrence, that I will not even allude to them. Our voyage, however, offered some variety to the usual monotony of a mere passenger ship, from our having troops on board. This naturally gave rise to numerous incidents which afford topics of interest, especially to military men. We, of course, had regular parades both for the sake of discipline, and to ascertain that the men were sober and clean. The men had, too, specific duties assigned to them—keeping watch, etc.

The object of placing the troops in watches, in time of peace, is, that they may assist in pulling and easing the ropes. They are confined to duties on deck only. If there should be an old sailor among them he may, of course, occasionally reef and unfurl sail. It is obvious that the addition of some fifty or sixty men to the crew of a merchant vessel of 600 or 700 tons burthen, is a great advantage in bad weather, as it enables almost the whole of the ship's crew to be employed aloft. In case of necessity a soldier or two will also assist the man at the wheel, or those at the pumps, by order of the quarter-master, or of the officer on duty, or of the captain himself.

Another advantage from having soldiers on board is in the case where the crew might be inclined to mutiny; when they would be restrained by the military. The troops being told off in watches, those on the morning watch assist in cleaning, or, what is called *swabbing*, the quarter-deck; but the rules for merchant ships are very imperfect in this respect.

Having troops on board necessarily adds much to the safety of the vessel.

It will probably be in the recollection of many of my readers, that two ships taken up in Australia as transports, were wrecked on the Great Andamans, islands on the east side of the Bay of Bengal, in the year 1844. These vessels would have been totally lost, but for the assistance rendered by the officers and men of the 80th Foot, the regiment which so nobly distinguished itself, the following year, at the battle of Ferozeshah, where many of those brave fellows who helped to save these vessels, yielded up their lives for their country.

To ensure regularity and a perfect understanding between the commanding officers of troops and captains of ships, a copy of rules for the guidance of the commanders of merchant-ships, should be given to the officer commanding the troops; and a copy of the regulations for troops of Her Majesty's forces, and the East India Company's service, given to the commander of the ship. The captain of a free-trader is not allowed to flog his men; but he may stop a sailor's grog and his pay for any crime of which he has been guilty. He may also put a culprit in irons, and lose the man's services.

Without stopping to describe my first impressions of India, or the countries which I traversed, after landing upon its far-famed shores, I will proceed at once to Cawnpore, where I found that my regiment was quartered, and where I first joined it.

On the 17th of October, 1845, my regiment, the 9th Queen's Royal Lancers, set out on its march from Cawnpore to Meerut, a distance of 266 miles. The Artillery received orders, at the same time, to hold themselves in readiness to proceed to the north-west. We reached Meerut on the 12th of November, and encamped near the lines of the 16th Lancers, to await further orders. We stayed only a few days in this place, which is situated in the province of Delhi. It is a very large town, of some antiquity, lying about forty miles to the north-east of the city of Delhi, and is one of our principal civil and military stations.

On the 23rd, our corps received orders to march the next day to Umballa, a large military station, a distance of 126 miles. We accordingly set out on the morning of the 25th, and marched to Sirdhana, eleven miles. On the 26th we encamped on the right bank of the river Hindon, at Nougawa Ghât, nineteen miles from Meerut. On the 27th, just as the corps was about to proceed onwards—for the trumpet to boot and saddle had already been sounded—we received a sudden order, by an express camel, to return and encamp on our old ground at Meerut. On the 28th, the regiment halted; the following day it re-crossed the river, and encamped at Sirdhana; and on the 30th returned to Meerut.

Here we were quartered till the 10th of December, when the Queen's Royal Lancers received an unexpected and peremptory order, at half-past eight P.M., to march immediately to Umballa. We accordingly again set out for Sirdhana, which we reached the next morning; and whilst at Shamlee, four marches from Meerut, and twenty-eight miles from Kurnaul, we received, between three and four o'clock P.M., an express direct from the Commander-in-Chief, with the following important intelligence:—

"That the 9th Lancers were to proceed at once to Ferozepore, agreeably to an enclosed route; and that the 43rd and 59th regiments of Native Infantry, which were to leave Meerut the same day as the Lancers, were to proceed thither also: the whole to be under the command of Colonel Campbell, of the latter corps."

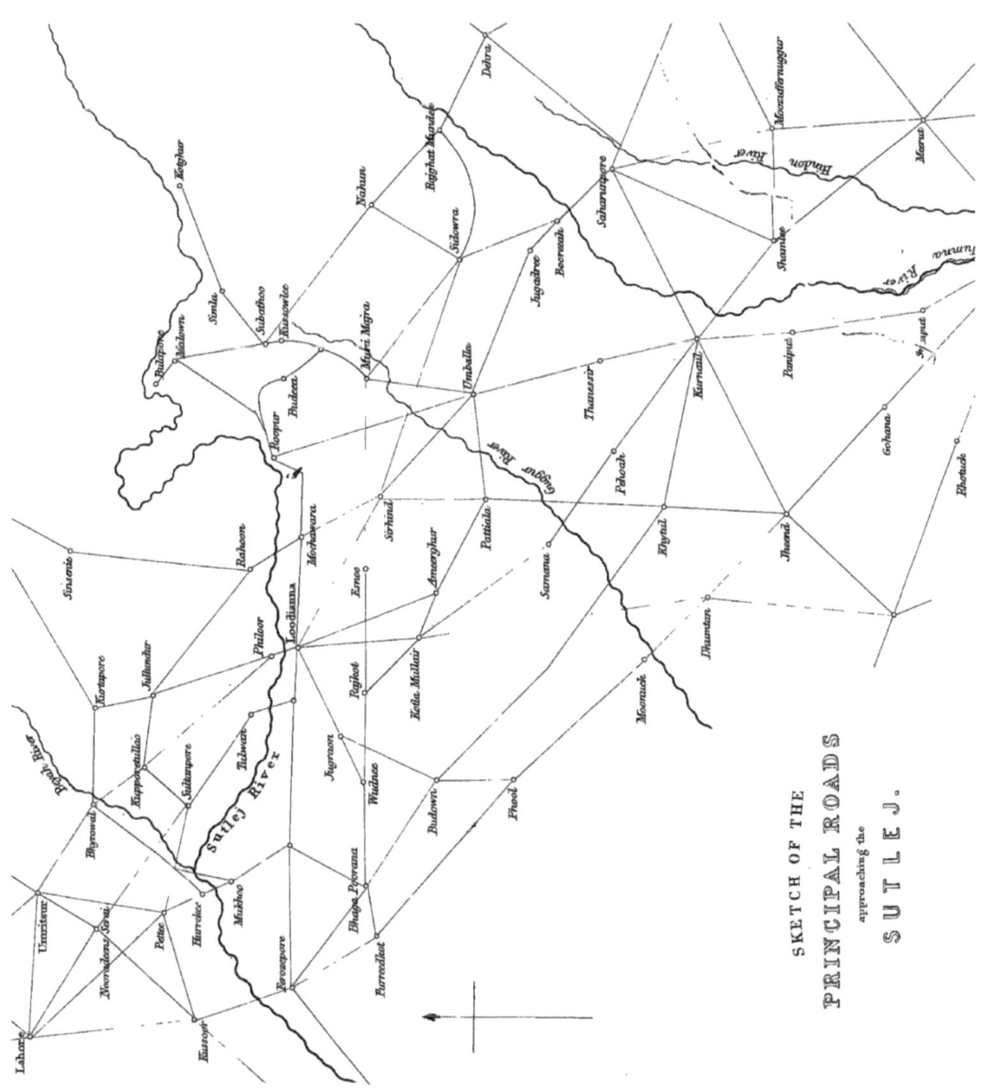

SKETCH OF THE PRINCIPAL ROADS APPROACHING THE SUTLEJ.

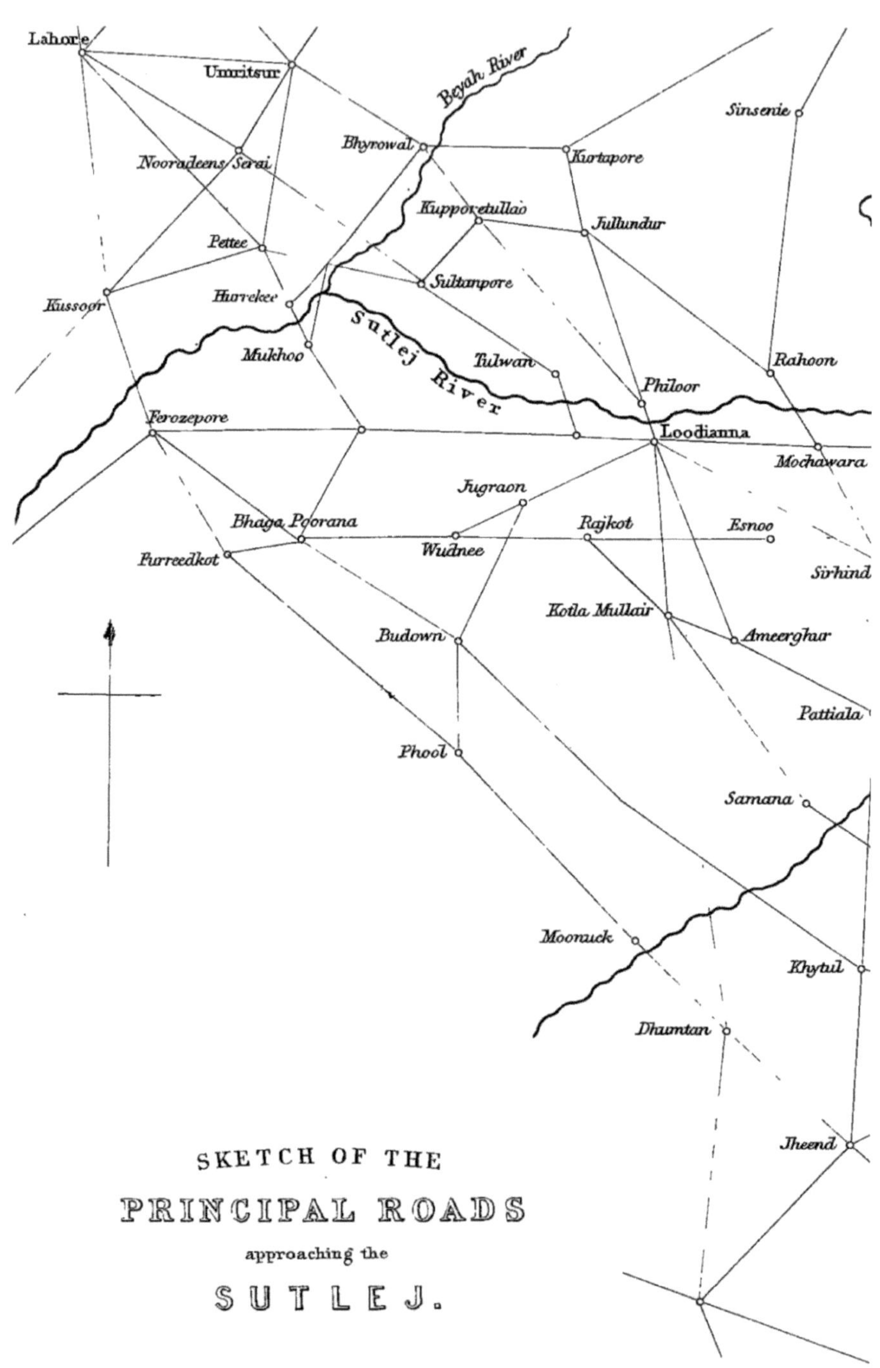

Sketch of the Principal Roads approaching the Sutlej. (*Enlarged - Left*)

Sketch of the Principal Roads approaching the Sutlej. (*Enlarged - Right*)

On reaching Kurnaul, we halted on the 18th, in order to make preparations for forming a depôt at Umballa; to which place all the superfluous heavy baggage, and the young horses, were immediately sent, under the charge of Cornet R.W. King, with instructions to rejoin head-quarters as soon as he had reported himself to the officer commanding at Umballa.

At this time, it was not yet known at Kurnaul that the Sikhs had crossed the Sutlej—an event which took place as early as the 13th of this month.

I may here remark, that the extensive cantonments of Kurnaul had been abandoned about three years before, by order of Lord Ellenborough, then Governor-General. The officers' bungalows were now nearly all roofless, and the neat little church going to decay. In 1852 it was entirely dismantled, and the materials conveyed to Umballa, to assist in building a station-church there. The immense parade-ground, large enough to allow for the exercise of 12,000 men, is about the best in India.

The route of the 9th here changed; for instead of proceeding to Umballa, we marched as follows:—

On the 19th of December to Suggah, 10 miles.
On the 20th of December to Khol, 14½ miles.
On the 21st of December to Pehoah 14 miles.

These three villages were in the protected Sikh states: the two former are small and insignificant; the latter is larger, and of more importance.

The whole tract of country, on either side of our line of march, was one continued jungle, and as level as a bowling-green.

The force under the personal command of Colonel Campbell, exclusive of officers, amounted at this time to 2,833 men, with twelve iron twelve-pounders, each drawn by an elephant. Brass guns of this description are usually drawn by ten, or even twelve, bullocks; brass eighteen-pounders by fourteen bullocks; and brass twenty-four-pounders by eighteen bullocks. An iron twenty-four-pounder is drawn by twenty-six bullocks; an iron eighteen-pounder by twenty-two bullocks; and an iron twelve-pounder by eighteen bullocks. Singly, therefore, that noble animal, the elephant, will draw a gun for which ten or even more bullocks are allowed.

These and the following remarks regarding cattle, are given for the purpose of showing the number used in dragging guns and carrying loads. By the regulations of the service in Bengal, it is directed that no elephant shall be taken into the service under twelve years of age, nor under seven feet in height. A committee is appointed to examine and report whether the animals are fit for service; but it not unfrequently happens that infantry or cavalry officers, or both, are put upon these committees, who know nothing at all of the matter. Sometimes, however, the animals are so palpably inefficient and diseased, that, as one of the committee-officers exclaimed, "This camel speaks for itself." No elephant is employed unless the committee can report that he is capable of carrying at least 20 maunds of 80 sicca weight, or 1,600 pounds = 14 cwt. 32 lbs.

Camels admitted into the service by a committee, must never be under five, nor more than nine, years old; and capable of carrying a load of at least 6 maunds, or 480 lbs. Bullocks are admitted into the service not under five, nor above eight, years of age. Draught-bullocks must be fifty inches in height; those for carriage, not under forty-eight inches. The former must be capable of carrying 210 lbs. avoirdupoise weight, besides the gear. The comparative value of these animals will be seen by the following scale:—

An elephant carries	1,600 lbs.
A camel carries	480 lbs.
A bullock carries	210 lbs.

In wet weather a camel, which, in dry weather, carries six maunds of tents, etc., will carry only four maunds, one-third being allowed for the difficulty which the camel finds of keeping on his legs in wet ground.

A six-pounder gun is drawn by six horses, and when bullocks are used, by six of these animals. This shows the relative value as to draught. Now a single elephant pulled along by himself one of the iron twelve-pounder guns, or, as they were more properly styled, "nine-pounders *reamed* up to twelves," which may be thus explained. Knowing that the Sikhs used guns of large calibre, the Government had ordered that these guns should be sent to the Delhi magazine, to be re-cast and reamed up for the occasion; and they did good service. They were a fraction lighter by this process than the nine-pounders were before.

On the 21st of December our troops halted at Pehoah. It is a large town, containing a succession of brick-built houses, the high walls of which, without any apertures, face the back streets, being evidently intended as a defence against marauders.

It will be seen, by reference to the map, that the original route by which the troops were ordered to march to Umballa, would have caused us to make a considerable *détour,* indeed, one of about thirty or thirty-five miles, for Umballa is nearly direct north of Kurnaul, while Ferozepore is north-west.

The Sunday at Pehoah was not kept as is customary on the Lord's-day in cantonments. We had no chaplain with us; and hence divine service was not performed. It would appear proper that, in the absence of the chaplain, some officer should take his place. This is the case in several European regiments, where the commanding or some superior officer reads the service to the troops. As on board of ship, when there is no chaplain, the purser reads the service, so I think, in the army, the paymaster should discharge this duty. A graduate of either University, if there be one in the corps, would be, from his education and training, the most desirable person to read a selection of prayers from the church service. A chaplain accompanied the Bengal and Bombay columns, which went to Afghanistan in 1838-39.

We have a noble instance of voluntary dedication to the duties of chaplain to an army on active service, in the case of the Rev. W.J. Whiting, M.A., during the second Sikh campaign. The arduous and invaluable services which this excellent clergyman rendered during that campaign called forth the grateful thanks of the Governor-General, the Commander-in-Chief, the Bishop of Calcutta, and the Court of Directors. He has left an indelible impression, on all engaged in that war, of the importance of his benevolent, as well as spiritual ministrations.

By the warrant for prize-money for the navy, dated 1846, naval chaplains share in the prize money. There appears to be no positive regulation for army chaplains; but the analogy between the two services will point out the propriety of its existing in the latter case; and the warrant being by royal authority, no doubt ought to exist on the subject. It is pleasing to hear that the Rev. George Robert Gleig, M.A., Chaplain-General to the Forces, formerly a subaltern during the Peninsular war, and author of several entertaining and instructive military works, has not only received his medal, with two bars, but has worn it at Court over his canonicals, and does wear it at all times in the pulpit.

By the navy warrant, passengers on board a man-of-war, if they desire to join in an action, receive a share of the prize money. The navy prize rules are fairer than those of the army. The army rules were made—I am speaking of India—by the Prize Committees, assembled at Seringapatam, Agra, etc., in 1799 and 1803; and, being composed of senior officers, they took good care of their own grade, while the juniors got a very disproportionate share.

I return from this digression to the bellicose signs of the times. Colonel Campbell's detachment marched, on the 22nd December, to Goelah, sixteen miles distant. Here, in consequence of rumours that the Sikhs had crossed the Sutlej, and having heard, in the afternoon, a distant noise resembling the sound of cannon (which subsequently turned out to be the explosion of mines), Colonel Campbell ordered all the troops under his immediate command to join and march together.

On the following morning the advanced guard consisted of a troop of the Royal Lancers—the light companies of the 43rd and 59th regiments of Native Infantry—some sappers and miners—and four 12-pounders. The main body consisted of the 9th Lancers—43rd and 59th regiments of Native Infantry—and six 12-pounders. The rear-guard consisted of a troop of the 9th—one company from each of the Infantry regiments—and two 12-pounders: Captain Spottiswoode, 9th Lancers, an able and most intelligent officer, acting as major of brigade. Here was a respectable force of nearly 3,000 men and twelve guns, or four to each thousand men, being above Napoleon's proportion, which was only three to 1,000.

It will be seen that we began the campaign with an artillery very inferior to that of the Sikhs. In fact, if calibres are reckoned, we, probably, were in the minority as one to three. I shall, in the sequel, prove these facts. But to proceed:

It will appear strange to the European reader when he hears that the whole tract of country between the Sutlej and the Jumna, including the protected Sikh states, which were under our control, as well as our protection, had been in the possession of the East India Company since the year 1809, or for thirty-six years before this period; and that, nevertheless, troops marching to join the army, in a direct line, sixty miles off, were not even aware that the Sikhs had crossed the Sutlej; and that, moreover, two battles had been fought, that of Moodkee, on the 18th, and that of Ferozeshah on the 21st and 22nd of December, the latter being one of the most deadly contested actions ever fought in India. I have before stated that the 9th Lancers had been ordered from Meerut, and did march on the 25th of November; that this line corps, being unfortunately ordered back, did not leave Meerut the second time until the 11th of December. Here was a loss of sixteen days: hence it is clear, that, as the regiment heard firing, or sounds arising from the explosion of powder mines on the 21st of December, it would have been present in the battles of Moodkee and Ferozeshah, had not its march been countermanded.

Now the order to return to Meerut was received on the 27th of November. To what circumstance was this to be attributed? The Sikhs did not cross the Sutlej until the 13th of December, or sixteen days after the 27th of November; and, allowing the order for the return to be dated the 25th of November, there certainly was not any crossing of the Sikhs at that time. It is positively stated, by a staff officer, that Lord Hardinge did not send the order. Although a Governor-General can send such an order direct, yet all military men here know that the Commander-in-chief is the channel for transmitting such orders. At the same time it is an established rule in the Indian army that a Commander-in-chief cannot order any troops on service without the sanction of the Governor-General, or of the government. Even in the common biennial or triennial relief the order is prefaced with the words: "With the sanction of government." The Governor-General being, in the present instance, on the field, was, *de facto*, the government. As Louis XIV. said: *L'état? C'est moi.*

Great uncertainty if not mystery prevailed in our army as to the probability of the Sikhs crossing the Sutlej. The Blue Book comes to our aid in deciding upon such a probability. It was argued that in 1843 the Sikhs did threaten to cross, but thought better of it and forebore; and therefore they might do the same now. But all the politicals knew well enough that the Punts and Punchees were no longer under the control of the Durbar as they were in 1843, but were more likely than not, to act in open defiance of it.

There were two officers, however, of great political talent, whose official position enabled them to know more of the feelings of the Sikhs, and of the probability of such a step than most others; one was Major G. Broadfoot of the 34th Madras Native Infantry, who had held the office of British Agent for Sikh affairs since November 1844, and who had acted as engineer in the celebrated defence of Jellalabad, the heroes of which obtained the well merited Roman distinction of a mural crown; the other was Captain P. Nicolson, 28th Bengal Native Infantry who had been appointed his assistant. Captain Nicolson was in Affghanistan in 1838-39, and was deputed to conduct the traitor Dost Mahomed Khan to Calcutta, and afterwards to Saharunpore. This officer had had seven years' experience of the politics of the Affghans and the Sikhs. At this juncture he was with Major General Sir John H. Littler at Ferozepore. He was in the daily receipt of intelligence from Lahore, and knew that the Sikhs would cross, for he wrote to Calcutta on the 9th of October, 1845, that "he believed the Sikhs would cross." What! because Major Broadfoot knew that the Sikhs had made an empty threat to cross in 1843, was it therefore improbable, that, being encamped for a long time, on the right bank of the Sutlej, menacing the Durbar at Lahore, from whence they marched in defiance of their government and of their chief, whom they compelled to join them, they would execute their threat under these circumstances?

Major Broadfoot was the Governor-General's agent, and as such was the officer to whom he looked for intelligence, Captain Nicolson was his subordinate; the Major doubted the Captain's intelligence, because he had received no other information to induce him to believe that the rebellious and infatuated Khalsa (or royal) troops would dare to cross. If they threatened to cross in 1843 without carrying that threat into execution, why might they not do the same in 1845? But this was not good logic; the inference was against him; because in 1843 they were obedient to the Durbar, and in 1845 they acted in defiance of it.

It would be useless at this distant period to enter into the discussion which arose in India, and was afterwards taken up with much warmth in England, as to the correctness of the views entertained by these officers on the crossing of the Sutlej by the Sikhs. The relative views of those two officers were then and are still sustained by their respective friends; but as far as we can individually offer an opinion, and as it seemed to many at the time, there is great difficulty in arriving at a decision as to the rights of the question at issue. It is true that Major Broadfoot, as the superior officer, might be presumed to be in a position for obtaining access to sources of information from which his subordinate was debarred. In a military point of view, this position must always carry its due weight in the scale of probable authentic intelligence, and should have a preponderating influence in ultimate proceedings, especially in such a country as India, and among such a people as we were then dealing with.

On the other hand, it is by no means uncommon for a subordinate in an important position, to have access directly, and indirectly, to authentic intelligence from which his superior may be shut out, and such a subordinate, knowing his duties and his means of intelligence, can constantly elicit facts in a variety of ways, especially from a hostile source, from which his superior is excluded.

Now, in reference to the position of Captain Nicolson at this juncture, and for a long period antecedent, we are decidedly of opinion that his information and impressions were correct: at the same time we do not consider that the admission of this circumstance can warrant any one to seek, or in justice desire, to disparage the opinions of Major Broadfoot. He, no doubt, had strong grounds for arriving at the conclusion that he did, as the information upon which he acted coincided with his own predilections, and for persisting in these views, even in the face of equally strong opinions on the part of Captain Nicolson.

Officers will, and must, differ on points like the one at issue; but we do not hesitate to say, that Major Broadfoot's views have subjected him to no small share of obloquy and censure. It is, however, important to bear in mind, that in no country, and among no class of people in the world, is there so much cause for a difference of opinion as among military men in India, especially on such a question as that under consideration. The character of the Sikhs, their former empty and vacillating tactics, made the crossing of the Sutlej a matter of uncertainty, even up to a few days of their actual transit; and, to the very last moment, some of their own people were doubtful on the point. This has always been a piece of oriental policy.

It cannot be denied, that the Sikhs had considerable cause for provocation. The sequestration of the two Sikh villages near Loodianna, by the British government, early in November, was the culminating point, and left no doubt of our aggressive intentions on the minds of the Sikhs. Their suspicions had long been awakened by our proceedings—by the rumours of boats preparing at Bombay, to form pontoons across the Sutlej—of our equipping troops in Scinde, for a march on Mooltan—and reinforcing our frontier stations with men and ammunition. They persuaded themselves that the policy of our government was territorial aggrandizement, and that war was inevitable. This feeling was shared by the mass of the Sikh population. The Durbar sitting at Lahore, however, knew well enough that the British government would not take the initiative; but it had completely lost the confidence and allegiance of the army by its internal dissensions, and the supine weakness and luxurious indolence of the chiefs of the Punjaub. The Sikh soldiery used to assemble in groups round the tomb of Runjeet Singh, vowing to defend with their lives all that belonged to the commonwealth of Govind—that they would never suffer the kingdom of Lahore to be occupied by the British strangers, but stand ready to march, or give the invaders battle on their own ground.

Thus, led on from one step to another, the Sikhs declared war on the 17th of November, and by an overt act broke the solemn treaty of alliance with our government; they crossed the Sutlej on the 13th of December, and on the 14th took up a position in the immediate vicinity of Ferozepore.

This treaty of alliance between the British government and the Maharajah had been concluded in April, 1809; being occasioned by the aggressions of Runjeet Singh upon the territories of the chiefs of the Cis-Sutlej provinces, who claimed the British protection.[1]

In Sir David Ochterlony's proclamation,[2] which was issued at the same time, it was especially stated, "That the force of cavalry and infantry which may have crossed to this side of the river Sutlej, must be recalled to the other side, to the country of the Maharajah. This communication is made solely with the view of publishing the sentiments of the British, and of ascertaining those of the Maharajah. The British are confident that the Maharajah will consider the contents of this precept as redounding to his real advantage, and as affording a conspicuous proof of their friendship; that with their capacity for war, they are also intent on peace."

There can be no question, that so long as Runjeet Singh held the government, this and subsequent treaties would have remained inviolate. He knew the power and influence of the English well enough to desire their friendship, rather than their enmity. But this was not the case with his successors, whose policy was guided by views of self-aggrandizement, rather than by the weal of their people, by which they lost their hold over them.

[1] See Appendix I.

[2] See Appendix, II.

Up to this time, the British had adopted only precautionary measures for the protection of their frontier states. The Governor-General, Lord Hardinge, had joined the Commander-in-Chief, Sir Hugh Gough, at Umballa, early in December; and as soon as the rumour gained ground, that the Sikh forces were marching towards the Sutlej, the troops in the upper provinces received marching orders, and all were speedily on the move. The corps stationed at Umballa, Loodianna, and Ferozepore, amounted to about 30,000 men, with 70 field-guns; and as Ferozepore, which was then occupied by Sir John Littler, was the most exposed, the troops from Umballa were sent to his support, and only a small garrison was left at Loodianna, in order that as large a body of available men as possible, should be placed at the disposal of Sir H. Gough to give battle to the Sikhs, should they carry out their threat of crossing the Sutlej.

This, as we have seen, they actually did on the 13th; but so great was the influence which Captain Nicolson exercised over some of their chiefs, that he prevailed upon Lall Singh to divide his forces; and it was only a division of the Sikhs which fought at Moodkee on the 18th of December.

The Sikh army numbered from 35,000 to 40,000 men, with 50 pieces of heavy artillery, besides a reserve force stationed near Loodianna, to act according to circumstances. The army of invasion consequently more than doubled that of the British. Notwithstanding the jealousy, mistrust, and treachery which prevailed in the Sikh army, in one thing they were agreed, that they would rid the commonwealth of Govind, of their hated British allies; and that in order to accomplish this, it behoved every individual to act as if the result depended upon himself alone. The Sikhs were commanded by Tej Singh, an officer of considerable talent. They took up an entrenched position at Ferozeshah, an inconsiderable village about 10 miles from Ferozepore and the same distance from Moodkee.

General Sir John Littler was, as we have stated, lying at Ferozepore with a garrison of about 10,000 men. As the Sikhs appeared to threaten the town, the gallant general immediately led out his men, and offered them battle; this they declined, mainly it would appear, from the double dealing and artful conduct of Lall Singh and Tej Singh, who, uncertain as to the result of the present movement, were anxious to remain friends with both parties.

The head-quarters of the Commander-in-Chief were at Umballa about 150 miles from Moodkee. His Excellency[3] broke up his camp on the 11th, and by forced marches arrived at the village of Moodkee on the 18th. The Governor-General was a little in advance of his Excellency, and rode over to Loodianna to inspect the troops. Finding that post secure from an attack, he dispatched about 5,000 of the garrison to guard the important grain depôt of Bussean.

On the 18th of December, the Commander-in-Chief, with the Umballa division of the army arrived at Moodkee, and was immediately joined by the Loodianna division. On reaching Moodkee there was no longer any doubt as to the whereabouts of the Sikh forces. Orders were immediately issued by the deputy adjutant-general to a brigadier, that he should be ready for duty next day; in other

[3] The Commander-in-Chief is always so styled; the Governor-General never.

words, that he should command the advance guard. This was about twelve o'clock in the day, when the officers were in the mess tent at *tiffin*. Two young officers of the 16th Native Grenadiers overheard the order: "You are brigadier for to-morrow; the army will march early in the morning to attack the Sikhs, who are known to be ten miles off." They were still discussing the glorious prospect of an encounter with the Sikhs, when orders arrived in camp for "all hands to turn out," Major Broadfoot having received intelligence that the Sikhs were near. The order had been sent by Lord Hardinge,—every inch a soldier, but who at that time had not yet been appointed second in command to the Commander-in-Chief.

The cavalry and horse artillery darted off to the right front; the infantry followed; it was a short affair. Lord Gough did not at first credit the report: "The Sikhs are coming!" Like a true Irish soldier, he would have a view of them before he could make up his mind—but he was soon convinced of the reality of the rumour. Major Broadfoot, galloping up to their position, was fired on; both the Governor-General and the Commander-in-Chief were, it is said, at one time nearly captured. The Governor-General, on the other hand, promptly put the troops in motion: being himself an old Peninsular officer, he was an excellent judge of the matter. His Excellency the Commander-in-Chief could not have done otherwise, but there was not time to send to him: the urgency of the occasion satisfies the mind of all military men; by a delay the Sikhs might have attacked the British.

Napoleon and other great generals "always anticipated the attack." They who attack have the advantage of deciding on the form of attack; those who await it, have no certainty where it may be made.

The battle of Moodkee was, as we have said, a short affair. The Sikhs headed by Lall Singh, opened with a heavy cannonade, but were answered by a brisk fire from the English; the enemy's rear was then attacked by a brilliant cavalry movement which routed him; and night put a stop to the carnage. The Sikhs were defeated with a loss of 17 guns. That of the British was very great; they had 215 killed, and 657 wounded. Among the killed were Sir Robert Sale and Sir John McCaskill. It is doubtful whether the addition of the 9th Lancers would have been of service at the battle of Moodkee, because there was no extended field for cavalry movements: at Ferozeshah, however, they would have been of eminent use, for on the the second day (December 22nd,) Tej Singh advanced with a large force of horse artillery; and I have heard it deeply regretted by officers present in this action, that we were not at hand to complete the rout of the brave Sikhs.

CHAPTER II.

Colonel Campbell's Advance—Provisions required—Camp Followers—Samana—The Doabs—Gooroo Govind—The Akalees, their quoits—Sikhs attack Ahmed Shah—Maha Singh—Maharattas—General Thomas—Runjeet Singh—Holcar—Sir Charles Metcalfe—Ochterlony's Proclamation—The Akalees routed—Generals Allard and Ventura—Treaty with Runjeet—Runjeet's Army—Runjeet's Death—Shere Singh Murdered—Dhuleep Singh—Ajean Khan—Battle of Moodkee.

In the meanwhile the force under Colonel Campbell was rapidly advancing to the scene of action. It was as we have stated, nearly 3,000 strong, and attended by about 10,000 or 11,000 camp followers, so that we were in all 13,000 or 14,000 assembled in camp, besides numerous elephants, camels, bullocks, horses, ponies, &c. I will here remark for what purposes camp followers are allowed. Every officer, according to his rank, will have from ten to twenty or twenty-five servants; the Bengal officers and others have more than those of Madras and Bombay; but the latter servants cost as much as the Bengalese. If a polki (or palanquin) be kept, then six bearers well be required; for every horse two servants, namely a groom and a grass-cutter;[4] for every elephant, two; for camels, one to every three is the usual number; for every two bullocks, one servant is allowed. Besides these there is a host of tent pitchers, store Lascars, etc.

Let us next consider the quantity of provisions required for our force; calculating the 9th Lancers at 800 horses (including officers' chargers,) the consumption of gram, a kind of vetch, daily would be, 800 × 5 = 4,000 seers, or 8,000 lbs. = 71 cwt. 48 lbs. The reader may hence form some idea of the quantity of corn required for 3,000 or 4,000 cavalry horses, or including horse artillery, waggon and private horses, say 5,000, and there would be a consumption of about 440 or 450 cwt. of gram daily. Then each elephant consumes 30 lbs. of atta (flour) cakes;[5] each camel public and private is allowed 6 lbs. of gram, and a bullock 5 or 6 lbs. daily. The elephant likewise gets forage, such as the leaves of trees; and if he can meet with the branch of a tree he is all the happier, for with it he gracefully fans away the flies from himself or his driver: the poor animal suffers greatly from the mosquito bite. The Mahāwat, or elephant-keeper puts the rice in a whisp of rice straw, making

[4] In the Dragoons, one groom is allowed by Government for every two horses, the other being paid by the soldiers themselves.

[5] In Bengal Proper, rice. These cakes are made just like those eaten by the men, but thicker and of coarser flour. No bad food on a pinch.

a kind of bowl for the food, which is boiled. The camels, too, get bhoosa, or split straw, when it can be procured, otherwise the leaves of trees: they prefer those of the Imlee, Peepul, Babool, and Burh (fig-tree). The bullocks eat bhoosa or karbi, the stalk of Joar or Bajra (the Holcus Sorgum and Spicatus). If we calculate the quantity of grain consumed in an army of 10,000, 30,000, or 40,000 men, the result will be enormous, and we can only marvel where such supplies are obtained.

The Duke of Wellington[6] when in India, often marched with 30,000, or 40,000 bullock-loads of grain, or 600,000, or 800,000 lbs. or 53,571, or 71,428 cwt. His grace's plan was never to open these grain bags so long as he could get supplies from the villages.

Let the reader imagine an Indian army of 20,000 men with its 60,000, 70,000, or even 80,000 camp followers, all of whom must be fed daily. Again, the number of hackeries, or carts, with an army of 20,000 or 25,000 men, varies from 700, to 12,000 or more, (for much depends upon whether there is a siege train), drawn by two, three, or four bullocks each, carrying shot, shells, and stores, and moving at the rate of two miles an hour, the whole line of march from the old to the new ground. Allowing 10 doolies, or light palanquins, for every European troop or company, for the conveyance of the sick or wounded men, there would be 80 required for the 9th Lancers, and as each dooly needs 6 bearers we had 480 bearers in our corps alone. In a European infantry regiment of 10 companies there will be 10 × 10 = 100; 100 × 6 = 600 bearers. A native corps is allowed only one for a troop or company, but some extra ones accompany the field hospital. Now such an army would have at least 5,000 dooly bearers, besides those which are required for luxurious officers, who have been seen, though, I am happy to say, rarely, to ride in palanquins.

The English waggon train establishment is said not to be good. A veterinary surgeon has published a work on the use of a light cart, with cross seats on springs; but before it can be generally adopted, the roads must be improved. In the Affghan war they used Kajawahs, that is a frame-work on each side of the camel, for two men.

On the 23rd of December, our force marched to Samana, a large old town, now completely in ruins, in the province of Delhi. It is in the Rajah of Pattiala's country, and is about seventeen miles distant from Pattiala, and seventy miles from Kurnaul. It was a very fatiguing march; the road during the last few miles being bad, rough and sandy; this greatly impeded the elephants who dragged the guns, and our progress was very slow; so slow indeed that at six o'clock in the afternoon the men had not dined. In cantonments one o'clock is the usual hour, but in marching to meet an enemy the dinner hour is uncertain. Yesterday and to-day we were obliged to breakfast upon what chance threw in our way.

On service with Lord Lake, it is said that frequently neither officers nor men got any breakfast at all, but broke their fast at sunset; similar privations no doubt often occurred in the Peninsula; but this is very undesirable when it can be obviated, for especially in hot countries, European soldiers require more nourishment than in colder climates.

[6] Vide Despatches.

Samana contains a large brick-built fort; it appears at one time to have been very strong, but is now falling to decay. There are many of these forts, and their origin is long anterior to 1809, when the British obtained possession of the protected Sikh states. They were built by Runjeet Singh, when he was lord and master of the country on the left bank of the Sutlej, governing, in fact, the whole district between the Jumna and the Sutlej. At that time he fortified all the towns and villages, to defend not only the inhabitants against the attacks of their neighbours, but also to prevent the cattle sheltered under the walls, from being carried off by marauders.

Before proceeding further on our route, we will take a brief survey of the territory of the Sikhs, and of the history of the singular race whom we were marching to encounter.

The Punjaub, or country of five waters, from *punj*, "five," and *āb*, "water," forms the northern portion of the plain of the Indus. It covers an area of 6,000 geographical miles, and extends from the lower ranges of the Himalaya mountains to the confluence of the Chenāb with the Indus. The four streams or arms of the Indus which rise in the Himalayas, namely, the Jelum, the Chenāb, the Rāvee and the Sutlej, intersect the country, and, with the Indus, divide it into four Doabs or Provinces.

The first Doab ("country between two rivers"), lying between the Indus and the Jelum, is 147 miles in breadth; this Doab is intersected with defiles and mountain chains, and covered with thickets. It is the worst cultivated, the most barren and thinly peopled of all the Doabs.

The second Doab is formed by the rivers Jelum and Chenāb. At its narrowest breadth it is forty-six miles across; this country is flat, except the low range of hills terminating the beds of rock salt that run through the Jelum. It is capable of very improved cultivation.

The third Doab lies between the Chenāb and the Rāvee. This Doab might with the greatest ease be converted into a most fertile country, were the land irrigated by the mountain streams, which could be conveyed in artificial canals. It is seventy-six miles in breadth at its widest part.

The fourth Doab is considerably the smallest, being only forty-four miles in breadth. It, however, comprises some of the most important cities, namely, Lahore, Umritsur and Kussoor. It lies between the Rāvee and the Sutlej.

Besides this fine country, the rule of the Sikhs at this time extended over the rich Province of Mooltan, on the right bank of the Indus. The territory under the sway of the Maharajah might be estimated at 8,000 geographical square miles, with a population of about 5,000,000 inhabitants, and an annual revenue of between £2,000,000 and £3,000,000 sterling.

The Sikhs, or "Disciples," were originally a religious sect, which arose among the inhabitants of the Punjaub as late as the close of the fifteenth century. Their leader was Nānak, who succeeded in drawing thousands of enthusiasts after him. He was a disciple of Kahir, and consequently a Hindoo deist; he upheld the principle of universal toleration, calling upon his followers to worship the one invisible

God, and to lead a virtuous life. He died at the age of seventy, in 1539. His doctrines and writings tended greatly to elevate the mind, and reform the morals of his disciples. The Sikhs believe that the soul of Nānak has transmigrated into the body of each succeeding Gooroo, or teacher.

The spirit of religious toleration adopted by the Sikhs, was odious in the eyes of the bigoted Mahomedans, and Arjoon, their chief, who was celebrated not only for his piety, but for his wisdom and skill as a legislator, was falsely accused, and put to death, by the Mogul, in 1606. Arjoon converted the obscure hamlet of Umritsur into a city of great importance, by making it the seat of his disciples, and the place of the Sikhs' pilgrimage. His cruel death transformed the quiet and peaceable Sikhs into a warlike nation; their spirit was roused, and, led on by Hur Govind, the son of their murdered priest, they determined to avenge themselves upon his assassins. The Mogul, however, was too mighty for them; and they were forced to retreat into the mountain districts beyond Lahore.

After a series of sanguinary engagements, in which the Mahomedans were successful, a powerful opponent to the infidel faith and arms, was raised up, in the person of Gooroo Govind, grandson of Hur Govind, in 1675. He effected a radical change in the character, laws, and institutions of the Sikhs, by the abolition of caste, and the introduction of religious, social and military reforms. Amidst the surrounding spiritual darkness, Govind had comparatively enlightened views of the Deity; he abhorred idol worship, and declared that there was but one Lord, and that the invisible God, the Creator of heaven and earth, could not be represented by any painted or graven image; and that as He could be seen only by the eye of faith, He must be worshipped in sincerity and truth. Fearful that he himself might hereafter become an object of religious adoration, Govind denounced all who should regard him as a divinity, alleging that it was his highest ambition that his spirit should return to God after his death.

In the full persuasion, that the only hope of successfully opposing the Mahomedan power was by throwing open the ranks of the army to men of every grade and profession, he adopted the wise and politic measure of abolishing the system of caste. This step was at first highly offensive, especially to the Brahmins, and many quitted the community; but the majority of the Sikhs rejoiced at the breaking down of this barrier to all social and religious intercourse. His expectations, however, were more than realized; vast multitudes joined his ranks, he caused each of his followers to wear a peculiar dress, to adopt the name of Singh, or soldier, and to suffer their beard and hair to grow; he completely reorganized the army, divided his followers into troops and bands, and placed them under the command of able and confidential men.

A special corps was formed of the "Akalees," the Immortals, or Soldiers of God, they wore a blue dress and steel bracelets, and were provided with a quoit, which they carried either round their pointed turbans or at their side; this quoit is a flat iron ring, from eight to fourteen inches in diameter, the outer edge is extremely sharp; they twirl this weapon round their finger or on a stick, and fling it to a distance with such dexterity and precision, that the head of the destined victim is often severed from his body.

In proportion as the Mahomedan power declined, that of the Sikhs rose into importance. They were bound together by the strong ties of a fervid common faith; and this gave them unity of purpose, and consequent strength in operation.

After various struggles for independence, in which they displayed heroism amounting even to martyrdom, they boldly attacked Ahmed Shah, the king of Affghanistan on his first invasion of India, in 1747. They were, however, dispersed by Mere Munroo, and expelled from Umritsur by Timoor, the son of Ahmed Shah, who was appointed governor of the Punjaub. Strong in the faith of Govind, and in his all-prevailing name they rallied their forces, drove out the Affghans, and re-occupied Lahore in 1756.

About this time they called in the aid of the Maharattas, gained several victories, and fortified their towns. In 1762, they were again attacked by Ahmed Shah, who completely routed them, but with their native energy and warlike prowess, they once more gathered their scattered forces, and in 1763 slew the Affghan governor, and defeated his army in the plains of Sirhind, when they took undisputed possession of the country from the Sutlej to the Jumna, and partitioned it among their chiefs.

They successfully defeated a seventh attack made by Ahmed Shah; and after ejecting the governor of Lahore, they took possession of the territory from the Jelum to the Sutlej. Like the former acquisition, it was divided among their chiefs.

During the brief period of peace which now intervened, the Sikhs settled the boundaries of their respective districts, and more firmly established their federal government, which, properly speaking, may be styled a theocratic feudal confederation, inasmuch as they considered God as the Head and Leader of their confraternity. They held stated councils, or conclaves, which they called "gooroo-moottas," in which they settled their civil and religious affairs. The nation was divided into twelve confederacies or "misls," from an Arabic word signifying "equal," each "misl" being under the control of a sirdar or chief.

Their respite from war was not, however, of long duration; for in 1767, Ahmed Shah made an eighth and last attempt to reconquer the Punjaub. Being, however, deserted by 12,000 of his own troops, he was compelled to retire, and had scarcely re-crossed the Indus when he was besieged at Rhotas, by the grandfather of Runjeet Singh; and the Sikhs took possession of this stronghold in 1768.

Timoor, the son of the veteran Shah, had various conflicts with the Sikhs; and in 1779 reconquered the city of Mooltan, which they had taken seven years before. He died in 1793, leaving the Sikhs undisputed masters of the Upper Punjaub.

Maha Singh, though originally an obscure sirdar, soon rose by his military skill to be the most influential chief in the Punjaub. With the view of cementing his power, he espoused his only son, Runjeet Singh, to the daughter of Sudda Kour. Maha Singh died at the early age of twenty-seven, leaving Runjeet Singh to succeed him in the government. He was a boy of only eleven years of age, having been born in 1792, at Gujeranwalla, forty-seven miles from Lahore.

From a very early age, Runjeet Singh began to display that wisdom and valour, combined with prompt decision and firmness of character, which distinguished him through life. He carved out with his sword his own colossal position in the Punjaub; and, at the age of twenty, expelled the Sikh chiefs, Ischet Singh, Muhuc Singh and Sahib Singh, who opposed him. On the second invasion and retreat of Shah Zeman, king of Cabool, Runjeet Singh acquired the object of his ambition—the wealthy kingdom of Lahore, with the royal investiture and title of Maharajah.

About this time the star of the Maharattas again rose in the Northern Provinces, under their able leader, Madhajee Sindhia, who, in 1785, formed an alliance with the Sikhs, and threatened the kingdom of Oude, then under the protection of the British. Runjeet, however, soon became jealous of his allies; and finding that they were likely to prove troublesome, he had recourse to the strongest measures to check their growing influence.

One of the generals of the Maharatta forces was an English adventurer, named George Thomas. He came to India in 1781, in a British man-of-war; he was originally a common sailor, but rose to be quarter-master, and on his arrival in India entered the service of the native chiefs. He was sent to oppose the combined forces of the Sikhs. Leaving a competent force for the defence of Jeypore, which was then threatened with an attack from another quarter, he marched to Kurnaul, where the Sikhs lay encamped. Here four successive engagements took place, in which the Maharattas lost 500 men, and the Sikhs about 1,000. Both parties at last inclining to peace, a treaty was concluded, by which the Sikhs agreed to evacuate the Province. In 1800, General Thomas again entered the Sikh country, with a body of 5,000 men and sixty pieces of artillery. He was now opposed by the youthful Maharajah, Runjeet Singh; but the issue was adverse to the Sikhs. Nor was it surprising that General Thomas with a well disciplined army of 5,000 men, and sixty guns[7] should defeat a young chief of twenty-two years of age.

The British government was not ignorant of the warlike character and growing power of the Sikhs. As far back as the year 1784, Warren Hastings placed a British agent at the court of Delhi, in order to watch the Sikhs, and deter them from making any attempt upon the kingdom of Oude.

The Sikhs, however, finding the Maharattas too powerful for them, applied to the British Resident, to enter with them into a defensive alliance against their common foe, at the same time placing at the disposal of the British a body of 30,000 men, whom they had stationed at Delhi to watch the Maharattas.

In the year 1805, the ambitious spirit of Holcar, the enterprising Mahomedan leader of the Maharatta forces, determined him to invade Upper India, and to invest Delhi. He met with a powerful resistance from Lord Lake, who drove him beyond the Sutlej, where he expected to find support from the Sikhs. Runjeet Singh had penetrated the Doab, between the Chenāb and the Indus. He had a meeting with Holcar at Umritsur, but finding it more to his interest to make friends with the English, the wily Maharajah put Holcar off, under the pretext that he must first reduce the Pathans of Kussoor. Friendly relations were then established with the British;[8] Runjeet Singh visited Lord Lake's camp in disguise, and a treaty was

[7] See Appendix III.

[8] See Appendix IV.

concluded, by which the English agreed not to encroach upon the Sikhs' territories so long as the chiefs of the Punjaub continued to maintain friendly relations.

Runjeet Singh, speaking of this circumstance some time afterwards to Sir John Malcolm, remarks, that he "was very glad to get rid of two such troublesome guests," namely, Holcar and the British. It was a curious coincidence that both Runjeet Singh and Holcar had each but one eye, but those eyes were piercing, nor were they disliked by the fair sex, if report speak true.

The news of the intended invasion of India by Napoleon, in 1808, spread a panic through the country, and the British government took instant measures to ascertain how far they could rely on the support of the various native princes. The most powerful and important of these was Runjeet Singh; and Sir Charles Metcalfe was accordingly despatched to the court of Lahore as British Envoy. The Maharajah was at that time engaged in the subjugation of some of the petty independent Sikh princes. His continued aggressions upon the Cis-Sutlej states, several of which he had made tributary, induced the princes of Sirhind to place themselves under British protection, and the envoy was charged with a remonstrance to Runjeet Singh upon this subject.

He received the envoy at Kussoor, which he had just conquered, and seemed more intent upon the enlargement and defence of his own borders, than alive to the dangers of a French invasion. So far from entering into the views of the British government on the necessity of a defensive alliance between them and the Sikhs and Affghans, in order to oppose the ambitious designs of Napoleon, Runjeet Singh replied, that, as the head of the whole Sikh population, and as master of Lahore, he had an indisputable right to the enlargement of his own territories, and scorned the attempts of the British to confine him to the right bank of the Sutlej. He abruptly broke off the negotiation, and made a third invasion into the Cis-Sutlej territory; the British envoy remonstrated against these open acts of hostility, and remained on the banks of the Sutlej until the Maharajah returned victorious from the conquest of Fureedkot and Umballa.

The British government hereupon again remonstrated, and declared to him, through Sir Charles Metcalfe, that they would not tolerate any superior authority in these parts, as the whole country, from the Jumna to the Sutlej, was under their protection. To give efficacy to this remonstrance, they despatched a corps under Colonel Ochterlony, and a reserve corps under Colonel St. Leger. The former advanced to the Sutlej, and in the beginning of February, 1809, he issued a proclamation declaring the Cis-Sutlej states to be under British protection.[9] The proclamation ordered that the fortresses on the left bank of the Sutlej should be razed, and the lands restored to their ancient possessors: that all the troops which had crossed the Sutlej should be recalled by the Maharajah to his side, and that in future they should never advance into the countries of the chiefs situated on the left bank of the river, who had placed themselves under the protection of the British government. That the British government would maintain perpetual friendship with the government of Lahore, and have no concern with the territories and subjects of the Rajah to the north of the Sutlej; but that in the event of any violation of these

[9] See Appendix V.

stipulations, the treaty should be null and void.

An apparently trivial circumstance, coupled with the apprehension lest the remaining independent states might break their allegiance with him for that of the British, favoured the demands of the envoy, and convinced the Maharajah that the British soldiers far surpassed his own. Sir Charles was at this time in the Sikh camp at Umritsur, and was attended by an escort of only two companies of native troops and sixteen horsemen. The festival of the Muharram was being celebrated by his Mahomedan attendants. The Akalees looked upon this as an insult, collected a body of the Sikhs, and attacked the envoy's camp with a round of musketry. The small escort immediately seized their arms; and, though their assailants were ten times more numerous than themselves, they completely routed them with considerable loss. Runjeet Singh was attracted by the uproar, and arrived just as the little band of brave Sepoys had gained the victory. Their valour had a great effect upon him; he apologized to the envoy for the insult offered by his people, expressed his high admiration of the discipline and courage of the British troops, and declared himself ready to sign the wished for treaty, which he accordingly did on the 5th of April, 1809.

Two years after, in 1811, when the Goorkhas threatened to invade his dominions, and asked the British to aid them in their attempt, Runjeet Singh obtained permission from the Governor-General, not only to cross the Sutlej and fight the enemy in their mountain recesses, but received the assurance, that, if the Goorkhas should descend into the plains of Sirhind, he should receive the assistance of British troops, in maintaining inviolate the passage of the Sutlej.

This assurance allayed his apprehensions and jealousy, of the influence and power of the British. He continued incessantly engaged in extending his dominions and increasing his army. Sword in hand, he conquered Mooltan and Cashmere; while his warfare with his formidable foes, the Affghans, was unabated, till he finally succeeded in obtaining possession of Peshawur, through the treachery of the brother of Dost Mahomed, whom Runjeet had bribed with the large promise of an annual pension of two lakhs. The continued intestine disputes of the minor states, induced the British government to issue the proclamation of 1811.[10]

It was in 1822, that Runjeet first received into his service two foreign officers, MM. Allard and Ventura; the former being a Frenchman, the latter an Italian. After the fall of Napoleon, these officers had in vain sought an honourable employment in Persia, and, therefore, turned to the warlike chief of Lahore. He gave them a most cordial and brilliant reception, and commissioned them to organize his army on the French system; which they did with great success. Each of these officers had a salary of 50,000 rupees, or £5,000. sterling annually. Four years afterwards, they were followed by Generals Court and Avitabile. It was to these officers that the Sikh chief owed the highly efficient state of his army, which consisted of a well disciplined body of 50,000 men, besides 100,000 Irregulars. Lahore and Umritsur were made the depôts of arms; and here cannon foundries, powder magazines and arsenals were established.

---

[10] See Appendix VI.

At times Runjeet, and still more his chiefs, felt jealous, lest too much authority should be given to these European officers; for which reason he rather wished them to instruct than to command,[11] fearing they might prove dangerous to the state.

In the summer of 1831, his late Majesty King William IV. despatched Sir Alexander Burnes to Lahore, to take charge of a splendid present of horses from His Britannic Majesty to the Maharajah. Runjeet Singh was then at the height of his power; respected by his friends, and dreaded by his foes. The veteran hero was flattered by receiving this distinguished honour from the monarch of a nation which he highly venerated, and whose superiority in every respect he acknowledged. He gave Sir Alexander Burnes a brilliant reception; and the esteem which he thus manifested for the English, led to several interviews between himself and the Governor-General, Lord William Bentinck, at Rooper, in October, 1831.

The result of these interviews was a treaty of commerce and navigation, to which a supplementary treaty was afterwards added, between Runjeet Singh and the British, by which it was agreed, that the merchants and traders should pay a certain fixed duty, in lieu of the former arbitrary exactions.[12]

The meeting at Rooper, in October, 1831, between the Governor-General and Runjeet Singh, caused a great display of British and Sikh troops. An officer who was present on this occasion, told me that the movements of the Sikh battalions were very slow, and to the beat of drum: the cavalry, mostly wearing bright cuirasses, looked glittering and showy; whilst many of the gun carriages seemed as if a long march over a rough road would break them down. The word of command was always given in French.

In March, 1837, the Commander-in-Chief, General Sir Henry Fane, G.C.B., visited Lahore, on the occasion of the marriage of Runjeet's grandson, Nou Nehal Singh. The entertainment was on a magnificent scale, and cost between ten and eleven lakhs of rupees, or between £100,000 and £110,000 sterling. Here there was again a grand military display, and feats of arms. On this occasion, Runjeet Singh established an order of Knighthood, called "the Star of the Punjaub." He bestowed the Order upon Colonels Torrens, Churchill, Lumley, and Dunlop; the Adjutants-General, and Quartermasters-General, of the Queen's and Company's armies respectively. The investiture, with the Order, took place afterwards at Simla, at the head-quarters of Sir Henry Fane. All these individuals, donor and receivers, are now dead. It was the *setting star* of Runjeet Singh, for he died about two years after, in June, 1839.

The appearance and discipline of Runjeet's army, was the admiration of all military beholders. In December, 1838, before the Bengal column marched from Ferozepore to Cabool, *viâ* Scinde and Candahar, there was a review of the British

[11] In 1845, Allard was dead; Ventura, Court and Avitabile were in Europe; Cortland, son of Lieut.-Colonel Cortland, late of H.M. 31st Foot, who had entered the service of the Sikh leader, came over to the British. Colonel Hurbon, a Spanish officer, erected the works at Sobraon; still he was not a regular officer in the pay of the Sikh government, but was employed for the occasion by the troops.

[12] See Appendix VII.

troops under the Commander-in-Chief, Sir Henry Fane. Several Sikh soldiers who were present, were heard to make very insolent remarks, and twisted their moustachoes, a gross affront to any one, especially to an officer. They asserted that their troops could manœuvre much better, etc. A day or two afterwards the Sikhs gave a review, and actually copied all the British evolutions, with the greatest accuracy and precision. The infantry movements were also more rapid than at Rooper, in 1831.

Lord Auckland, Governor-General of India, in the same month, visited Runjeet Singh, at Lahore, when another display of English and Sikh troops took place. It was on the occasion of the review of our troops, that his Lordship, who was a bad rider, had a serious fall from his horse. His death would have been a great blow.

Lord Auckland, at that time, asked permission of the Maharajah to allow the British troops a free passage through his territory, on their march to Cabool, and to join his forces with those of the British, in this expedition into Affghanistan. This Runjeet Singh acceded to rather as a matter of necessity than of choice. Though only 59 years of age, his mind and body had become so enfeebled by his irregular course of life, that during his interview with Lord Auckland, his speech was already affected. He sank rapidly, from dropsy, and was finally carried off by paralysis.

When the death of their great chief was approaching, the army was drawn up in a line, and the dying monarch was carried in a litter through the ranks. As the procession moved slowly along, his favourite minister, Dhean Singh, appeared, to receive orders from his expiring sovereign, and informed the army, that Runjeet Singh declared, that his son, Khurruk Singh, should succeed him, and that Dhean Singh should be the chief minister of the kingdom. The soldiers received this intimation in perfect silence. According to the custom of the Sikhs, the body of the Maharajah was burnt the next day, before the gates of his palace, in the presence of all the great persons of the kingdom, and of the assembled troops. Four of his wives, two of whom were only sixteen years of age, and endowed with great personal beauty, together with seven of his concubines, committed themselves to the flames with his body. Dhean Singh also made a semblance of profound grief, and appeared to be in the act of throwing himself upon the funeral pile, but was forcibly withheld by the family of the Maharajah.

The death of Runjeet Singh occasioned considerable difficulty in the management of the auxiliary Sikhs under Colonel Wade, the British agent at Lahore who was now with the British army, and had the command of the column that was to force the Khyber pass. This glorious achievement he accomplished from the 22nd to the 27th of June, when he made himself master of Ali Musjid. He was nobly sustained in this campaign by the troops of Runjeet Singh; and on the 6th of August, the army of the Indus entered Cabool and forced Dost Mahomed to fly to Bokhara.

Runjeet Singh was succeeded by his son Khurruk Singh, then thirty-seven years of age. He was a weak and luxurious prince, and was totally incompetent to the affairs of government. Soon after his accession he was seized with a severe illness, of which he died, in November, 1840. His son, Nou Nehal Singh, and the chief minister, Dhean were supposed to have been not altogether innocent of his death.

Nou Nehal Singh, who was nineteen years of age, inherited his grandfather's ambitious spirit, and could scarcely conceal his joy, even at his father's funeral pyre, on finding himself sovereign of Lahore. He hated the English, and dreaded the effect of their policy in procuring a clear passage for their troops through the Punjaub, and thus, by a chain of consecutive alliances, effecting a union between the southern provinces of India and the West of Europe. He was determined to give proof of this on the first favourable opportunity that might present itself; but the royal sceptre which had so long fired his youthful breast soon passed to another, for the same day that elevated him to the throne, saw him a corpse! On leaving the pile he thought to wash away his sins in the Rāvee, and as he was riding through the outer gateway of the palace, a large portion of the archway fell upon him, killed the friend who was riding at his side, and so severely wounded the young prince in the head, that he expired in three hours. For several days his death was kept a secret; by some, in order to give his mother time to come up, and by others, to secure the succession to Shere Singh, the reputed, and afterwards adopted, son of Runjeet Singh. After a fierce contest between the queen mother and Shere Singh, the latter ascended the throne.

Shere Singh, though he had compelled the troops to recognise him as king, was incapable of commanding them. They soon became insubordinate and committed the most violent excesses; and their lawless conduct gave rise to apprehensions of a general insurrection.

This so intimidated the merchants and wealthy inhabitants on both sides of the Sutlej, that they appealed to the English for protection. The Maharajah was fully sensible of the critical state of his position, and though he deprecated the interference of the British power, he considered it best to yield to the necessities of the case and listen to the advice of the British. For though educated at the most magnificent and warlike court in India, amid events which were calculated to call forth a chivalrous spirit, Shere Singh never manifested either valour or firmness of character, but was carried along by the tide of events, and swayed by the dominant minds of the age. He felt his own incapacity as a ruler, and for a long time was completely under the control of Dhean Singh.

During the disastrous campaign of Cabool in 1842, Shere Singh rendered great services to the English in the relief of the distressed garrison of Jellalabad, and provided more than the stipulated corps of 5,000 men on payment of the sum of two lakhs of rupees.

The Governor-General, in consequence of the state of Affghanistan, determined to place an army of reserve at Ferozepore, and took this occasion for proposing an interview with Shere Singh. The Maharajah, however, apprehensive of the result of such an interview, declined the proposed honour. Lord Ellenborough took offence at this, and Shere Singh despatched Dhean Singh and his own son, Perthaub Singh, to make an apology in person, which was accepted; and his Lordship returned the visit of the young prince.

The military Sikh escort which accompanied, them crossed the Sutlej, which was much swollen at the time by the late heavy rains, with a rapidity and skill that excited the admiration of the British officers. The prince was permitted to review the British forces, soon after which the Governor-General broke up the encampment, and Shere Singh was relieved from his dreaded foe.

Shere Singh was addicted to drunkenness and vice, and succumbed to the influence of unworthy favourites. He had become suspicious of Dhean Singh, and, at their instigation, was induced to sign a royal warrant for his execution. This order was shewn to Dhean Singh by the very men who had procured it. Incensed at the treachery and ingratitude of the man whom he had raised to the royal power, Dhean Singh, as prime minister, immediately signed an order for the assassination of Shere Singh himself, and placed it in the hands of Ajeet Singh, the favourite who had supplanted him, and who had before threatened to kill Shere Singh.

Both Shere Singh and his hopeful son, Perthaub Singh were treacherously murdered on the next day, September the 15th, 1843, by Ajeet and Lena Singh; and the wily minister, Dhean Singh, who had joined with them in the conspiracy, met with the same fate, at their hands, before the close of that very day.

Heera Singh, the son of Dhean Singh, called upon the army to avenge his father's murder. Ajeet and Lena Singh were surrounded the same night, and both met with their well-merited fate before the morning's dawn.

Dhuleep Singh, the reputed son of Runjeet Singh, who was only a few months old at the time of his father's death, and, consequently, now only four years of age, was proclaimed Maharajah. His mother, Chunda, appointed her brother, Jowahir Singh, prime minister; but he was disliked by the army, and cruelly murdered by them. The military were now masters of the state, and sought to make Goolab Singh, the oldest of Runjeet's favourites, vizier. Goolab being fully aware that his great wealth was the bait, kept them in a state of uncertainty as to his resolve; but, in the meantime, instigated them to march upon the British territories, with the intent of invasion.

Deceived by the promised support of Goolab, and buoyed up by exalted notions of their own military prowess and discipline, as well as animated by the desire of pillage, the Sikhs made sure of success. Though they had never seen the British troops in battle, the Khalsa soldiers considered themselves fully equal to contend against them. There is no doubt, and it is necessary to make the remark in order to account for the presumptuous conduct of the Sikhs, that our sad reverses at Cabool in 1841, and our retreat in 1842, had greatly affected the *prestige* of the British military character. Just as the failure of Lord Lake before Bhurtpore, in 1805, even after his victories in 1803 and 1804, had left the impression on the minds of the native princes, that we could not take forts.

Now the Sikhs under Runjeet Singh had defeated the Affghans under Ajean Khan, the elder brother of Dost Mahomed Khan, at Noushera (half way between Attock and Peshawur), in 1823. They imagined themselves superior, as soldiers, to the Affghans, and knew that the latter had defeated the British. They did not, however, bear in mind that our troops were destroyed in the retreat by the frost and snow. Lady Sale says, the first snow fell on the 26th of November. They, therefore, argued thus:—They had beaten the Affghans, and the Affghans had beaten the British; therefore the British were not invincible, and might be overcome by Sikh troops.

The disturbed state of the Lahore government during the latter part of the reign of Runjeet Singh, up to the present moment, had compelled the British government to introduce various precautionary measures for the protection of the British frontier, on a scale which was opposed to the terms of the treaty of 1809. It is true that the British government had recognised their boy-king, Dhuleep Singh, who had been proclaimed by the army, but being of a naturally suspicious character, the Sikhs considered themselves in danger of invasion, and resolved to anticipate the British, and wage war, by crossing the Sutlej. They appointed Lall Singh, prime minister, or vizier, and Tej Singh, an officer of considerable talent and experience, commander-in-chief of the Sikh forces.

The British government demanded an explanation of this movement, but none being given, the Governor-General issued a proclamation,[13] declaring all the possessions and territories of the Maharajah Dhuleep Singh on the left bank of the Sutlej to be confiscated and annexed to the British dominions; calling upon the inhabitants and their rulers to second the British government, he assured all who were peaceably disposed, of the protection of that government.

Thus the war was begun. The Sikhs, as we have seen, crossed the Sutlej with their heavy artillery on the 13th, on the 14th, marched to Ferozeshah, and, on the 18th, met the British forces, under the command of Sir Hugh Gough.

The battle of Moodkee, on the 18th of December, was their first battle with the English. This engagement they themselves allowed to be a defeat; but in that of Ferozeshah, three or four days later, they claimed the victory. Indeed many British officers have told me that it was a very desperate affair, and that it was fortunate the Sikhs were ignorant of their own power and resources. If this fact be held in recollection, when the reader comes to the battle of Sobraon, seven weeks later, he will see the necessity for a grand effort on their part; for another defeat or retreat would have been ruin to the Sikh cause.

Colonel Campbell's force was, as we have stated, nearly 3,000 strong, but the loss of the English in the battles of Moodkee and Ferozeshah, amounted to 3,291 men killed and wounded, and 804 horses; so that the arrival of this force would not replace the numbers lost. It was, therefore, necessary to draw troops from other quarters also, and concentrate them at the place of action.

[13] See Appendix VIII.

CHAPTER III.

Nidampore—Christmas-day—Munsorepore—Kotla Mullair—Phurawallee—Bussean—Surrender of Wudnee—Cession of Ferozepore—Bhaga Poorana—False Alarms—Roree Bukkur—Sir John Littler—Sir H.M. Wheeler—Ferozeshah—Aliwal—Sikh Forces—British Forces—Sikh Entrenchment—Returns of Killed and Wounded—Sir H. Hardinge—Battle of Ferozeshah—Sudden Attack by Tej Singh—His Blunder—Appearance of a field of Battle—Fate of the Wounded.

To resume our route. On December the 24th, Colonel Campbell's force marched to Nidampore, a small village; a distance of nine miles. Here we halted, with the prospect of spending a quiet Christmas Day. On this day, however, we received intelligence, in camp, of the battle of Ferozeshah, which had taken place on the 22nd of December; and that the Sikhs, driven from the field, had retired across the Sutlej. This day, therefore, instead of breathing peace and love, was employed in preparations for war with our determined foes: unlike the Romans at the siege of Jerusalem, when no operations were undertaken against the Jews on their Sabbaths and Holy days. In Europe, however, and indeed all over the world in the present age, all days are alike in regard to war. The heathen Sikhs, who keep sacred no day in the week, might attack us on any day, and at any hour; so that it was necessary in self-defence that we should be prepared for the enemy. Accordingly the services of the armourer-sergeant and his men were put in requisition to sharpen swords and lances, and all was ready for starting the next morning.

On the 26th, our troops began their march to the village of Munsorepore, a distance of ten miles, through a country abounding in jungle, which rendered it necessary to observe great caution on the march; and flanking parties were sent out to prevent a surprise. Our route lay through two villages, which appeared to be thinly peopled: the walls of the houses were in a state of decay, and altogether they presented a desolate and deserted appearance. This, however, was not extraordinary; for as the Sikhs had been located on the south side of the Sutlej for fourteen days, it was to be expected that the people would abandon their homes and fly to the desert.

On the 27th of December, our troops marched to Kotla Mullair, a distance of sixteen miles. This town is very long and densely built; the main street being peculiarly narrow.

On the 28th we marched to Phurawallee, the country of the Nabah Rajah, twelve miles over a flat country, and by an unmade road, but by no means bad. This was Sunday; and still no public service. Last night, a private of the Lancers shot himself dead; such an event is happily of rare occurrence, and it produced a deep impression upon both men and officers.

There was a report abroad in the bazaar to-day, that another battle had taken place; but there was no foundation for the rumour. The Sikhs, it will be seen, did not meditate fighting again so soon.

On the 29th, we proceeded to Bussean, a long twelve miles' march through a flat and open country. The detachment had under its charge 4,300,000 rounds of ball (musketry) cartridges. This would give for 20,000 infantry, 215 rounds per man; and, as it is said that one shot in 100 kills, there were rounds sufficient to destroy 43,000 of the enemy. Independently of this, we had round-shot, shrapnell, canister and grape.

Our next march was to Wudnee or Budnee, fifteen miles and a half, by a very sandy route, which was consequently quite unfit for hackeries.

On the road, the commanding officer received an Express from the Governor-General, ordering us to take the fort of Wudnee, should we find it occupied by Sikh troops. Captain Rose, of the Lancers, was accordingly sent in advance of our force, to surround the Avails with his troop. To his great regret, the garrison offered no resistance, and about 5,000 rupees, and a few half-starved horses were given up to us. Two companies of the 59th Regt. of Native Infantry were left in charge of the fort.

Only a few days before, the whole of this district had been under the sway of the Maharajah of Lahore; but by the proclamation of the Governor-General it was now incorporated with the British dominions.

About ten years previous to these events, the demise of the female chief of Ferozepore without issue, gave us possession of that place; the rule in such cases being, that the estates of those chiefs who die without heirs become escheats. Thus this city fell to the East India Company. Runjeet Singh had previously objected to cede to us any of the ferries; but we had now for some time past been permitted to make use of them, both here and along the course of the river. On the cession of Ferozepore, however, his jealousy was aroused anew, and studiously fostered by his officers, at our occupation of a territory so near his own capital; and his chiefs constantly urged upon him the necessity of excluding us. Thus, with the possession of Ferozepore, we had gained the ferry at that place, and subsequently also secured one opposite to Loodianna.

This was an important point, for by it we obtained the right to cross whenever we chose. The Sikhs, however, as we have seen, were not prevented from crossing over to us. It was a very anomalous position for the British rule to be placed in, for, while we were protectors of the estates of four Sikh Rajahs, the estates of other chiefs were under the government of the Lahore Durbar. It is obvious that the circumstance of the Sikhs having a right to visit the estates of those chiefs who owed allegiance to the Durbar, and none to the British government, must have been a source of considerable inconvenience and annoyance, to say the least of it. Hence there is no doubt, that they sent over guns and ammunition to the left or south bank of the Sutlej, long before they crossed themselves, and when they did venture over, we confiscated the said estates.

To return to our narrative. On the 31st of December, the detachment under Colonel Campbell marched twelve miles to Bhaga Poorana, a small native village in the possession of the Alloo-walla Rajah, who held lands on both sides of the Sutlej. Here the Colonel received an order from the Commander-in-Chief to proceed to Loodianna, instead of to Ferozepore, the object of which change we could not in the least understand. In the evening, while we were at mess, we were suddenly disturbed by the report that some thousands of Sikhs were approaching our camp, and indeed had actually entered it. Our dessert was left untouched upon the table; the whole regiment was soon mounted, and drawn up at the head of their lines. After waiting about half an hour, and seeing no enemy, all retired to bed. In less than half an hour after, we had a second false alarm, from the firing of some sentries, belonging to the picquets of the Native Infantry corps. Such mistakes, with all their concomitant annoyances, are by no means unfrequent. An alarm has been occasioned by a few bullocks crossing a nullah near a camp during a dark night. In such a case, a Sepoy sentry receiving no answer to his challenge, "Who come dare?" (who goes there?), fires his piece, and the whole camp taking this as a signal of danger, is instantly in motion.

A false alarm of this kind occurred at Roree Bukkur, in Scinde, when the Bengal column under Major-general Sir Willoughby Cotton, was *en route* to Candahar, in February, 1839. The musket of one of the sentries went off by accident; the others immediately fired, whereupon the whole of the troops turned out.

Looking at the map, it would seem as if the recent "Express" to move on Loodianna had in view to command the road from Delhi, though just then no convoy was, it is believed, on the road from that city. Again, troops had been marched from Loodianna, and Runjoor Singh had not then crossed. The sudden appearance of the Sikhs in the neighbourhood of our frontier, threatened the two advanced posts at Ferozepore and Loodianna, both on the south bank of the Sutlej, and distant from each other about seventy miles. Major-General, now Sir John Littler, commanded at the former place; and, when summoned on the 23rd of December, 1845, to join the Commander-in-Chief, had about 10,000 troops. He left a small force at that post, and joined head-quarters at about 1 o'clock, P.M. At Loodianna, Colonel, now Sir Hugh Massy Wheeler, K.C.B., commanded. At Subathoo, fourteen miles up the hills, the Honourable Company's 1st European regiment was stationed. Loodianna is about equi-distant from Subathoo and Moodkee.

The battle of Ferozeshah, on the 21st and 22nd of December, 1845, has been the subject of discussion both as to the time and form of making; the attack. In regard to time, it is the opinion of the French marshal, Marmont, in his "L'Esprit des Instructions Militaires," p. 151, that "it is best to begin a battle early in the morning if certain of success; but if uncertain, in the middle of the day." Some assert that it was not necessary to commence the attack on the 21st, and that it would have been far better to have deferred it till early the next morning. Then again it is maintained, that had the attack been deferred till the morning of the 22nd, Tej Singh would have joined the main body of the Sikhs. However, early next morning the attack was renewed, and the rest of the entrenchments soon taken. It also appears that Tej Singh did actually come up before Ferozeshah at nine o'clock in the morning—at an hour when the British had possession of the place—and Major-General Littler was ordered to hold it at all risks.

I have before said that the cavalry were taken off in the direction of Ferozepore, with the exception of the 3rd Dragoons. Here, again, I may remark on the absence of the 9th Lancers, which was a general subject of regret among the officers present in the battle; a regret which I have heard repeatedly expressed both at the time and since. It is not possible to calculate the value of the services which this strong corps might have rendered in the hour of need; instead of which they were marching backwards and forwards between Ferozepore and Loodianna. Yet it is very probable that Tej Singh may have been aware that the 9th and 16th Lancers, and other corps, were on their march to join the main army, and hence have hastened his retreat.

Another objection to delay was the great scarcity of water; there being, it is said, no water at Ferozeshah, except in the village held by the enemy, and but little in the villages near it. Others, again, assert, that had the troops fallen back a little they would have found a supply of water, and that the Sikhs, moreover, would then most probably have come out of their entrenchments, and attacked the English on even ground.

At the battle of Aliwal, which took place subsequently, namely, on the 28th of January, 1846, the Sikhs did leave the little entrenchment which they had thrown up, and took up a position, their right resting on a village of the same name; their left on a circular entrenchment; and their centre on some heights. Again, it is whispered that the Governor-General and the Commander-in-Chief were desirous of making an immediate attack, in order to prevent the Sikhs from marching upon Ferozepore or Loodianna. Of Loodianna, however, there was no danger, because they would naturally attack that place by crossing at Philoor; there was far more reason to have expected an attack upon Ferozepore, for three good reasons.

1st. Because the Sikhs had fallen back to Ferozeshah, only a few miles from Ferozepore.

2ndly. Because, as has been before stated, Runjeet Singh's Chiefs were very averse to the English having possession of Ferozepore, from which there is a direct road to Lahore, their capital; and

3rdly. Because, by their retrograde movements from Moodkee, the Sikhs joined the other infantry.

The object in not attacking till the next morning, would have been to gain information respecting the nature and strength of the enemy's entrenched position at Ferozeshah. The late Captain P. Nicolson, the assistant political agent, is said strongly to have recommended an attack on the rear of the enemy's entrenchment. Major Broadfoot, when he reached the spot, where Major-General Littler joined about noon, exclaimed, "We will now drive them out of that entrenchment."

It is said that there was a great deal of jungle about Ferozeshah, but that the ground immediately around was open. By a brief delay, it might have been ascertained that the rear was undefended by guns. It is not to be supposed that the Sikhs would have thought of an advance beyond their then position, until they had gained a victory.

Again, it is broadly asserted that the Sikhs would never have left their entrenchments, and might have strengthened them, had any delay taken place.

The Sikh force is said to have been as follows:

	Battalions.		Corps.	Guns.
French Brigade Infantry,	4	Regular Cavalry,	2	26
Buhadoor Singh's Infantry,	4	Regular Cavalry,	1	16
Mertab Singh's Infantry,	4	Regular Cavalry,	1	18
	12		4	60

The Infantry were 7,200 men.

	Irregular Cavalry.
Charaganee Horse	4,500
Orderly Horse	3,500
Lall Singh's Horse	1,800
Heera Singh's Horse	3,500
Moolraj's Horse	550
Bala Singh's Horse	200
Nehing's Horse	1,000
Utter Singh's Horse	700
Pindeewalas	900
Dogras[14]	200
	16,850
4 Corps of Regular Cavalry, about	2,000
Irregular Horse, about	16,850
	18,850
Infantry	7,200
Total	26,050
Artillery Field Guns	60
Heavy Guns	28
	88
Zumbooruks (Camel Guns)	250

[14] The Jummoo Chief is called Dogra.

The above force, with 3,000 detached Infantry, and the greater part of the Irregular Horse, marched to Ferozeshah, for the purpose of holding Moodkee; reaching this place in the evening, they fought the battle of the 18th of December, with a force of 17,000 or 18,000 men.

The British force at Moodkee was about 13,000 men, and 48 guns, 36 of which were horse artillery: the action was sudden, and there was no regularity; the corps moved off in echelon, but owing to the dust, confusion, and lateness of the day, some infantry corps fired into each other. I have heard that a native infantry corps fired by mistake into H.M. 50th foot. Many of the officers, and all those of the staff who were killed, were shot by Sikh soldiers from the branches of trees, where they had stationed themselves. The Horse Artillery and Cavalry opened the encounter; but the dust which these troops raised, caused the Infantry, which came up last, to grope as it were in the dark, and to make serious mistakes.

The Sikhs having been defeated at Moodkee, called upon the troops before Ferozepore, and the Nuggur Ghât to join them, which made their force as under:

Battalions.	Infantry.		Cavalry.		Guns.
10 Additional,	6,000	Additional,	500	Additional,	55
12 Before	7,200	Before	2,000	Before	60
	13,200		2,500	Heavy Guns	28
					143

This, including the 16,850 Irregular Cavalry, gives 32,550 men, of whom the Regular troops were 15,700 men; and, deducting the seventeen guns taken at Moodkee, the enemy ought to have had 126 guns at Ferozeshah, besides the 250 Zumbooruks. These were not very great odds against the British as to numbers.

The number of British killed and wounded was 2,419; namely, 2,269 non-commissioned officers and privates, and 150 officers, which gives one officer to every fifteen men; and as the usual proportion is one to twenty, or twenty-five, this was the greatest proportional loss in the four battles.

At Ferozeshah, including the Sikh force detached to Moodkee, there were 13,200 infantry; deducting, say 1,200 killed and wounded at Moodkee, there remained, say 12,000 men; to these add an additional reinforcement of 6,000 men and we have 18,000 infantry, which appears to have been the amount of the Sikh forces in the entrenchments at Ferozeshah on the 21st of December 1845; also 126 guns, of which twenty-eight were heavy guns, which likewise agrees with the returns; the enemy's cavalry could scarcely have exceeded 8,000 or 10,000 men. The entrenchment was about a mile in length, and half a mile in breadth, but as there was a village within those limits, the space for the troops was of course greatly diminished by it.

It will be for the military reader to form his own judgment, as my experience does not warrant me in giving an opinion of the motives and actions of my superiors. I have trusted a great deal throughout my accounts, to officers who were actually present in this remarkable campaign. It is curious to note the opinions of others. One thing however seems tolerably clear, that the only mode by which a really true account of any battle can be given, is to obtain a statement from some competent officer of each corps, troop, or company of artillery, etc., actually present in the field.

The practice, in this respect in the Indian army is this: each brigadier reports to the major-general commanding his division, upon the efficiency and prominent services of each regiment in his brigade, noting also the disposition of each corps; the major-general in a similar manner makes a report to the Adjutant-General for the information of the Commander-in-Chief, of the state of each of his brigades, and the particular services rendered. It is from these divisional reports that the Commander-in-Chief draws up his despatches.

It is obvious, that after a great battle, particularly if there be a pursuit of the enemy, no correct return of the killed and wounded can be given for two, three, or four days; for those who are killed lie on the field, and those who are wounded will get into a village, if near, and remain concealed there.

The Sikhs having thus, as we have stated, drawn their various forces from Moodkee, Ferozepore, and Nuggur Ghât, concentrated them at Ferozeshah, and formed their entrenchments, which in several places they threw up breast high.

Lieutenant-General Sir Henry Hardinge, the Governor-General, who was second in command, shared all the fatigues and dangers of the army with the Commander-in-Chief. Orders had been despatched to Sir John Littler to join head-quarters immediately. He accordingly left only a small garrison at Ferozepore, and, with a body of about 5,000 men and twenty-one guns, effected the junction, about noon on the 21st of December. Measures for a general attack were at once planned; but a considerable delay occurred, and much time was lost, as we have stated, in consequence of the conflicting views of competent officers, as to whether it was desirable to make an immediate attack, or to defer it till the following morning. The former was ultimately resolved upon.

The British marched in even ranks, and commenced the action with a brisk fire of artillery at a distance of about a mile from the enemy. The Sikhs made a gallant defence. The British artillery advanced steadily till they were within a few hundred yards of the entrenchment; but the Sikhs kept up an incessant fire from their heavy guns; in consequence of which our infantry were ordered to advance, and, in the face of a murderous fire, to take the batteries. Night put a stop to the carnage, but not to the awful state of confusion which prevailed in the British camp, which arose partly from the severe losses and the scattering of the different regiments, with the uncertainty as to whether any advantage had been gained, and partly from the incessant firing kept up during the whole night by the Sikhs upon the wretched soldiers who were lying wounded upon the field of battle, or who were cowering around their scanty fires, worn out with cold, fatigue and excruciating thirst.

Sir Henry Hardinge, finding that a large Sikh gun occasioned much annoyance to our troops, brought up the 80th Foot, who soon took it. He then passed among the different European corps, which greatly cheered and reanimated them under their intense sufferings. It was a night of terrific suspense and anxiety to the two British Chiefs, both of whom nobly resolved to fight and conquer, or perish in the attempt. The British lion was roused, and his vast strength was all centred in one final attempt. The die was cast. The Governor-General gave the word, and Britons struck home the death-blow.

The village of Ferozeshah appears to have been held during the night of the 21st of December, partly by the British and partly by the Sikhs. One of our divisions under the gallant Major-General, Sir Harry Smith, kept up a fire during the greater part of the night. The other divisions bivouacked at some distance, no one knows where. Had a concerted movement been necessary, it would have been quite out of the question; for, by some mistake or oversight, no place of rendezvous had been fixed on. I am told that the men belonging to two or three of the European corps got clubbed together, and were so found the next morning; nay, even the whereabouts of the Commander-in-Chief himself could not be found. A certain Major-General was anxious to communicate with him, and an engineer officer, who had just been with Sir Hugh Gough, offered to shew him the road; but, to his surprise, he could not find it: either His Excellency had moved his position, or the night was too dark to enable the officer to trace his way back.

The morning light revealed the fact that the Sikhs were still masters of a large portion of their entrenchments; the British retaining only that part where they had bivouacked during the night.

The Commander-in-Chief now drew up his forces; the Infantry forming into a line supported on either side by the horse artillery. His Excellency took the command of the left wing, the Governor-General of the right. The engagement opened with a brisk cannonade from the centre. The Sikhs renewed the deadly fire from their heavy guns, screened by their masked batteries, scattering death and destruction among the British troops. Both the left and right wings of infantry advancing under their able commanders, charged the Sikhs at the point of the bayonet, and took possession of the village of Ferozeshah.

At this juncture, when victory seemed to be decided for the British, Tej Singh, the commander-in-chief of the Sikh army, suddenly appeared on the field with his army of reserve, consisting of 30,000 men, and a large park of light guns. He charged into the midst of the British troops, and attempted to recover the entrenchment, but without success. He then opened a fire upon us from his guns, but, unhappily, all our shot were expended. It was one of those unexpected cases which demand the greatest promptitude and judgment; and our artillery are said to have fired blank ammunition.[15]

The British cavalry had been ordered by a certain staff officer, in the Adjutant-General's department, to move off to Ferozepore. This, I suppose, must have been before Tej Singh came up. It is also reported that Tej Singh conceived that this move was made in connection with some deeply concerted plan, with the inten-

[15] When Sir Archibald Campbell, who commanded the expedition against Ava, in 1824-26, headed a Portuguese brigade of infantry in the Peninsular war, he was informed upon one occasion, that only a few rounds of shot were left. He immediately ordered a charge in line, his object being to conceal his want of ammunition.

tion of getting into his rear. Whatever may have been his opinion, he contented himself with firing a few shots from his light guns—none other had he—by which a few of the British were killed and wounded. Had the cavalry not been ordered off, the whole of which, I understand, moved away, with the exception of that noble regiment the 3rd Light Dragoons, who had previously, in this same action, performed prodigies of valour in charging batteries and entrenchments,—acts unparalleled in cavalry tactics,—Tej Singh might have been attacked to advantage. Thus much is certain; that the officer above alluded to was allowed to retire from the service. The whole affair of the morning of the 22nd cannot be either unravelled or explained; and I have discussed the matter with many officers who were present on that occasion, but have never met with one who could solve its mysteries. It savours more of romance than of reality. "Truth is strange—stranger than fiction." Goolab Singh, now Maharajah of Cashmere, speaking to a European officer, of Tej Singh's advance, as above described, observed that: "Tej Singh committed a great blunder; he should never have gone near you, but should have marched at once upon Delhi!"

Many, however, are of opinion, that the sudden attack of Tej Singh, with his 30,000 troops, was a mere feint. It was well known that he was in correspondence with Captain Nicolson; and it is even affirmed, that he had privately furnished an officer with a plan of the intended operations of the Sikh army. It was his object to ingratiate himself with both parties. His position as leader of the army demanded that he should make the attack; while at the same time he foresaw that the British would ultimately triumph in the Punjaub, and that it would be for his interest to make friends of them. Therefore, after firing a few shots, the Commander-in-Chief of the Sikhs fled from the field of battle, at the very moment when the failure of the enemy's ammunition, and the departure of their cavalry to Ferozepore, gave him an advantage which might have turned the tide of victory in his favour. After the desertion of their general, the Sikhs made several ineffectual attempts, to recover the entrenchment, but before night-fall, were compelled to retreat across the Sutlej.

The view of a field of battle awakens the noblest sympathies of our nature. Even the stern Napoleon has had his cold heart touched by such a scene. The first survey is overwhelming; and the heart of even the stoutest soldier shrinks within him, and sickens at the sight. On a nearer inspection, we find the dead and the dying, friend and foe, lying side by side; their furious contest suddenly cut short by the cold hand of death—while the cries and moans of the wounded till our ears with sounds of lamentation and woe, and our hearts with pity and commiseration.

We lament the fate of the slain, and grieve that his career is ended; yet it is the death of the brave soldier who has gloriously discharged his duty to his country, and whose fame remains imperishable, that calls forth our deepest grief, admiration and gratitude. "*Dulce et decorum est pro patria mori.*" Well did Lord Hutchinson, in reporting the death of the brave and lamented Abercrombie, express the feelings of a soldier, when he said: "His name shall be embalmed in the memory of a grateful country."

Thoughts of a future state are powerfully impressed upon the mind, as the eye wanders over the battle-field of the slain. As we gaze upon those who have distinguished themselves, not only as the liege soldiers of their king, but as the faithful soldiers of the King of kings, our heart insensibly finds relief. While the spark of life yet flickers in the mortal tenement, we watch by the side of our wounded comrade, and, like king David, we fast and weep, and say: "Who can tell whether God will be gracious to me that he may live;" but when the dread fiat has gone forth, and the spirit no longer dwells within its house of clay, like David we restrain our grief, and looking beyond the grave, exclaim in faith: "Wherefore should I weep? Can I bring him back again? I shall go to him, but he shall not return to me."

Before quitting the field of slaughter, I would make a few remarks respecting the wounded. The fate of the private soldier is often very hard: by the loss of limbs he is rendered useless for life as a soldier, his means of subsistence are curtailed, and what is yet dearer to him, his military career is blighted for ever. The officer may do duty again if he lose an arm, or what is almost the same thing, if he be wounded and unable to have the ball extracted. This was the case with my father, who, having been hit in both shoulders at the battle of Waterloo, did duty in his most gallant regiment the old 95th, now the Rifle Brigade, for nearly three years after, although, as the ball remained in the shoulder, the left arm was rendered useless.[16] Some officers even continue in the service after they have lost a leg, and receive a good pension. This is the case with Field-Marshal the Marquis of Anglesey.

The disabled rank and file are what is styled "invalided," that is to say, they are sent to England and elsewhere, where they obtain a pension, fixed and determined by a board of officers.

The late Queen's Inspector-General of Hospitals in Bengal, states a fact which ought to be generally known, "The number of those who are wounded and die in consequence, cannot be ascertained fully under the lapse of a year, because there are cases in which a gun-shot through the lungs has superinduced affections of the brain, fevers, etc." It is likewise worthy of remark that gun-shot wounds are more dangerous than sabre cuts.

[16] See Appendix IX.

CHAPTER IV.

Return to Bussean—Sir John Grey's Detachment—Battle of Assaye—Sindiah's Troops—Generals Allard and Ventura—General Lloyd's Observations on the Art of War—Tactics of the Sikhs—Runjeet Singh's Discipline—Sikh Artillery—Goojerat—Moodkee—Sir Joseph Thackwell—Bootawalla—Pontoons—Their Value to an Army—Great Rise in the Price of Food.

On the 2nd of January, 1846, Colonel Campbell's force marched to Bussean, a retrograde movement; but in times of war, such counter movements are occasionally unavoidable, and their utility can be known only to the superintending eye of the Commander-in-chief.

In the course of the day, soon after we had finished our long and fatiguing march, we were surprised to find that we were to return in the direction of Ferozepore, in company with Major General Sir John Grey's detachment, which, at this time, was a march or two in our rear. This detachment consisted of three troops of horse artillery, H.M. 16th Lancers, 3rd Light Cavalry, H.M. 10th Foot, three regiments of Native Infantry, a company of Sappers and Miners, and the 4th Irregular Horse. This formed a force of about 7,500 men. There were besides, twelve twelve-pounders and eighteen horse artillery guns; in all thirty guns, or four to every thousand men, a force as large as that with which the Duke of Wellington fought the battle of Assaye, on the 23rd of September, 1803; for, excluding the 3,000 Mysore, etc., cavalry, he had only 4,500 men. The enemy was defeated with the loss of 120 guns taken, destroyed, or lost; the captured guns amounted to above 100.

It may be asked, why, when the Duke of Wellington, with a mere handful of soldiers, attacked some 35,000 men and gained such an action, we could not utterly eradicate even the very name of Sikh? The reasons are threefold. The battles of Moodkee and Aliwal were field actions; those of Ferozeshah and Sobraon were storming entrenchments. The strength of the entrenchments at Ferozeshah was not equal to those at Sobraon. The number of killed and wounded at Ferozeshah amounted to 2,419, and at Sobraon 2,383. At the former battle, the enemy had more than one hundred, at the latter sixty-seven guns, and two hundred camel-swivels; besides, at Sobraon, the Sikhs had two strong batteries in the rear of the right and left flanks of the entrenchment; for there were entrenchments and works within one another. We made three good attacks. The attack in front by Major-General Gilbert's division was not originally designed. There was a bank or mound of earth between this division and the entrenchment. The brigade, of which the 29th Foot composed a part, got jammed up, and formed into a wedge, something like the Roman form. It was at first intended that this division should wait as a reserve, and act if required, There was a failure in the right attack on the enemy's left.

Secondly, the troops of Sindiah and of the Berar Rajah, at the battle of Assaye had indeed been drilled, but they had not then had the advantage of having French officers; besides which, they, the Sirdars, were unable to act by themselves; nor had their men, like the Khalsa troops, been disciplined by such distinguished officers as were in the service of Runjeet Singh. The older French officers had died off, and the others were mere adventurers, very different from Ventura and Allard, who had served in the wars of the great Napoleon; the former having been in the retreat from Moscow. Sindiah's European officers were simply drill-sergeants; the merely being able to advance in line, or to execute some common evolutions will not gain a battle. A practised military eye for planning a battle, and marking out the details, is the indispensable requisite for such an achievement. As General Lloyd truly observes, in his able work on the Art of War: "No art or science is more difficult than that of war. It may be divided into two parts: the one mechanical, which may be taught by precepts; the other has no name, nor can it be either defined or taught. It consists in a just application of the principles and precepts of war in all the numberless circumstances and situations which occur; no rule, no study or application however assiduous, no experience however long, can teach this part; it is the effect of genius alone. As to the first, it may be reduced to mathematical principles; its object is to prepare the materials which form an army, for all the different operations which may occur: genius must apply them, according to the ground, number, species, and quality of the troops, which admit of infinite combinations. In this art, as in poetry and eloquence, there are many who can trace the rules by which a poem or an oration should be composed, and even compose according to the exactest rules, but, for want of that enthusiastic and divine fire, their productions are languid and insipid: so in our profession, many are to be found who know every precept of it by heart; but alas! when called upon to apply them, are immediately at a stand. They then recall their rules, and want to make everything, the rivers, woods, ravines, mountains, etc., subservient to them; whereas, their precept should, on the contrary, be subject to these, which are the only rules, the only guide we ought to follow. Whatever manoeuvre is not formed on these is absurd and ridiculous. These form the Great Book of War, and he who cannot read it, must for ever be content with the title of a brave soldier, and never aspire to that of a great general."

The discipline and training of the Sikh army had, as I have observed before, undergone a complete transformation and improvement under Runjeet Singh, so that the troops under Sindiah, in 1803, could not bear comparison with those of 1845, who had been disciplined by Ventura and Allard. Runjeet Singh himself was a great warrior; and from the time that he visited Lord Lake's camp, in 1805, he became convinced of the superiority of the discipline of the British army, and at once resolved on re-forming his own. He had a good material to work upon in the native hardihood, bravery and energy of the Sikh character. His primary attention was given to the formation of a regular infantry; and in this he was greatly aided by some deserters from the British service, to whom he confided the drilling of his troops. After that, he enlisted the Goorkhas, whose able resistance to the English had given him great confidence in their mode of discipline.

The opposition of his officers and troops, especially in the adoption of a new dress, would have daunted a less resolute character; but Runjeet Singh, conscious of the power of example, took part in all the military exercises and drill, and even wore the unaccustomed dress of a British foot-soldier; thus making himself master *de facto*, and not merely *de verbo*, of the new principles of war. After this, Ventura, Allard, and other European officers, carried out and perfected that discipline, which made the Sikh army what it was, when led under Tej Singh against the British forces, in 1845.

Let the reader bear in mind how fatal the trap, laid by the Sikhs for our troops at Ramnuggur, had proved to those gallant cavalry officers, Colonel Cureton,[17] Lieutenant-Colonel Havelock, and Captain Fitzgerald; the two latter were my brother officers in the 4th Queen's Own Light Dragoons, at Bombay. At the battle of Goojerat, on the 21st of February, 1849, the Sikhs moved more than once to try and turn our flank. Was such an attempt ever made in 1803? No! It was at Assaye that the Duke of Wellington fought his hardest and best battle (I am speaking of India), for he had five to one as odds against him. In guns, the enemy had seven times the number, besides several 16-pounders and heavy guns. The Duke had none but 17 pop-guns; for 6-pounders, when brought into action against 16 and 12-pounders, deserve no better name.

Thirdly, The Sikhs fired their guns in the ratio of thrice to our twice, which multiplies most fearfully the battering power of artillery, and raises the calibre of a six into a nine-pounder. At the battle of Ferozeshah, the Sikh guns were served with extraordinary rapidity and precision. The infantry stood between and behind the batteries, and lay on the ground behind their artillery, priming their muskets, and actively discharging their pieces in the face of the British force, thus forming an almost unprecedented shower of balls, carrying destruction and death with irresistible force. Recollecting that in 1845 and 1846, the enemy's artillery was double that of the British, we might rather ask how it came that so many escaped its deadly effects, than wonder how it was that so many were destroyed.

At Goojerat, where we had the greatest number of guns, the victory was complete; for after three hours' constant firing, our troops advanced, the enemy's guns were taken, and they fled.

Referring to the history of the battles in India in earlier times, from 1780 to 1792, we find that Hyder Ali Khan and Tippoo Sultan, used 18-pounder guns as field-guns. Sir Eyre Coote was obliged to use the same, which taught the British the necessity of having large guns; but, till very recently, we had departed from the practice of using guns equal in calibre to those of our enemies. It is a curious fact, that the British had 2,419 killed and wounded at Ferozeshah, and 2,383, or 36 less, at Sobraon: also, at the former battle, 694 killed, and at the latter, only 460,

[17] See Appendix X.

being a difference of 50 per cent. less. How can we account for this, but from the circumstance of our having had more guns at Sobraon? At Goojerat, the British loss was 807, out of which number 96 were killed, or not one-eighth. At Moodkee, the English lost 872 killed and wounded, of which number 215 were killed, or nearly one-fourth. At Goojerat, nearly 90 guns had been playing for three hours upon the Sikhs, before they gave way and the British advanced to take their guns. At Moodkee, the 36 Horse Artillery guns were the only ones brought into play. Except at the battle of Aliwal, where the loss was 589, the British suffered less at Goojerat than in any other battle with the Sikhs.

Lord Gough, in his Despatch,[18] says that the enemy had 60,000 men (perhaps overrated), and 59 guns. His lordship had 84 guns, according to the return, and these were of heavier metal than those of the enemy.

Surely, after these proofs, and when we have lost 10,788 men, killed and wounded, and 1,899 horses, in seven battles and one siege, viz., Moodkee, Ferozeshah, Aliwal, Sobraon, Ramnuggur, Chillianwallah, Goojerat, and the fort of Mooltan, we ought to be prepared on every point on our North-West frontier.

When I left India, in 1846, after the decisive battle of Sobraon, it was the general opinion that not another shot would be fired again in India for many years to come, whereas, in little more than two years after, we had, instead of a campaign of two months' duration, that is from the 18th of December, 1845, to the 10th of February, 1846, an uninterrupted warfare of ten months' continuance.

To resume our narrative. On the 3rd of January, Colonel Campbell's force marched for the third time to Wudnee, a distance of seventeen miles. The fatigue and tedium of marching to and fro, began to be sensibly felt, and many of our camp followers deserted. Among them was my *Bihishti*, or water-carrier, who had accompanied me on the march from Cawnpore. Then, too, there was so much heavy baggage, that instead of the indispensable refreshment of an ablution at the end of a dusty march, our officers could not get their towels and soap till a late hour in the afternoon.

On Sunday, the 4th of January, we marched back to Bhaga Poorana. Here we experienced a scarcity of water; and what little there was, was very bad. On the 5th, we marched at a quarter to five, A.M., on Moodkee, fifteen miles distant.

Here we encamped on the battle-field, which was still covered with the fragments of soldiers' clothing and appointments, carcases of camels and horses, and the bodies of friends and enemies, who had been slaughtered here on the 18th of December. The atmosphere all round was greatly tainted, which, combined with the horrible sight before us, made our hearts sick, and our heads faint.

About a month ago, this large village, containing about 4,000 inhabitants, belonged to the Lahore Rajah. It was now in the possession of the English: the scene before us proclaimed the price at which it had been bought. But even amid the ruins, the soldier as well as the Christian, looks forward with hope to the future: the one to the promotion of his country's glory, the other to the spread of the Gospel among the heathen.

[18] See Blue Book, p. 597.

In the evening, we received an unexpected order to join the "army of the Sutlej"; our Horse Artillery and Cavalry to proceed together; the Infantry and Elephant Battery to halt. On the 6th, we made a forced march of about twenty miles, to Aurufkee. On the road, we saw several corpses of British and Sikh soldiers, in a state bordering on decomposition, and plundered of their clothing.

Colonel Campbell[19] having been appointed to a brigade of Cavalry, as also Colonel Scott, Major and Brevet Lieutenant-Colonel Fullerton[20] assumed the command this day, of the Queen's Royal Lancers.

Our camp was pitched at a distance of four miles from the river Sutlej.

On the 8th, I called on Major-General Sir Harry G.W. Smith, K.C.B., commanding the first division of the army of the Sutlej, an old brother rifleman, and friend of my father's.

The cavalry was commanded by Major-General Sir Joseph Thackwell, K.C.B. (now Colonel of the 16th Lancers), who is very much liked by all who have the honour of knowing him. He is considered one of the ablest officers in the British service; and his experience of military operations in India has always rendered his advice and assistance indispensable in all the late campaigns. Sir Joseph, I am happy to find, has been invested with the highest class of the Bath, and never did a braver or kinder man receive this distinction. His services during the campaign of which I am now treating, were most invaluable, none more so; and yet his reward was slow. Colonel Campbell, having, as I said before, been made a Brigadier of Cavalry, was appointed to the 2nd Brigade, consisting of the 9th Lancers, 11th Light Cavalry, and 2nd and 8th Irregular Cavalry.

On the 9th of January, about 10 a.m., we distinctly heard the roar of the Sikh guns. During the greater part of the previous day, the Sikhs, who were encamped in great apparent regularity, on the right, or opposite side of the river Sutlej, were practising their guns. They were evidently preparing for another encounter. In the course of the day, I called on Major-General Sir Joseph Thackwell, Major-General Sir Robert H. Dick, K.C.B., Lieutenant-Colonel Gough, Acting Quarter-Master-General to H.M. forces, since then Colonel and Aide-de-Camp to the Queen, and Lieut.-Colonel Havelock, Persian Interpreter to the Commander-in-Chief.

On the 10th, the cold was intense, when we were out at a general watering parade, at eight o'clock in the morning. Encamped on an arid plain, we found the dust extremely troublesome, the west wind, which usually prevails at this season, blowing very hard.

Sunday, January 11th. This morning at two o'clock there was an alarm. Every man of the 9th immediately turned out, and, having saddled and bridled, stood by his horse until the *reveillé*. I sent off all my superfluous baggage to the house of

[19] Colonel Campbell, C.B., and K.H., died suddenly in London, of quinsy, March, 1850, a few days after his arrival from India.

[20] Lieutenant-Colonel Fullerton, C.B., died on the 28th of April, 1850, on his way to visit Cashmere, whither his body was conveyed on the following day, and deposited in the Royal Gardens. By his death, the regiment was deprived of a most just, warm-hearted, and honourable man. A simple tablet marks the spot where he is interred.

Lieutenant Fullerton, 14th Regiment Bengal Native Infantry, at Ferozepore, distant fourteen miles. He is a cousin of Lieut.-Colonel Fullerton, my commanding officer, and he had kindly offered to give it shelter. The Lieutenant, who had acted as aide-de-camp to Major-General Littler, at the battle of Ferozeshah, was at this period in charge of the Sudder (chief) Bazaar, at Ferozepore. The weather about this time was still intensely cold.

On the 12th of January, we changed ground to Bootawalla, less than two miles distant from the Sutlej: our position was on the left of the army. It is usual to change ground every now and then, because an encampment becomes dirty in a few days, and likewise because it is desirable to be nearer to the forage. When an enemy is close, however, these changes are made with much caution, since it is highly expedient not to give up a good position in exchange for a bad one. Such niceties are reserved for marches in times of peace, or where no enemy is at hand.

January 13th. We marched at two p.m. about three miles out from camp, in the direction of the bridge of boats, erected by the Sikhs; when, after a little cannonading on both sides, we returned by six o'clock p.m. The object of such a movement was this, to try our rockets in the enemy's camp, and to ascertain the range of his guns. But, suppose we had found our enemy off his guard, that there were but few sentries, and no battery to defend the bridge on our side, our plan would then have been to destroy the bridge, and station a guard to prevent its reconstruction.

The advantage of a pontoon bridge consists in your being able to place it at any part of the river. When Major-General Littler heard that the Sikhs were likely to cross, he sunk our pontoon bridge.

And here I may be permitted to digress a little, to give some account of this pontoon bridge, which was made at Bombay. The Duke of Wellington, in 1803, ordered forty boats, each twenty-one feet in length, to be made at Bombay, and transported on a carriage with four wheels. This step was taken with a view to the operations of our army on the river Toombuddra against the Maharatta territory, and to enable him to cross and re-cross the river whenever he chose.[21] The Ferozepore pontoon bridge was sent thither in 1844. My object in mentioning this bridge is, that it forms an argument why the Sikhs expected us to attack them, for they said that the bridge of boats was a clear proof of our design. It is not a little singular, that in all the wars from 1803 to 1844, or for above forty years, the British had never used a pontoon bridge; none have ever been seen in the Delhi magazine. When opposite to Ramnuggur, in 1848, on the Chenāb, the Commander-in-Chief detached a large force to operate against the right flank of the Sikh army, it was found necessary to proceed twenty-five miles up the river, before this force could cross. Thus making a march of fifty miles before it came up with the enemy, and when ranged on the opposite bank, nearly in face of the British camp, that single division stood completely isolated, without the possibility of being supported in case of need. Whereas, had the army of the Punjaub possessed a pontoon train, this force might have crossed above the Sikh entrenchment, and been in a position to receive support from the main army. The Commander-in-Chief could easily have received prompt intelligence of their advance and progress, and instantly on

[21] See Despatches, vol. iii. p. 64, 10th of April, 1803.

hearing that they had engaged the enemy, transported his army across the ford, or, by means of a second pontoon train, he might have defeated Shere Singh's army at once, and deprived him of all his guns. The moral effect of an attack carried on under such circumstances is incalculable; the chances are that it would have decided the campaign.

Besides, had the British possessed a pontoon train they might have destroyed all the enemy's boats, and prevented him from crossing, except at fords, which are few and often imperfectly known.

But it is not every one who is gifted with the genius of a Wellington; at the battle of Assaye his Grace sent some staff-officers to find a ford at a place where there was a village on each side of the river; and when a ford was found, he remarked: "I thought it probable that the people would not have built villages there unless a ford existed."

The want of a pontoon train caused a complete stand-still of the whole army at Ramnuggur. The artillery, cavalry, and infantry might be said to have been immovable, and therefore, useless, because they could not cross an ordinary river.

Let us consider how they act on the continent of Europe. Windischgrätz crossed the Danube to Vienna, with 150,000 men, by means of a pontoon train. The French army have a special corps of pontoniers. The Russian guards have a movable force of 50,000 men, complete in every branch, with a magnificent pontoon train, exclusive of the other pontoon trains, attached to the other divisions of the mighty army of that vast empire.

Every military man knows that the transport of an army, with its immense quantity of artillery and baggage, across the rivers which intersect its line of march, is one of the most difficult as well as the most important operations in military tactics, especially in India, where the camp followers are so numerous.

History, both modern and ancient, teaches us that the success of a campaign often depends on the rapid conveyance of troops across the rivers that intersect their march. As far back as the days of Darius a floating bridge was thrown across the Bosphorus, and afterwards across the Danube, while Xerxes threw one over the Hellespont at the time of his ill-starred expedition to Europe. The most celebrated pontoon of modern times, was that constructed by the engineers of the British army across the Adour, in the south of France, in 1814, the river being 110 feet across.

During the retreat of Napoleon from Moscow, the whole of his immense army must have been captured or destroyed on the banks of the Beresina, had it not been for the extraordinary care and vigilant forethought of the principal French engineer, in preserving the materials required in the formation of a pontoon.

A pontoon train, such as the Duke of Wellington employed in India, in 1803, composed of forty boats, would require forty carts and 160 to 170 bullocks. The Duke, in his Despatches,[22] states that for some streams he had basket boats ten feet in diameter and three feet deep, and covered with double leather.

[22] Vol. i. p. 136, April 8th, 1803.

When the Duke of Wellington's bridge of boats was brought to Ferozepore in the autumn of 1845, Major Broadfoot, who was charged with its transport, aroused the suspicion of the Sikhs, and in their opinion, virtually acknowledged that hostilities existed between them and the British, by manifesting extraordinary vigilance for its safe keeping, placing it under the escort of a strong guard of soldiers, and by employing the pontoniers to construct it, on the arrival of the boats at Ferozepore.

To return to my journal. On the 14th of January, 1846, the cavalry received orders to hold themselves in readiness to march at a moment's notice. We remained in this state of suspense from eight in the morning till one o'clock in the afternoon, when we again marched towards the Sikh bridge, and did the like execution with our guns as yesterday. The Sikhs having crossed over to our side of the bridge, were busily employed in making an entrenched camp.

On the 15th gram sold at sixteen seers or thirty-two lbs. for the rupee, a rather dismal prospect for a large army. The 9th Lancers had 600 fighting men, and the camp followers amounted to 3,600 men which gives six to every fighting man. After deducting 1,600, the number of followers required for 800 horses, including officers' chargers, and 480 dooly bearers, there would still remain 1,520 followers to be accounted for, and if we again allow the officers about forty in number, say 500 servants,—a very fair portion,—there would then be left 1,020 whom we must conclude to have been elephant and camel drivers, tent lascars, cooks, bazaar people, etc.

On the 18th the Lancers again held themselves in readiness to turn out at a moment's notice, owing to the enemy's crossing the river in large numbers. On the 19th we changed our ground, five miles to the right, and on our arrival the troop of the 9th, to which I belonged, was sent on picquet to a distance of nearly two miles to our right front, and pretty close to the Sutlej; indeed a picquet of the enemy was clearly seen on the other side. Had the enemy crossed, or rather, attempted to cross, the officer in command would have sent information to the camp, and in the meanwhile made arrangements to retard the force in the best manner he could, so as to allow the army time to come up to his support. To gain time is an officer's chief object, under such circumstances; nor must he in any case retire, unless driven in.

CHAPTER V.

Hurrekee Ghât—Chain Bridles—Sir Thomas Dallas—Victory of Sir Harry Smith at Aliwal—Umballa—Preparations of the Sikhs—Capture of Dhurmkote—Loodianna—Runjoor Singh—Buddiwal—Sirdar Ajeet Singh—Invalids at Loodianna—The Pattiala Rajah—Alarm at Loodianna—Siege-train in Danger—Convoy inadequately protected—Sikh Artillery at Aliwal—Major Lawrenson—Singular Formation of the Sikh Infantry at Aliwal—16th Lancers—Desperation of the Sikhs—Colonel Cureton—Charge of Lancers—Marshal Marmont's Opinion—Sikhs evacuate Buddiwal—Rapid Movements of the Sikhs—Brigadiers Godby and Hicks.

The Governor-General and the Commander-in-Chief inspected the 9th Lancers on the morning of the 21st of January. An incessant report of guns of a heavy calibre was heard all day, from the other side of the river. This afternoon I rode in company with my commanding officer to the Hurrekee Ghât, near which was our picquet, to enquire about two boats, said to have been captured by the enemy. We, however, saw only a couple of old boats and a great many unarmed people near them.

On the 23rd a false alarm caused the Commander-in-Chief to order us out, and we all stood to our horses at the head of our lines, from twelve till four o'clock, P.M.

On the 25th several of our officers had chain reins made for their regimental bridles, because in the last action the enemy had cut some of the bridles of the 3rd Light Dragoons, with their swords, by which their riders became powerless, having lost all command over their horses.

This brings to my recollection an anecdote told me of the late Lieutenant-General Sir Thomas Dallas, of the Madras Cavalry, well known in the wars with Hyder Ali Khan and Tippoo Sultan, as the best horseman and most experienced swordsman, in the Madras army, having often proved himself the victor in single combat, and killed his man. One of the enemy was noted for possessing a scimitar of the first quality; Sir Thomas, then a Captain, and this man made an agreement to this effect, that they were to fight together, and that the native was not to cut the Captain's reins, nor he to use his pistols. After a long encounter the man violated the engagement and cut the Captain's reins, which were not of steel, upon which the latter drew his pistol and shot his opponent dead on the spot.

In a country like India every officer should go on service, furnished with a chain rein, for without it many a man has lost his life; besides, it is neither heavy nor inconvenient. The dragoons and troopers should also be supplied with them. The natives use them as well as coats of chain armour, and many of the Sikhs, as I myself witnessed, wore even breast plates and back pieces of steel. I picked up a steel helmet in the Sikh camp at the battle of Sobraon, which now serves to decorate my father's dining-room.

On the 28th of January, the Royal Lancers were in readiness the whole day to turn out at a moment's notice, as the Sikhs shewed themselves in great force, and appeared as if bent upon mischief.

January 29th. Intelligence was received in Camp of the splendid victory gained by Major-General Sir Harry Smith over the Sikhs under the command of Runjoor Singh, at Aliwal, on the 28th. The force under Sir Harry having captured the whole of the enemy's guns, forty-eight in number, and put to rout their army of 24,000 men, our whole line turned out at sunrise, when a royal salute was fired in honour of the day. After the salute, the Governor-General and Commander-in-Chief passed up the line, and the former addressed each regiment separately. These addresses are not unusual in India.

The battle of Ferozeshah, it will be remembered, was fought on the 21st and 22nd of December, 1845, so that about five weeks had elapsed since the last feat of arms. More troops were now advancing to the frontier, and several hundred hackeries, laden with shot, shells, powder, and stores of all kinds, were coming up. Engineer officers, too, were in great request; for it now became known that our assiduous enemy was fortifying Sobraon, on the left bank of the Sutlej, between Loodianna and Ferozepore. In fact the Sikhs were working hard at their entrenchments day and night.

We had not as yet received our military stores and supplies from Delhi. A well-stocked magazine, was apparently much needed. Many considered that Umballa was the most advantageous spot for establishing such a depôt, being 150 miles from Ferozepore, and seventy-one from Loodianna. Ferozepore was thought too isolated; delay, therefore, was imperative, and it was of no use to anticipate events.

The reader may easily conclude that the Sikhs, seeing our additional troops, guns and stores moving up to the army, did not remain idle, for they had a great game at stake, being no less than the future fate of a kingdom. They were buoyed up by their success at Buddiwal; the whole army under Tej Singh had re-crossed the Sutlej. The bridge-head, which secured so important an advantage, was enlarged; and, in the very face of the British army, they unremittingly carried on their warlike preparations. They seemed confident of victory, and ready to carry war and destruction into the very heart of their enemy's country, when our unlooked-for and glorious victory at Aliwal, proved to them that they were not invincible.

The announcement in our camp, on the 29th, of Sir Harry Smith's victory at Aliwal, caused considerable sensation. As for myself, I must confess that it was a great disappointment to me not to have taken a part in this engagement. I had written just before to Sir Harry Smith, who, as I have already observed, had been in the Rifle Brigade with my father, during the Peninsular war, expecting that he would have some fighting, and asking to be employed as his aide-de-camp. It was now too late. The news of the brilliant victory came, and put an end to all chance of my witnessing a battle in that quarter.

The object of Sir Harry in moving from our camp was doubtless to prevent the Sikhs from marching towards Delhi and intercepting our supplies. He succeeded in taking the little town and fort of Dhurmkote, which was filled with grain, and thus secured the regular supplies of the army. Having accomplished the reduction of the place, he received intelligence from head-quarters, that Runjoor Singh had crossed the Sutlej with 40,000 Sikhs, and had taken up a position on the road to Loodianna, for the purpose of intercepting our supplies from that town, which he threatened with an attack. This was accompanied by an order to Sir Harry Smith to proceed immediately to Loodianna.

Four regiments of infantry, three of cavalry, and eighteen guns composed the whole of the detachment under the command of this brave general, when on the 21st of January he proceeded to Buddiwal, a small garrison close to Loodianna, which was occupied by Runjoor Singh, and 10,000 of his men. Sir Harry Smith endeavoured by a détour to reach Loodianna, and effect a junction with the Brigade stationed there, before undertaking any engagement with the Sikhs. The latter, however, relying upon their superior numbers, provoked an attack by a brisk fire from their formidable artillery. A severe contest followed, and the British General after sustaining heavy losses, deemed it prudent to fall back upon Loodianna. This he effected by a very skilful evolution, and succeeded in holding the place.

Dr. M'Gregor, in his history of the Sikhs,[23] states that Runjoor Singh, younger brother of Lena Singh Mujetheea,[24] commanded the division of the Sikh army destined to act against Loodianna, as well as to seize the siege-train in progress to join our army, which were the two objects to be held in view by Sir Harry Smith. Dr. M'Gregor says: "Had he (Sir Harry) stopped to return the fire of the Sikhs at Buddiwal, all fear for Loodianna might have been removed; but then there was the risk, that if discomfited, Runjoor Singh might have crossed the country, and captured the siege train, which was escorted by only a Native Infantry regiment, and the 11th Light Cavalry, with a few Artillerymen. The condition of Sir Harry Smith was such, that he could not hope effectually to drive Runjoor Singh across the Sutlej that day, and he probably considered—like a good general, brought up in the school of Wellington, and disciplined in a corps like the immortal old 95th—that half measures were worse than useless. Besides, though making a great sacrifice of baggage, and even of lives, there was the hope that his forbearance would be construed into fear by the Sikhs, who might, in consequence, be induced to meet him in a fair field, where he would have an opportunity of accomplishing the two objects which he had in view; namely, the defence of Loodianna, and the safety of the train, closing all, perhaps, with the entire discomfiture of the Sikhs, when his

[23] Vol. ii., p. 133.

[24] Lena Singh had left the Punjaub before the Sikhs crossed the Sutlej, and went to Benares, and subsequently to Calcutta. At one time he was placed under surveillance, after his brother's attack on Loodianna. Lena Singh, no doubt, hoped to prevent the confiscation of his estates on this side of the Sutlej.

troops should be a little refreshed." The whole of the Sikh force was not, it was believed, at Buddiwal, therefore the apprehension of Sir Harry Smith, doubtless, was that the other division might get to Loodianna. Buddiwal was at the time in the possession of Sirdar Ajeet Singh, a chief under our protection, who, after the operations at Moodkee and Ferozeshah, burnt a portion of the barracks of H.M. 50th Foot, at Loodianna, and then took possession of Buddiwal, where he made prisoner Assistant-Surgeon R.G.D. Banon, 62nd Foot (now Surgeon of the 96th Foot), and kept him in confinement for twenty-five days,—twelve of which in irons. The Sikhs in vain tried to induce him and the other Europeans who were in the fort, to join their army. They were released after the battle of Sobraon.

It is said, that though Sir Harry Smith was ordered not to fight before he had made a junction with Colonel Wheeler's detachment, yet that as the Sikhs had been moving to the south of Buddiwal, an action must inevitably have ensued, to prevent their advance towards our convoy. There were said to be three roads from Buddiwal to Loodianna. Buddiwal lies to the south-east of Aliwal and between it and Sirhind. Runjoor Singh's force was double that of Sir Harry Smith, besides which he had a large number of guns.

The fort at Loodianna contained all the sick of H.M. and the H.C. troops, which had marched from thence to join the army, as well as the ladies, women, and children belonging to those regiments. The only troops left there were the two Goorkha corps, the Nusseeree and Sirmoor Battalions,[25] but they were afterwards increased by the arrival of the 30th Native Infantry, the 1st Light Cavalry, and about 1,500 of the Pattiala Horse. The Pattiala Rajah was under our protection, and was one of those chiefs who early rendered assistance to our army, both in men, money, and supplies. He died very suddenly, soon after the battle of Ferozeshah, not without suspicion of having been poisoned, which is by no means an unusual method of securing the succession to a Rajahship. It is not impossible that he may have been killed by some of the true Sikhs, for his strenuous support of the British. A mystery hangs over this affair; and if we were to discard mystery from the records of Indian narratives, we should have little left to relate. The deceased Rajah's successor more than fulfilled the expectations of the Governor-General, and was, at the close of the campaign, confirmed in the possession of his estates, and invested by Lord Hardinge with the style and title of Maharajah, in consideration of his important services.

The alarm at Loodianna was natural, for a Sikh force having burnt down part of the cantonments, the appearance of a second, and more powerful force would be conclusive in the minds of most persons as to the fate of the station. *It fama per urbes Subathoo et Simla.* At Umballa the alarm was still greater. Dr. M'Gregor, in his History of the Sikhs, p. 136, writes: "We may smile at the fears which prompted this fugacious movement,[26] but had Sir Harry Smith not advanced to Loodianna, there is every reason to believe that the siege-train might have been lost, Loodianna

[25] These corps were raised in May, 1815, soon after the late Sir David Ochterlony's victories at Malown. The Goorkhas are the bravest and most active native troops in India. They are also excellent shots at game.

[26] No smiling affair, we should think! Ladies, women and children, flying to Meerut, Saharunpore, and Mussooree.

pillaged and burnt, the hill stations destroyed, and Umballa, and even other places in the Provinces, sacked and occupied; so that the movement of the 1st division was one of the utmost importance, and not only prevented such sad disasters, but was followed by one of the best managed actions on record." That the train was in some danger is evident, from the fact that the Commander-in-Chief despatched for its security the 3rd Infantry Brigade, under the command of Brigadier Taylor, towards Dhurmkote, which lies to the west of Aliwal, and about half way between Loodianna and Ferozepore. On the 30th of January, this Brigade returned to camp.

Now, if we look at the map we shall see, that on the 28th, the day of the battle of Aliwal, the convoy would have been but a short distance south-west from Dhurmkote, perhaps twenty miles. And, again, if we suppose a line to be drawn from Dhurmkote, in a direction twenty miles to the south-east, which extreme point is called Bussean, we shall find that the Sikh troops at Buddiwal were very near to the convoy, on the night of the 27th of January. The escort for the convoy was extremely weak; for a corps of Native Infantry, and another of Native Cavalry, would not (after the late actions), have been above 1,200 men strong. This convoy was very inadequately protected, and such as our brave Commander-in-Chief would not have sent. Until joined by Taylor's brigade, from the neighbourhood of Kurnaul, it was in imminent danger. Had the Sikhs seized the convoy, the battle of Sobraon could not have taken place when it did; moreover, from delay, the season would have been sickly; and great loss must have ensued from this cause alone.

There are some circumstances which occurred at the battle of Aliwal, deserving of prominent notice. The enemy had a great many guns, which were playing with considerable effect upon the British troops. Major, now Lieutenant-Colonel G. S. Lawrenson, C.B., who commanded the Brigade of Horse Artillery, finding his men and horses falling, to save the delay of waiting for orders, instantly galloped up his brigade of guns to within a short distance of the Sikhs, wheeled round, unlimbered, and, by a brisk cannonade soon forced their gunners to quit their guns for a time. Had the cavalry charged at the same moment, I am assured they would have taken the guns. It was one of those exhibitions of decision and promptitude in war, which well merits, and did receive its reward. It was probably the suddenness of the movement which prevented the immediate support by troops.

The Sikhs made a singular disposition of their infantry in this battle for receiving the charges of the British cavalry. Instead of forming in squares they were arranged into triangles, the apex being in front and opposed to the British, the men also in the rear, or base line, knelt down, so that when the 16th Lancers broke through the front face they were received by fixed bayonets. The French system was followed in these dispositions; and a few French officers were alone wanting to animate the enemy with hopes of success, however futile such hopes must have proved. For, opposed to a force commanded by one of our ablest and most experienced generals, nothing but ruin and utter destruction could, under any circumstances have fallen to the lot of our rash, though brave foe.

The 16th Lancers suffered greatly, for the Sikhs fought with the most obstinate bravery. Preferring a voluntary death, even when all hope of resistance was at an end, they determined that their lives should be purchased at a high cost. Captain

Bere of that gallant regiment was most successful in his efforts, having been seen to charge through the wedge of Sikhs, and back again more than once. And cordially do I congratulate a brother officer, Lieutenant T.J. Francis, on having had the good fortune to be present in this glorious action. He had but lately returned from England, and, at the commencement of the campaign, was on his way to the upper provinces with a detachment of recruits. Being anxious not to lose the opportunity of seeing service with Sir Harry Smith's division, Lieutenant Francis hastened up, and arriving opportunely for the battle, obtained permission to accompany the 16th Lancers to the field. After the action, Brigadier Cureton, who commanded the cavalry, thanked Lieutenant Francis for his valuable services, which commendation I had the pleasure of reading from a copy of an extract from the brigade orders a day or two after.

The late Colonel Cureton of the 16th Lancers, who was unfortunately killed at Ramnuggur, had been known to say that Lancers should never be employed in charges with the enemy in less than a squadron, and from the results of this battle many cavalry officers have questioned whether the lance is the best weapon for cavalry in India. In the charges at Aliwal the Sikhs have been known to receive the point into their bodies and then to kill their adversary by cutting him down. The Sikh could not extract the lance, nor had the Lancer time to draw his sword.

There is no doubt that Lancers should never charge in small parties. Nothing less than a wing should attempt to break squares of infantry.

The charge in line, of a broken enemy is another thing. Marshal Marmont, in his "Esprit des Instructions Militaires," p. 45-50, says: "Cavalry should have one pistol; heavy cavalry, with lances and sabres and some few carbines, should be employed to fight infantry, the light cavalry to finish. The hussar or light cavalry soldier will, single-handed, beat the lancer. Cuirassiers should be armed with the lance and straight sword. The first rank should charge with the lance couched, and the second rank with the sabre in hand. As soon as the shock is effected, and the ranks are mingled, the sabres must do their duty. Lancers are equally successful against cavalry in line, especially if the enemy have only sabres. The cavalry in line should have lances chiefly, the sabre as an auxiliary."

Though Marmont was educated as an artillery officer, his great military experience entitles his opinion to be received with due respect, no matter to which branch of the profession he may refer. The Lancers were not employed in the Peninsular war, nor yet at Waterloo, consequently the 16th is the first Lancer regiment which has had the honour of testing the lance in open conflict, and against bodies of hostile infantry.

After the engagement at Buddiwal on the 22nd of January 1846, the Sikh troops under Runjoor Singh suddenly evacuated that place, and proceeded in the direction of Loodianna, keeping close to the river, where they secured a number of boats with the apparent intention of re-crossing to the right bank to join the main army. Whether this was a feint, or whether Runjoor Singh, having received intimation of the advance of reinforcements with whom his forces might not be equal to cope, desired to secure the means of a hasty retreat; or, whether he was following the example of Tej Singh, and acting a double part, remains uncertain. However this may be, Sir Harry Smith lost no time in taking possession of the place which had been evacuated by the Sikhs, who were soon after joined by a large reinforcement of their own body. The troops under Runjoor Singh, amounting to between 15,000 and 16,000 men, were immediately on the move, and preparing for fresh aggressions.

Sir Harry Smith saw that a collision was inevitable, and his own strength having been reinforced from head-quarters, he proceeded, on the morning of the 28th to reconnoitre the enemy's troops, and, if compelled, to give him battle. Sir Harry encountered them near the village of Aliwal, on their way to Jugraon, with the intention of occupying that town. The Sikhs, finding that Sir Harry was about to outflank them, suddenly changed their position, and drew up along a ridge with their right flanking the village of Aliwal, and their left resting on their own entrenched camp. With the extraordinary agility and rapidity of action which characterized the Sikhs throughout their engagements with the army of the Sutlej, the centre division of the Khalsa troops instantly threw up entrenchments, behind which they hastily placed their strong artillery, and opened a murderous fire upon the British.

Sir Harry's force amounted to only 11,000 men, being a fourth less than that of the enemy, but like an able tactician, knowing that by the superior activity and disposition of his troops he could bring more men into action against the different salient points of attack, than the enemy who opposed him, he overcame the odds of numbers.

Notwithstanding the sharp fire of the Sikhs, he ordered a halt while he took a rapid survey of the nature of the country, and the position of the troops. His quick eye instantly recognised and decided on the mode of attack. He saw that by carrying the village of Aliwal, he should be able to throw himself upon the enemy's left and centre. This was effected with great promptitude and valour, by Brigadiers Godby and Hicks, who captured two guns. The general then made a skilful and effective charge upon the right wing, where the enemy was worsted; but the contest with the left was for some time doubtful, and the onslaught deadly. Three times did our British Lancers charge into the midst of the closely serried ranks of their brave opponents, whom they literally cut to pieces. To the very last their indomitable spirit did not forsake the Sikhs, they fell back in a body to a distance of a few paces, discharged a full volley into the faces of their conquerors, and then retreated towards the ford on the Sutlej. Although beaten, they were not dismayed; and although their leader, Runjoor Singh, was the first to fly and basely quit the field, leaving his brave followers to conquer or die, their courage never quailed. Again they rallied and made one last and vigorous effort. Though defeat had made them desperate, and they fought like men who jeoparded all, it was a defeat, and they were compelled to give way.

It was a magnificent and hard-fought battle: as ably conducted as it was skilfully planned.

CHAPTER VI.

Richard Bond, the Messman—Sikh Grass-cutters—Choice of Camps—General Lloyd's Opinions—Lieut.-Colonel Irvine and Sir H. Maddock—Position at Sobraon—Brigadier E. Smith's Plan—Colonel Irvine's Plan—Goolab Singh's Policy—Sir Robert Dick's Division—Major-General Gilbert's Division—Sir Harry Smith's Division—Brigadier A. Campbell—Sir Joseph Thackwell—Brigadier Scott—British Batteries—Rockets—Sikh Batteries—Assault on the Sikh Entrenchments—Brigadier Stacey—Captain Cunningham's Account—The 10th Foot—Lieut.-Colonel Franks—Sikh Entrenchments stormed—Sirdar Sham Singh destroys the Pontoon—Sikh Retreat cut off—Great Loss of the Sikhs—Peace Principles inapplicable to India—Sikhs driven across the Sutlej—Tej Singh.

On the 30th of January, 1846, about noon, we moved out and proceeded a distance of two miles, expecting to meet the Sikh cavalry, who were encamped by the bridge of boats, but after having waited for two or three hours we were doomed to be again disappointed.

On the 1st of February, our mess-waiter, Richard Bond, died, he had been for some weeks past in bad health, yet, being anxious not to be separated from his regiment, in which he had served for many years, the poor man accompanied us from Cawnpore, and though apparently of an Herculean frame, an insidious malady gained upon him; and on the 1st of February poor Bond was numbered among those who have been. *Mors sola fatetur quantula sint hominum corpuscula.* He was an old and meritorious servant: and as a member of the Mess Committee at this period, I feel happy in paying this passing tribute to his memory.

Whilst on an out-line picquet on the 2nd, I heard most distinctly the Sikh drums from the camp in our right front, about six o'clock in the afternoon. During the day also my patrols brought in five grass-cutters in the employ of the enemy. After having questioned them I released them with a warning not to appear near our camp again. This was by no means an uncommon ruse de guerre, while pretending to cut grass they were in fact spying out the land.

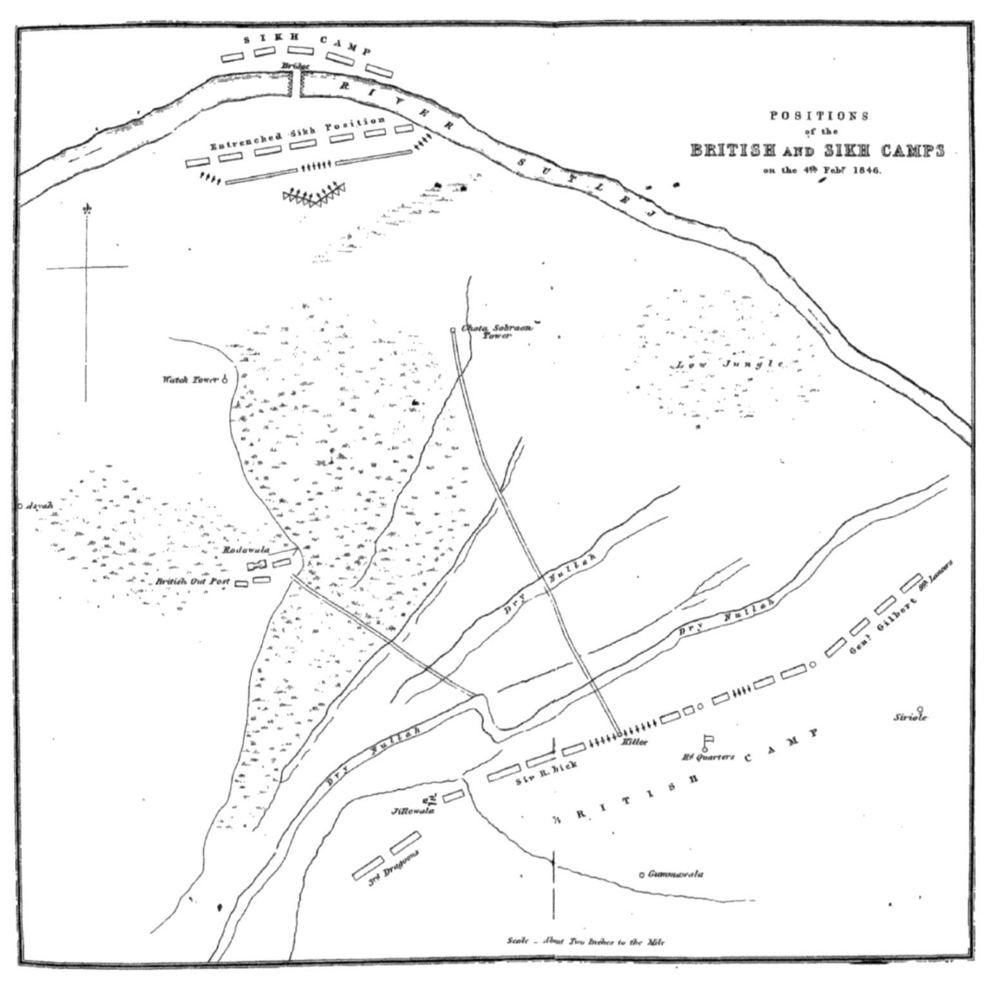

POSITIONS OF THE BRITISH AND SIKH CAMPS ON THE 4TH FEB. 1846.

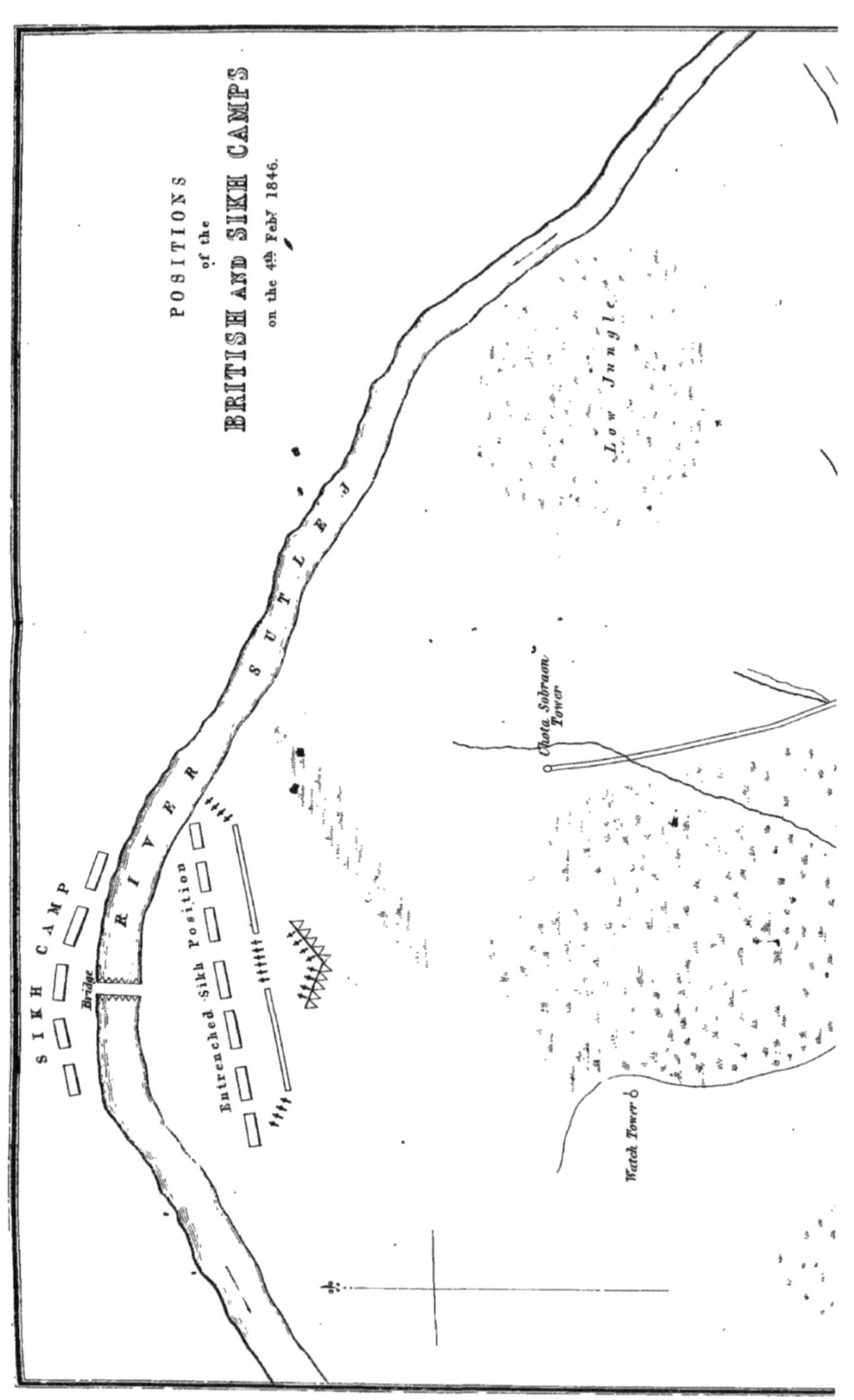

Positions of the British and Sikh Camps on the 4th Feb. 1846. (*Enlarged - Top*)

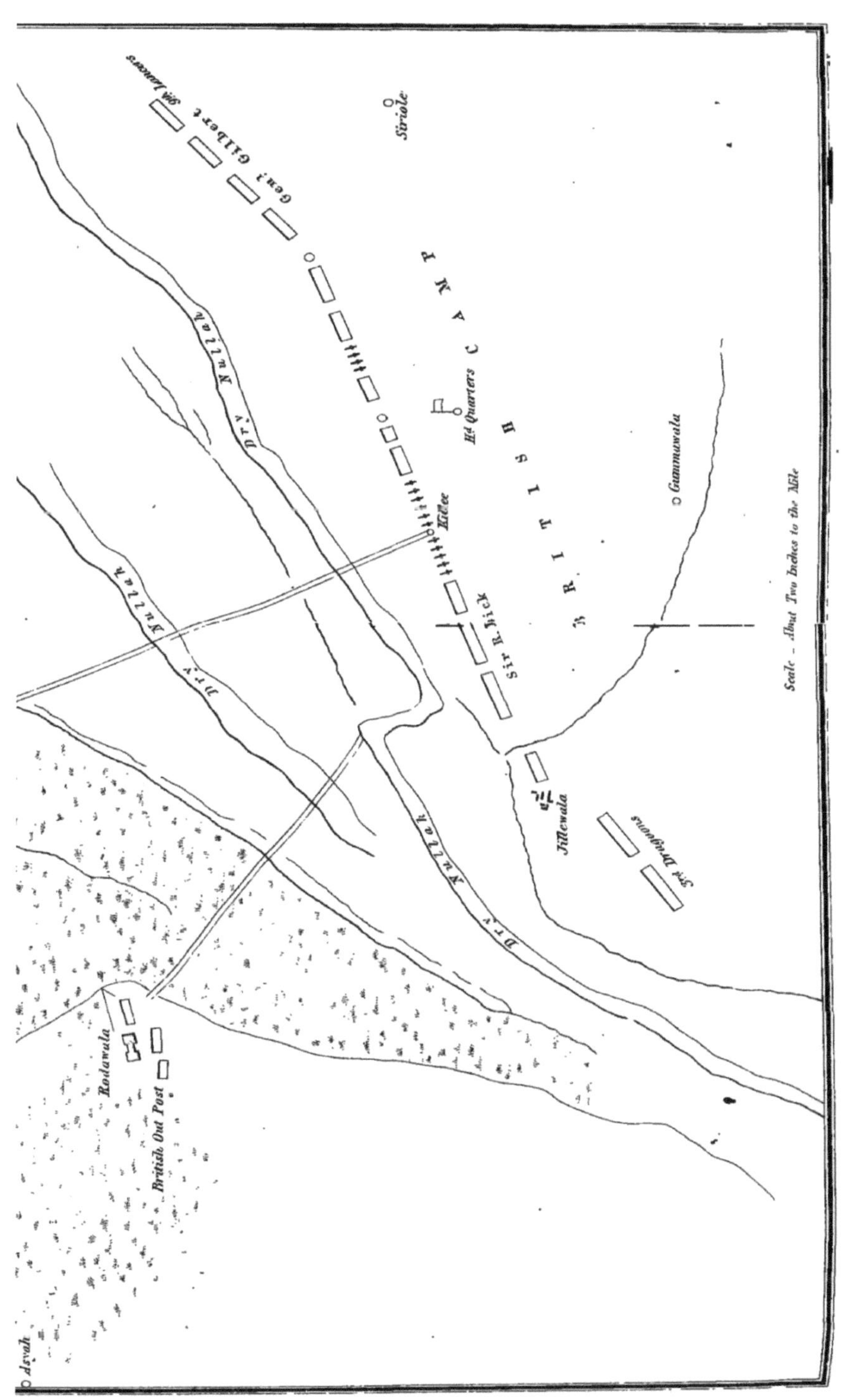

Positions of the British and Sikh Camps on the 4th Feb. 1846. (*Enlarged - Bottom*)

On the 7th of February, our regiment again changed ground, from the right to the extreme left. The whole army was encamped in a line nearly parallel to the river Sutlej, from which it was distant not more than a mile and a quarter, and in some parts even less. It is a rule in forming a camp, not to make it within reach of the fire of the enemy's guns; and at the same time to shew as extended a front as possible, both for the purpose of overawing the adversary, and of watching his movements. The same rule applies on having crossed a river, to avoid exposure to the fire of the enemy who occupies the bank which you have quitted.

In reference to the choice of camps, I may perhaps be excused if I again refer to the able and very scarce work on the Art of war by the well known author of the "Seven Years' War in Germany."

"The choice of camps," he says, "depends on two principles: the one geometrical and the other the effect of genius. The first consists in calculating the distance relative to the number and species of troops which compose the army; the other in seeing all the combinations that may be formed on a given piece of ground, with a given army, and in the choice of that precise combination which is most advantageous. This unacquirable and sublime talent is much superior to the other, and independent of it. Great geniuses have a sort of intuitive knowledge; they see at once the cause and its effect, with the different combinations which unite them—they do not proceed by common rules successively from one idea to another, by slow and languid steps. No, the *whole* with all its circumstances and various combinations is like a picture, all together present to their mind: these want no geometry, but an age produces few of this kind of men; and, in the common run of Generals, geometry and experience will help them to avoid gross errors.

"The perfection of our art would be, no doubt, to find a construction or an order of battle equally proper for all kinds of ground. But this being impossible, the only thing remaining for them to do is to find such a construction and such a formation of the troops as may, with the greatest simplicity, and, consequently velocity, be adapted to those numberless circumstances which occur. This should be the constant subject of their studies, but can never be obtained without geometry."

February the 8th. Sunday. Dined at half-past six, with my brother officers, at the mess of the 3rd Light Dragoons. They are encamped on our right, at the distance of about a quarter of a mile. As in the field, so at the mess-table, the Lieutenant-Colonel of this fine corps, Colonel White, C.B. (now aide-de-camp to the Queen), appeared to be beloved by his officers; indeed they have no small reason to be proud of one, so universally esteemed and respected by the cavalry division of the army of the Sutlej.

The battle was at hand: already were preparations making to meet those gallant men, the Sikhs, in mortal combat. On the evening of the 9th, Lieutenant-Colonel Irvine, of the engineers, came into the camp, having been sent to the frontier at the recommendation of Sir Herbert Maddock, Deputy-Governor of Bengal. Troops had been detached from the army to meet the large convoy coming from Delhi, with ammunition and stores; for the operations against the enemy at Moodkee, Ferozeshah, and Aliwal, had exhausted the greater part of our gun ammunition.

Indeed, as I have already observed, that on the 22nd of December, 1845, when Tej Singh came before Ferozeshah, the British had no shot left. The force under Brigadier Campbell, however, brought up 4,300,000 rounds of musket ball cartridges, and twelve 12-pounders, with shot and other missiles, otherwise my gallant friend, Sir Harry Smith, would not have had the means of fighting the splendid battle of Aliwal.

And now we come to the 10th of February, the day on which the memorable battle of Sobraon, the crowning battle of the Sikh campaign of 1845-46 was fought, and which most persons expected would be the last.

The fate of the Punjaub seemed to hang by a thread; from the 22nd of December, 1845, to the 28th of January, 1846, no military operations had occurred till Sir Harry Smith gained the battle of Aliwal. The Sikhs' strongly entrenched position at Sobraon still remained to be taken; defended as it was by 30,000 regular troops, besides being equally strong by nature and art. By nature, as situated on the banks of the river, in the form of a half moon, having many and great impediments in its front; by art, the triple form of the entrenchments, bristled with a triple row of guns, which must be silenced before an entrance could be effected; a bridge of boats in its rear, by which the besieged might retire if they chose; and, moreover, batteries commanding the rear of the flanks of the entrenchment, which enabled them to fire upon any troops attempting to storm the works: added to which, the men could come over the pontoon bridge to assist in serving the guns in the works; and this they actually did.

Major-General, Sir Harry Smith, after the battle of the 28th of January, in which he had lost 589 killed and wounded, joined His Excellency, the Commander-in-Chief, on the 8th of February. It was judged expedient to wait for his arrival before the attack on Sobraon could be safely made. Part of the siege train, too, had arrived, to ensure the safety of which, it may be recollected, was the principal object in detaching Sir Harry Smith.

A plan had been proposed by the late Brigadier E. Smith, C.B., Chief Engineer, but when the nature of the proposed attack was explained to Lieutenant-Colonel Irvine, a senior officer, who had been sent by Sir T. Herbert Maddock, to join the army, which he had only reached on the 9th, the day before the battle, he is said to have taken a different view.

It is recorded, that in the year 1776, Sir W. Howe, in a despatch on the American entrenchments, wrote: "If I could have made approaches I could easily have taken the enemy's entrenchments."[27]

Whether Colonel Irvine proposed to make approaches I cannot say; certain it is, that it was agreed to follow the plan laid down by Brigadier Smith, Colonel Irvine being of opinion that it would be better to leave the conduct of the affair in the hands of the officer who had formed a digested plan. Had Brigadier Smith been superseded, a delay of two or three days at least must have ensued. Now, without knowing the exact cause for the delay, it is stated in the "Blue Book" that certain proposals had been made by the Lahore Durbar, or by some of the principal chiefs.

[27] Field of Mars, 1801.

Some say, that the celebrated Goolab Singh of Cashmere had made certain offers, to which an answer was required in three days. An officer of artillery remarked to the Commander-in-Chief, that the remainder of the supplies, stores, etc., from Delhi, would reach camp in two days. Lord Gough, in his Despatch of the 13th of February, says:—"Part of my siege train having come up with me, I resolved, on the morning of the 10th, to dispose our mortars and battering guns," etc.[28] This waiting of two days or more would have consumed more time than it was thought politically right to expend. We must remember that an answer was required in three days. Now, if Goolab Singh was the real proposer of these terms, it would seem that it could not answer to grant them. Perhaps he undertook to pay us the expenses of the war, to reduce the Sikh army, and to accept a British Resident at Lahore; these conditions, or something like them, must have been proposed.

Such offers could not have satisfied the government of India, because, when after the treaty of 1846, we took a slice of the Punjaub (Jullundur), and allowed the Sikh Durbar to keep up an army of 32,000 men, they raised more, either openly or covertly; hence, if they acted thus under our own eye, while holding the reins of government at Lahore, it is not unreasonable to conclude that they would follow up the plan *in extenso* in our absence, for a Resident would have been no adequate check.

Goolab Singh was evidently playing a game for himself: if he could be the means of saving the country, then Cashmere ought to be his reward; but, when affairs went in a contrary direction, he was forced to be no longer an actor on the scene. But, distrusting Goolab Singh, and supposing him to have been a traitor to his country, yet might he not be meditating the destruction of the English? He had his own troops with which he could turn the scale against us. Thus, whatever were the terms, or the nature of the terms, they were clearly less than we could accede to.

Colonel Irvine, as I have remarked, instead of acting as Chief Engineer, became an aide-de-camp, and partly a spectator.

The reader will doubtless imagine, and justly so, that we had more shot and shell on the road to join us; but time—that important element in our lives, which when once lost cannot be recalled—time, in military matters is everything. This was a well-known saying of Napoleon's, and the truth of it is evident to less able soldiers. The old plan, therefore, and not the new mode of attack, was the order of the day.

Owing to the peculiar form of the enemy's entrenchment, it was decided that the battering-train and disposable field-artillery should be put in position in an extended semi-circle, embracing within its fire the works of the Sikhs. On the morning of the 10th, a heavy mist prevented the intended cannonade from beginning at daybreak as was proposed. It must be borne in mind, that, strictly speaking, the attack on a strong entrenched position is usually made in the same way as upon a fort or outwork: for forts are, sometimes, surrounded by entrenchments, thus making the fort a kind of citadel, as it were, though it may not be so called

[28] War in India, Despatches of Lords Hardinge and Gough. Second Edition. London, 1846; p. 116.

technically.

This mist, though unfavourable for artillery is often favourable for troops, for enabling them to form under cover near such works and entrenchments.

Major-General Sir Robert Dick's division was placed on the margin of the river Sutlej, ready to commence the assault. The 7th Brigade belonging to this division, and led by Brigadier Stacey, was to head the attack, supported by the 6th Brigade of the same division, at a distance of two hundred yards. A reserve which was entrenched at the village of Rodawalla, was in readiness to move forward if required.

In the centre, Major-General Gilbert's division was deployed for support or attack, with its right resting on Little Sobraon. With regard to this division, it has been stated by an officer of an infantry corps, that it was not intended that it should attack in the first instance, but it so happened that Major-General Gilbert[29] with that decided conduct which marked all his actions, finding that the left attack on the enemy's right had not succeeded, determined at once to make his attack in front.

As I have before observed, there were impediments in the front, of which we were ignorant; they were in the nature of an embankment, and when our troops came up, this embankment, lying between them and the entrenchment, prevented the British from easily mounting it and entering the enclosure; the only means, therefore, by which they could effect this, was by moving to the right and left of this impediment. It will not be a matter of surprise therefore, that a little confusion occurred, and that our troops were in some slight degree jammed together. But we must defer the result to its proper place, and proceed with the order for the movements of the other troops.

Major-General Sir Harry Smith's Division was formed near the village of Guttah, with its right thrown up towards the Sutlej. It was determined to threaten by feigned attacks, the enemy's horse, under Rajah Lall Singh Misr, which was stationed on the other side of the river. There was a ford at Hurrekee Ghât at which were drawn up the 16th Lancers, who would thus have been enabled to cross over and attack the Sikh cavalry, if circumstances had called for aid. Besides, as there was a ford there, the enemy might have thought of crossing himself, for the purpose of attempting to turn our left flank.

Brigadier A. Campbell took up an intermediate position, between the divisions of Major-General Gilbert's right, and Major-General Sir Harry Smith's left. Campbell's brigade was to the rear of Sir Harry's division, the better to effect this object, for it is desirable, on occasions like these, not to place the cavalry within reach of cannon shot.

Major-General Sir Joseph Thackwell, K.C.B. commanding the cavalry division, had under him Brigadier Scott, C.B.,[30] who held a reserve in the first brigade on

[29] Afterwards, Major-General Sir Walter Raleigh Gilbert, Bart., G.C.B. (since deceased).

[30] Lieutenant-Colonel, 9th Lancers, and formerly Lieutenant-Colonel in the 4th Light Dragoons, from which, like the author, he was removed into his present corps, when the 4th was put on the English establishment, on its return from Bombay in 1842. Colonel and

our left, ready to act as circumstances might render necessary. Brigadier Scott, as well as the Major-General, had commanded cavalry in the Affghan campaign, when Ghuznee was taken, in July 1839, and proceeded to Cabool; so that, should the presence of Sir Joseph Thackwell have been required in any other part of the field of action, he had as his second in command, an officer whom he well knew, and in whom he could place the most implicit confidence, for it must always be recollected that it is of great advantage to have an officer in the field, who has had experience in Indian warfare. It cannot be supposed that an officer just come from Europe can all at once, be prepared to command a brigade composed of Lancers, Dragoons, and native Cavalry. Surely a little experience is requisite. Besides in India, from the nature of the service, a Lieutenant-Colonel often commands a Brigade; while in Europe that command would generally devolve upon a Major-General.

Our battery of 9-pounders, twelve of which had been reamed up to 12-pounders, opened their fire near Little Sobraon, a village a short way in advance, between Major-General Gilbert's and Major-General Sir Harry Smith's divisions. Our artillery was thus placed,—five 24-pounder howitzers on our right, three 12-pounders (reamed) on the right of the 29th Foot, No. 19 battery on the left of Major-General Gilbert's right brigade; then between General Gilbert's left and the 62nd Foot there were six 8-inch howitzers, and six 5½-inch howitzers; on the left of the 62nd Foot there were eight 8-inch howitzers and five 18-pounders flanked by the 9th Foot and the 26th regiment of Native Infantry. On the extreme right there were forty-eight guns and howitzers, besides twelve guns, etc. on the right and left of Major-General Sir Robert Dick's division. In fact Major-General Sir Harry Smith's division was wheeled up to its left, so as to throw a flanking fire into the enemy's left. Also, Major-General Sir Robert Dick's division on the left, wheeled up to its right, so as to fire into the enemy's right.

Owing to the mist before mentioned, it was half-past-six A.M. before the whole of our artillery fire was brought into full play; the object of this fire was to silence the enemy's guns and to destroy their works before we assaulted the place. There was also a rocket battery. It must be remembered that the enemy had upwards of a hundred guns to fire against our sixty-two guns and the rocket battery. Rockets, the reader must be aware, were formerly much used in Indian warfare among the native armies. They were tried at Hattrass in 1817, with the force under the command of the late Major-General Sir W.S. Whish, K.C.B., but there was too much wind. On the present occasion the wind was not unfavourable. As the enemy's camp on the other side of the river was set on fire, the means by which that important service was effected may be disputed.

We must bear in mind that the Sikh guns were like those of a fortress, protected by walls, not *en barbette, i.e.* open all round. Besides this there was a triple line of trenches. The Sikhs also had two batteries on the other side of the river. When these batteries were silenced, the gunners came over by the bridge of boats, to the works on our side, to aid and to replace the gunners who had been killed or wounded. The bridge was said to be mined in case of accident, that is to say, if they

A.D.C. to the Queen.

were pursued in the retreat they could have blown it up to prevent our pursuing them.

It is clear that the mist had delayed the practice of the batteries, but still the artillery played upon the enemy's works for two hours. A more powerful battery would have been desirable; and it is said that this was Colonel Irvine's reason for proposing the delay. However, in all battles, there are two main points of consideration; first the military delays, and then the political delays, we know are sometimes dangerous. No doubt a casual observer would have exclaimed, "Why not wait for more guns? Recollect Ferozeshah; you tarried fifty days for this attack, during which time the enemy strengthened his position. You have more guns, more shot and shell coming up. Recollect also, you fell short of shot on the 22nd of December at Ferozeshah!" The late Captain J.D. Cunningham, of the Engineers, who was present at the battles of Aliwal and Sobraon, wrote thus: "The officers of artillery naturally desired that their guns, the representatives of a high art, should be used agreeably to the established rules of the engineers; or that ramparts should be breached in front and swept in flank, before they were stormed by defenceless battalions; but such deliberate tediousness of process did not satisfy the judgment or the impatience of the commanders, and it was arranged that the whole of the heavy ordnance should be planted in masses opposite particular points of the enemy's entrenchments, and, that when the Sikhs had been shaken by a continuous storm of shot and shells, the right, or weakest part of the position, should be assaulted in line, by the strongest of the three investing divisions, which, together mustered nearly 15,000 men," the enemy being 30,000 men.[31]

A military friend of mine, Major W. Hough, of the Bengal establishment, formerly a deputy Judge-Advocate, and author of some most valuable works on Military Law, and other subjects, has suggested that the attack in column is the more usual mode of assault, and has adduced many proofs that such a system has been at different periods acted upon, both in ancient and modern warfare.

Now let us look at the other side of the picture. Proposals had been made by the Sikh Sirdars, some say by Goolab Singh, which were refused. Had Goolab Singh's troops mutinied and refused to obey his orders, he would have said that he was helpless; it was possible that these same troops might be anxious to join Sham Singh in the entrenchments, a movement which it was the great object of the British chiefs to prevent.

As to the artillery, which is not surpassed by any artillery in the world, in celerity of movement, in precision of fire, or in any of the qualities which render this branch of the service illustrious, they could not perform impossibilities. They were deficient in that indispensable desideratum, shot. To have continued firing till all our shot was expended, and thus have exposed our want of it to the enemy, would have been very unwise; for, had the infantry failed in the attack, they might have retired, and our artillery resumed their fire. Hence it was that the British artillery ceased for a while to send forth its missives of death.

After two, or two and a half hour's firing, and at about nine o'clock, Brigadier

[31] History of the Sikhs, p. 319.

Stacey's Brigade, supported on either flank by two batteries of Foot and a troop of Horse Artillery, moved to the attack in good order, with Brigadier Stacey at their head. This gallant officer was armed with sword and buckler, the most effective weapons for such an attack, where you may come into personal contact with men who, after the custom of their country, are armed in this peculiar manner.

> *'Ἀμφί σάρ 'ώμοισιν βάλετο ξίφος ἀργυρόηον,*
> *— —αὐτάρ ἔπειτα σάκος μέγα τε στιβαρόν τε.*
>
> *Homer. Iliad* III. lines 334-5.

The troops marched in line. Captain Cunningham[32] says:—

"The left division of the British army, advanced in even order, and with a light step to the attack; but the original error of forming the regiments in line instead of in column, rendered the contest more unequal than such assaults need necessarily be. Every shot from the enemy's lines told upon the expanse of men, and the greater part of the division was driven back by the deadly fire of muskets and swivels and enfilading artillery.

"On the extreme left, the regiments effected an entrance amidst the advanced banks and trenches of petty out-works, where possession could be of little avail, but their comrades on the right were animated by the partial success; they chafed under the disgrace of a repulse, and forming themselves instinctively into wedges and masses, and headed by an old and fearless leader, they rushed forward in wrath." Major-General Sir Robert H. Dick, K.C.B. and K.C.H., was mortally wounded close to the trenches whilst cheering on his men; but we must reserve to a future page a further mention of this brilliant and noble officer.

The artillery took up positions to aid these divisions at a gallop. Brigadier Stacey's Brigade drove the Sikhs in confusion before them, within the area of their encampment. The 10th Foot, headed by their dauntless leader, Lieut.-Colonel T.H. Franks, entered; and here the work of carnage commenced, for now it was that hundreds of our indomitable foe fell under the withering fire of this gallant corps, Lieut.-Col. Franks having particularly cautioned his men not to fire until within the works of the enemy.

Let the reader pause and imagine the thunder of 120 guns on both sides reverberating for a length of time

> "As if the clouds their echo did repeat,"

and he will have but a very faint conception of the mighty grandeur of those awe-inspiring sounds. Never shall I forget the majesty of the whole scene.

> "No pen can write, no pencil trace the sound."

Seeing that Brigadier Stacey's Brigade might incur the whole weight of the attack, the centre and right divisions were ordered to advance. The centre division experienced great difficulty, for the mound in front was a very serious impediment. The Sikhs, sword in hand, strove to regain the points of the entrenchments which they had lost: it was not until the cavalry of the left wing under Major-Gen-

---

[32] History of the Sikhs, p. 325.

eral Sir Joseph Thackwell advanced and dashed into the entrenchments, in single file, through the openings effected by the pioneers in the mound, re-forming as they passed; and finally the full weight of three divisions of infantry with every available field-gun had been brought to bear against the resolute enemy, that victory crowned our efforts. The work was gloriously achieved. The insult offered to the British arms was avenged; and England stood triumphant.

For the important services which Brigadier Scott rendered in this action in leading his brigade into the enemy's entrenchment, he was honoured with the gratifying distinction of being appointed aide-de-camp to Her Majesty the Queen. At the taking of Ghuznee, July 23rd, 1839, Sir Joseph Thackwell and Brigadier Scott were employed in destroying the enemy who had escaped from the fort; they were, therefore, not novices at their work.

At Sobraon, our cavalry could not pursue the enemy as he retreated across the river; and, to have proceeded by Hurrekee Ghât, the nearest ford, would have been too late. The veteran Sirdar, Sham Singh, who commanded in the entrenchments, was engaged at his devotions when he first heard of the attack. As he must have known that our stores had not all arrived, for the Sikhs had accurate intelligence of our movements, he did not anticipate an attack from us so soon. Summoning his chiefs, Sham Singh reminded them of the great stake at issue, and bade them fight nobly and exterminate the infidel Feringhees (English). He assured his officers and men that the way of glory lay before them; and, to prevent their retreating, boldly commanded the two centre boats of the bridge to be cut away, so that his army could not pass over the pontoon. The order was obeyed; and, when forced to fly, the enemy in vain attempted the bridge, and were constrained to take to the river. Encumbered with arms, many attempted to swim across the river, which had risen seven or eight inches a day or two before; but all their efforts were unavailing. Hundreds and hundreds were drowned, or fell under the fire of our guns.

The press in England have condemned this general slaughter of our defenceless foe; but the answer, in extenuation, is, I believe, that the Sikhs had cruelly and relentlessly cut to pieces our wounded men at Ferozeshah.

If we regard the morality of the measure, we must not, at the same time, overlook the consequences which would have ensued from our sparing this resolute foe; for, at this time, we had yet to cross this river; and we were by no means certain but that we should have to fight another battle.

Messrs. Cobden and Co. must discover some golden rule for keeping the peace in India; for it would be a hard matter to find a single Sikh chief who is not ready to fight. The Rajpoot would laugh and say: "Sirs, it is my trade, as the calico line is yours; we were born soldiers." This universal Peace Association is, I have no doubt, a very amiable fraternity; yet let not its members, being deceived themselves, try to deceive others. The world still lieth in wickedness. Some divines understand the words of our Saviour, when he said, "I came not to send peace upon the earth, but the sword," to signify, there are very many religions in the world, and these will give rise to fighting. The Sikh would say: "You English have come and conquered the best and fairest portions of India, and now you are trying to annex the rest of the country; can you wonder that every man's hand is lifted up against you?"

Even Mr. Cobden must allow that to fight *pro aris et focis*, is not a very despicable employment. Until all nations and lands are prepared to join the league—until the time that all standing armies shall be dispensed with—and until right and might can keep their place—away with such empty talk! We must fraternize at home before we can hope to do so abroad. The natives of India do not understand those fine-drawn distinctions of our European policy. They know that the strongest will attack them if they can, and that the only plan of defence is to maintain armies.

The continent of Europe may be likened to India in one respect. Comprising various sovereignties, as in India, there are many independent princes. The native chief, like Alexander the Great, sighs when no more conquests are to be made! India, besides, is not a commercial country, like Europe; and all its inhabitants cannot plough or work at a trade. India has been, for centuries, the arena of strife. From the year 1187, when Delhi was seized by a Mahomedan conqueror, to the present year, anarchy, rapine, and war, have been stalking over the land. Thrice three thousand times blessed will be that period when every man of every nation shall have "turned his sword into a ploughshare, and his spear into a pruning-hook!" Until then, in order to ensure peace, let us be armed for war.

In Europe a sovereign loses a portion of his dominions, when it is taken by a monarch more powerful than himself. The league of the Holy Alliance contracted by four kings, in 1815, has not been able to preserve peace. The principle of *uti possidetis*, or, "as you are," of 1815, is not recognised in 1854. The Russians and Austrians have attacked Hungary, and Hungary has fought for her independence. The Neopolitans have sent an expedition to Sicily, and the Sicilians have sighed for independence. The French are masters of Rome, and Rome has longed for a republic, and thus we might multiply examples. Independence, the natural right of all countries, cannot generally be obtained except by war.

But *revenons à nos moutons*, the Sikhs again succumb. The battle of Sobraon has been fought and lost by them: at noon on the 10th of February, not a living Sikh remained on the left bank of the Sutlej.

At about two o'clock P.M., I rode leisurely through the enemy's entrenchments, and witnessed the horrible slaughter that had taken place; even at that time, a few determined artillerymen occasionally sent a ball across the river, to the dismay of our plundering camp followers. A mine, too, would now and then explode, and hurl the heedless and inquisitive into eternity, for the entrenchment was completely undermined; and during the following night and morning, explosions were every now and then heard in the camp.

During the action, the 9th Lancers advanced at about eleven o'clock A.M., under a heavy fire, in two lines, for the purpose of charging the enemy, when I commanded the left troop of the second squadron; after a time, however, as no opportunity to charge was allowed, we again fell back. The 9th Lancers left their camp at four o'clock A.M., and returned to it between five and six o'clock P.M., not a little tired, as the reader may imagine.

Thus the day, which rose so bright upon the landscape, after the mists of the early morning had been dispelled by the brilliant rays of the sun, was darkened by a battle and slaughter and death, ere the shades of evening closed upon it. The indomitable Sikhs, whose bravery was but the more aroused by the defeat at Aliwal, and whose feelings had been harrowed by the sight of the corpses of their unavenged comrades slain in that battle, who were still borne along the stream, and who had entered upon the contest with the resolve to conquer or die, these brave fellows were now lying in hundreds, or rather in thousands upon thousands, on the field of carnage, or floating along the sweeping flood of the Sutlej, while others fled in wild confusion before their victorious foe. But where were now their leaders?—the men who had instigated the revolt, and who with dastardly duplicity sought their private interests by simulated friendship with both parties? Where was Tej Singh, the chief commander of the Sikh forces? When the British opened the assault, Tej Singh commanded the entrenchment, but as soon as we had effected breaches in the mound, and the fire from his batteries began to slacken, when his followers were falling thick around him, when the British, led on by their gallant commanders, fought resolutely for every inch of ground, Tej Singh, instead of manfully leading on fresh troops, and animating them by his example, like a base traitor, again deserted his post; he fled at the first brush, and, as at the battle of Ferozeshah, abandoned his troops, and, in their destruction, sought, and effected his own escape; Goolab Singh, who had played his cards so well, was at the side of the Maharannee, counselling the adoption of such measures as would virtually promote his own interests; while the intriguer, Lall Singh, lay with his cavalry higher up the river in a careless, unmilitary position, conscious of being closely watched by the English.

Far different was the conduct and deportment of Sirdar Sham Singh, of Attaree. In accordance with the vow so solemnly made to his men that he would die in the conflict, and thus offer up himself as a propitiatory sacrifice for his country's weal to appease the wrath of Govind, he clothed himself in a white garment, as one who had devoted himself to death, and calling upon all around to follow him, he unflinchingly led on his rapidly thinning ranks, with the assurance of the Gooroo's eternal reward to those who should fall in defence of their country; and, at last, covered with wounds, the fine old veteran sunk down a lifeless corpse, amidst the slaughtered bodies of his brave followers.

The Commander-in-Chief estimated the loss of the Sikhs in this decisive battle at from 12,000 to 15,000 men; while that on the side of the British was, 320 killed, and 2,063 wounded, making our total loss 2,383.[33]

[33] See Appendix XI.

CHAPTER VII.

The Advanced-guard cross the Sutlej—Burial of Sir Robert Dick—Bridge of Boats—Kussoor—Surrender of the Sikhs—Dhuleep Singh—Lulleanee—Lahore—Runjeet Singh's Monument—The Summer Palace—The Governor-General's Address.

On the night of the victory of Sobraon, some of our advanced brigades crossed the Sutlej, opposite Ferozepore: they met with no resistance on landing, the whole place was abandoned, and not an enemy was visible. They hastened on to Kussoor, where they took possession of the fort.

Early on the morning of the 11th of February, we were once more on the move. The Commander-in-Chief appointed one division to remain behind and take charge of the sick and wounded, with orders to bring them on to Ferozepore; together with all the guns, etc., which we had taken from the enemy. These amounted to sixty-seven cannon, and 200 camel-swivels, or, as they are generally called, "zumbooruks;" together with immense quantities of ammunition and stores, and many of the Sikh standards.

The 9th Lancers accordingly started for Attaree, a distance of fourteen miles. On the 12th, we left our old encamping ground at Attaree at four o'clock A.M., and at eight o'clock A.M., we reached our new halting-place at Khoonda Ghât, about two miles distant from Ferozepore.

Soon after eight o'clock this morning, we heard the discharge of eleven guns, in the direction of Ferozepore, which we were informed were being fired over the grave of the late lamented Major-General Sir Robert Dick.

Not a month before the battle of Sobraon, I had called upon poor Sir Robert in his tent. He was then all life and animation, highly pleased with the Division to which he was about to be appointed, and which he asserted was the finest in the army. Not having had the opportunity of seeing a hostile shot fired in India, this noble soldier was in ecstasy at the thoughts of meeting the Sikhs in actual warfare. Conspicuous for his gallantry, when commanding the 42nd during the Peninsular War, Sir Robert was determined not to be out-shone; and placing himself at the head of his Division, the 3rd Infantry, he fell gloriously whilst mounting the enemy's entrenchments, in the very moment of victory. Never fell a General more regretted by his troops, nor one who in life was more beloved. The coolness of his temper in the battle-field, was only surpassed by the warmth of his hospitality in quarters; thus adding one more proof to the many on record, that the noblest and bravest heart is ever united with the gentlest and kindliest spirit.

To testify the estimation in which Sir Robert was held by his brother officers, a subscription was immediately set on foot among the officers throughout the army, and a large sum was collected for the purpose of erecting a monument to his memory, in the church of his native village of Tullymet, in Perthshire. The officers and men who have had the honour of serving under him, will not forget him; and the only consolation we could feel was, that he died, as I really believed he wished to die, fighting for his country, *exegit monumentum ære perennius*.[34]

Our bridge of boats having been completed, the Commander-in-Chief, with the whole of the army, crossed the Sutlej on the 13th. We passed over in single file; and after a tedious march of about eleven miles, arrived at Kussoor.

In the immediate vicinity of the Sutlej, the country is in a high state of cultivation, the valley being covered with a rich, soft verdure, but scarcely a tree is visible till within three miles from the banks; then the scene changes completely, and for miles and miles the eye rests upon nothing but immense tracts of jungle, interspersed with bushes, low tamarisks and tamarinds, with here and there the picturesque view of some ancient mosque or tomb. Close to Kussoor, lie the ruins of a large city scattered about in wild confusion; here mosques, domes, minarets and columns, tell of the departed glory of the Mahomedan era, when the arts and civilization were in their prime. The road runs through the town, which stands on a lofty eminence, and completely commands the place, and the ancient citadel of Kussoor. The town was formerly divided into twelve parts, each surrounded by a wall; and tradition says, that the founder gave one of these divisions to each of his twelve sons. Major Hough states that an army might make a good stand here, because there are not only heights, but each division of the town could be converted into a fortified position. But I am of opinion, that in the event of a hostile attack, it would not be capable of standing either a lengthened siege or a vigourous defence; it consists of a low wall, surrounded by narrow moats and projecting bulwarks. The town itself is surrounded by a very high wall, flanked with towers, and is densely built of brick. We encamped under the walls of the ancient town. The Governor-General joined the army early on the morning of the 14th. Kussoor is situated about sixteen miles from Ferozepore, and thirty-two from Lahore.

On the following morning, after some previous negotiation, the Maharannee of Lahore, who had appointed the Rajah Goolab Singh and some of the council to confer with the British army, sent her embassy to our head-quarters. They were intrusted by the queen mother with full powers, upon the condition that the treaty should embrace the continuance of the Sikh government at Lahore. The Governor-General surrounded by a brilliant staff of officers, received the Lahore embassy in his own tent. The deputation was then referred to Major Lawrence, now Sir Henry Lawrence, K.C.B., and since President of the Board of Administration for the affairs of the Punjaub, and Mr. Currie, now Sir Frederick Currie, Bart., and late Member of the Supreme Council of India, with whom they had a conference which lasted several hours. The Sikh chiefs being at first extremely reluctant to enter into the terms proposed by the English, their negotiations were prolonged far into the night. The following are the terms which were proposed by the English, and final-

[34] See Appendix XII.

ly agreed to by the Sikhs.

The complete surrender of the whole of the territorial possessions of the Sikhs, lying between the Sutlej and the Beas: the payment of a million and a half sterling, as a partial indemnity for the expenses of the war; the disbandment of the Sikh army, and its reorganization on the footing established by Runjeet Singh; the surrender of all the guns used against the British, and the assumption of full powers by the Governor-General to settle the frontiers and to fix the internal government of Lahore. The youthful Maharajah, Dhuleep Singh, the son of the Maharannee, being still regarded as an Ally, was required to meet the British army on its entering Lahore, and tender his submission. It was further stipulated, that the Sikhs should not have the power of raising any armed force, without the consent of the British government.

On the 18th of February, the 9th Lancers reached the little mud-walled village of Lulleanee, a distance of ten miles, during which I was on baggage guard. It stands in the midst of corn fields and jungle. It is about thirty-four miles from Ferozepore, and about midway between that place and Lahore.

This evening, agreeably to the stipulation, the infant Maharajah, Dhuleep Singh, came into the camp of the Governor-General. His council sought forgiveness for the late act of aggression on the part of the army. The Maharajah did not receive any military honours from the Governor-General until he had made his submission; but after having done so, he was treated with the style becoming the rank of a prince, and remained in camp till the entry of the army into Lahore.

While we were at Lulleanee, we suffered much from scarcity of water. On the 19th, we reached the village of Kankuch, a distance of ten miles. Both yesterday and to-day the 9th Lancers were on the advanced guard of the army. On the 20th of February, we marched to Lahore, a distance of ten miles, and encamped on the celebrated Meanmeer, three miles from the city—the ground where the Sikh troops used to be drilled. Through the kindness of Major Lawrence I obtained a pass out of camp, and an escort of two Sikh horsemen, for the purpose of visiting Lahore, the renowned Sikh capital.

The appearance of the city is very imposing at a distance, from its numerous mosques, with their azure domes and sparkling minarets rising majestically above the palaces, houses and gardens, the far distance being bounded by the bold outline of the snow-capped Himalayas. To the south, lies the ancient city of Lahore, completely in ruins, interspersed with the remains of caravansaries, sepulchral monuments, towers and domes, overshadowed here and there by the lofty crowns of the graceful date-palm.

These splendid buildings carry the mind back to a bye-gone age, when wealth and grandeur reigned in Lahore, under the first Mahomedan conquerors of Hindoostan, before they succeeded in establishing themselves in the central Provinces of India. Lahore was the residence of Humayoon, the father of Akbar, who greatly enlarged and improved the city, which during his reign is said to have been three leagues in length; even to this day it is of considerable extent.

The modern city of Lahore lies close to the Rāvee, and contains about 80,000 inhabitants. It is surrounded by a massive brick wall, twenty-five feet in height, and fortified at regular distances with bastions and towers. Runjeet Singh greatly improved and strengthened the fortifications; and, like a good general, carried a moat completely round the outer side of the wall, and circumvallated this moat with a line of strong ramparts, fortified by out-works and heavy artillery, running in a circumference of seven or eight miles round the city. It gives the impression of a once impregnable place, and even now presents an appearance of considerable strength, though many of the bastions and works are going to decay.

The bright illusions which have previously filled the imagination of the stranger with visions of grandeur and magnificence, vanish like a dream the moment he enters the city gate. The principal street is very narrow, and extremely dirty, with a kennel running through the middle of it, into which is thrown the refuse from the neighbouring houses. Here, too, the streets are unpaved, and in such a wretched condition, that they are almost inpassable in wet weather. The houses are chiefly of brick, and though lofty, present a mean appearance. Like most of the Oriental houses, they have flat roofs, where the inhabitants pass the cool of the day. They are surrounded by dead walls, and present nothing of architectural interest; the only redeeming feature being an elegant arabesque carving, which runs along the wooden balconies and windows.

My first visit was to the citadel, which lies to the North-West of the town. It contains the barracks, extensive magazines, and military stores, together with the Hazuree Bagh, the noble winter palace of the late Maharajah, which was commenced by Akbar, and completed by others of the Mogul emperors. At an angle of the Maharannee's apartments, close to the gate, is the magnificent tomb of Runjeet Singh, together with those of the other members of his family. I visited this fine marble mausoleum, which is built in the Arabesque style, and was erected by Shore Singh, on the spot where Runjeet Singh, his son, and his grandson, together with their wives and female slaves, were consumed on the funeral pyre. This monument is just outside the lofty gates of the Hazuree Bagh. It was while passing through the ruins of these gates that Nou Nehal Singh was crushed to death, by the sudden dislodgment of a ponderous stone, as he was proceeding to the Rāvee to wash away his sins, immediately after the burning of his father's corpse.

The Hazuree Bagh was, in ancient times, the residence of the Mogul emperors. It is an immense pile, built of red granite, and consists of three large quadrangles, surrounded by arched corridors, magazines, and stores. From each of the four angles rises a lofty minaret, 150 feet in height; while the Western-side of the principal quadrangle is occupied by the Mosque, of red sand-stone, built by the emperor, Aurungzebe. This quadrangle, which is 500 paces in length, leads to the garden court or Hazuree Bagh, which is likewise surrounded by vaulted corridors, now in ruins. A pavilion of white marble stands in the centre.

The fort, or citadel, is in the third quadrangle. It is surrounded by numerous buildings, among which is the palace of the late Maharajah. The appearance is striking and unique, as it has a winding staircase rising above the highest platform.

The bazaars, which in all Eastern cities are the most animated parts of the town, presented nothing of interest; and instead of the varied display of costly oriental manufactures, in gold and embroidery, there was little else but sweetmeats and eatables.

There are some fine buildings in the immediate vicinity of Lahore. The principal is the tomb of the emperor, Jehangeer. It is of white marble, and red sandstone, and rises in the centre of a beautiful garden. The Arabesques, above the arches of the piazza, which surround the tomb, are executed with great skill, and are in a state of perfect preservation, while the rest is going to decay. The tomb occupies a square building, 66 paces each way, the piazza being 1,800 feet square. I must not forget to mention the summer palace, or Shalemar. It was the residence of the emperor, Shah Jehan in 1627, and bears the inscription, "House of joy." It is constructed of white marble, in the same style as the Shalemar, at Cashmere, and stands in the middle of a lovely garden, tastefully laid out, with flowers, fountains, shrubberies, magnificent trees, and orange groves.

On my visit to the house of the Maharannee's German physician, I was introduced to Colonel Van Cortland, late of the Sikh service. In my rambles, I went over the house of General Ventura, since the residence of the Chief Commissioner, Sir Henry Lawrence. It is a spacious building, and presents a more European character than any in the city. In the gun-sheds, I saw only seven guns. The Infantry barracks were tenantless. The few soldiers, too, whom I saw in the place, had a mortified and disconsolate look.

Great alarm naturally prevailed in Lahore, in consequence of the defeat of the Sikh army, the arrival of our victorious troops, and the occupation of the citadel by an English garrison. The Governor-General, anxious to allay the ferment, issued a proclamation, which had the desired effect.[35]

On the 9th of March, the Governor-General signed the important treaty between the British and Lahore governments.[36]

I was on duty at the Governor-General's tent, with a troop of my regiment as a guard of honour, for the reception of the young Maharajah of Lahore, who had arrived from the capital attended by his principal Sirdars, and a numerous retinue, for the purpose of signing the treaty between the Government of the Company and that of the Lahore Durbar. Three royal salutes were fired from our 12-pounders, namely, one salute on the arrival of the prince, another at the signing of the treaty, and the third on his Highness' departure.

After the treaty was ratified and signed, the Governor-General made the following speech:—

"For forty years it was the policy of Runjeet Singh to cultivate friendly relations between the two Governments; and during the whole of that period, the Sikh nation was independent and happy. Let the policy of that able man towards the British Government, be the model for your future imitation. The British Government in no respect provoked the late war. It had no objects of aggrandizement to obtain by hostilities. The proof of its sincerity is to be found in its moderation in

[35] See Appendix XIII.
[36] See Appendix XIV.

the hour of victory. A just quarrel, followed by a successful war, has not changed the policy of the British Government. The British Government does not desire to interfere in your internal affairs. I am ready and anxious to withdraw every British soldier from Lahore. At the earnest solicitation of the Sikh government, I have reluctantly consented to leave a British force in garrison at Lahore, until time shall have been afforded for the reorganization of the Sikh army, by whose assistance the stipulations of the treaty may be more easily carried into effect. In no case can I consent that the British troops shall remain in garrison for a longer period than the end of this year. I state this publicly, that all the world may know the truth, and the motives by which I am actuated in this matter."

At the conclusion of this address, the young Maharajah, who had thus been virtually recognised as the Sovereign of Lahore, under the protection of the English, was re-conducted to his palace by British regiments, under a royal salute.

CHAPTER VIII.

Review of the Army—Eastern Mode of Adoption—Cashmere assigned to Goolab Singh—Defeat of Affghan Cavalry—Major John Cameron Campbell—Security of the North-west Frontier—Fertility of the Punjaub—Infantry introduced into the East—Hyder Ali's Notion of English Power—Runjeet's Craftiness—Improvement in the Punjaub—Dhuleep Singh professes Christianity—Dr. Login—Dhuleep baptized by the Rev. W.J. Jay—Dhuleep Singh's Sincerity.

On the 10th of March, the whole army was reviewed by the Governor-General, the Commander-in-Chief, the Governor of Scinde (the late Lieutenant-General Sir Charles J. Napier, G.C.B.), the Maharajah Dhuleep Singh, Goolab Singh, and many of the Sikh Sirdars. The troops formed line in masses of brigades; the second Brigade of Cavalry, being on the extreme left in open column of squadrons, at quarter distance: there were about 22,000 men on the ground. The conqueror of Scinde, having left behind his 16,500 men and fifty guns, had joined the head-quarters of the army, and was present at this review. The Sikh chiefs also were present, more humble than in former days. They, poor men, with few exceptions, were only the forced actors in the late drama. The Punts and Punchees[37] having decided upon fighting, the chiefs and Sirdars were constrained to gird up their loins for action.

The Governor-General, Sir Henry (now Viscount Hardinge, G.C.B.), was well aware that there were 20,000 Khalsa troops under arms in another part of the Punjaub. Conversing with a field officer, and looking at our European troops, the Governor-General remarked, "See those men, there are only 3,200 fit for duty;" which observation was at the time interpreted somewhat thus: "Out of 7,000 or 8,000 Europeans at first employed in this army, see the reduced remnant; had I not made the treaty, I could not at this season have continued the war."

The young and handsome Maharajah gazed upon the magnificent spectacle before him, with a kind of childish indifference, little concerned about the slice carved out by our swords from the dominions of his putative father; he is ignorant of his paternity, neither does he know whether he can legally call the Maharannee his mother. The Eastern mode of adoption is a very easy mode of providing a successor, for if a Rannee has no sons, others have, who may supply the place. Child-stealing, moreover, is very common in the Punjaub. Report assigns Jummoo as the place of his Highness' birth. The Rajah had a brother. I must leave the unravelling of the mystery, however, to those of my readers who feel an interest in

[37] See Appendix XV.

tracing genealogies, with as much likelihood of success, at least, as the Sikh chiefs who tried the puzzle.

On the 10th of March I was on escort duty with my regiment, from half-past two to six in the afternoon, accompanying the Governor-General to and from a visit to the Maharajah, in the palace at Lahore.

On the 12th of March, the army of the Sutlej was broken up, and our kind-hearted Commander-in-chief bade it farewell.

Let us consider our position at the present time, with respect to our late enemy. A treaty has been concluded: we garrison Lahore with our troops, and form a government of Sikh chiefs, superintended by a British officer, namely, Sir Henry Lawrence. We declare that we must withdraw our force from Lahore by the end of the year. The Sikh chiefs entreat us to remain, which we at last agree to, and enter into another treaty to govern until Dhuleep Singh shall be of age, which will be in September, 1854.[38] This period was fixed, because as the Company's charter expires on the 30th of April, 1854, an act of indemnity would otherwise have been required from Parliament.

We first of all take possession of the Jullundur Doab; assign to Goolab Singh the rich and fertile valley of Cashmere,[39] whose productions are those of the temperate zone. The Sikhs are to disband their present army and organize a new one, which is not to exceed 32,000 men, 20,000 of which shall be infantry; and furthermore, we compel them to pay to the British government 22 lakhs of rupees, or £220,000 sterling per annum. Next, a deep conspiracy is discovered at Lahore, and two British officers are murdered at Mooltan. The Sikhs, under Moolraj, Chutter Singh and Shere Singh, raise large armies. The Maharannee is at the bottom of this conspiracy. We send troops in December, 1848, and take Mooltan in February, 1849. We fight at Ramnuggur, and fall into a trap. At Chillianwallah, we take the bull by the horns, but at Goojerat, on the 21st of February, 1849, with eighty-four guns against the enemy's fifty-nine, we gain a victory complete in every point, the Sikhs being battered by our overwhelming force of artillery for three hours. The Affghan Horse, under the command of a son of Dost Mahomed Khan, of Cabool, are routed after a noble charge, by a squadron of the 9th Lancers, and a party of the Scinde Irregular Horse, under the command of Captain J.C. Campbell,[40] of the Lancers, in which he was ably supported by Lieutenant F.J. M'Farlane, of the same corps, a stalwarth and powerful officer; and the whole army of the enemy having been put to flight and pursued for many miles, we finally annex the Punjaub to the British dominions.[41]

Now how would the leader of the British Anti-War Association have acted? The Sikhs cross the Sutlej and attack us. Would that gentleman have reasoned with them, or would he have attacked them? Whatever he may make of Europe,

[38] See Appendix XVI.

[39] See Appendix XVII.

[40] For this gallant charge, Captain Campbell obtained the brevet rank of Major, since which time he has, however, retired from the army, by the sale of his commission, after a long period of service.

[41] See Appendix XVIII.

we cannot at present rule India otherwise than by the sword. India has to look to a possible invasion from the North, but none from the South. It is true, Admiral Suffrien did, in 1783, tell the King of France that the French might invade India from the Burmese territory; and he was right. But in 1826, we secured ourselves against such an event by Treaties. The Queen of England is ruler of the Mauritius, and the Cape is subject to her sway. On our North-West lie Scinde and the Punjaub, which two countries protect us against invasion from Candahar direct; and from an attack by the circuitous route of Cabool, we can always secure the Bolan and Khyber Passes; and those of Dhera Ghazee Khan and Dhera Ismael Khan are in our hands whenever we choose, for Mooltan would cover the operation.

Thus has the last Sikh campaign rendered our North-West frontier as safe as we could desire. Time will make the conquest valuable, and it must be our aim to conciliate a new people. Francklin (p. 66) says: "The Punjaub yields to no part of India in fertility of soil; it produces in the greatest abundance, sugar-cane, wheat, barley, rice, pulse of all sorts, tobacco, and various fruits, and it is also well supplied with cattle. The principal manufactures of this country are swords, matchlocks, cotton-cloths, and silks, both fine and coarse."

This description was written in 1802: it is useful to compare the past with the present. The Punjaub still (1854) supplies all the necessaries of life, and the district between the Indus and the Jelum contains salt-mines. In regard to commerce, as well as to manufactures, such as those of cotton-cloths, various stuffs, curious carpets, etc., the Sikhs are behind the other nations of India; yet, considering they are a military people, they shew less contempt for the occupations and amusements of civil life, and the peaceful cultivation of the soil, than might have been expected.

There can be no doubt that this country will become very flourishing under British rule. European art and science will be applied to the improvement of trade and agriculture, and above all, afford that greatest of incentives to industry, the certainty that, "what a man soweth, that shall he also reap." The Sikhs were more anxious to acquire other lands than to improve those which they already held; besides, in the constant scenes of anarchy and warfare, which have desolated this fine country, no man could ever feel certain that he should gather all his produce. Francklin, speaking of the Sikh army, in 1802, says (p. 67): "It has been remarked, that the Sikhs are able to collect from 50 to 60,000 horse; but to render this number effective, those who do not take the field, or who remain at home to guard their possessions, must be included."

The following is Francklin's statement, which comprehended the districts from the Attock to Sirhind:

	Cavalry.
The districts South of the Sutlej	15,000
The Doab, or country between the Sutlej and the Beyah (Beas)	8,000
Between the Beyah and Rowee (Ravee)	11,000
Force of Buyheel Singh, Chief of Pattiala	12,000

The countries above Lahore, the inhabitants of which are chiefly under the influence of Runjeet Singh	11,000
The Force of Nizam-ud-deen Khan	5,000
Ditto of Roy Elias	1,300
Ditto of other Pathan Chiefs in pay of the Sikhs	800
Grand total	64,100

The Chief of most consequence was Runjeet Singh. If we suppose that two-thirds of this force might take the field, there would be 42,730 horsemen.

The above writer also says, that the repeated invasion of the Punjaub by small armies, of late years, affords a convincing proof, "that the national force of the Sikhs cannot be so formidable as has been represented." "It was successfully invaded by the Maharatta armies of Ambajee, Bala Row and Nana Furkiah, who drove the Sikhs repeatedly before them." No mention is made of the Sikh artillery.

It is to be remarked of the Sikhs, as of other native states (indeed, it is an old remark, and has been made by some of the best informed natives themselves), that Hyder Ali Khan, and Tippoo Sultan, of Mysore, Sindiah, Holcar, in fact, all the native Chiefs of India, were victorious over their native enemies by means of large masses of horse. Infantry of some description they had; but the regular battalions, drilled by Europeans, were only introduced as a system about 60 years ago, by French, German, and Italian officers.

The principal use of Infantry was to defend their forts. Seeing the advantage of regular and well-disciplined Infantry, under the British and French, the leading princes and chiefs adopted the same plan, and at length resolved to have Brigades of Infantry; as, for example, Sindiah's Brigades, under Duboignie, and the Nizam's, etc., etc.

Before this period and until the chiefs had regular corps, the British marched over the country for hundreds of miles, the enemy flying before them. But, in 1803, Sindiah brought many disciplined brigades of infantry into the field, perhaps 8,000, 10,000, or even 12,000 infantry, and seventy, eighty, or one hundred guns, besides horse. Our losses were sustained in taking the guns. Thorn, in his "History of the Maharatta War, 1803," says; "the Maharatta armies in three of their greatest battles were as follow:—

	Infantry.	Cavalry.	Guns.
At Delhi	8,000	6,000	68
Assaye	10,500	30,000	100
Leswarree	7,000	4,500	72."

It will be seen that except at Assaye, they had more infantry than cavalry. While the enemy mustered the above numbers, and always had about one fourth of their guns of large calibre, the British only brought seventeen, twenty-five, and thirty small guns into the field. Runjeet Singh's views were different from those of the native princes. Captain Meadows Taylor, in his "Life of Hyder Ali," says;

"In December, 1782, just before his death, Hyder Ali Khan of Mysore, called for his confidential adviser and said, 'What signifies the loss of Colonel Baillie's detachment of 3,000 or 4,000 troops? The English can get more by sea; unless I can build a navy to compete with the Feringhees, and stop them from landing, I cannot destroy them. They come as fast as you cut them down.'"

The Maharatta Chiefs thought differently. The power of the English, whose ascendancy in India dates from about the year 1803, had supplanted that of France. The French having rejected the application for European troops, made by Tippoo Sultan in 1799, a brief pause followed upon Napoleon's expedition to Egypt, but on the renewal of the war with England in 1803, Napoleon, in his projected invasion of India, engaged the assistance of the powerful Maharatta chiefs, who entered warmly into the war, and Sindiah's troops were placed under the direction of French officers sent out for the purpose.

M. Perron, in 1803, had 43,000 Infantry and a powerful Artillery, with which he held Allygurh, Agra, and Delhi. He designed, moreover, by degrees, to supersede Sindiah's authority, but Lord Lake's and Sir Arthur Wellesley's battles defeated the scheme. The Maharattas, or rather their troops under French officers, governed Delhi at this time, the Emperor Shah Allum being a captive prince and blind. Runjeet Singh, although a young man, knew all these facts, he therefore, caused his troops to be disciplined by European officers, for the purpose of fighting his battles against the Affghans, and other native enemies; but he never desired to lead them against the English, nor did he much like to entrust his European officers with commands in his wars. General Avitabile had charge of Peshawur, as civil, not as military, governor.

In 1825, when the British attacked Bhurtpore, the Rajah wished Runjeet to aid him, but the crafty fox refused. Some time after, asking Captain Wade (now Lieutenant-Colonel Sir Claudius M. Wade, C.B.) "what the English would have done had he joined the Rajah:" Captain Wade replied, "We should have attacked you first, and then have gone to undertake the siege." "Indeed!" said Runjeet, "I thought so. I shall not quarrel with the English; they are my friends."

Thus the Punjaub, which had been for centuries the tempting lure of a succession of invading hordes, and a prey to anarchy, rapine, and oppression, has passed, like its far-famed "Mountain of Light," into the possession of Queen Victoria; and from the marvellous success which has already crowned the efforts of the British Government to improve this new domain, I have no doubt that it will soon shed as much lustre on the British name, as this brilliant jewel over the royal brow.

When the Punjaub, paralysed and withered under the military authority of Runjeet Singh, first became ours, it never entered into the imagination of the most sanguine, to conceive the change which a few short years of wise and enlightened rule would produce in the outward face of the country. Whole tracts of forest and jungle have been cleared and brought under cultivation; canals, hundreds of miles in extent, and at an outlay of millions of rupees, are in course of excavation; commerce and agriculture are encouraged, and every possible facility is afforded to the native mind to develop the resources which nature has placed within the reach of its inhabitants.

We cannot but feel that it is only a Christian power, which could have exercised this happy influence; for Christianity has been in all ages, and under all circumstances, the pioneer of enlightenment and civilization. Circumstanced as the British government were, they could not well make any direct efforts to establish Christianity among the Sikhs, and indeed their usual caution and feeling rather lean to the reverse. And yet without any such efforts or encouragement on their part, and no one can tell exactly how, the first fruit of the Gospel among the native sovereigns of India, is the young Maharajah, Dhuleep Singh, the son and successor of the mighty Runjeet Singh.

As this event, so important and significant under any circumstances, but doubly so under the present shaking and waning attachment of the Sikh population to their own religious rites, is deeply interesting to the British public, I will here give an extract from a speech delivered by Archdeacon Pratt, in Calcutta:

"The baptism of Dhuleep Singh is an encouraging event, and although perhaps the less said about it the better, for the young convert's own mind, yet as so many false accounts have gone abroad regarding him, it is well briefly to state the circumstances which led him to seek baptism. His desire to become a Christian has generally been attributed to the influence of Dr. Login, who has charge of the young prince. But this is altogether a mistake. Dr. Login has acted the part of a wise and consistent Christian, in the delicate and responsible charge committed to him, but no overtures were made by him to induce the youth to become a Christian. It is believed that an early disgust of his own countrymen, was created in his mind by the horrible assassinations which he witnessed as a child at the Court of Lahore; and the personal kindness which he afterwards met with from Lord Dalhousie and the officials, up to the time of his quitting the Punjaub, gave him a favourable impression of the English.

"But the first impulse in his mind in favour of Christianity, was occasioned by his Brahmin attendant reading the Scriptures to him, during Dr. Login's absence in Calcutta.

"The Brahmin had learnt English in a missionary school, and like many of his countrymen, was himself convinced of the truth of the Word of God, but had not courage to stem the torrent of opposition, which an open avowal of his convictions would have created. His reading, however, awakened the young prince's mind to the value of the Bible; and Dhuleep Singh wrote to Dr. Login that he must have a copy of the Scriptures; and also, that he intended forthwith to break his caste. From this last step he was wisely dissuaded, till he should be better informed.

"The whole matter was made known to the Governor-General and to the Court. It was determined, that if he finally desired to become a Christian, no impediment should be placed in his way, when he was perfectly prepared for the rite. The chaplain of the Station was directed to give him the necessary instruction, should the prince desire it; and his mind has been growing and maturing under the wise superintendence of Dr. Login, and the instructions of his English tutor and the chaplain; but no more progress in advance has been made without his own desire. His attending divine service, both in private and afterwards in public, in the Mussouree church, was of his own seeking and urging.

"I have seen a good deal of the youth, and feel persuaded that he has been led by a higher hand than human, and that the work is of God. He is only a youth; but his character in every respect is a most interesting one; more especially when we remember who he is, and the darkness out of which he has come. If God keep him steadfast, and to this we should direct our prayers, his conversion may have an important influence on missionary prospects."

After a careful examination into his knowledge of those truths which he professed to believe, the Maharajah was formally admitted into the Christian church by baptism, on the 8th of March, 1853, by the Rev. W.J. Jay, Chaplain of Futtyghur. At this interesting ceremony, which took place in the Maharajah's own house at the station, were present all the civil and military authorities, and the American missionaries, as well as a number of his own attendants, on whom the solemnity of the occasion appeared to make a deep impression.

The "Friend of India," in its notice of this event, remarks:—

"It will, of course, be observed, particularly in England, that it would have been more advisable to postpone this irrevocable renunciation of Hindooism, until matured age should have given the young Maharajah the knowledge and experience necessary to enable him to make a permanent decision; but according to Major Smyth's 'Reigning Family of Lahore,' Dhuleep Singh was born in 1837, and he is therefore already sixteen. A lad of this age in India is a man, with as great a capacity for estimating the merits of different creeds, as he is ever likely to possess. From the time that he was placed under the charge of Dr. Login, his education has been most carefully provided for; and the boy who, when rescued from Lahore, could not even read, is now almost English in language, ideas, and feelings. His conduct, with reference to the ceremonial salutes, and his visit to the Governor-General, are sufficient proofs that his judgment is not beneath his acquirements, and that he has been fairly rescued from those influences which warp the minds of the *Porphyrogeniti* of the East. Sixteen is the age at which the Law Courts acknowledge the right of a native youth to judge for himself; and this last act of the Maharajah has been performed entirely of his own free will. He has been neither coaxed nor frightened into Christianity. Indeed, the Government had every motive for retaining him in his old creed. An Asiatic Christian prince, with £40,000 a year, might excite an interest in England, which it has hitherto been the policy of the home authorities to avoid, but they doubtless felt that it was not for them to interpose obstacles in his way. He was simply left to his own discretion; and that he has chosen rightly will, we think, be allowed even by those who are not given to 'Missionary fanaticism.' His conversion, will, at least, save the palace of Futtyghur from becoming like that of Delhi, a place where all evil naturally seeks shelter; and a native Christian noble, with his vast wealth, may accomplish far more good than a hundred ordinary converts.

"With the exception of 'Prester John,' in whom, despite Marco Polo, our faith is exceedingly limited, and a Roman Catholic Ziogoon of Japan, Dhuleep Singh is the first of his rank in Asia who has become a Christian. His example may, perhaps, give confidence to many who remain in Hindooism, rather from a vague dread of the consequences of abandoning it, than from any belief in its tenets; and we may see Christianity reverse its ordinary course, and descend from the highest to the lowest ranks. We have little hope of such a result; but it requires no religious belief to prove that it would be of the highest advantage to themselves and the people. The mere fact that there then would exist oaths by which they could be bound, and principles which they would scruple to violate, would bind their subjects to them, with a chain stronger than any which the ablest of their number have yet been able to forge."

The editor of the "Oriental Christian Spectator," observes: "From the persuasion which we have of the Christian judgment and prudence of Dr. Login, whose instructions have been blessed to this great result, we have every confidence that this conversion is of the most satisfactory character.

"The Sikh Prince, in the path he has pursued, appears before us, as no inappropriate specimen of his nation, and of what may be expected from them, if only at the present juncture suitable opportunities be presented. Their national discomfiture has been the overthrow of that fanaticism, under the standard of which they hoped to find themselves invariably the conquerors, and progressing rapidly to universal dominion. It has disappointed them; its prestige is gone; it has lost all hold upon them. If we neglect to meet adequately the present crisis, they will become rapidly absorbed in Hindooism, or Mahomedanism, and infusing a new and energetic element into those decayed systems, may re-invigorate them, and prolong their existence for a season. But if we go forward on a liberal and comprehensive scale of action, to the improvement of the remarkable opportunities now presented to us, there is hope that, as a nation, they may follow the example of the young ex-Maharajah, whose profession of Christianity, at the present moment, is calculated to exercise upon them a very important influence."

CHAPTER IX.

The Army of the Sutlej broken up—Set out on a Tour—Dhool—Ferozepore—Grandeur of the Himalayas—Misri-Wala—Ferozeshah—Moodkee—Bhaga Poorana—Bussean—Phurewallee—Kotla Mullair—Munsorepore—Samana—Goelah—The River Cuggur—Pehoah—Khol—Kurnaul—Military Stations—Transport of Artillery—Ali Merdan's Canal—English Church—Malaria—Sir David Ochterlony—Gurounda—Minarets—Somalka—Paniput—Battles of Paniput—Baber—Ibrahim Lodi—Ahmed Shah—Defeat of the Maharattas—Nadir Shah—Capture of Delhi—Mahomed Shah—Troops engaged—Native Armies—Sunput—Change in the Weather.

THE army of the Sutlej being broken up, the different corps took their departure for the various stations assigned to them, my own regiment, the 9th Lancers, being ordered to Meerut. I set out on the 14th of March, 1846, and commenced a march of 704 miles, intending to ride quietly to Allahabad, and thence proceed by steam to Calcutta. I had obtained leave of absence to England for a period of two years, from the day of embarkation, and four months to Calcutta, from the date of leaving my regiment.

On the 14th, therefore, as I said, I bade "adieu" to my regiment, and commenced my journey attended by my own servants fourteen in number, two camels, and two three-bullock hackeries, my Khidmutgar having engaged to supply me with my meals. On the first day I rode to Kankuch, a distance of ten miles. On the 15th there was a violent storm of wind, rain, thunder and lightning, from four to six o'clock in the morning, which made it unadvisable for me to proceed, as my only tent, a hill-tent, was completely saturated.

On the 16th, I rode to Dhool, about sixteen miles; through Lulleanee, and left Kussoor on my right hand. The next day I made a longer journey, and rode twenty miles to Ferozepore. On my way thither, I met a train of 500 hackeries and 4,000 camels, laden with provisions for the force which was to garrison Lahore. Ferozepore was distant about ten miles from the bridge of boats, by which I crossed the Sutlej. There were formerly two of these pontoons, each nearly 300 yards long, the boats themselves being of the ordinary flat-bottomed sort, with very broad ends, called "dandy boats," which are used in the navigation both of the Indus and Ganges, as well as of the Sutlej. The two bridges consisted respectively of fifty-nine and forty-seven such boats, but Sir J. Littler sank the smaller of them. They are, or rather were, so strong, that the heaviest weight might pass over them with the greatest ease and security. It was interesting to watch the elephants; they put down their proboscis, and then successively each of their fore-feet with extreme caution, to try the strength of the bridge, and when they had satisfied themselves that it would bear their weight, they crossed without the least hesitation.

Ferozepore is one of our large military stations; it derives its present improved state from our occupation; for it was formerly a desolate and ruinous place, the houses deserted and dilapidated, and the country round waste and uncultivated. Now all is animation and progress. The dismal-looking town stands on a rising ground in an immense plain, a couple of miles from the river. Like nearly all the Indian towns, it is surrounded with walls, which were erected chiefly as a protection to their cattle, against the predatory hordes that infested the vicinity, the animals being driven out in the morning, and brought home at night. It contains a very handsome tank, close to an elegant pagoda surrounded with trees. The great detriment here, is the want of water; there are plenty of ditches and a dry arm of the Sutlej, and if the inhabitants would only dig twenty-five or thirty feet for water, the whole face of things would be changed at once.

The cantonments are about three miles to the south of the town. They are divided into streets, which cross at right angles. The officers' bungalows are picturesquely situated in the midst of pretty gardens which combine the flora of the eastern and the western hemispheres; the barracks, both for the European and native regiments, are not particularly good; the magazines and stores are built of stone and have a very durable appearance.

But to the lover of nature, the great attraction is the distant range of the snow-capped Himalaya mountains. Neither pen nor pencil can describe their splendour amid the gorgeousness of an eastern sunset. Earth and sky are covered with a veil of liquid gold; the clouds, as they traverse the deep blue vault, gradually assume the most varied and brilliant tints, and the majestic Himalayas, girdled round their base with a robe of gold and crimson, rear their silvered crests in line relief against the bright effulgence that surrounds them. How different are the feelings inspired by gazing upon such a scene, and those aroused by the din of battle, the sight of slaughter and death which I had so recently witnessed!

"Aye, there they stand, as in creation's prime,
Above the mouldering wrecks of sin and time!
Man's fatal fall, which all beneath them cursed,
Hath left them standing as they stood at first:
Unchallenged, still they keep their place in heaven,
And wear the diadem their God hath given;
And change and death sweep on o'er sea and land,
And find, and leave them changeless: there they stand!"

On the 19th I journeyed to Misri-Wala, ten miles. On my arrival there, I rode over to Ferozeshah, which is only about a mile and a half off, as I was anxious to see the battle-field. It was a horrid sight. After an interval of three months it was still covered with the unburied bodies of the Sikhs, on whom hundreds of Pariah dogs and birds of prey were feasting; dead camels, horses, and bullocks also seemed to invite them to a plentiful repast. The odour was dreadful, even more so than on my former visit.

20th. Proceeded to Moodkee, ten miles and a half, and pitched my tent on the edge of the battle-field, close by the fort, which was then occupied by a company of the 51st regiment of Native Infantry. Three months had just elapsed since the battle, which was fought here on the 18th of December, the first of the four engagements between the army of the Sutlej and the Sikhs. Within that short period no less than 1,449 of our troops had fallen, and 4,926 had been wounded, many of whom have since died; while the destruction of the Sikhs is fearful to contemplate. In round numbers they are said to have lost about 20,000 men.

On the 21st I went to Bhaga Poorana, a distance of fifteen miles. On my route, I again met a train of 400 hackeries laden with stores for the troops at Lahore. Next day I marched to Wudnee. On my arrival, I examined the square brick-built fort; the battlements command a fine view of the surrounding country. The eye wandered over a vast extent, without hill or mountain to intercept its wide spread range. All nature seemed to be at peace, and the Sutlej, which had so lately been stained with the blood of the slain, now flowed down in a pure and silvery current, bearing along with it health and refreshment from its rise in the table land of Thibet, to its junction with the Indus at Mithunkote.

On the morning of the 23rd I made an early start, and was on the move at a quarter to three for Bussean, fifteen miles and a half distant: it lies midway between Lahore and Umritsur, and is about twenty miles from each place. On the 24th I rode to Phurewallee, fourteen miles. On the 25th to Kotla Mullair, ten miles. Here the Dewan, or steward, of the Rajah of Nabah called upon me for a certificate that I had been well treated on my way through his master's territories, a request with which I willingly complied.

On reaching Munsorepore, a distance of sixteen miles, on the next day, I found my tent pitched close to a mosque; yesterday it had been placed near a Hindoo temple—and I was sadly disturbed at sunset by some barbarous sounds on a horn, made by a Brahmin. On the 27th I started, at two o'clock A.M., for Samana, a distance of nineteen miles, which I was desirous to make that day. I was, however, no gainer by my early start, for my guide lost his track in the dark, and I was delayed more than half-an-hour before we found our way. The road, moreover, was exceedingly heavy, neither more nor less than a bed of sand, in consequence of which, part of my establishment did not come up till two o'clock P.M. The Thanadar[42] of Samana furnished me, at his own particular request, with four chokedars, or watchmen, for I had only asked for one.

On the 28th, I rode to Goelah, a distance of twelve miles, and forded the Guggur or Cuggur River, about half way on my journey. After passing the towns of Bunnoor, Seyfabad, Pattiala, Jowhana, and Jomalpore, the Guggur enters the country of the Bhatties at the town of Arwah, formerly the capital of the district.[43]

[42] Thanadar, keeper of a public station. The word likewise means commandant of a military post.

[43] Francklin's Life of George Thomas, p. 66.

About sixty miles south of the Sutlej, the Cuggur flows parallel with it, till opposite to Loodianna, where it runs in a straight direction, and is lost in the sands of the desert. It might easily be restored. Mr. Thomas, whilst residing at Bhatneer, could perceive but little vestige of what was called the ancient bed of the river. The natives declared that it formerly extended as far as the Sutlej, which it joined in the vicinity of Ferozepore; now the Sutlej runs south-west of Loodianna.

There is another river which formerly ran from the Jumna to the Sutlej; I understand that the Government intends to open its channel, which would indeed prove an immense benefit.

29th March. Rode to Pehoah, sixteen miles. Travelling alone as I now did, I found the appearance of the country very different to that which it presented when I marched along this same route with the troops. Then all was life and animation—the measured tread of the soldiery—the tramp and neighing of the horses—the heavy step and snort of the elephants and camels—the confused jargon of the immense rabble of camp-followers—the motley sight—the picturesque dresses—the clouds of dust, and, in the midst of all this apparent confusion, the loud, peremptory orders putting all in motion, and keeping all in order, presented an almost inconceivable contrast, to the calm repose of a solitary traveller passing noiselessly along, with his small retinue of twelve or fourteen attendants.

On the 30th, I rode to Khol, fourteen miles, and on the 31st to Suggah, fourteen and a half miles. I have already spoken of these several places, and shall therefore pass them without further mention.

April 1st. Rode to Kurnaul, ten miles. This town is about seventy-eight miles north-west of Delhi. It appears that it was first made a military station in 1806, when a corps of native infantry was quartered here. In 1807, it became the head-quarters of the third or north-west frontier division; Saharunpore and Loodianna being dependent commands. A depôt was also formed here; and in July, 1809, four large platform boats of 700 maunds (25 tons) were established at Khoonda Ghât, for the ferry across the river Jumna. Meerut is seventy miles distant by the road; the Cawnpore road being on the other side of the river. In 1831, H.M. 31st Foot, was sent to Kurnaul, where they encamped till the barracks were built, they being the first European corps stationed there. In 1840, Kurnaul contained a troop of Horse Artillery, a light or horse field-battery, having six guns each, one European regiment of Foot, two regiments of Light Cavalry, and three regiments of Native Infantry, being an establishment of about 5,000 men. It was for many years the head-quarters of the Sirhind division.

A troop of Horse Artillery, on the Bengal system, musters 169 horses, but on detachment the number has been as high as 230. A 6-pounder gun and carriage, with ammunition and stores, loaded and packed ready for service, weighs 23 cwt., not including the wheels, which weigh 238 lbs. each. Each horse carries seven stone of harness, besides the man. The horses are told off as follows, by regulation:

	Horses.	Total Horses.
6 Pieces of Ordnance	14 each.	84
6 Ammunition Carriages	8 each.	48
4 Spare Ammunition Carriages	7 each.	28
Staff of the troop		9
		169

Their actual distribution, however, is about as under; the four spare waggons being drawn by bullocks.

	Horses.
1 Staff-Sergeant.	1
6 Sergeants.	6
2 Trumpeters, 2 Rough-Riders, 2 Farriers, 1 Saddler, and 1 Native Doctor	8
6 Guns, at 13 each.	78
6 Waggons, at 12 each	72
Spare	4
	169

Six horses to a gun, and four to a waggon, was the order laid down some years ago as the draught power; but of late the weight of the carriages has been so much increased as to equal that of the guns. On the line of march, both guns and waggons have latterly been worked with teams of eight horses, which, although not giving the horses daily relief, answers extremely well, as I am assured by my informant, Major E.J. Pratt, 9th Lancers, Assistant-Adjutant-General of the Cavalry in the Sikh campaign of 1848-49. A 6-pounder takes into action, on its own limber and waggon, 128 rounds in horse draught, besides 96 rounds on its spare waggon, in bullock draught; making 224 rounds present in troop-park.

The remaining stations were: Hansi, 84 miles distant from Kurnaul, where, on the 1st of January, 1849, was the Hurrianah Light Infantry; Loodianna, 120 miles from Kurnaul, containing a Company of Foot Artillery, head-quarters and right wing of 34th Regiment of Native Infantry, and the Sirmoor Rifle Battalion. Ferozepore, 70 miles from Loodianna, to the West, where were stationed, a troop of Horse Artillery, and the 32nd Native Infantry; and lastly, Subathoo in the hills, where there was also, in the same year, a Detachment of the Nusseeree Rifle Battalion.

All these stations had just supplied troops for the Punjaub, and were consequently, at the period of which I am writing, very ill-garrisoned. In the month of January 1840, there were above 13,000 men in the Sirhind division.

At Kurnaul there is a canal, called Ali Merdan Khan's canal, running from the Jumna, which is within three miles of Delhi, and, passing close to the right flank of the old cantonments, near the house built by the late Major-General Sir David Ochterlony; this officer likewise erected a house at Loodianna, and another at Neemuch.

The barracks for the European Infantry are at right angles with the old cantonments. A Church was also built here in 1836; a neat little structure, with a singular tower, close to the parade ground. In 1828, this station was considered very unhealthy, in consequence, it was said, of malaria, generated by the grass growing on the banks of the canal, yet from 1829 to 1836, it was as salubrious as Meerut. In proof of this, it may be stated that H.M. 31st Foot, lost fewer men at Kurnaul, than at Meerut, their next quarters. Now Meerut is reckoned one of the healthiest military stations in the Bengal Presidency.

Whether the malaria which appeared at Kurnaul, in the autumn of 1842, was owing to the clearing out of the great canal, which runs through the city, or whether it was merely a passing evil, confined to a particular quarter, is still an open question; so much is certain, that it broke out among the European troops, and was confined to one locality, precisely where their barracks were situated. Kurnaul has now, unfortunately, ceased to be a military station.

The extensive cantonments, as well as numerous elegant bungalows and villas, in the midst of parks and gardens, stretch in a semi-circle of three miles around the town, and present a unique and extremely picturesque *tout ensemble*. The cantonments are traversed in every direction by good roads, shaded by avenues of trees.

At the time of my visit, in April 1846, the barracks were deserted; the roofs, in many instances, had fallen in, the frame-work with the doors and windows had been removed, and the compounds were overgrown with weeds and jungle. The only exceptions are the houses built by Sir David Ochterlony, both of which are the property of Brigadier-General Thomas Palmer, commanding the Cawnpore division of the army. These two houses are in fine preservation; one, called the banqueting-house, is a noble building, situated in the midst of English park-like grounds, with coach-houses, etc., in good taste and perfect keeping. The other, the dwelling-house, is built somewhat after the Eastern style; the garden surrounding it is most delightful, being filled with a luxuriance of the richest shrubs and flowers I ever saw, its gallant owner being one of the best botanists in India.

The town of Kurnaul is dirty and closely built. The houses are chiefly of brick; and, like most of the old Indian towns, it has a dingy look, and is surrounded by a high wall.

During the time of the Earl of Ellenborough's government, the station was so sickly, that his lordship, ever alive to the well-being and comfort of the army, peremptorily ordered it to be abandoned.

Being situated so near to the frontier, only fifty-three miles from Umballa, it was the practice, during the Sikh campaign of 1845-46, for reinforcements, marching up from Meerut, Delhi, and other stations, to assemble at Kurnaul for the purpose of forming depôts, etc., and then to march forward in a body.

Officers were frequently sent up by Dâk, at the expense of government (at a cost, it is said, of about £20,000), to join their corps, from every part of the Bengal presidency, particularly from Calcutta. They were often detained here twelve or fourteen days, waiting for a convoy for protection.

A re-mount depôt was established at Kurnaul, about nine years ago, by Viscount Gough, which imparted some signs of re-animation to this station, which, in my estimation, is one of the most pleasant quarters in India. The head-quarters of the Sirhind division have been removed to Umballa.

On the 3rd of April I struck my tent and rode to Gurounda, a distance of twelve miles, in a dense jungle, through which a road had been cut. After leaving Kurnaul, the distance was marked at every two miles by the celebrated ancient minarets, which were erected by Akbar the Great, from Delhi to Cashmere. These elegant mile-stones, tapering from their circular pediments to a height of twenty feet, are, notwithstanding their age, kept in a tolerable state of preservation by the inhabitants, from a religious feeling. After a ride of six miles, I came to a handsome bridge, which was built over the canal by the emperor Humayoon. It is lofty, and arched; and looks all the more picturesque from a remarkably large cotton-tree which grows close beside it, and seems to have had its origin about the same time as the bridge. Gurounda itself is an insignificant place, presenting nothing of interest, except the ancient caravansary. It is large, and has lofty turreted gates, which are in fair preservation.

On the 4th I rode to Somalka, twenty-two miles, having passed through Paniput, the scene of two of the fiercest encounters which this country ever witnessed. Paniput is about ten miles from Gurounda, and, like the majority of the cities and towns in this part, a mass of ruins. The road again lay through a tract of jungle, and the greater part was ankle deep in sand. I pitched my tent in the area of a large and once elegant serai; but now, alas! in a state of dilapidation. These serais are public buildings, erected for the convenience of Eastern travellers, where they may eat, drink, and repose, and then go on their way with a thankful heart.

Paniput is a spot of too much celebrity to be silently passed over; for both in a military and political point of view, it fills an important place in the annals of India. It is about forty-eight miles from Delhi, the capital of the emperor of Hindoostan. It was formerly surrounded by a brick-wall, and at its greatest extent is little more than four miles in circumference. Paniput is famous as the scene of two great battles, which were attended with most decided effects upon the fate of Hindoostan. The first took place in the year 1525, between the Sultan—more usually called the Emperor Baber—and the Delhi Pathan emperor, Ibrahim Lodi; the latter was slain, and his army totally routed, which put an end to the Pathan dynasty of Lodi, and introduced the Mogul empire of Timoor, of whom Baber was the great grandson.

The life of the Emperor Baber was written by himself, a beautiful translation of which has been made by Mr. Erskine, formerly of Bombay. This illustrious conqueror was king of Cabool, and equally famous as a warrior, poet, and historian. At the battle of Paniput Baber's army consisted of only 12,000 men, including followers; whereas Ibrahim had 100,000. The former, however, had guns, the latter had none; and we must conclude that the artillery greatly contributed to secure the victory for Baber.

I must not omit the mention of Nadir Shah's invasion of India, in 1739, which preceded the second great battle to which I have alluded. Nadir Shah, having plundered Delhi of several millions sterling of property, retired through the Khyber Pass, where he paid a lakh of rupees as a security against plunder. Being assassinated by one of his attendants, Ahmed Shah Abdallah seized a convoy of treasure on its way to Candahar, and, raising the standard of rebellion, proclaimed himself king of Affghanistan.

It appears, that about A.D. 1720, the Affghans conquered Persia, but were expelled by Nadir Shah, who in turn subjugated their dominions; and in 1739, after the capture of Delhi, annexed Affghanistan to the Persian empire. Ahmed Shah Abdallah, in 1748, occupied the Punjaub and invaded India, but being repulsed, renewed his attempt in the year 1751. In the declining state of their empire, the Moguls called in the Maharattas, a sure sign of weakness in a Mahomedan government, when it craves the aid of the Hindoos to assist in settling its disputes.

Ahmed Shah again invaded India, in 1756, when he took Delhi. He invaded India for the fourth time in 1759, which brings us to the second great battle of Paniput; which was fought on the 6th of January, 1761, between the Maharattas and the army of Ahmed Shah. The Maharatta cavalry, commanded by the Bhow, consisted of 55,000 troops, in regular pay, with at least 15,000 predatory Maharatta cavalry,—the Pindarries,—and 15,000 infantry, of whom 9,000 were disciplined Sepoys, under the command of Ibrahim Khan Gardee, a Mussulman deserter from the French service. He had besides 200 guns, numerous wall pieces, or "zumbooruks," fired from the backs of camels, and a great supply of rockets, the rocket being a favourite weapon with the Maharattas. This army of 85,000 men, with its innumerable followers, made the number within his lines amount to 300,000 men.[44]

Ahmed Shah, on the other hand, had about 40,000 Affghans and Persians, 13,000 Indian Horse, and a force of Indian Infantry, estimated at 38,000, of which the division, consisting of Rohilla Affghans,[45] would be very efficient; but the great majority consisted of the usual rabble of Indian foot soldiers. He had also thirty guns, of different calibre, chiefly belonging to his Indian allies, and a number of wall pieces.

Now, if we reckon the Maharatta force at 70,000 regular troops and 200 guns, and the Dooranees[46] at 44,000 regulars and thirty guns, there will appear great

[44] Grant Duff, in his History of the Maharattas, agrees with Casi Rai in making the paid horse and infantry as in the text, and estimates the predatory horse and followers at 200,000. Casi Rai makes the whole number to have been 500,000. *Asiatic Researches,* vol. iii. p. 123.

[45] Roh means a hill; the Rohillas are the Affghans, who settled in Rohilkund on the return of Ahmed Shah to Cabool.

[46] The Dooranees were so called from Ahmed Shah Abdallah, who assumed the name of Dooree Dooraun, "Pearl of the age," when after seizing the sovereignty of Affghanistan,

odds against the Dooranees. The Dooranees estimated the number of the army that crossed the Indus at 63,000 men; but Mr. Elphinstone thinks this force is exaggerated, considering that there were only 40,000 Affghans, and 2,000 horse and 2,000 infantry, furnished by the Indian allies.

The camp followers were in overwhelming numbers.

The Shah pitched his camp eight miles from the enemy, and his small red tent was placed at the head of the army, in order that he might see every movement in the enemy's front. At night he surrounded his camp with an abattis of felled trees. At one time flour sold in the Shah's camp for two rupees, or 4*s.* a seer (2 lbs.), owing to the Maharattas having intercepted the supplies.

The Maharattas, as usual, took the field after the Dusserah,[47] the 17th of October, in 1760; and three actions, of partial success, were fought before the great battle. The two armies daily turned out in battle array; but at length the Hindoostanee allies of Ahmed became impatient and urged him to engage. Then it was that Ahmed Shah gave them the memorable rebuke, "This is a matter of war with which you are unacquainted. Military operations must not be precipitated. At a proper time I will bring the affair to a successful termination."[48] He was resolved to have no councils of war, and used to say to his Hindoostanee allies, "Do you sleep; I will take care that no harm befalls you."

Ahmed Shah was a cautious and vigilant general. Taking with him forty or fifty horsemen, he used, in company with his son, Timoor Shah, to visit daily every part of his army, and reconnoitre the enemy's camp. At night, a body of 500 horse advanced as near as possible to the enemy's position; remaining under arms till daybreak; whilst other bodies went the rounds of the whole encampment. On the day of the great battle, the Dooranees marched from their camp to the attack, when objects were only just visible. The Maharatta army was drawn up facing the east, a great mistake on their part, as they thus had the sun in their eyes; whilst the Dooranees fronted the west.

The Maharattas entered the field with determined courage, each having taken a betel-leaf in the presence of all his comrades, and sworn to fight to the last extremity.

The Shah ordered his trumpets to sound to battle. Breast works of sand had been thrown up, under cover of which the Nawab Vizier's troops advanced; upon which the bildars, or pioneers, proceeded half musket-shot in advance of the cover and threw up another; and in this manner the troops progressed about two miles, until they were within long musket-shot of the enemy. The Rohillas fired volleys of rockets,[49] as many as 2,000 at a time, which not only terrified the horses by their

---

he was crowned king at Candahar, in the year 1747.

[47] A day kept as a holiday by Hindoo Princes, when, if war be intended, the campaign is opened.

[48] *Οὐκ ἀγαθὸν πολυκοιρανίη: εἷς κοίρανος ἔστω,*
Εἷς βασιλεύς.

Homer's Iliad, ii. 204, 205.

[49] The British used rockets on a small scale in 1817, against the Fort of Hattrass; but

dreadful noise, but did so much execution, that the Maharattas could not advance to charge them. The Mussulmans did not make much use of their guns.

The Dooranees were men of great bodily strength, and their horses, which were of the Toorkee breed,[50] were rendered hardy by constant exercise.

Casi Rai Pundit, who was an eye-witness and attached to Ahmed Shah's allies, says: "About noon, the Shah received advice that the Rohillas and the Grand Vizier's division had the worst of the engagement, upon which he sent for the Nesuckchees—a corps of horse, wearing a peculiar dress and arms, and who were always employed in executing the Shah's immediate commands—2,000 being assembled, he sent 500 of them to his own camp to drive out all the armed people and fugitives whom they should find there, that they might take part in the action; the remaining 1,500 he ordered to meet the fugitives from the battle, and to kill every man who should refuse to return to the charge. This command they executed so effectually that, after killing a few, they compelled 7,000 or 8,000 men to return to the field."

Meanwhile the Shah sent for the reserve corps, of these he despatched 4,000 to cover the right flank, and 10,000 to support the Grand Vizier, with orders to charge the enemy sword in hand, in close order, and at full gallop; at the same time he gave directions to Shah Pussund Khan and Nujeeb-ud-Dowlah that as often as the Grand Vizier should charge the enemy, those two chiefs should at the same time attack him in flank. The advantage still inclined to the side of the Maharattas, when Ahmed, after successfully rallying the fugitives, gave orders for an advance of his own line, at the same time ordering the division on his left, to take the enemy in flank. The manœuvre was decisive, and a terrible conflict ensued, especially in the centre, commanded by the Bhow and Biswas Row. The latter was wounded and unhorsed, which being reported to the Bhow he ordered him to be taken up, and placed upon his elephant,[51] when the Bhow himself continued the action at the head of his men. They fought fiercely on both sides with spears, swords, battle-axes, and even daggers; when Biswas Row expired from his wounds. Suddenly, as if by enchantment, the whole Maharatta army turned and fled at full speed, leaving the battle-field covered with heaps of the dead and dying.

The victors pursued the flying Maharattas with the utmost fury; and, as they gave no quarter, the slaughter was terrific, the pursuit being continued in every direction for fifteen or twenty miles. According to Grant Duff, the whole number of the slain is said to have amounted to 200,000 men, which must have included the losses in both armies, as well as the followers; for the highest numbers given were 176,000 fighting men, which we find reduced to 114,000, including both sides. Never was a defeat more complete. Grief, despondency, and despair spread over the whole Maharatta people. The wreck of the army retired beyond the river

---

they have never tried them against troops.

[50] See Appendix XIX.

[51] Chiefs often ride on war elephants to be better seen by their troops. An Indian queen has thus led her van in the battle field. Should the elephant be struck down, or the chief fall wounded from his elephant, the fortune of the day is generally decided.

Nerbudda, evacuating all their acquisitions in Hindoostan.[52]

The battle lasted about nine hours. Besides the loss in slain and wounded, 40,000 were taken prisoners, and the plunder was enormous. In front of the door of each tent, except that of the Shah and those of his principal officers, an immense pile of heads was placed as a trophy.

Ibrahim Khan Gardee, the Mussulman General of the Maharattas, having, on one occasion during the action, ordered his men and musketry to cease firing, advanced with seven battalions of disciplined Sepoys, to attack Doondy Khan and Hafiz Rahmut Khan's divisions with fixed bayonets. The Rohillas received the charge with great resolution, and fought hand to hand. About 8,000 Rohillas were killed or wounded; and the attack told so severely upon them that a few only remained with their chiefs. Their force originally consisted of 15,000 foot and 4,000 horse. In this action, however, six of the seven battalions of Ibrahim Khan were entirely cut to pieces. This gallant general was covered with wounds, and being taken prisoner, afterwards fell a sacrifice to Ahmed Shah's vengeance, for fighting against his own faith.

Nearly all the great chiefs were either killed or wounded. Malhar Rao Holcar, who was accused of too early a retreat, was wounded. Sindiah, afterwards the founder of a great state, was lamed for life; and Nana Furnavese, who long averted the downfall of the Peishwah's government, narrowly escaped by flight.

The confederacy of the Mahomedan powers dissolved on the cessation of these common dangers. Ahmed Shah returned to Cabool without attempting to profit by his victory; nor did he ever afterwards take any share in the affairs of India. This victory, however, put an end to the Mogul empire.

"Most of the Maharatta conquests," says Mr. Elphinstone, "were recovered at a subsequent period; but it was by independent chiefs, with the aid of European officers and disciplined Sepoys."

The Mogul empire, which had now received its death-blow, had been in a tottering state for more than half a century; for its decline commenced with the death of Aurungzebe, in 1707. Having been viceroy in the Deccan, which he left to proceed to Agra, for the purpose of dethroning his father, Shah Jehan, he assumed the royal authority in 1661, with the arrogant title of "Alumgeer," or "Conqueror of the World." From the death of this crafty and cruel man, in 1707, till 1760, no less than six emperors of Delhi had been dethroned, assassinated, or poisoned, besides two children, who reigned only a few months. This proves the state of the Delhi empire at that period; and it was this internal weakness which allured Nadir Shah, in 1739, to advance to the capital and plunder Delhi. Elphinstone[53] says, "The divided government would have fallen an easy prey to the Maharattas, had not circumstances procured it a respite from the encroachments of these invaders."

The Maharattas, whose early history is involved in much obscurity, were a warlike race, inhabiting the mountain provinces as far as Guzerat and the Nerbud-

[52] Hindoostan commences north of the Nerbudda; south of that river the country is called the "South of India," and "The Deccan."—See *Malcolm's Malwa*. vol. i. pp. 120, 121.

[53] Vol. ii. p. 598.

da, a large tract of country on the west coast, between Surat and Canara. In 1720, they were invited by the governor of the Deccan, who aimed at the establishment of an independent monarchy in India, to ravage the territories of the Mogul, and attack the city of Delhi. This predatory race gladly undertook a task which offered such a prospect of booty. They committed great ravages throughout the country, and finally attacked the city of Delhi. Although they sustained a defeat, they so far succeeded in spreading the terror of their name, that the generals of the Mogul army, concluded a dishonourable treaty with them. The Governor of the Deccan, disappointed in his expectations, readily found cause for a quarrel with the Court of Delhi, and induced the disaffected nobles, who were disgusted at the treaty concluded with the Maharattas, to call in the aid of Nadir Shah, the usurper of the throne of Persia.

Nadir Shah, one of the most distinguished, but at the same time most atrocious, men recorded in history, was born in 1687. While General of the Persian forces, he quitted the military service, and became leader of a formidable band of robbers. His military talents, however, were so distinguished, that the king of Persia, not only pardoned this audacious step, but took him again into his service, and gradually raised him to the office of Commander-in-Chief of the Persian forces, with the title of Khan, being the highest dignity he could bestow.

By his intrigues, Nadir Shah soon succeeded in gaining the whole army, and when the Shah of Persia concluded a peace with the Turks without his advice, Nadir basely dethroned his sovereign, seized the regency in the name of the infant prince, who was still in his cradle, and, after a sanguinary victory over the Turks, he was, on the death of his Ward, chosen king of Persia, in 1735. From that day he adopted the name of Nadir Shah. His arms were everywhere victorious; but he shed torrents of blood, and inflicted even upon his own subjects, the most unheard-of cruelties. His soldiers, whom he had enriched with the splendid spoils of many a victory, were so devoted to him, that none of his disaffected subjects, durst place himself at their head. Even the priests, who were incensed at his oppression and cruelty to their own body, and at his attempt to establish the Soonie creed instead of the Shiah form of Mahomedanism, which was the national religion, were utterly powerless, and every conspiracy that was formed to hurl the usurper from the throne, was crushed in its birth. His greatest, but at the same time his most cruel, campaign, was that against the Great Mogul, in 1739, of which we have already spoken.

Being invited by the Grand Vizier, and by those nobles who were indignant at the ignominious treaty concluded by their sovereign with the Maharattas, whom he had induced by a large bribe to retire from the capital, and the promise of an annual tribute in money and treasure, on condition of their not renewing their assault, or plundering the territories of the Great Mogul, Nadir Shah, who was bent upon revenge for the protection afforded to some of his Affghan enemies, lost no time in obeying the summons. He placed himself at the head of his army, and crossed the Indus before Mahomed Shah, the emperor of Delhi, had even heard of his impending approach. Mahomed immediately collected his army, and fortified his camp, near Paniput, but hearing of Nadir's approach, he went out to meet him, and offered him battle in open field. It was a bloody contest. Both sides fought with desperate valour, but Mahomed Shah was beaten; 20,000 of his valiant men were wounded or slain, and Mahomed, to stop the sanguinary strife, went with his chief men, and offered himself and his treasures to appease the conqueror.

Nadir received his fallen foe, with more compassion than might have been expected. He promised to reinstate him in his dominions, on condition that he should give up his treasures and jewels, and that his nobles and people should pay an enormous sum, as some indemnity for the expenses incurred in this inglorious war. The dejected sovereign, glad to be reinstated in his kingly power, had neither the heart nor the means to resist the dictates of the conqueror, and returned with him to his capital. Little did he anticipate the horrible scenes about to be enacted there, in levying the cruel exactions of Nadir, whereby he lost thousands of his subjects, and his already shattered power received a blow which prevented it from ever rallying again. Victor by the power of arms, and by the treachery of Mahomed's nobles, Nadir Shah, sacked and devastated the conquered empire, fired and destroyed the city of Delhi, and slew 200,000 inhabitants. This fearful slaughter was occasioned by a false report of the death of Nadir, which caused the inhabitants to rise *en masse*, and fall upon the soldiery. Nadir immediately gave orders for a general massacre, which were instantly obeyed. The carnage commenced at sunrise, and lasted till noon, when it was at length put a stop to at the earnest entreaty of the Emperor of Delhi. Nadir Shah carried off the imperial treasures which had been accumulated by the Mogul rulers for upwards of two centuries.

Thus the arrival of Nadir Shah, preserved for a short time longer the existence of the Mogul Empire, by the restoration of Mahomed Shah to the imperial dignity; otherwise it must have succumbed to the Maharattas. When Ahmed Shah first invaded India in 1748, the Vizier of the Emperor of Delhi had recourse, as I have already remarked, to the humiliating expedient of calling in the Maharattas. The state of the Mogul Empire in 1756, was much the same as that of Calcutta when it was attacked by Suraj-ud-Dowlah, the Subahdar of Bengal, in June of the same year. No mandate of the Emperor was obeyed: the Nawab of Oude, the actual Vizier of the Empire, had raised the standard of independence: the power of the Maharattas was at its zenith, and that of the Mogul Empire at its lowest ebb.

Now the proper country of the Maharattas is the south of India. When Aurungzebe left the Deccan about 1658, he appointed a deputy, who, however, was unable to control the Maharattas. Even Aurungzebe himself when he went in pursuit of Sevajee, the founder of the Maharatta Empire, was often baffled by the wily chief who would suddenly retire into his hills and mountain fastnesses.

On the decline of the Delhi power at the death of Aurungzebe, the Maharattas began to extend their operations to the north of the Nerbudda; they gradually threatened all parts of Hindoostan, and even visited Calcutta. At that time, what is called the Maharatta ditch was thrown up to protect the city against these invaders, an ingenious device of the Calcutta factory, and well enough for a body of merchants. The origin of the term "ditchers," as applied to them, is derived from this Maharatta ditch; though it would be as difficult to determine its locality, except on paper, as that of the Black Hole.

The number of elephants and camels with the two armies, is not stated. Elphinstone says, "that the force ascribed to the Indian kings is probably exaggerated. Porus, one of the princes who occupied the Punjaub, is said to have had 200 elephants, 300 chariots, 4,000 horse, and 30,000 efficient infantry, which, as observed by Sir Alexander Burnes, is, substituting guns for chariots—exactly the establishment of Runjeet Singh, who is master of the whole Punjaub, and several other territories." Burnes must have referred to the year 1831, when he was in the Punjaub; in 1848 Runjeet Singh's force was supposed to be 50,000 men, besides irregulars for garrisons. Neither Polybius nor Arrian's history of Alexander's expedition, mentions the number of elephants or cattle with any of the armies. Humboldt in his "Cosmos"[54] writes: "According to the testimony of Polybius, when African and Indian elephants were opposed to each other in fields of battle, the sight, smell, and cries of the larger and stronger Indian elephants drove the African ones to flight. The latter were probably never employed as war elephants in such large numbers as in Asiatic expeditions, when Chundragupta had assembled 9,000, the powerful King of the Prasii 6,000, and Akbar an equally large number. These armies must have been much larger than those engaged at the battle of Paniput in 1761."

We read that the elephants were placed in the front of the army, and that they often turned back and killed more friends than foes. Now 9,000 elephants in a single line, allowing each to take up 12 feet would reach 20 miles, and 6,000 elephants would extend 13 miles and 1,120 yards. It is said there were 50,000 camels with the army of the Indus[55] in 1838 and 1839.

It may be interesting to the reader, to see the following statement of the native armies in the time of Akbar, in 1582, as given in the Ayeen Akbaree, by Abul Fazel, Prime Minister:—

Province of	Cavalry.	Infantry.	Elephants.	Boats.
Agra	50,600	477,570	221	—
Allahabad	11,375	237,870	323	—
Bahar	11,415	149,350	—	100
Delhi	18,275	125,400	—	—
Oude	1,340	31,900	—	23
Ajmere	8,000	38,000	—	—
Bengal	1,100	142,920	1,100	—
Total	102,105	1,203,010	1,644	123

Thus we find that the cavalry and infantry in the seven Soobahs of Agra, Ajmere, Allahabad, Bahar, Bengal, Delhi, and Oude amounted to 1,305,115; and if to these we add two others, viz., Lahore and Mooltan, the number of men will be

[54] Vol. ii. p. 540, note.

[55] The return of those lost was 30,000: one commanding officer said 50,000. Lieutenant-Colonel Burlton discredits the amount, but one of his own departmental officers gave in that number. The Government bought fresh camels in the room of those which died or were lost.

increased to 1,965,116, or of cavalry alone, to 170,370, for

Province of	Cavalry.	Infantry.
Lahore	54,480	426,086
Mooltan	13,785	165,650
Total	68,265	591,736

Making about 2,000,000 of fighting men from Lahore to Bengal: and if we estimate the population at that time (1582) at 35,000,000, there would have been one soldier out of every seventeen inhabitants.[56]

At present the population of the

North Western Provinces is	23,199,668
Punjaub	1,75,0000
Bahar and Bengal	24,000,000
Total	48,949,668

According to Diodorus, Alexander heard that he was to be opposed on the banks of the Ganges by 20,000 cavalry, 200,000 infantry, 2,000 chariots and 4,000 elephants. Megasthenes mentions Alexander's visit to Sandrocottus, monarch of the Prasii, when encamped with an army of 400,000 men. When Aurungzebe died, in 1707, two of his sons took the field with 300,000 men each, which appear to have been the largest armies assembled within the last 150 years in India.

Sultan Baber, as I have before observed, in 1525, with 12,000 men and guns, defeated Ibrahim Lodi, the emperor of Delhi, who had 100,000 men and no guns. In the battle of Paniput, in 1761, when the Maharattas strove for the ascendancy over the Mahomedans, there were not above 150,000 men on either side. The infantry in Akbar's time were very indifferent soldiers. Elphinstone says:[57] "that it is mentioned in the Akbarnama that the chiefs of Scinde employed Portuguese soldiers in this war; and had also 200 natives dressed as Europeans." These were, therefore, the first Sepoys in India. The same learned author states,[58] under the year 1692, only about fifteen years prior to the death of Aurungzebe, that: "In spite of all Aurungzebe's boasted vigilance, the grossest abuses had crept into the military department. Many officers only kept up half the number of their men, and others filled their ranks with their menials and slaves."

Whatever credit, therefore, may be due to the statement of the number of troops in each Province in 1582, it is evident that in the year 1692, we should, by the like reasoning, have to reduce the royal standing army from 2,000,000 to 1,000,000 men. The cavalry was the most efficient force. The infantry, though ten times more numerous, yet we may reckon that not one-fourth were of much use in action. The cavalry in Akbar's time amounted to 170,000 men, and the infantry to

[56] The population of Great Britain and Ireland during the late war, was about 18,000,000; out of which number 1,000,000 were employed in the army, navy, marines, militia, volunteers and yeomanry.

[57] Vol. ii. p. 261.

[58] Vol. ii. p. 494.

about 1,800,000: but if 500,000 could take the field, it was probably the maximum; wherefore, if we were even to allow 700,000 men for all Hindoostan, from Cabool (for it had been made a Province) to Cape Comorin, the force would not greatly exceed many of the Continental armies. The East India Company's armies at one period numbered 302,797 men, including the royal regiments.[59]

Folard, and many other judicious writers observe, that in proportion as infantry is bad, and the military art declines, the number of horse increases in our modern armies; because, say they, "An able general at the head of a good infantry, can do anything, and wants but a small cavalry." It is certain that when the infantry is good, much may be done with it; and if it is bad you must increase your cavalry to keep the enemy at a distance, as you must have a great quantity of heavy artillery for the same purpose.

I must now take leave of Paniput with the remark, that formerly a treasury was established there, Kurnaul furnishing the necessary guards.

About this time there was a considerable change in the weather. The days for the most part were hot and oppressive, and towards noon even sultry. On the 5th of April I rode to Sunput, about seventeen miles. On the 6th I started, at half past two in the morning, in the midst of a complete hurricane, and proceeded to Barah Duree, a Chokey, or Police Station, near Alepore. The road was excessively sandy and fatiguing, the distance being sixteen miles and a half. On the 7th I rode to Delhi, eleven miles and a half, and encamped outside the walls of this famous royal city of the Moguls, close to the Cashmere gate.

I had now travelled 313 miles and a half, since I quitted Lahore, a distance which I accomplished in twenty-two marches.

---

[59] Captain Walter Badernach, p. 4, table 1, 1826.

CHAPTER X.

Delhi—Mahmood of Ghuznee—Shah Jehan—Gates of Delhi—Mosques—The Palace—Hall of Audience—Chapel of Aurungzebe—The Gardens—The Jumma Musjeed—Khoonee Durwaza—Protestant Church—The Observatory—Tomb of Zufder Jung—The Cootub Minar—Allah-ud-Deen—Gheias-ud-Deen—Mahomed Togluk—Humayoon—Nizam-ud-Deen—The Cantonments—Mahomedan College—Delhi—Produce of Delhi—Shah Allum II.—Lord Lake—Monsieur Louis Bourgion—Sir David Ochterlony—Holcar—Lieutenant-Colonel W. Burn—Mr. E. Thornton—Allahabad—Marquis Wellesley—Defence of Delhi—Mahomedan Population—Colonel Ochterlony's good Generalship.

Delhi, or Dilli, in Sanscrit Indraprastha, an ancient Hindoo city, founded by Delu, was, according to tradition, built more than 300 years before the Christian era. The Rajahs of Dilli, or Indraput, are mentioned by the Mahomedan historians as early as A.D. 1008. In 1011 the city was taken and plundered by Sultan Mahmood, of Ghuznee, but afterwards it was restored to the Rajah as a tributary.[60] It is reported to have covered a space of twenty miles, and the ruins now are very extensive. It is scarcely possible to conceive anything more striking and picturesque than the first appearance of Delhi, situated on its rocky mountain chain, with its mosques, monuments, palaces, and tombs rising in perfect beauty amid the widely scattered ruins of bye-gone days and former greatness, environed with verdant gardens, corn-fields, palms and cypresses; while the silvery Jumna flowing in the luxuriant valley imparts a bright relief to the whole scene. To see the magic grandeur of the *tout ensemble* the traveller should ascend the lofty Cootub Minar which is about seven miles from the city. The effect produced on the mind by this grand panorama is quite indescribable.

In the year 1631, the Emperor Shah Jehan founded the city of New Delhi, on the west bank of the Jumna, and named it Shahjehanabad, but it did not long retain his name. It is about seven miles in circumference, and is surrounded on three sides by a wall of brick and stone, in most beautiful preservation, with, as far as I could judge, not a stone displaced. The wall is furnished with embrasures, and has been more strongly fortified by the English, who surrounded it with a moat. It has seven gates built of freestone, each indicating by its name the direction in which it lies; thus the Lahore gate points to the city of Lahore; the Ajmere gate to

[60] Ferishta, Rennel, Francklin, etc.

the city of Ajmere. The other five gates are named Agra, Turkoman, Delhi, Mohur, and Cashmere.

The modern city is built on two rocky eminences. It is divided into two parts, the old and the new; the streets are inferior and narrow, except two, the one leading from the palace to the Delhi gate, which is thirty yards broad, and 1,900 yards long, with an aqueduct along the middle of its whole extent, supplied with water from Ali Merdan Khan's canal, and the other leading from the Lahore gate which is still wider and handsomer, being forty yards in width and a mile in length.

Ali Merdan Khan, the Prime Minister, brought the above-named canal from the Jumna, where that river approaches Kurnaul, to Delhi, a distance of more than 100 miles; but it became choked up after the Persian and Affghan invasions; in consequence of which, in 1810, the English undertook to clear and repair it. It was not finished till 1820, and is said to have cost £35,000. It furnishes the inhabitants of Delhi with a supply of fresh water, the water of the Jumna being much impregnated with salt below Kurnaul. And here I would mention, by the way, that it is owing to this circumstance that the overflowing of the Jumna does not improve the soil like the inundation of the Ganges and other Hindoostanee rivers, the deposits of which are of a very fertilizing nature. The restoration of this canal proved an immense benefit, the country around having become scarcely habitable from the deleterious effects of the water.

Delhi contains about forty mosques, and many splendid palaces and residences of rich natives, surrounded with gardens, baths, and other out-buildings. The palace of the Great Mogul, commenced by the Emperor Shah Jehan in 1640, and finished in 1648, has two noble entrances, flanked by massive towers, over the principal of which is the residence of the officer commanding the palace guards, from whom it is necessary to obtain leave for visiting the palace. The palace is all that now remains to the king, of the glory and splendour of his ancestors. It lies on the west bank of the Jumna on some low cliffs; it forms an irregular quadrangle, enclosed by a wall of red sand-stone, between thirty and forty feet high, and about a mile in circumference, with forty-five small bulwarks and towers. Immediately below the wall is a deep moat. A pretty garden extends from the eastern side of the wall to the Jumna.

Passing through the massive portals which I have already named, a long, dimly lighted vaulted passage and gateway, brought me into the first court, which is 300 paces square, enclosed by walls, and traversed by a canal. A large gate led me into another square, containing the hall of audience, which is an open quadrangular terrace of white marble, the façade of the hall being formed by a double row of twenty marble columns, and the sides by eight, in the Arabic-Byzantine style. Here stands the throne, which is also of white marble, ornamented, and, like the hall, adorned with arabesques, Florentine Mosaic, and sculptures in relievo. Here the Great Mogul used to give audiences to the ambassadors and nobles of the empire, who, on these state occasions, always rode on elephants. The docile animals marched in a particular order, and were drawn up in array behind the barrier, which was sufficiently capacious to admit 200 elephants.

Through another white marble court I entered the Khas, or chief hall of audience, which is also of white marble, and the vaulted ceiling supported by thirty-two white marble columns in double file. Here stood the celebrated peacock throne. The throne itself was of gold, covered with diamonds and precious stones, supported on either side by a peacock, whose brilliant outspread tail glittered with jewels, while above the throne was a parrot the size of life, cut out of a single emerald, with wonderful skill. The value of the throne was estimated at between six and seven millions sterling. We all know that Timoor carried off the precious rubies, and that Nadir finished the work of demolition by removing all the other jewels. It is now a simple seat standing on a platform ornamented with gold, and a few worthless jewels, while the canopy which hangs over it bears the following inscription in Arabic: "If a paradise ever existed on earth, it is here, it is here." Alas! for the man who seeks his paradise here below!

Close by this hall is the chapel of Aurungzebe: it is of white marble, very small, but of the most exquisite workmanship. Altogether this pile of building presents a combination of splendour and elegance, with its gardens and fountains, mosques and columns, halls, balconies, corridors and minarets, which awaken feelings of melancholy as we recall to mind its former grandeur, of which the glory is now departed. The gardens are said to have cost Shah Jehan a million sterling; it would have been far too expensive to keep them up in their former style, and they are now rather like a neat park in England than an appendage to an Indian palace.

The Jumma Musjeed is a noble pile, built by the Emperor Shah Jehan, and finished in 1656 at a cost of £100,000; it is raised upon an equilateral foundation, composed of blocks of red sand-stone, about 30 feet above the level of the ground. It is said that the Emperor employed several thousand men for six successive years in its construction. It is, as the word Jumma or "gathering" denotes, the place of worship where all the Mahomedans are expected to meet on Fridays. This building is one of the finest and most perfect specimens of the Arabic-Byzantine style, and is constructed of white marble and red sand-stone, inlaid with arabesques. The massive portico, with an elegant minaret on either side, leads into the marble hall under the principal cupola. In the centre of this hall is a limpid fountain for the ablutions of the worshippers; and the whole is lighted by ever-burning lamps.

Quitting this mosque by the northern gate, I proceeded down the Dureeba Street, in the neighbourhood of which are the principal bankers and jewellers, and issued by the Khoonee Durwaza, or Bloody Gate, so named from the scene that took place during the massacre of 200,000 of the inhabitants by the tyrant Nadir Shah, into the Chandee Chowk, a place where an officer is stationed to receive tolls and customs. Leaving on my left a small mosque called the Roushen-ud-Dowlah, built in 1721, and ornamented with gilt cupolas—where the despot sat unconcerned, while the inhabitants were being slaughtered around him—I traversed the whole length of the street, went out of the Lahore Gate, round the outer wall of the City, and returned to the Cashmere Gate.

Close to this gate, and just inside it, is the Protestant Church, called the Church of St. James. It was built by the late Colonel James Skinner,[61] in 1837, at an expense

[61] Son of the late Colonel Hercules Skinner of the Bengal Infantry. Colonel James

of £12,000. It is a miniature resemblance of St. Paul's Cathedral, and is certainly a very elegant little place of Divine worship.

I also visited the Observatory, which was built in 1730 by Rajah Jey Singh, of Ambheer, a favourite minister of Mahomed Shah, and a great lover of astronomy. The troublous political events of this period, prevented the completion of this noble work. It is now dilapidated, and is surrounded by buildings, which have shared a similar fate, some more, some less in ruin. I saw, however, enough of the general design, and of the genius of its founder. The sun-dials and quadrants are on an immense scale, and rest upon huge red sand-stone arches.

The fine tomb of Zufder Jung, which was built in 1754 at a cost of £30,000, stands in the midst of an extensive garden. The King of Lucknow caused a suite of apartments in one of the large summer-houses of this garden, to be fitted up at a considerable cost for the convenience of travellers. The Mausoleum, is like many of the Delhi edifices, of white marble and red sand-stone, in alternate perpendicular stripes. The cornices of the building are ornamented with small towers and graceful minarets.

April 8th.—Being anxious to obtain a good panoramic view of the city, I hired a horse and buggy, and went to the celebrated Cootub Minar, which, as I said before, is situated about seven miles from the gates of Delhi. This wonderful and gigantic monument stands in the midst of ancient buildings and temples. Some, dating from the times of the Hindoo dynasty, and dedicated to the service of Buddha, indicate the great prosperity of that era, and the perfection which the arts had attained. The richly sculptured friezes, delineating events descriptive of their history and religion—combats—processions—and ceremonies—are alike interesting and instructive.

The Cootub Minar is so called from Cuttub-ud-deen, "The Pole-Star of religion," the favourite of the emperor Mahomed Gauree. He was originally a slave, and was purchased by that monarch, in whose favour he gradually rose from one office to another, till, on the death of the sovereign, he ascended the throne with the title of Shums-ud-deen Altumsh. He was the first Pathan, or Affghan sovereign. He erected this noble minaret to commemorate his successes over the infidels. It was commenced in 1214 and finished in 1228. It was repaired by Sultan Feroze the Second in 1368, again by Sultan Secunder Ben Lodi in 1503; and, lastly, by the British Government, after the dome had been shattered by an earthquake, in 1803. It is not certain whether the original structure consisted of five stories, as at present, or of only three; for the style of the two upper, does not by any means correspond with the lower portions. It is the loftiest column in the world, being 250 feet (some say 265 feet) in height, with a diameter, at the base, of about 40 feet. A spiral staircase, of 381 steps, leads to the summit of the Cootub Minar, from which I enjoyed a glorious prospect. The late Brigadier Smith, of the Engineers, in repairing the Cootub, restored it, as far as his ingenuity went, to its original appearance. There are various inscriptions, in Persian, on this building. One of these says:—"The prophet, on whom be the mercy and peace of God, has declared, 'he who erects a temple to the true God, on earth, shall receive six such dwellings in

Skinner, for many years commanded the 1st Local Horse, then called Skinner's Horse.

Paradise.'"

Close to the Minar are the remains of an old mosque, to which it is supposed to have belonged, the decorations of which are admirably executed. But the most beautiful and interesting object, after the Minar, is the square domed building on the south-east, erected as a gateway; the lofty Saracenic arch of which, coupled with the graceful and beautiful style of ornament, surpasses anything in the neighbourhood. It was built in 1243, by Sultan Allah-ud-Deen, whose now ruinous tomb is close at hand.

The poor emperor, who is now a pensioner upon the British Government, passes some months every year in this vicinity, where he can ruminate in silence on his fallen greatness.

Having spent a considerable time among these noble erections, which immortalize their founders and the era that produced them, I returned to my buggy, and drove a distance of eight miles, to the ancient and long deserted city of Togluk-abad, built by Gheias-ud-Deen Togluk in 1321; it is remarkable for the rude and massive grandeur of its fortifications.

In the midst of a small level plain close by, stand the tombs of Gheias-ud-Deen and his son Mahomed Togluk. Near the river is a decayed building, two stories high, deeply imbedded in the terraced roof of which stands the famous pillar, Lath or Monolith, formed of a single stone, which, according to the inscription upon it, as deciphered by the late gifted Mr. James Prinsep, was one of eight similar monuments erected at Allahabad, Hissar, and other places, somewhere about the year B.C. 250, by a sovereign of all India, named Asoka, and was removed from its original site, in the vicinity of Sadowra, by Shah Feroze, to adorn his new residence.

Two miles further is the fort of Deenpunna, built by the emperor Humayoon, in 1531, which contains a highly-ornamented mosque of a peculiar style, built at the same time as the fort. A couple of miles beyond this, is the mausoleum of the emperor Humayoon, son of Baber, whose tomb is at Cabool. This magnificent pile was erected between the years 1565 and 1571, at an expense of £150,000, by his son the famous emperor Akbar. Besides the central dome it contains a number of small chambers, in which are the tombs of members of the royal family, amongst which are those of the Bunoo Begum, mother of the emperor Akbar, and the emperor Alumgeer the Second, who was assassinated in 1756. There is a fine view from the top. Near this Mausoleum is a tomb with a marble screen, to the memory of the poet and historian Ameer Khosroo, who died in 1325. A walled tank, some fifty feet in depth, was dug here by the saint, Nizam-ud-Deen. This is now a place of great public resort for the beggars and idlers of the neighbourhood, who exhibit various feats of diving headforemost, for any coin which the traveller may throw to the bottom for the benefit of the diver.

All these interesting buildings have been so often described, as to render any further account of them unnecessary; but they will long live in my recollection as peculiarly striking and splendid. In them we may read a sad but useful lesson, on the utter nothingness of this world, and learn that the most magnificent creations of puny mortals, are in a world's existence to be compared only to a passing shadow.

Their present imperial master is now a mere pensioner upon the bounty of the British government,[62] and his sway is bounded by the walls of his own palace. The semblance of royalty is all that remains to him. I was told by the sentries at the Cashmere Gate, that as a mark of respect, I must close my umbrella in passing through; no camels or carts are allowed to enter by that particular gate.

At a short distance from the Cashmere Gate, lie the cantonments. Two Native Infantry corps, and a Horse Field-battery are now stationed here. There is also a large magazine for military stores. Close to the cantonments is a bridge of boats across the Jumna, which is in constant use.

Some years ago, there was a Madrissa or Mahomedan college in Delhi; but it is now in disuse, and instead of it there is a college for the instruction of natives in the English language. Mohun Lall, of Cabool celebrity, was educated here.

Delhi is a place of great antiquity and importance, having been the capital of one of the greatest of the Hindoo sovereigns, long before the invasion of India by the followers of the Prophet. In 1011, as I before remarked, it was taken by the Mahomedans, and became the seat of the Affghan monarchs. In 1525, the Mogul dynasty was founded by Baber, when he slew the last of the Affghan kings in battle; and as the deliverer of his people ascended the vacant throne. Under the Mahomedan sway, it became one of the most magnificent cities of Asia; and in the time of the illustrious Aurungzebe, it contained a population of upwards of two millions of inhabitants. According to Shakespear's Statistics for 1848-49, Delhi contained 137,977 inhabitants at that time. It continued under the Mahomedan power till the establishment of the English in India. Since it has been under the British government, it has recovered somewhat of its ancient importance, being one of the principal channels of the Oriental trade with Britain and the Western world.

Delhi is famous for its jewels, shawls, scarfs, medallions, and painted drawings of noted kings, queens, and buildings. I would here venture to offer a word of caution to the traveller, to beware of being duped, for, in the purchase of these articles, there is a vast difference both in the price and value of the materials; and he will often find that what may be considered very good and cheap here, could have been procured in London at a more moderate cost, and of better workmanship.

Ever since the disastrous invasion of Nadir Shah, the emperors of Delhi had been either dethroned or assassinated; in 1761, Shah Allum II. ascended the throne; he attacked the British possessions, but was defeated; and having surrendered himself, remained under their protection till 1771, when he repaired to Delhi under a Maharatta escort. He ascended the throne, and became a puppet sovereign, the Maharattas paying him insulting homage. He remained a prisoner in the hands of the French officers who commanded the Maharatta army till 1804, when Lord Lake defeated the Maharattas, and entered the capital on the 12th of September.[63]

M. Louis Bourgion, who commanded Sindiah's troops, had crossed the Jumna on the night of the 10th of September, with sixteen battalions of regular infantry,

[62] The East India Company allow him an annual pension of £120,000.

[63] Thorn's History of the Maharatta War, p. 110.

13,000 in number, and 6,000 cavalry, making a total of 19,000 men, and 70 guns. The British had about 7,000 men, and 22 field-pieces. Victory, however, soon declared on the side of the British. General Lake restored Shah Allum to his throne; but his power was merely nominal. He had been deprived of his eye-sight by the Rohilla chief, in 1788. It is not usual among the Mahomedans for a blind sovereign to succeed to the throne; but Shah Allum had previously been emperor for forty-two years. His death occurred in December 1806. The present emperor is his grandson.

The late Major-General Sir David Ochterlony was the Resident at Delhi, at the time when it was found necessary to undertake military operations for its protection against the Maharatta chief, Holcar. He had refused to join the confederation of Sindiah, and the Berar Rajah, and now came forward, single-handed, to fight the English, who had destroyed the armies of two chiefs more powerful than himself. Colonel Ochterlony began to put the defences of the city in order, and planted guns on the ramparts. Holcar, escaping the vigilance of General Lake, appeared before the city of Delhi about the 2nd of October, 1804.

At this time there was only one corps of Native Infantry, the rest being irregulars, not above 2,500 men altogether, at Delhi. Lieut.-Colonel W. Burn, 2nd Battalion 14th Native Infantry,—now 29th Bengal Native Infantry,—commanded the troops; and, when Holcar's army appeared, Lieut.-Colonel Ochterlony made over the command of the city to him. Holcar having erected batteries, the troops made sallies and destroyed them; upon which he constructed others, but more distant. At length the enemy, having made some gaps in the walls, determined to storm the place; for which purpose they brought several ladders. But the British having thrown them down, they did not attempt another assault, but kept up an incessant fire from their guns. General Lake, who had heard of the state of affairs at Delhi, marched towards that city; whereupon Holcar began to retreat on the night of the 8th of October.

Mr. E. Thornton, in his History of British India, intimates, that the Resident did not consider that it was possible to defend the city, but that Colonel Burn took a different and bolder view of the means of defence. A certain Lieut.-General, still living, was then a subaltern in the 14th Native Infantry, and present at the siege; from him, and others, we know that Sir David Ochterlony did plan the defence, and that Colonel Burn thanked him for his ability and advice. Mr. Thornton might have seen Lieut.-Colonel Ochterlony's report to General Lake, stating what he had done for the defence of the imperial city, as well as Colonel Burn's letter of thanks and report of the siege. It is singular, too, that Mr. Thornton was not aware that the *Resident* was afterwards the celebrated Sir David Ochterlony, G.C.B., the pride of the Bengal army; distinguished no less for his gallantry, than for his political conduct; for he was, when he died, in August 1825, the Governor-General's Agent for the North-west Provinces, an office which has been changed into the designation of Lieut.-Governor of the North-western Provinces.[64]

---

[64] As Lieutenant, he accompanied the Bengal force under the late Colonel Pearse, which marched to Madras in 1781, and was present in the battles with Hyder Ali Khan. At the siege of Cuddalore, in 1783, Sir David was wounded; as was also the late King of Swe-

In 1806, Lieutenant-Colonel Ochterlony was removed from the post of Resident at Delhi to the command of the fortress of Allahabad, in consequence of an order from the Court of Directors, that no military officer should be the Resident at any Native Court. He was, however, granted the allowances of Adjutant-General of the army, as he had, by being Resident, lost his promotion to the head of that department. The Marquis Wellesley had appointed chiefly military men as Residents, which, in a country like India, seems to have been the best arrangement; for a divided authority in an unsettled country has generally proved injurious.

I have thought it right to make the above digression, because Mr. Thornton's omission might lead some to suppose that Colonel Ochterlony had entertained erroneous military notions, and was deficient as a military man. The defence of Delhi depended on two circumstances; firstly, the walls of the city, and secondly, the prevention of an outbreak among the Mahomedan population; for, the people having been under British rule only one year, it was to be apprehended that the disaffected would rise and join Holcar. It was, therefore, Colonel Ochterlony's military skill, together with his knowledge of the native character, his temper, and cool judgment that saved the city of Delhi.

den, Bernadotte, then a sergeant in the French army.

CHAPTER XI.

Ghazenuggur—Secundra—Allyghur—The Fort—The Church—Monuments—The Gaol—Akbarabad—Meerun-ke-Serai—Kanoge—Tombs—Ancient Coins—Language of Kanoge—Supposed Site of Palibothra—Population of Benares—Streets of Benares—Singers and Musicians—Productions of Kanoge—Poorah—Cawnpore—Court Etiquette at Lucknow—Nawab of Oude—His Regal Rank—Military Depôt at Cawnpore—Saddlery—Sirsole—Dâk Bungalows—Arapore—Lohunga—Allahabad.

On the morning of the 11th of April, I bade adieu to the far-famed city of Delhi, after a most agreeable stay of only four days, during which, however, I had made the most of my time.

Quitting the city from my encampment at the Cashmere gate, I set out for Ghazenuggur, a distance of fourteen and a half miles. I passed over the river Jumna, about five miles from Delhi, by the bridge of boats of which I have already spoken. The bed of the river being unusually broad at this time, these boats were exceedingly numerous. Half way *en route* to Ghazenuggur, or perhaps rather less, I crossed the river Hindon by an iron bridge.

On the 12th, I rode to Secundra, a distance of twenty-three miles, the scenery being very tame and uninteresting. On the 13th, I continued my route as far as Koorjah, seventeen miles and one-eighth; and on the 14th, to Somnagunge, fourteen and a half miles.

On the 15th I reached Allyghur, or Coel, as the town is called. On my arrival, I immediately visited the Great Mosque, with five cupolas, and a large pillar close by it, called the Minar. It is in a ruinous state, and a very poor resemblance of the renowned Cootub Minar, at Delhi. I ascended as high as was practicable by the spiral staircase in the interior, and counted eighty-one steps. An intelligent native, who accompanied me, told me that the founder intended that it should rival the beautiful column at Delhi; but some accident prevented its completion.

I next visited the Fort of Allyghur, taken by Lord Lake, in 1803. It is built of mud, faced with kankar, or limestone, of a square form, and surrounded by a very deep and broad fosse filled with water, and abounding in fish. Within the gates nothing now remains of this chief stronghold of Sindiah but a few huts, and small bomb-proof magazines; the fortress having been stormed by the British troops under Lord Lake in 1803, and dismantled by Lord William Bentinck.

The church, built at the expence of a liberal and pious civilian, is very small and neat; near it is a monument erected to the memory of seven officers of H.M. 76th Foot, who were killed in action against the army of Sindiah. At no great distance are two low pillars, each encircled by a wall, in memory of two French officers, in the service of Dowlut Row Sindiah; and, close by, a faithful Mussulman Khidmutgar, or butler, lies interred beneath a flat stone. On one side of the church is a European burial ground, nearly covered over with tombs and pillars.

A few minutes' walk conducts the visitor to an enormously large gaol, in which all the culprits in the district of Allyghur, about 700 in number, were at this time confined.

The station appeared to be an exceedingly pleasant one; the bungalows to the north are surrounded with fine tropical trees, which give it a very cheerful appearance. During my stay here, my tent was pitched in an ancient Mahomedan burying ground.

On the 16th of April, I rode to Akbarabad fourteen miles and a half. The hot winds having now set in, and travelling in the day-time being almost insupportable, I started at eleven o'clock the same night, and arrived at Budwas, a distance of twenty miles at half-past-four o'clock on the morning of the 17th. On the 18th I rode to Naia Serai, twenty miles; and on Sunday, the 19th, to Korowlee, thirteen miles and one-eighth; on the 20th, to Bowgong, sixteen miles; on the 21st, to Chiberamow, twenty-one miles; on the 22nd, to Goorsaigunge, fourteen miles.

On the 23rd I rode to Meerun-ke-Serai, a distance of fourteen miles. On my arrival, I visited the ancient city of Kanoge, by diverging two miles from the main road, to my left. An old man of ninety years of age was my guide through the ruins, accompanied by his son apparently as aged as himself. The father's name was Oodee Ram. Kanoge is abbreviated from Kanyacubja.[65] It is a town of great antiquity and celebrity, in the Province of Agra, having been the capital of a powerful kingdom, at the time of the first invasion of the Mahomedans. It is situated on the west of the river Ganges, in Lat. 27° 5′ north, and Long. 79° 52′ east. The Ganges runs about two miles off, and, by means of a canal which makes a bend towards the town, the sacred stream is brought close to the citadel.

The town, at present, consists of only one street, but along an extent of six miles, the fragments of small pieces of brick earth, and the occasional vestiges of a building, point out the site of this ancient capital of Hindoostan. I may mention a peculiarity in the Hindoo buildings, that they are composed of very small bricks, worked in with a great portion of cement, which is harder, and requires more force to break it, than the bricks.

I here saw the tombs of two Mahomedan saints, who lie in state in two Mausolea on an elevation covered with trees. From the terrace which surrounds them I enjoyed a pleasant prospect over the plain, scattered with the ruins of temples and tombs; little images broken into fragments, are lying about in all directions under the trees. Ancient coins of an irregular shape are frequently found among the ruins; they are inscribed with Sanscrit characters, the original language of In-

[65] Kanya, a damsel, and cubja, a spinal curve.

dia, and, sometimes have the figure of a Hindoo deity on one side. We nowhere read of any one having ever collected these coins, much less of having translated the inscriptions upon them. Surely it would be worth the trouble to send some one to dig them up out of the heaps of rubbish which cover them. Coins are the books of antiquity, for the art of printing was not known even in Europe till about 400 years ago. The coins found in the Tope at Munnikala in the Punjaub, have led to the belief, that such structures as those at Kanoge were not raised by the natives of the country. It is true that the search for coins in that district has not always produced genuine ones, for the cupidity of the natives has led them to sell modern copies of ancient coins to Europeans not versed in the knowledge of these antique deposits; they see that they are of Bactrian origin, but cannot distinguish the true from the false coins. General Ventura, who opened the Tope, had the advantage of a first discovery, for spurious ones could not have been originally deposited there.

Kanoge, in the remotest times of Hindoo history, was a place of great renown, and the capital of the powerful kingdom of Hindoostan, which existed down to the period of the Mahomedan invasion, which is about coeval with that of England by William the Conqueror. The name Kanyacubja, has reference to a well-known story related in the Hindoo mythological poems. The language of Kanoge appears to have formed the ground-work of the modern Hindoostanee known also by the appellation of Hindee or Hindivee, it is a graft on the Sanscrit; the Oordoo is a mixture of Hindee and Persian. Oordoo means a camp, hence Oordoo is the Camp or Court language of Delhi and Lucknow, where it is spoken with the greatest purity. Kings formerly often lived in Camp with their troops.

The Rajahs of Kanoge are mentioned by Ferishta as early as 1008. The town was conquered, though not permanently retained, by Mahmood, of Ghuznee, A.D. 1018. The late Lieutenant-Colonel W. Francklin, Bengal army, in his "Enquiry into the Site of the Ancient Palibothra," calls it "Kennouj, or Kanycacubja." The learned Mr. Maurice, in his Indian Antiquities (p. 36), observes, of this city, that it was enclosed by walls fifty coss, or one hundred miles, in circumference; and, in page 42 of the same work, states, on the authority of the Ayeen Akbaree,[66] that, in the beginning of the sixth century, under the reign of Maldeo, it contained 30,000 shops where betel-nut was sold, and 60,000 bands[67] of singers and musicians, who paid a tax to government. The extent of the city might reasonably allow of a population of from two to three millions of souls. If these positions be admissible, we surely need not cavil at the extent of the city of Palibothra, as assigned to it in the Hindoo records. Colonel Francklin writes of Bisnagur (Beejanuggur), "of this city, Cæsar Frederic, a Venetian merchant, who was there in 1567, says, 'that it had a circuit of ninety-four miles, and that it contained within it a number of little hills and pagodas.'" Major Rennel, the well-known Surveyor-general of India, in his Dissertations, agrees with the Venetian, that these hills and pagodas were within the boundaries. Of course, there were many temples at Kanoge; and there seems to be no reason whatever for disbelieving the fact of its having been one hundred

[66] A work written by the command of Akbar. It contained a statement of the revenues of all the districts and towns, the amount of the troops, and the number under each commander.

[67] Tyfeeah, "a band," or set of Natch girls.

miles in circumference, or of there having been 4,000 souls to a square mile.

Now, let us take the city of Benares. The late Mr. James Prinsep,[68] between the years 1824 and 1827, found the population to be 183,491; or, 34,621 to the square mile. The census was taken under peculiar difficulties. Benares, or Kasi, is the most sacred Hindoo city in Hindoostan. In the late census, taken in 1848-49, the population was allowed to stand the same as when taken in 1824-27. The lapse of more than twenty years will give a great increase of population, even supposing that there had been an over-calculation.

Let us test the point by English statistics. In Middlesex[69] they quote 5,590—98 souls to a square mile. Now, if we say three millions for Kanoge, it will give about 4,800 souls to a square mile. Then it must be recollected, that the streets of Benares are so very narrow, that if one person enters a street at one end on an elephant, and another comes from the opposite end similarly mounted, neither can pass, but one must back out, which implies that the streets are not twenty feet wide. Besides which, the native houses in Benares are several stories high. It is a fact, that a great portion of the sickness of that city, as of others which I have seen, arises from the circumstance that the sun's rays never penetrate the street. Therefore, if Kanoge were peopled to anything like the extent even of Middlesex, we may believe the number of inhabitants to have been as great as suggested by Maurice. If the Venetian be correct, we may assert that, if Beejanuggur extended ninety-four miles, Kanoge, the most ancient Hindoo city of Hindoostan, was one hundred miles in circumference. It is to be borne in mind, that the population of the world, at the period referred to, was greater than in times before the Christian era. Lord Lake had his head-quarters at Kanoge before his army took the field in 1803.

The late Lieut.-Colonel Thorn, in his Memoir of the War in India, 1803-6, says: "Kanoge, which modern writers suppose, though certainly on very problematical grounds, to be the site of the celebrated Palibothra;" but this will be noticed again when I speak of Allahabad, which some deem to be the identical site of Palibothra.

The 60,000 bands of singers and musicians is a more puzzling problem: because each band has never less than four persons; two girls and two men. Now, 2,500,000 divided by 60,000, gives a "natch" or dancing set to about every forty-two persons. It proves at least the musical taste of the Hindoos, and their fondness for singing and dancing in those days. We must, however, recollect that singing enters into their religion, and forms a necessary part of their sacred festivals. Again, if we take a brick house to contain six people, and a mud house four, there would be a band for every eight or nine families.

Kanoge is celebrated for its attar of roses, rose-water, and sweetmeats; of the last I purchased fifteen seers, or thirty lbs. for my servants, thus giving two lbs. to each man.

On the 24th of April, I rode twenty-three miles to Poorah; on the 25th, to Kullianpore, nineteen miles and three-quarters. My next stage was to Cawnpore, a

[68] Statistical Survey of Berar, p. 155, table xxx. Statistics, North-west Provinces. By A. Shakespear, Assistant Surveyor-General.

[69] Shakespear's Statistics, North-west Provinces of India, table ii. p. 172.

distance of seven miles, where I put up at the Bungalow, next to the one I occupied when I was stationed at Cawnpore with my regiment last year. The change from my tent to a Bungalow was exceedingly agreeable, for latterly I had found it almost intolerable, on account of the dust and heat.

Cawnpore is a large military station, situated on the right bank of the Ganges, between Kanoge and Allahabad. The circumstance of its becoming a military station, was the result of a treaty with the Nawab of Oude, by which the British East India Company agreed to keep a Brigade at Cawnpore for the defence of the Nawab's dominions. It is about forty-nine miles from Lucknow, the capital of the King of Oude. About the year 1818, the Governor-General, the late Marquis of Hastings, suggested the title of King in lieu of that of Nawab. The Company, it seems, had borrowed money from his Highness, as he was then called, to pay the expences of the Nepaul war; and as the Nepaul frontier bordered on Oude, there appeared to be some tangible reason for asking for a part of the outlay. His Highness lent two "crores," or two millions sterling: one of which was afterwards repaid, and the other was partly absorbed in the kingly title.

The Nawab, as Vizier, had been the servant of the Emperor of Delhi; and at the time of which I am treating two of the Emperor's sons were living at Lucknow, and used to be supplied with money by the Nawab. Now the court etiquette was such, that whenever his highness met their royal highnesses, the princes of the blood of Delhi, his highness was constrained to make his elephants kneel down, if so mounted; which deportment was considered degrading in the presence of his liege subjects at Lucknow, and called for a remedy. It was therefore, intimated to the Nawab, that he and the Honourable Company might make an amicable agreement, by the government of India conferring upon him the title of Majesty.[70] The Nawab jumped at the proposal, and was dubbed "King and mighty Sovereign." Besides these advantages, he was not only raised in rank above the princes of the blood royal; but he was also king as well as the great Mogul, whose style was "Shahun Shah," or "King of Kings." The Emperor, however, was greatly incensed; what now was to be done? He complained that his income of ten lakhs, or £100,000, was not meet and sufficient to keep up his royal dignity;[71] whereupon the Company, in order to conciliate his majesty, at once raised his pension to £120,000 per annum. Money carries everything in the East, as it does for the most part in the West—it can do anything short of a miracle.

The investiture of the Nawab of Oude with regal dignity is, however, by no means incongruous. Mooltan, for instance, we find from old historians, covered an area of 3,273,932 beegahs, or 1,636,966 acres of measured lands; and again those of Oude were 2,796,206 beegahs, or 1,398,103 acres. Now, as there was formerly a king of Mooltan, the size of which is only 238,863 acres larger than Oude, there seems to be no reason why its ruler should not bear the style and title of King of Oude. Oude is estimated to be 250 miles in length, and 100 in breadth, from which it appears that it is as large as Scotland and much larger than Hanover.

His Majesty has disbanded his disorderly troops, and maintains two corps of

[70] Vide Oude, Parliamentary Papers.

[71] See Appendix XX.

Infantry, disciplined and appointed by British officers, stationed at Sultanpore and Seetapore. At Lucknow itself there is a Horse Field-battery and three battalions of East India Company's Sepoys. Visitors to Lucknow should go to the late General Martin's palace and the Dil-Khoosha. The Residency is situated two-and-a-half miles from the cantonments. There is a bridge over the Goomtee river, and an iron bridge near Dil-Khoosha. In the neighbourhood of Lucknow are many fine palaces, which well deserve two or three days' inspection.

At Cawnpore there are two companies of Artillery, a corps of Native Cavalry, a European regiment of Infantry, three corps of Native Infantry, and an Infantry recruiting depôt; whereas formerly, there used to be a troop of Horse Artillery, a regiment of British Dragoons, a corps of Queen's Foot, two companies of Artillery, a corps of Golundaz, a regiment of Native Cavalry, and three regiments of Native Infantry. The cantonments are of great length and very straggling; the distance from the magazine to the end of the Native Artillery lines being seven miles. Looking from the river, the regiments used to stand thus:—The European Infantry on the left; next to which come the European Foot Artillery, then the Native Infantry; next the Dragoons and Native Cavalry, and, lastly, the Native Artillery. The civilians live chiefly at Nawabgunge, about two or three miles to the left of the cantonments. In the midst of the cantonments are the Church, the Theatre, and the Assembly Rooms, the latter consisting of two rooms parallel to each other and about 100 feet in length, where public meetings are held. Besides the church here spoken of, a neat little chapel was built close to their lines, for the use of the Dragoons, when they were stationed here.

There is an hotel at Cawnpore, kept by a Mr. Duhan, pleasantly situated on the banks of the river. It is a great convenience to travellers, but, owing to the want of sufficient patronage, it will, probably, be soon broken up. Not far from the hotel is the European burial ground, crowded as usual with pillars and slabs, marking out the last resting-place of beloved relatives and friends.

Cawnpore, although very hot and dusty, is, in my opinion, not an unhealthy station; for, during my stay there, from the 28th of April, 1844, to the 17th of October, 1845, I found that, with common prudence, a person might enjoy very tolerable health. There is a fine race-course, which used to afford an exciting amusement during the cold months. The officers' bungalows, pleasantly situated in large compounds,[72] surrounded by walls, are very comfortable. The one which I occupied, while stationed here, and for which I paid only £96 per annum rent, was, perhaps, rather adapted for a general officer than for a captain of Dragoons. The saddlery made at Cawnpore is celebrated throughout India, as particularly good; and the Native Cavalry are chiefly supplied with it. The extension of our frontier has, however, done no small injury to Cawnpore, for it will never again enjoy the large and important commerce which it used to possess. To continue my route:—

On the 30th of April, 1846, I rode to Sirsole, fourteen miles, and put up at the Dâk, or Stage Bungalow. These Dâk Bungalows are stationed along all the principal roads in India, at a distance of about fifteen or twenty miles apart, are a great

[72] From *Campaô,* a Portuguese word, signifying an enclosure round a house, or bungalow.

comfort to the weary traveller; for, as there are few hotels on the route, he thankfully avails himself of such fare as these afford. Here he enjoys the luxury of a bath, accommodation, and attendance, for the trifling sum of 2s. per diem. The traveller must bring his own provisions, which the Dâk Khidmutgar will prepare *à son goût*. These establishments are under the control of the government post-masters. The word Dâk signifies post; and the Inland Mail is transferred from one part of India to another not by railway and mail coaches, but by such conveyances as are best adapted for speed in different localities. Thus, in some districts camels are used; in others, horses; and, in others again, mail-carts; while the most ordinary method of transmission is by a runner, who carries the letter-bags, generally at the end of a bamboo pole poised over his shoulder, and shifts it upon those of another runner, who stands, waiting in readiness, at a distance of ten or twelve miles, and who, in his turn, transmits it to another, and so on, till the whole distance is accomplished. These Dâk post runners keep on at a regular speed of four or five miles an hour.

On the 1st of May I rode to Kullianpore, a distance of seventeen miles, and the next day to Futtehpore, sixteen miles. I was on the point of taking my customary ablution this morning, when my Bihishti, or water-carrier, discovered a deadly cobra de capella, partly concealed and asleep, under one of the earthen jars which I was just going to use. I felt very thankful for my escape.

Futtehpore is an extensive Mahomedan city; it is in a lamentable state, and the ruins of tombs, mosques, houses, and walls lie spread over a very large space. It has been a civil station since 1826; and it also contains a very large gaol.

On the third of May, I started for Arapore, a distance of sixteen miles, and proceeded the next morning to Lohunga seventeen miles off. I arrived at Kusseah on the 5th, after a ride of sixteen miles, and having rested till five o'clock in the afternoon, I commenced a long march, but halted for about half-an-hour at the Travellers' Bungalow at Koela, fifteen miles, to allay a burning thirst with some tea, and finally reached Berrill's Hotel at Allahabad at a quarter to one the next morning, being a distance of twenty-nine miles.

Thus I rode the whole way from Lahore to Allahabad, a distance of at least 704 miles in fifty-four days, including the nine days I halted.

CHAPTER XII.

Allahabad—Pilgrimages—The River Jumna—Hurdwar—Akbar—Allum II.—Fortifications—Inscriptions on Column—Military Depôt—Lieut.-Colonel A. Abbott, C.B.—Colonel Kyd discovers a Cave—Ancient Palibothra—Arrian's Account—Megasthenes—Dr. Adams—Heeren—Chundragupta—Patna—The Sacred Rivers—Bhaugulpore—The Mandara Hill—The Chundun—Palibothra—Rajmahal—Antiquity of Kanoge—Allahabad—Extent of Asiatic Cities—Mahomedan Invasion—Extent of Hindoostan.

THE hotel at which I took up my residence at Allahabad, was very pleasantly situated: my rooms faced the Jumna, whose clear blue water was most refreshing to the eye, the hotel standing on the right bank of that noble stream.

Allahabad, which literally means the "Abode or City of God," is by the Brahmins called Bhat Prayag, or by way of distinction it is designated as "Prayaga," also "Praag," or "Prayagas," or "sacred confluence of rivers."[73] The River Jumna takes its name from Yumna, which in Sanscrit means, meeting, or confluence. Some of the religious ceremonies enjoined upon the Hindoo pilgrims must be performed in a vast subterranean cave, which is situated in the middle of the Fort—it is supported by pillars, and is believed by the vulgar to extend under ground as far as Benares, a distance of fifty-three miles, and to be infested by snakes and poisonous reptiles—granting the cave really to extend thus far, who could possibly live to go through to its termination!

Allahabad is one of the most celebrated places of Hindoo pilgrimage, and the deluded devotees come here by thousands to wash in the sister streams to purify themselves, or to carry some of the precious water to their distant homes. Nay, many annually drown themselves at this celebrated junction of the Ganges and the Jumna; they are conducted into the middle of the stream in a boat, and then sunk by having earthen pots tied to their feet. This reckless sacrifice of life would no doubt have sooner been put a stop to, had not the native governments derived considerable advantage from it, for they used even to levy a tax upon the pilgrims for the privilege of bathing in the sacred stream. The debates in the East India house regarding the tax levied at Juggernauth led to a change in the system; and it has since been abolished.

Allahabad and Hurdwar are the two most noted places of pilgrimage. At the

[73] The late Bishop of Lichfield and Coventry, Dr. Samuel Butler, in his Ancient and Modern Geography, p. 267, called it also Helabas. In India some speak of it as "Illahabas."

latter city a fair is held annually where thousands of people go to bathe, and although the river Ganges, is very shallow there, many lose their lives. The great fair is held every twelfth year, when several companies of sepoys are generally present both to keep the peace and to prevent accidents. About thirty years since, innumerable lives were lost by the sudden rush of pilgrims down the great ghât leading into the river. Hence the troops have special charge to hinder any large number of persons from congregating together.

Akbar was very partial to Allahabad and founded the modern city, intending it as a stronghold to overawe the surrounding country, for which it was extremely well adapted by its natural position. This enterprising emperor also built Agra, which he styled Akbarabad. Allahabad was taken in 1765, by the British army, under Sir Robert Fletcher; soon after which (1766) the Nawab of Oude, to whom it belonged, having been defeated at Buxar, and in subsequent battles, assigned it by treaty to the East India company.

The Emperor of Delhi, Allum II., who was then a fugitive, had joined the Nawab, and, together with him, made his peace with the British. He was placed under their protection; and they agreed to allow him twenty-six lakhs, or £260,000, per annum. Upon receiving in perpetuity the revenues of Bengal, Bahar, and Orissa, it was agreed that the royal share of those revenues, twenty-six lakhs of rupees, should be annually paid to him by the Company; but when he accepted the aid of the Maharattas to replace him on the throne of Delhi, he was informed that the tribute of those provinces would be no longer granted to him. Mill, vol. iii. p. 579, says:—"The discredit of this transaction belongs to the Directors of the East India Company." It must however, be borne in mind that the Government strongly advised the Emperor not to go to Delhi.

The Emperor of Delhi resided, under the guardianship of the English, in the Fort of Allahabad until the year 1771. In 1765, an imperial grant was issued, constituting the East India Company Dewanny, or receivers of revenue, of Bengal, Bahar, and Orissa, which grant gave the Government the virtual sovereignty of these countries. The Dewanny yielded about two millions sterling a year. The Emperor also confirmed the English in all the titles conveyed to them by the Subahdar, or Viceroy, of Bengal, whose successor is now Nawab only of Moorshedabad.

The city of Allahabad does not present a very striking appearance, as there are only a few brick buildings without any kind of ornament. The fort is placed at some distance, on a tongue of land, the one side being washed by the blue waters of the Jumna, and the other nearly approaching the dull yellow stream of the Ganges. It is lofty and extensive, and completely commands the navigation of the two rivers. Both the river fronts are defended by the old walls, with the addition of some cannon and semi-circular bastions; the third side, near the main land is regular and very strong; it has three ravelines, two bastions, and a half-bastion, and stands higher than any ground in front of it. The gateway is Grecian, and very elegant.

In the centre of the fort rises an ancient granite column, thirty-six feet high, with Pali and Sanscrit inscriptions. The Sanscrit is almost obliterated; it gives the genealogy of Akbar, and states that the column was erected by him. The British have added a third inscription, giving the date of its transfer to them in 1765, and its final cession in 1801, together with the province. In the same line with the fort is another building, which has been modernized and converted into barracks for the garrison staff sergeants. The sums expended upon the fortifications, up to 1803, were something quite enormous, and are said to have amounted to more than twelve lakhs. They have now been rendered quite impregnable against the attacks of a native enemy; and even by a European force its capture would be a matter of no small difficulty.

Allahabad was at one time the grand military depôt of the upper provinces. During the Sikh war of 1848-49, the principal commissary of ordnance was located there, and most of the contents of the arsenal in Fort William, Calcutta, were transferred to Allahabad.[74] The present principal commissary is Lieut.-Colonel A. Abbott, C.B., of the Artillery, distinguished for his services at Bhurtpore, in Affghanistan, and at Jellalabad. The following anecdote will serve to exhibit his energy and promptitude under difficulties. In October, 1848, it was found that the store of musket-ball ammunition at Ferozepore, etc., was damaged; upon which application was made to Colonel Abbott for a fresh supply. By relays of bullocks, he managed daily to send up 100,000 rounds, which reached Umballa, a distance of 529 miles, in fourteen days. He continued this until he was informed that no more were required. This trait of zeal in the public service is given, not only as an instance of the expeditious mode of forwarding supplies, but as an act of justice to Lieutenant-Colonel Abbott, and as shewing the importance of placing in such a post of difficulty, an officer who has seen a great deal of hard service.

There is a place for the manufacture of gunpowder at Papamow, between two and three miles from the cantonments; also another at Isharpore, near Barrackpore. At these two depôts all the Company's gunpowder is made, and a two-years' supply is generally kept in store. The cantonments of Allahabad are about three miles from the fort, and appear very comfortable.

I may here mention an interesting discovery made by Colonel Kyd, of the Engineers, during the restoration of the fort. While forming the glacis, he discovered a cave, which contained a number of images belonging to the tribe of Serawagy, of the sect of the Jains, which were soon after claimed by some persons, who asserted that they had been deposited there by their ancestors, during the persecution of the Hindoos by Aurungzebe in 1680. In the entrance of the cave is a sacred tree, which is said to have flourished there from time immemorial, and is held in great veneration by the Hindoos. There is also a tank of water, which is in high repute among the pilgrims.

The English church is a very neat building, with a light and handsome spire. The rides in the vicinity are numerous and pleasant; and the roads, which extend in various directions for thirty miles, skirted with trees of abundant foliage, are excellent. Indeed there is no other station in the Bengal Presidency which contains

[74] There is a magazine at Chunar, which serves for Benares and the stations immediately below it. The river from Chunar to Allahabad is not suited for a speedy transmission by boats, because the stream for about thirty miles below Allahabad is full of shoals.

so many good roads. They are made by the prisoners, of whom, unhappily, there are always a great number in the Allahabad gaol. It is said, that the allowance of food is so liberal in the gaol, that some contrive to gain admittance there, as into a comfortable asylum; however they are made to work pretty hard, and the government sells the produce of their labours. It has been remarked of Sydney, that if no convicts had been sent thither, there never would have been a road two miles long. The same may be said with equal truth of Allahabad.

The troops now stationed at Allahabad, are a Company of Native Foot Artillery, two regiments of Native Infantry, and a depôt for H.M. regiments of Foot, under the command of a Lieut.-Colonel. Formerly there were two companies of European Artillery in the fort, of which a general officer was always in command. In 1817, just before the Maharatta war, a European Flank Battalion, composed of companies of royal regiments, was quartered in the fortress. At this time a circumstance occurred which created great alarm; for one evening, whilst the officers of the Flankers were at mess, several of them were suddenly taken ill. The cholera had been known in India in 1781 and 1783, but not since; so that it was concluded to be an attack of that fearful and fatal contagion. Upon investigation, however, it appeared that the cooking pots, which it was customary to have fresh tinned every twenty or twenty-five days, were not clean. Many thought it was a premeditated attempt at poisoning; hence it is necessary in India, more particularly on the line of march, to "look before you cook."

Before quitting Allahabad, I must redeem my promise of laying before the reader some statements confirmatory of my view, that the ancient city of Palibothra was the site of Allahabad, and not, as some suppose, Kanoge.

There are many theories in existence respecting the site of ancient Palibothra. Some of them are so improbable as to be unworthy of notice; but others, propounded by learned and ingenious writers, may fairly claim consideration in this place. Before I enter upon the examination of these it will be proper to state such information, with regard to position and other circumstances, as we may gain from early historians.

In the first place we have the statement of Strabo (lib. xv.), that Palibothra was situated at the confluence of the Ganges with another river; but he does not mention the name. Arrian says:[75] "The capital city of India is Palimbothra, in the confines of the Prasii (or Prachi of Sanscrit writers) nigh the confluence of the two great rivers, Erannoboas and Ganges. Erannoboas is reckoned the third river throughout all India, and is inferior to none but the Indus and Ganges, into the last of which it enters." He further states: "Of the two great rivers of India, the Ganges and the Indus, Megasthenes assures us that the first is by far the largest, for it arises great from its very fountains, and receives many great rivers; namely Cainas, Erannoboas, Cassoanes (Coosah?) Sonus,[76] Sitocatis and Solomatis. All these are navigable; and, besides these, the Condochates, Sambus, Magones, Agoranis, and Omalis."

To determine which is this said third river of India, we must premise that the

[75] Rooke's Translation of Alexander's Expedition.

[76] Sanscrit, the Sone or Golden River.

Berhampooter was not known to Alexander the Great, or his successors, nor was it known in Europe until A.D. 1765.

Megasthenes states also "that the length of this city is eighty furlongs, the breadth fifteen, that it is surrounded with a ditch thirty cubits deep, and occupying six acres of ground, the walls being defended with 570 towers and six gates."

Such is the evidence furnished on this subject by early writers, and the question resulting from it is, which of the many rivers flowing into the Ganges are we to consider the third river in India, at the confluence of which Palibothra was situated? It does not appear that Megasthenes has given the rivers in the order of their size; for he omits all mention of some of the largest, and the first river he speaks of, the Cainas, is certainly smaller than the fourth on his list, the Sonus. The only rivers, of any consequence, entering the Ganges on the right bank, are the Jumna and the Sone, of which the former is by far the more considerable.

A very current opinion, entertained and supported by several respectable writers, makes the modern Patna to be the site of the ancient city. Thus Dr. A. Adams[77] says:—"Patna, the capital of Bahar, built along the south bank of the Ganges, an extensive and populous city, supposed to be the ancient Palibothra." Heeren[78] also says: "Palibothra must be sought in, or near the modern town of Patna, where its ancient appellation still survives in the name of a certain district called Patalputhra." Major Rennel also in some places affirms his opinion to be decidedly in favour of Patna, and in others speaks doubtingly to the same purpose,—"S'il est vrai que Palibothra ait été située où est aujourd'hui Patna, et les dernières découvertes rendent cette opinion probable."

Now Patna is situated near the confluence of the Sonus with the Ganges, in a very favourable position for a city of importance: and it appears to be pretty certain that it is the site of a very ancient city, but *not that of the city of Palibothra.* We must recollect that there is an Upper and Lower Ganges, the latter of which would be below Patna. Now, though the ancient kingdom of Maghada included Patna, it is not probable that there was a capital so low down. Heeren declares that the empire of the Prasii extended beyond the junction of the Jumna with the Ganges, and we may infer from this that the said junction was not much short of the limits of the empire. And, speaking of particular towns, he names Ayodhya, Kanoge, and others. Also mentioning Pataliputra (Patna) the same author says: "The scene of these fables (Hitopadesah, or Pilpay) is laid in the city of Pataliputra, by no means the most ancient in India."

Arrian tells us that Palibothra was in the confines of the Prasii. But Pataliputra was the capital of King Chundragupta, who reigned long before the kingdom of the Prasii was established. Heeren[79] says: "Compare the accounts of Chundragupta given by Wilford in the 'Asiatic Review, vol. v. p. 264.'" In the list of kings arranged by Sir William Jones[80] the reign of Nauda is placed in 1602, and of Chundragupta in 1502 B.C.; the latter, therefore, must have lived 1200 years before

[77] Ancient and Modern Geography, p. 522.

[78] P. 300.

[79] Page 3, note 1.

[80] Works, vol. i. p. 306.

Sandrocottus. Will any one pretend that there was another Chundragupta?

Arrian tells us simply that the city of Palibothra is in the confines of the Prasii: he does not say that it had been thus distinguished as the capital of Chundragupta, which he would no doubt have done if the fact had been so, and the very antiquity of Chundragupta destroys the possibility of his capital being Palibothra, which was built so many years after. We conclude, therefore, that Patna, as is generally allowed, is the site of the ancient Pataliputra, the capital of Chundragupta; and that it is *not* the same as Palibothra, but a much more ancient city.

It has been stated by some, that Pataliputra and Palibothra are one and the same place, and that the latter name is simply a corruption of the former. But Buchanan well remarks on this subject,[81] "This city (Patna) is indeed allowed by the Pundits to be called Pataliputra; but Pataliputra has no great resemblance to Palibothra; nor can Patali be rationally considered as a word of the same origin as Pali, said to be an ancient name of this country, and of its people and language." There is no doubt that the use of the word Pali, in this connection, is derived from the Pali language of the Buddhists, who have a temple at Gya.

And further, as to the derivation of this name, we read that a Brahmin, having married Bhoom Deo (the earth-god), had two sons, one of whom, Bukshun, married Soormut, and had a son called Pootur (or son), who married Patlee, the daughter of the king of the Singhaldees. In the case of Hindoos, the men do not take their fathers' names. Supposing that these joined their names, we have Pootur-patlee, which will not answer, because the young man calls himself Patlee-pootur, taking the wife's name, which is contrary to Hindoo usage. The story states further, that Patlee-pootur planted his staff, and a beautiful city sprang out of the ground, which in honour of his wife he called Patleepoora, or Patleepooturpoora, a name truly royal in its length! The pair died, leaving a son called Puttum, and a daughter named Putnie, from whom the modern name Patna is said to have been derived. In the absence of more definite evidence we may rest a strong presumption on these traditions, and whatever part of them we may accept or reject, they certainly contain some amount of historical evidence to prove that Pataliputra must not be confounded with Palibothra.

In the eleventh century a play is supposed to have been written, the Mudra Rakshasha, the principal scenes in which are laid at Pataliputra, the capital of Chundragupta. Buchanan[82] says, that other traditions preserved in the Skund Poorana derive the name of Patna from the Sanscrit word meaning *a cloth*; from the circumstance of the goddess Parbuttee having dropt her mantle on the spot, in her flight to Kylas (the sky).

So much with respect to the derivation of the names Patna and Pataliputra. From what has been stated, it may be clearly seen that Palibothra cannot be a corruption or modification of Pataliputra, and that the modern name of Patna is traceable to a very remote period.

To proceed with the proof that Patna is not the ancient Palibothra:—An opin-

[81] Vol. i. p. 26.
[82] Vol. i. p. 146.

ion has been expressed by one who appears to be a competent judge, Mr. E.C. Ravenshaw,[83] that the distance from Patna at which the Sone now runs into the Ganges is so great that it cannot be said to be at the point of confluence, and therefore does not answer to Arrian's description as before quoted.

But a better argument is this,—that the river Sone has no particular sanctity attached to it by the Hindoos; it does not convey sacred water to the district of Patna, such as is supposed to flow in the Ganges, and many other Indian rivers. We know that the most sacred streams issue from the Himalaya mountains, the region of the gods and of Brahma. The Ganges, the Indus, the Jumna, the Gograh, the Coosah, the Gundruk, and others, come from that holy source; but the Sone and the Nerbudda rise in the table-land of Omerkuntuc in Gundwana,—in lat. 22°, 35′ N.; long. 82°, 15′ E.[84] Now it is very certain that the Sone, lacking this sacred character, could not have been reckoned as the third river in India; superior to many streams which take their rise from the Himalaya, and inferior only to the Ganges and the Indus, both of which are regarded with the deepest reverence.

Thus, with regard to Patna, we are led to the conclusion, that, while there is great evidence to prove that it is a most ancient city, and to identify it with the former Pataliputra, the capital of the Gupta dynasty; yet it is quite as clear that it is not the site of Palibothra.

Another opinion, however, would place the ancient city further east, and not far from Bhaugulpore.[85] The late Colonel Francklin took a journey on purpose to examine this subject, and in his preface to the second part of his researches respecting the site of Palibothra, he writes:—"If then my assumption of the Mandara hill as the place recorded in the Puranas,[86] where one of the sovereigns of Palibothra was assassinated, be correct;—if the evidence afforded by the hills which appear in the neighbourhood of the town, and through a very great extent of what formerly constituted the Prasian kingdom, prior to the expedition of Alexander the Great;—if these and other connecting circumstances, as well local and historical, as traditional, be conceded;—it will, I think, be also conceded to me, that they apply in every instance throughout the discussion, as more naturally indicative of the town of Bhaugulpore possessing the site of Palibothra, and the metropolis of the Parsii (Prasii?) than either Rajmahal, Patna, Kanoge, or Allahabad."

The argument drawn from the assassination of this king of Palibothra on the Mandara hill, is really worth nothing. The circumstance that this took place near Bhaugulpore no more proves the site of Palibothra to have been there, than if the sovereign had been assassinated at any other of the places named. For if kings travel, particularly among enemies, and in times of anarchy, they are liable to be killed anywhere. Our first Richard was assassinated in Normandy, and our first Edward had a narrow escape in the Holy Land. Moreover, this murdered king of

[83] Journal of Asiatic Society. Vol. xiv. p. 137. Part I, Nos. 157-162.

[84] Hamilton's Gazetteer, Rennel, &c.

[85] Wilford, Asiatic Researches. Vol. v. p. 272.

[86] Elphinstone, in his history of India, says: "There are *eighteen* Puranas composed by different authors between the 8th and 16th centuries." Col. Francklin should have proved his author, and given his date.

Palibothra might have been taken to the Mandara hill as a fitting place of execution; so that we can gather from this occurrence no clue whatever, to the actual site of his capital city.

Again, there is no large river flowing into the Ganges at the point where Bhaugulpore is situated. Colonel Francklin states that at Dhurumgunge, five miles N.W. of Bhaugulpore he met with the river Chundun, but the confluence of the Chundun with the Ganges is at Champanuggur, thirteen miles from that town. He assumes this river to have been the Erannoboas of the Greeks; and, because it is to be found thirteen miles from Bhaugulpore and runs into the Ganges, he fixes the Mandara hill as the site of Palibothra. At the end of his journal, he adds, that, "in the words of Arrian, the Erannoboas was a river of the third magnitude among the rivers in India." But here the Colonel mistakes the meaning of his author; for Arrian says, not that it was a river of the *third magnitude*, but the *third river* throughout all India. It is thus that historical authority is sometimes falsely cited. The Chundun, even near its mouth, is only seven hundred yards in breadth, and this will not constitute a third-rate river in India. The Gograh, on the left bank, is in some places a mile broad, in many places half-a-mile, and of greater depth even than the Ganges. The Chundun is so inconsiderable, that we hear of no natives, except those of Bhaugulpore, who speak of it at all; and to identify this with a river said to be next in size to the Indus, is plainly absurd.

In a subsequent tour, the Colonel again visited Bhaugulpore, and about four miles south-east of that town, he found a commanding eminence, being 600 yards in circumference, and on which the site of bastions and the outer ditch of a fortification are plainly to be discovered. "The place," he says,[87] "is called by the natives Suffiegur; and here the surface of the ground in the front, as well as the neighbouring grove of mango trees, is overspread with a variety of stones of different kinds, cornelians, agates, flints, and specimens of beautiful veined stone, pieces of crystal and slabs of chalcedony; these evidently indicating the remains of a building of a superior order, at a remote period of time."

The Colonel again remarks—"In my humble opinion, I should assign it as one of the summer palaces of the sovereigns of Palibothra." But since, in that country, ruins are so numerous, and frequently of such a splendid character, we cannot allow this circumstance to be of any weight. Any other hill containing a few stones, and a few relics of ancient fortifications, might, as far as Colonel Francklin has given proof, have been the summer residence of the kings of Palibothra. There are two very singular round towers near the town of Bhaugulpore, in the direction indicated by the Colonel, which he may possibly have mistaken for the summer palace of the king.

We cannot suppose that if Bhaugulpore had been the ancient Palibothra, it would not have been revered as a sacred spot, even though it were in ruins. Kanoge, for example, although no longer in existence, is spoken of with veneration. But it does not appear that any particular sanctity is attached by the natives to Bhaugulpore, nor that they esteem it as more than a common city. And, if it had been what Colonel Francklin claims for it, it would, of course, have been the

[87] Part iv. p. 53.

capital of the Prasii. But we have no evidence whatever that the kingdom of the Prasii extended so far south; and supposing that it did, still it is most improbable that their chief city would be placed at the extremity of their dominions. If the Colonel's opinion were correct, would not Abul Fazel, who wrote in 1582, or some Hindoo writer of prior or subsequent date, have spoken of such a place? Would there not be a pilgrimage to it, as there is now to Allahabad, and other sacred places? Without doubt, such would have been the case; and therefore, taking all these things into consideration, it appears to me that we must reject Colonel Francklin's favourite theory, and that Bhaugulpore could not have been Palibothra.

Another opinion places the site of the lost city at Benares. This is no doubt also an ancient town; it was taken by the Sultan Mahmood of Ghuznee in A.D. 1017, and a mosque with two elegant minarets existing to this day, was built there by Aurungzebe to mortify the Hindoos. The river Birnah runs between the military cantonments and the civil station, across which a small stone bridge was thrown, about fifty years ago, by the late Major-General J. Garstin. This river is situated to the left of the city, where it enters the Ganges. It is a very narrow and inconsiderable stream, and could not bring Benares within the denomination of "a city with two large rivers;" so that we may dismiss this opinion also, as quite improbable.

Rajmahal has likewise been mentioned, as the place where the ancient city stood. But this is at a considerable distance below Patna, and it is not likely that the limits of the Prasii extended so far in this direction. A hundred years ago, Rajmahal was two or three miles inland; and though, by the encroachment of the current upon the land, it is now situated on the bank of the river, yet there is no other river near it, it does not stand at the confluence of any stream with the Ganges, and therefore does not answer to Arrian's description.

Of the opinions on this subject, which I deem erroneous, the only other worthy of mention is that which makes Kanoge the site of Palibothra. This is also a very ancient city, as is clear from the fact that Vicramaditya,[88] who lived in the year B.C. 57, resided alternately at Palibothra and at Kanoge. It is stated by Heeren[89] to have been founded by one of the kings of Ayodhya (Oude) who made it his capital. On the decline of Ayodhya, it rose in importance. Maurice[90] dates its foundation in B.C. 1000. But while we may respect the antiquity of Kanoge, we cannot assign to it the honour claimed for it. The rivers Ramgonga and Gurrah, whose united waters flow into the Ganges near its ruins, are very inconsiderable, and could not by any stretch of the imagination be looked upon as constituting the *third* river in India.

But now, having, as I hope, clearly shown the great improbability that any of the opinions already quoted are correct, and having proved also, how irreconcilable they are to the historical evidence which we possess on this subject, I will mention my own opinion as to the site of the ancient city of Palibothra. According to Arrian, as we have seen, Palibothra is at the confluence of the Ganges and Erannoboas, which Erannoboas is said to be the third river in India. Now the Ganges is called the *first*, the Indus the *second*, and in respect of size, no other river has so

[88] He was also Lord of Benares, and rebuilt Ayodhya.

[89] P. 295.

[90] Vol. i. p. 36.

great a claim to be ranked the *third*, as the Jumna. After the two streams just mentioned, the Jumna is certainly the largest in the country. This river and the Ganges may be termed twin-sisters, as their respective sources are within a few miles of each other. Its length is 780 miles, according to Rennel, exceeding by 280 miles that of the Sone.

Coming down to the point at which the Jumna flows into the Ganges, we find the city of Allahabad. And here I would place the site of Palibothra. Its centrical position as to Hindoostan, marks it as being most fitting and convenient for the capital of a kingdom. It is certain also that it was inhabited by the Prasii, and it was most probably in the very centre of their dominions.

The great sanctity of the confluence of the Ganges and the Jumna at Allahabad, as an annual bathing-place, revered by all Hindoos, is well known. The very fact of their being two great rivers, the first and the third in magnitude, would give it a sacredness not attachable to inferior rivers. The second river, the Indus, falls into no other stream. It is joined by the Cabool river at Attock, and after receiving the Punjaub rivers, empties itself into the sea. And the fact that the two greatest rivers are not confluent, tends, no doubt, to add to the high veneration with which the natives regard the confluence of the first and third rivers.

Several of the streams flowing into the Ganges which have been adopted by controversialists, are in reality very insignificant, and are considered by the natives as quite unimportant. But the Jumna is universally known and venerated throughout all India. When water is taken from the Ganges, to a distance, it is invariably either from Hurdwar, Allahabad, or Benares.

The late Maharajah Runjeet Singh always had water from a particular spot, which was considered the best in the Punjaub. A strict Brahmin of Benares, would present his guests with water drawn from the most sacred parts of the Ganges, nor, however hot the weather, would he cool the water with ice, for by so doing, he would mix two waters, the one holy, the other profane: the water of the Ganges, and the water of America.

No native would ever take the Ganges water from near the Chundun; no Brahmin living in Calcutta would ever use it. Allahabad is held in such reverence that a public tax was paid both to the Mahomedan government of the Nawab of Oude, and to the British government, by pilgrims at certain seasons of the year. There are different degrees of sanctity ascribed to the sacred cities of India; all places are not of equal sanctity, Benares is not so sacred as Kanoge, and neither is so sacred as Allahabad. The waters of the Ganges at this confluence are accounted of superior holiness, and special virtue is ascribed to them.

Here then, the description of Arrian, to which I have shown that none of the before-mentioned opinions conformed, is fully answered, and all probability points to Allahabad as the disputed site. The central situation of the city, its position on the right bank of the Ganges, the circumstance of its superior sacredness, and above all, the fact that the Jumna is the third river in India, which no one, who will compare the relative claims of the rivers, can deny; all these together yield more than presumptive proof in its favour. We may fairly conclude then, that the ancient Palibothra is at the junction of the Ganges and the Jumna, and that there appears no just ground for supposing that any other position on the right or left bank of the Ganges can be assigned as its site.

It may now be of interest to state what is known respecting the size of the city. Strabo informs us[91] that "its length is eighty stadia, its breadth fifteen,[92] and its form oblong; that it is environed by a wall of wood, in which are sundry holes to shoot through; also a ditch, both for the defence of the city and the reception of all the filth issuing from it; and that the people are called Prasii." In an appendix to his work, Francklin gives additional notes, extracted from a pamphlet which was printed, but not published, at Calcutta, wherein he says: "For the extent of the city and suburbs of Palibothra, from seventy-five to eighty miles have been assigned, by the Puranas, a distance said to be impossible for a single city." And adds: "so indeed it might, were we to compare the cities of Asia with those of Europe." He next states, that in A.D. 1567, Cæsar Frederic, a Venetian merchant, who was then at Beejanuggur (Bisnuggur), says that it had a circuit of ninety-four miles. Major Rennel makes the city of Gour, the ancient capital of Bengal, to be fifteen miles in length, extending along the old banks of the Ganges, and from two to three miles in breadth. Colonel Francklin (Appendix p. 59) quotes Babylon[93] as extending over 365 furlongs, being the number of days in the year; or forty-five miles and five furlongs. Herodotus allows the city to have been 480 stadia, or sixty miles in circumference.[94] Colonel Francklin makes Kanoge to have been 100 miles in circuit. London, the largest city in Europe, has been estimated at twenty-five, but at present, with the suburbs, it may be thirty miles round. Now it must be recollected, that in estimating the size of European and Asiatic cities, several distinguishing circumstances are to be borne in mind. For instance, though in London there are numerous churches, they occupy but little space, compared with pagodas, mosques, and mausolea; to which in an Eastern city, much ground and many buildings are usually attached. In Oriental cities too, there are many gardens and granaries, and the stables and studs for elephants occupy a great deal of room. It is calculated that the stabling for one elephant, occupies more space than would afford accommodation for a carriage and four horses.

The Mahomedan invasion of India, which effected so great a change in the character of the country, took place in the first quarter of the eleventh century. The Mahomedan empire was founded there by the Ghorè dynasty in 1157. I may fitly close my remarks on the site of this ancient city, by glancing at the geographical extent and condition of the country at this great era of a mighty change in Indian history. It is said by Rennel and other writers, that according to the testimony of the ancients, India, on the most enlarged scale, divided on the West from Persia by the Arachosian Mountains, bounded on the East by China, on the North by Tar-

[91] Lib. xv. p. 1028.

[92] The eighty stadia long by fifteen broad, would be equal to twenty-three miles and three quarters in circuit.

[93] Diodorus Siculus, vol i. pp. 120, 121.

[94] Francklin (Appendix p. 62.) gives Beejapore as thirty-six miles in circuit, and Nineveh as forty-seven miles. Diodorus Siculus makes Nineveh to have been sixty miles and Babylon only forty-eight.

tary, and extending South to the Sunda Isles, comprised an area of 40°, including a superficies almost as large as Europe: a statement which appears preposterous. The Mahomedan writers understood Hindoostan, under the sovereigns of Delhi, to include the twelve Soobahs or Provinces into which it was sub-divided in 1582; viz., Lahore, Mooltan, Scinde, Ajmere, Delhi, Agra, Allahabad, Bahar, Oude, Bengal, Malwah, Guzerat; Cabool, and the country west of India, was made a thirteenth Soobah, and again others were added: namely, the Deccan, including Berar, Khandeish, and Ahmednuggur, and afterwards Aurungabad.

According to the geography of the original Hindoos, Hindoostan is bounded on the North by the Himalaya ridge of mountains, including Cashmere, Nepaul, and Bootan; on the South by the Ocean; on the West by the Indus; and on the East by Chittagong. With the exception of Bootan, the primitive Brahminical religion and languages prevail in the above boundaries; nor are they to be found beyond them, save in Assam and Cassey, where Brahminical doctrines still prevail; but in Bootan the people are Buddhists.

The modern name Hindoostan, is a Persian appellation, derived from the word "Hindoo" (black), and "Sthan" (a place). The above limits give 1,020,000 geographical miles. Elphinstone[95] says, "India is bounded by the Himalaya mountains, the river Indus, and the sea. Its length from Cashmere to Cape Comorin is about 1,900 British miles,[96] and its breadth, from the mouth of the Indus to the mountains east of the Berhampooter, is considerably above 1,500 British miles. In its southern boundary it is limited by the Nerbudda."

According to the Hindoo calculation, India extends northward to the thirty-fifth degree of latitude. Cabool, which was included by Akbar in Hindoostan, is reckoned between the thirty-third and thirty-fifth degrees of north latitude. But Hindoostan is bounded on the West by the river Indus, which excludes Cabool and Scinde. Sylhet, and Chittagong are to the East of the Berhampooter, near the mountains, and must be included. The southern boundary is the sea.

[95] Vol. i. p. 1.

[96] China has 1,200,000 square miles, and is said to be 1,400 by 1,600 miles.

CHAPTER XIII.

Steamers on the Ganges—Native Pilots—Course of the River—Mr. Sims proposes Shields to the Banks—Shoals—Tributary Streams—Rapids—The Jumna—Mirzapore—Benares—Trimbuckjee Danglia—Chunar—Sultanpore.

There is a regular steam communication between Calcutta and Allahabad; but as the steamers proceed no further than that city, it may not be out of place to give the reader a few words on Steam Navigation, at least so far as the Ganges is concerned. Until steamers were introduced, the only way of proceeding by water from Calcutta to Allahabad, and the intermediate stations, was by boats, the largest of which are called budgerows and pinnaces. About twenty years ago, the East India Company ordered four steamers to be built for the navigation of the Ganges, much against the advice of many, who urged the impossibility of using steam in consequence of the shifting sands. They were accordingly built in England, and shipped in pieces to Calcutta, where they were put together by able engineers. For many years these government boats were the only steamers seen on the Ganges; but latterly two Companies have been started, the one called "the India General Steam Navigation Company," established in 1844, and the other, "the Ganges Company." The control of the government steamers is under the judicious management of Captain J.H. Johnston, R.N. The number of boats on the Ganges belonging to government alone, is as follows:—ten steamers, three accommodation, three cargo, and two troop-boats. On an average, one steamer leaves Calcutta every ten or fourteen days, having an accommodation-boat, or sometimes one or two cargo or troop-boats, in tow. This is a striking and novel sight. Every one is aware that a ship at sea will take another in tow, which is effected by the ship to be towed sending out hawsers; but in very bad weather they disengage themselves by casting off the towing-hawsers. Besides these hawsers for joining one with the other, there is a plank of wood, twenty-five feet in length, a foot in width, and six inches in thickness, placed between two short masts, one at the bow of the accommodation, cargo or troop-boat, the other at the stern of the steamer, to each of which it is bound by chains. This plank serves as a mutual convenience to the crews of the two vessels, without its being requisite to lower a boat; besides, if it were not for this more solid material, accidents would frequently happen by the vessel in tow running foul of her leader; whereas, as it is, should the steamer touch ground unexpectedly, the other sheers quietly alongside.

The steamers are of iron, and (I am now speaking only of those belonging to government) are fitted up with two engines of thirty horse power each, and carry sail. The fires are never wholly extinguished, for although the steamers anchor at sunset, yet they are again under steam at the first dawn of day. The fares and prices of the two Companies correspond exactly with those of the government; the charges for the whole trip from Calcutta to Allahabad, being for a first-class cabin, 300 rupees, for a second, 250, and for a third, 200. The charges for the downward passage are only two-thirds those of the upward.

The hours for meals are generally, breakfast at nine, luncheon twelve, dinner four, and tea seven. Anything required between meals, is charged extra. For supplying these, each passenger pays the Commander three rupees per diem. Wines, spirits, etc., are extra, and charged for according to the consumption.

The boats of the two private Companies are differently constructed from those of the Government; for, like the steamers on the American rivers, the steam and accommodation centre in one boat, but some of them, have one or two cargo-boats in tow. The Ganges boats, it is said, draw too much water. The Company's boats draw three feet, and their steamers three-and-a-quarter feet each. Hindoo servants, who are forbidden by caste to cook on board, are landed every evening, if practicable, as soon as the steamer casts anchor. From the Mahomedan servants, one of whom is allowed to each passenger, without cost for the trip, the Commander receives a quarter of a rupee a-day, which each has to pay for his food.

A native pilot is taken on board every twenty or twenty-five miles; he is responsible in some measure, that the vessel does not touch the bottom, or run upon a sand-bank. The poor men, who receive only a scanty pittance for this trouble, are extremely careful; and it is very rare indeed, for any serious accident or interruption to occur. The steamers have a commander, a mate, and about twenty Lascars, or native sailors, and the other boats about the same number. The cabins are generally light and airy, though many of them abound with mosquitoes, cockroaches and ants, and not unfrequently with rats. The dining-room is spacious, being the whole width of the vessel, and would be very comfortable if a punkah could be introduced. The cabins contain no furniture save a bedstead, so that the traveller is required to furnish it with a mattress, table, chair, chillumchee or wash-stand, and mosquito curtains.

The river Ganges is called by the natives "Gunga Jee;" "Gung" signifies *river*, and "Gunga" *the* river; "Jee" denotes *sir, lord, master, mistress*, and is used as a mark of religious respect, the Ganges being pre-eminently the king of rivers—the sacred river. The Hindoos swear by the waters of the Ganges, as we do on the Testament, or the Mahomedans on the Koran. The Ganges has a very uncertain channel, in consequence of its tortuous course; sometimes dashing across from the right to the left bank, and forming a new bed. To obviate this, various clever plans have been proposed; but I shall now merely allude to that of Mr. Sims, Civil Engineer to the East India Company, who was sent out some time back, to select and survey the district which he should consider suitable for a railroad. The scheme fell into abeyance, but is once more revived. A Board was appointed in England, comprising a committee, secretary, engineer, etc.; two of the official staff arrived in Calcutta in February, 1848, for the purpose of collecting the unpaid capital, and the money is fast coming in. Meantime, the Government has desired Mr. Sims to propose a plan for controlling the freaks and sudden changes of this river, which is at the same time one of the most beneficial in the world. The task is a difficult one, and the expense enormous; however, the first sod has been since turned up, and this is some earnest of its completion.

I collect from the Report, that Mr. Sims proposes to form extensive shields at certain points of the banks. Just as in fencing, we guard right and left where the thrust is expected, so the shields are to be erected on the right and left, according as the river rushes in. Brunel used shields in making the Thames tunnel, but they were above, while Mr. Sims's shields are to be perpendicular to the river, and parallel to the banks. Wherever a shoal may be forming, Mr. Sims proposes to make a diversion by means of a channel, which is to be kept open by bamboos and other material, so as to prevent the sand from filling up the excavations. The expense of the operation is not clearly ascertained; but the cost of each shield is £60,000! Until we know how many of these shields are required, we can have no means of estimating the total outlay.

Major Rowland Hill, late 70th Regt. Bengal Native Infantry, and commanding 4th Irregular Cavalry, when at Sultanpore, Benares, tried the following plan, in 1846. Placing several large boats with their prows facing up the river, he cut through the sand-bank, upon which the force of the current drove away the sand to the right and left of the boats.

There are so many points along the Ganges which demand the attention of the engineer, that nothing short of a careful examination of every hundred yards, on both banks, can solve the problem. Thus, having formed a shield in one locality, who can say where the next may be required? or, again, whether the river driving with full force to a new point, the evil may not break out at another? The natives never thought of such schemes in days of yore. Being a sacred river, the Ganges could do no wrong: if a man lost his boat, it was his destiny (*nuseeb*): the will of God in anger for his sins! Æsop's fables have been translated by a Brahmin; and an Englishman having read, to a Hindoo, the fable of the waggoner's complaint to Jupiter, the man shook his head and laughed.

It would seem possible, that by carefully examining this river during the dry season, from October to April, the channels might be found out. In the Bhauguretty, and smaller Indian rivers, dredging machines are used. The practicability of the plan could be ascertained, and that, too, at no great cost, by buoying off the river, and placing it in sections; this could be done by a native establishment, with some Europeans as supervisors.

The steam-boats often run aground, although they have native pilots, and are frequently not got off for several days. Sometimes, when the river is low, steamers can only reach Sirsah, twenty-six miles below Allahabad.

I must remind the reader, that the first rise of the river is caused by the melting of the snows in the Himalaya mountains during the warm weather, before the rainy season sets in, and that the rains afterwards keep it up to the high-water mark, until the month of October. The fall of rain in Assam, south-east of Calcutta, has been 240 inches in a year. At Bombay, up to the middle of August, 1849, it was eighty-six or eighty-seven inches; which is about the same quantity that falls in Calcutta during the whole of the rainy season.

I must not omit to mention, that some years since, an attempt was made to get a steamer up to Ghurrumkteesur Ghât, on the Ganges, about thirty miles from Meerut. But it proved a failure, for the Ganges from Allahabad to Cawnpore is shoaly, and above the latter place more so than below it, in addition to which hinderance, there was not a sufficient depth of water. By dint of great exertions, Captain Templeton did get the steamer up to Cawnpore; but he first took the precaution to unlade it. The steamers carry freight, as well as the cargo-boats; they are also more capable of enduring bad weather, yet during the rains of 1849, a gale blew so violently that the steamer turned aside, nearly to her opposite gunwale. In the month of August, the river is so rapid opposite Dinapore, that the steamers lose ground, or fall below their starting-point, even in crossing from one side of the river to the other. They go down the river at the rate of twelve or fourteen miles an hour.

There are many rivers that fall into the Ganges below Allahabad. The Ganges, I may remark, rises at Gangoutrie, in the Himalayas, that enormous chain of snow-capped mountains, which extends from Cabool along the north of Hindoostan to China. It flows for more than 1,200 miles through rich fields to the Bay of Bengal, which it enters by a delta of about sixteen miles in extent. In its course, it receives eleven tributary streams, none of which is smaller than the Thames. Below Allahabad, there are on the left bank, the Goomtee, Birnah, Koosee, Dewah, or Gograh, and the Great and Little Gundruk. On the right, at and below Allahabad, the rivers Jumna and Sone, all of which, except the latter, which rises near to the Nerbudda in the Deccan, flow from the Himalaya mountains. As there is no large stream which falls into the Ganges above Allahabad, it will easily be understood, that its greatest width and depth must be below that place.

The next attempt was to steam up the Jumna, but meeting with a shoal at Kulna, the steamer could proceed no further. The rocks which formerly existed in this river, were blasted by the late Lieutenant-Colonel Joseph Taylor, of the Engineers.

The question naturally arises, why the same remedy could not be applied as at Gottenburg, in Sweden, where rapids have been passed by making a canal outside; and why, in India, canals are never resorted to for out-flanking an impediment in a river? This, however, is an enquiry to which no satisfactory reply has ever yet been given.

The Nerbudda[97] offers similar difficulties, having rocks and rapids interspersed at intervals, in quick succession. It has a course of 750 miles, rising at Omercote, and emptying itself below Baroda into the sea. Attempts have been made to navigate the Nerbudda, from the centre downwards, where there are no rocks.

Having referred to Gottenburg, I will quote a passage from the Travels of the late Bishop James, of Calcutta[98]:—

---

[97] "Narmada," Sanscrit, "rendering soft," Colebrooke, Wilks, etc.

[98] See Appendix XXI.

"For the purpose of avoiding the falls or cataracts that for many ages obstructed the communications of the country, a navigable canal had been excavated in the solid rock of granite, which being near two English miles in length, and carried to a depth, in one part, of 150 feet, was a scheme that few minds would have originated, and still fewer even have ventured to put into execution. The great undertaking was completed, after six years' labour, in the year 1830; and it already pays, as we were informed, an interest of 42,000 rix-dollars per annum, upon a capital of 358,988 rix-dollars, originally expended: a return amounting to nearly 12 per cent., and sufficient to afford the most unequivocal testimony both of its success and of its great public utility."

This stupendous work was undertaken by a private Company unaided by the Government. It was necessary to float the timber down the river in order to save the great expense of land carriage. It is true that in the American rivers they contrive to stop the boats short of the rapids, unlade, and then re-ship the goods; but the Swedish plan is preferable. As a commercial speculation, where, the interest of money as in Sweden is two and two and-a-half per cent., it was a great result. The river Jumna abounds in shoals at certain places, but small canals overcome such impediments; for instance, near Kulna. As the railroad will, probably, not reach that portion of India for many years to come, the Jumna would transport goods thither. The course is estimated at 780 miles. It is fordable at times at Agra, and I believe also at Delhi. It is time, however, that I should resume my narrative.

At noon on the 20th of May, 1846, my servants with the baggage left Berrill's Hotel in a boat for the steamer "Megna," at Sirsah, the water being too low to permit the steamer to proceed higher, than within twenty-six miles of Allahabad, which, as I have before observed, is frequently the case. I left the hotel about 3 P.M., in company with the Commander of the "Soorma," accommodation boat, and reached that vessel in tow of the "Megna," about 9 P.M., at Sirsah. Before leaving the hotel I paid the Commander of the "Soorma" 217 rupees, 10 annas, *i.e.* 166 rupees, 10 annas, for a cabin to Calcutta; and 51 rupees for seventeen days' messing; being 3 rupees per diem, exclusive of wines, beer, and other extras: or £21 15*s*.

On the 23rd, at about 3 P.M., we anchored off Mirzapore, nearly ninety miles from Allahabad. It is one of the largest inland trading towns in Hindoostan, and the great mart for cotton. It is noted for its manufacture of carpets, somewhat resembling those of Turkey, and used all over India. I bought a very handsome bedside carpet, entirely made of wool, and as soft as velvet, for only six shillings. Silk is imported into Mirzapore from Bengal, and despatched to the west of India for sale, particularly among the Maharattas, and the central parts of Hindoostan. There are also fabrics of cotton manufacture, plantations of indigo, etc.

The town has many handsome European houses and native dwellings, with clusters of Hindoo temples, crowding the right bank of the Ganges, on which it stands. The appearance from the river is very imposing. Close to the main ghât stand two temples, the top of one of which is most elaborately and beautifully carved. On the other side of the river, which is here not very broad, stands the elegant residence of the Rajah of Benares.

As the steamers stop here to take in coal, as well as to land and receive passengers and goods, I took a stroll on shore. A traveller intending to visit Bombay and the west of India, should take the steamer as far as Mirzapore; this is better than going to Allahabad, which lies too far north; besides which, the navigation is not so pleasant, in consequence, as I have before observed of the shoaly state of the river between Mirzapore and Allahabad.

Mirzapore may be termed central between Allahabad and Benares, the distance from the former, by land, being forty-four miles, and from the latter, thirty-three miles, but situated on the left bank of the Ganges. There are six civilians at this station, and, at the time of which I am writing, a wing of the Shekawattee Battalion—an irregular Infantry corps—was quartered here and at Juanpore, on the opposite side of the river. The Church Missionary Society have a church and chapel here. A beautiful and magnificent Chowk, or Square, was in course of construction; and on my return, in September, 1849, when proceeding up the river, in the India General Steam Navigation Company's steamer, "General Macleod," I had the pleasure of seeing it completely finished. On this latter occasion, I again visited this bustling and thriving place, in company with my friend and fellow-countyman, Lord Frederick Montagu, at this time an officer in the 24th Foot. And here I may be permitted to render a tribute of thanks to Mr. Lord, a resident of Mirzapore, for the sumptuous hospitality with which he received his lordship and myself, both of us having been entire strangers to him previously.

The country around is pretty, and the officers' bungalows are most pleasantly situated on the bank of the river, in the midst of large compounds, or gardens, which are not exuberant with vegetation. The population of Mirzapore is between 70,000 and 80,000, the people are particularly industrious and active, and have great commercial enterprise. On leaving Mirzapore, on Sunday, the 24th, we mustered six in number, at the cuddy table, namely, Mrs. Lushington, Mr. T.A. Lushington, civil service, since deceased, Mrs. Swayne, widow of Major Swayne, killed during the rebellion at Cabool, in 1842, Captain G.R. Siddons, 1st Bengal Light Cavalry, Mr. W.R. Baillie, of the Bengal Secretariat, and myself.

On the 24th of May, at eight o'clock in the evening, we anchored off Benares, forty-nine miles from Mirzapore, having passed Chunar at about two o'clock. Chunar was acquired by the East India Company in 1775, along with the Zumindary of Benares. The fort is erected on a freestone rock several hundred feet in height, and is built of red Chunar-stone (limestone), and fortified after the Indian manner, with walls and towers. It is of considerable strength, and lies on the right bank of the Ganges, which runs close under the very walls and bastions of the fort, thus rendering it secure against the attacks of any native army. On the left, or opposite bank, the water is not very deep. The troops in the garrison are two Companies of European Artillery Invalids, and two of European Infantry Invalids, one European Veteran Company, and a detachment of the Shekawattee Battalion. It also contains a military magazine, which supplies Benares and the other adjacent stations with ammunition, arms, stores, etc. It was formerly used as a kind of state prison, and amongst the names of the compulsory inmates were Trimbuckjee Danglia, a fearful murderer, and the treacherous minister of the ex-Peishwah; and also Hadjee

Khan Kakur, who was instrumental in Dost Mahomed's escape, soon after the fall of Ghuznee and Cabool.

There is much treachery in the character of some of the high Hindoos; but the most infamous scheme to destroy an adversary was executed by Sevajee, the founder of the Maharatta Empire. He invited a certain Nawab, under the pretext that he had some urgent and friendly business with him, and requested him to give him a meeting unaccompanied by his suite, or any other person, stipulating that he himself would also be unattended. The Nawab agreed to the proposition. He arrived at the place of rendezvous, at the time appointed. He came unattended, and saw no person but Sevajee, who immediately went up and embraced him with the ardour of a friend; but he had iron claws about his arms. He clasped the Nawab and held him so tight that he could not resist, and then drawing his dagger, stabbed him to the heart. But Sevajee himself did not long go unpunished, for soon after he was seized by the emperor of Delhi and thrown into prison. Cunning and crafty, he determined on a plan of escape. He pretended to become very charitable, and daily gave away large baskets filled with food and sweetmeats. At length he bribed a man to personate him, and having made him lie down in his bed, he crept into one of the baskets, which was accordingly lowered from the window; thus he effected his escape from Delhi, and reached the Deccan or South of India in safety.

The cantonments for invalids at Chunar, are situated outside the fort. The houses are all built of stone, and are generally two stories high; the residence belonging to the stone-cutter, which stands near the crowded cemetry, is a handsome structure. This last resting-place for the dead, is situated on the slope of the hill, which is crowned by the fort; the white monuments contrasting forcibly with the red stone fortress. The Major-General commanding the Division used to reside in the fort, up to the early part of this century, and in 1807, the chaplain, the Rev. Daniel Corrie, afterwards Archdeacon of Calcutta, and lately Bishop of Madras, lived here. There is now a resident chaplain, and some missionaries.

The fortress, as I observed above, fell into the power of the English, in 1775. They had been repulsed in an attempt to assault it by night, but it surrendered shortly after, without a siege. It was formerly a place of great importance, but Allahabad being more north, has superseded it as a military depôt.

In the hills near Chunar, which run parallel to the right bank of the Ganges, and are clothed with heath and brushwood, are to be found some of the largest snakes in India; many of them, it is said, being eighteen feet in length and half the thickness of a man's thigh, but they are not venomous like the cobra de capella, and the short, thin, green snake. The difference between the bite of the snake and the sting of a scorpion, is contained in the following Oriental distich:—

"He that's bitten by a serpent sleeps:
But he that's bitten by a scorpion weeps."

Sultanpore, about four miles from Chunar, is prettily situated; a regiment of Native Cavalry was formerly stationed here.

CHAPTER XIV.

Benares—Bathing in the Ganges—Water-carrying by Women—Extent and Population of Benares—Attempted Tax—Mosque of Aurungzebe—Observatory of Rajah Jey Singh—Bazaars—Jewellery—Cultivation of Sugar—Secrole—Murder of Mr. Cherry—State Prisoners—The Maharannee of Lahore.

We anchored off the ancient and sacred city of Benares, at eight o'clock in the evening. The Sanscrit name of the district of Benares is Varanase, from "Vara" and "Nashi" ("two streams"); it is in the Province of Allahabad, and was ceded to the East India Company by Asophud-Dowlah, the Nawab of Oude, in 1775. Its national appellation was "Kasi," or "the Splendid." It is built upon the left bank of the Ganges, along which it stretches in a semi-circle for six or seven miles. On the outer side of the curve, which is the most elevated, stands the holy city of Benares. Generally speaking, the banks of every river are higher on the side where its course is convex, and they are always high alternately, if the river has a winding course, high on the convex side, and low on the concave of the curve which it forms.

It is customary with the natives to build on rising spots of ground, because such localities are more healthy, and can be easily drained.

Benares is seen to great advantage from Ramnuggur, on the opposite bank of the Ganges. Its appearance is strikingly grand and picturesque; the ground is covered with buildings even to the water's edge, and some of the ghâts, which are constructed of large blocks of red chunar-stone, have a flight of thirty or forty steps leading down to the river. Here a most animated scene generally presents itself. Men and women, boys and girls, may be seen bathing early in the morning, and evening, and, during the cold season, also in the middle of the day; for the cold does not deter even the gentler sex from adventuring into the river. Hither, too, resort the girls and young women of Benares, to fetch water from the sacred stream. Their figures are elegant and their stature erect. They all carry two or three water-pots on their heads, each successive pot being smaller than the one beneath it. Having dipped them into the stream, and filled them with water, they replace them upon their heads, and return homewards. This habit of carrying their gharahs, or jars, filled with water, from their early youth, may account, in a great measure, for their graceful carriage. They balance their pitchers so equally as not even to require any assistance from the hand. The sight of these women, with their water-pots, powerfully recalls to mind passages in Holy Writ;[99] and many of them refer to periods of so ancient a date, that we cannot avoid coming to the conclusion

[99] See Appendix XXII.

that the Hindoos are a people of great antiquity.

As I ascended into the city, I found the streets so exceedingly narrow that it was difficult to penetrate them, even on horseback. The houses are crowded close to each other, with turrets rising from their terraced roofs. They are built of stone, and some of them are six stories high. The windows are always extremely small, to keep the apartments cool, as the natives suppose, as well as to prevent their neighbours from looking in, for the opposite sides of the street approach very closely to each other, and, in some places, are united by galleries. The natives in eastern countries generally sleep on their flat roofs, in the verandah, or even in front of their dwellings. Here, again, the Bible illustrates the practice of sleeping on the roofs.

According to an old Brahminical legend, Benares was originally built of fine gold; but, owing to the depravity of its inhabitants, the gold was converted into stone; and as they degenerated more and more, the houses were transformed into brick and mud.

The number of stone and brick houses, from one to six stories high, was estimated in the year 1815 to be upwards of 12,000, and the mud houses above 16,000. I find by Shakespear's version of the Statistics of the North-Western Provinces[100] that the Hindoos of the city of Benares amounted to 147,082 persons, and the Mahomedans to 36,409, making a total of 183,491, giving 34,621 inhabitants to a square mile, which is the largest amount of population of any city.

Benares, as I have already observed, is a very crowded city. In speaking of Kanoge, I stated that, according to Mr. Maurice,[101] it was supposed to have been a hundred miles in circumference, with a population of 2,500,000 or 3,000,000. Taking the former number to be correct, there would have been 4,000 souls to every square mile. A country is considered to be well peopled which has 100 inhabitants to every square mile. Certainly, neither London, nor any city in Europe, can have an amount of population equal to one-fourth of Benares. The late Mr. James Prinsep took the census, between the years 1824 and 1827, and it is not called in question now. Recollecting, also, that there are many six-storied houses, not only along the banks, but rising in tiers, closely behind one another, with only a few feet space between them, the European traveller will not be so much surprised at the immense mass of habitations thus congregated together. In 1815, Benares was computed to contain 8,000 houses, occupied by the families of the Brahmins, who receive charitable contributions, and subsist chiefly on the daily offerings of the wealthy inhabitants and pilgrims, although many of them possess private property of their own.

In 1803, the supposed population of the city and suburbs of Benares amounted to 582,000, exclusive of the attendants of the three Mogul princes, who were reported to be 3,000, making an aggregate of 585,000 souls. At that time the Mahomedans were considered to be one to every ten Hindoos. The above return gives 36,409 Mahomedans to 147,082 Hindoos, or a total of 183,491 in the city of Benares, making the Hindoos to exceed the Mahomedans in the ratio of about four to one.

[100] 1848, p. 155, table xxx.

[101] Indian Antiquities, p. 36.

Mr. Prinsep took a census in 1824, and gave the returns at 181,482. It is probably now 200,000. Mr. Prinsep's census gives six as the average number of inhabitants to a chowk (yard or court), whether in the city or in the rural outskirts, seven to a pucka (brick) house, and four and a half to a kucha (mud) house.

In the year 1809, the Government resolved to impose a tax on all the houses in the city; upon which thousands of Brahmins and other inhabitants quitted it, and great excitement and uproar prevailed. A serious riot would inevitably have taken place, had not Mr. W.W. Bird, the late Deputy Governor of Bengal, an able and excellent officer, hurried to the spot and promptly quelled the disturbance. The inhabitants hereupon petitioned the Government; and vowed that if the tax were persisted in, they would represent the matter at Calcutta. The authorities, who had not displayed much judgment in the imposition of the tax, had the good sense at once to abolish the obnoxious impost; but in consequence of the *émeute,* the Government considered it prudent to have a European corps at hand, in the event of any future disturbance; and a royal regiment was accordingly stationed at Ghazepore.

Notwithstanding its dense, close, and crooked streets, taken as a whole, there are few cities that can carry off the palm from Benares, with its gilded pagodas, its temples, and its mosques, their slender minarets, rising in majestic grace amid countless domes and cupolas, all standing out in bold relief, among the varied forms and foliage of groves of mangoes, tamarinds, and plantains, the sombre cypress, and the beauteous palm, beneath the deep blue canopy of heaven, and lighted up by the glorious effulgence of an Eastern sun.

The most celebrated of these mosques is that built by the Emperor Aurungzebe. In order to mortify the Hindoos, he destroyed their most renowned temple, that of Vishnu, and not only raised his mosque upon its site, but, as if to heighten the indignity, caused the materials of their sacred edifice to be used in the construction of this rival temple, which was to celebrate the triumph of the Koran over the laws of Menu. What a contrast to the liberal spirit evinced by Akbar, in the exercise of his power. That great emperor, at the solicitation of his Brahmin prime minister, rescinded a caput tax, which had been imposed upon all his Hindoo subjects. History and experience teach us by many a lesson, how much we lose by harshly opposing the prejudices of others; and how much we gain by the adoption of conciliatory measures—provided no principle be involved—but alas! how slow we all are to learn this important lesson.

This mosque rises in the centre of the noble range of temples, ghâts, and edifices, that run along the left bank of the sacred Ganges. As seen from the river, it presents a most striking appearance. It stands at an elevation of eighty feet above the level of the Ganges, while its graceful minarets, tapering as they rise, tower to a height of 147 feet from their foundation. It is the most conspicuous edifice in the city, being visible for many miles round. The precise date of its erection is not known, but as the emperor died in 1707, we may assign 150 years ago as the period.

I ascended one of the two lofty minarets which flank the principal cupola. It had lately been restored to its original state by the British government, under the able superintendence of Mr. James Prinsep, British Resident at Benares. This was a most critical undertaking; for the minars were more than a foot out of the perpendicular. I enjoyed an extensive and magnificent view of the city and adjacent country, which for ten miles round is held sacred by the Hindoos. Indeed so highly is it venerated, that pilgrims resort to it from all parts of India, and those who, from age, or other circumstances, are unable to perform the lengthened journey themselves, send willing proxies, to whom they pay considerable sums. Many come there to wash away their sins; and not a few to die within its hallowed precincts.

Looking down from this dizzy height, upon the almost miniature world below, such a strange sensation came over me, that I could well conceive the propensity of certain minds to precipitate themselves from a lofty elevation. Several melancholy instances of this kind are said to have occurred here; a few perhaps from impulse, others from despair, and some from mere foolhardiness, with a view of immortalizing their names. Among the last, I was told, was a Fakeer, or devotee, who, whether by accident or design, contrived his fall so cleverly that it was broken by his being caught midway by the matting of a roof, and he alighted almost unscathed upon the floor. The people of course considered this as a miracle; and the Fakeer would doubtless have been idolized by them, had not his cupidity exceeded his love of notoriety, and induced him to make his escape with sundry articles belonging to the good Samaritan who had poured oil and wine into his bruises.

The city of Benares has long been known as the ancient seat of Brahminical learning; and to this day it retains its fame. The arts and sciences still flourish; and the schools and colleges for the training of the priests are yet celebrated, while the laws of Menu continue to be expounded in Sanscrit. But with all his erudition and research, the learned Brahmin is sunk in the most abject ignorance; and with all his wisdom, he degrades the nobler faculties of his mind, by bowing down to worship the most disgusting of monster-idols. Here, as elsewhere in our Indian possessions, the germs of Christianity have been sown under the fostering care of various British Protestant Missionary Societies, especially of the Church Missionary Society. Benares already boasts of fifteen missionary schools, one of them being founded by a wealthy Hindoo. All these schools are more or less frequented by Hindoo children; and the public preaching of the Gospel has been the means of making many of the natives acquainted with the superiority of the Christian religion.

Next to the mosque of Aurungzebe, the most conspicuous object in the city is the celebrated observatory of Rajah Jey Singh, of Jeypore, so renowned as an astronomer. He was likewise the builder of the observatory at Delhi. Here, too, everything is in character with the mind of its great designer, the instruments, etc., being on a grand scale. It is built of large blocks of red sand-stone; and, from its elevated position, commands an extensive prospect over the river and the surrounding country.

Benares is so well known, that I shall not attempt to give any further description of its numerous interesting buildings, nor of the strange sights and scenes which greet you at every turn.

Benares formerly possessed a mint for the coinage of rupees. It was under the direction of the late Mr. James Prinsep, who was the last mint-master. This gentleman was the youngest brother of a family, whose eminent services and varied talents, have identified them with the history of India. Mr. James Prinsep was a good Sanscrit scholar, and deciphered the Sanscrit inscription upon the stone pillar in the fort of Allahabad, as I said before, and which had baffled all previous attempts. In short his was a mind to grasp all things. When the mint at Benares was broken up, Mr. Prinsep was appointed assay-master at Calcutta, and so highly was he esteemed, both as a public servant, and as the liberal patron of everything good and noble, that upon his early death, in 1840, his fellow-citizens erected a splendid landing-place to his memory, one of the first objects of interest which attracts the eye of the traveller on sailing up the Hoogly. It is called Prinsep's Ghât.

I cannot take leave of Benares without saying a word or two about its bazaars, which are most attractive, not only from possessing the usual display of an Oriental mart and rendezvous of the most varied ranks, tribes, and costumes, but also from the extreme beauty and costliness of the native manufactures. Foremost among these, are the jewellery, and the exquisite works in gold and silver. These are made of the pure metal; and though they may not have the same strength and brilliancy as the alloyed, they are more intrinsically valuable, and are held in greater esteem by the natives. Many of these works are elaborate and highly finished. I was particularly struck with the ingenuity and delicacy displayed in the manufacture of a vine leaf, serving the purpose of a tea-ladle; every portion of which was so finely and minutely cut, as to leave only the slender fibres. The value of the labour bestowed upon this little article, was at least a hundred and fifty per cent. upon the cost of the original material. The price of the silver might be four shillings, and the cost of the labour about six. Precious stones, and especially the diamonds from the mines of Bundelkund, form an extensive article in the trade in jewellery which is carried on here, and are much sought after. The beautiful muslins and Benares scarfs, of red and gold, are the admiration and envy both of native and European ladies. The bazaars, too, abound in vessels of various metals, especially copper; and in manufactures in peacocks' feathers, and ingenious toys gaily painted, the colours of which are very durable, and in no danger of being effaced.

The district of Benares is also famous for its growth and manufacture of sugar; indeed, about half the quantity of sugar imported from Calcutta is raised in this neighbourhood. Thus this sacred city presents attractions to those who admire it on account of its antiquity, or sanctity; the richness of its manufactures, or the lucrativeness of its commerce.

The Rajah of Benares has a palace at Ramnuggur, on the right bank of the Ganges, about four miles from the city. It has been the residence of the Rajahs ever since the flight of Cheyte Singh from the city, in 1781.

The cantonments which are situated at Secrole, about four miles from the river, contain the second company fifth battalion, with No. 4 Light Field-battery, and third company fifth battalion, Foot Artillery, 48th and 65th Regts. Native Infantry;

and 3rd Infantry Recruit depôt. The church is a very good one. There is likewise a large theatre, and a fine racket-court. The Society at Secrole is very agreeable; independently of the military, it is the station of five or six civilians, a chaplain, and eleven missionaries. The station is large and very healthy; many of the residences are well built, and surrounded by pleasant compounds and gardens; the best are those belonging to the civilians, which, being situated across the Birnah, are united to it by a bridge.

Benares is the scene of the treacherous murder of Mr. Cherry, the British Resident, and three other gentlemen, in January, 1799, which being well known, I will only briefly allude to. Upon the death of Asoph-ud-Dowlah, Nawab of Oude, in 1797, he was succeeded in the government by his illegitimate son, Mirza Ali; but being much disliked he was deposed, and his uncle, Saadut Ali, placed upon the throne. Mirza was at first permitted to reside at Benares; but as he was suspected of hatching a conspiracy, the Marquis Wellesley determined upon his removal, under strict surveillance, to Calcutta. Mirza Ali was exceedingly indignant at the proposed change, and remonstrated with the government. But as his application did not meet with a favourable reply, he waited upon the British Resident; his bearing and language were so intemperate, that the Resident admonished him to be more careful, which so exasperated Mirza, that he rushed upon Mr. Cherry sword in hand. This was a signal for his attendants to follow his example. They made a general rush, and cruelly murdered him upon the spot. This assassination was followed by that of three other Englishmen; the murderers then made a similar attempt upon Mr. Davis, the Judge; but he made a desperate resistance to save himself, and his family. Armed with a short spear, he stood at the top of the narrow winding staircase, on the roof of his house; like all circular stairs, it only admitted a single person at a time. The first man who came to the top was speared, and his dead body blocked up the passage, and impeded the attack of those behind him. Mr. Davis succeeded in warding off the blows, till the arrival of a body of Native Cavalry, upon which Mirza and his attendants took to flight. The regiment was at that time stationed at Sultanpore, seven miles distant. Saadut Ali, notwithstanding the danger to which the suspected conspiracy against his throne exposed him, was too imbecile to use any efforts in aiding the British to capture the assassins, who successfully eluded the vigilance of the government for some months. Mirza Ali even succeeded in collecting a considerable number of adventurers; but upon some offence they abandoned him, and he took refuge in the court of a petty Rajah, who, however, refused to harbour him, and delivered him up to the British government.

Amid the many strange vicissitudes of Indian history, it is by no means unusual to find deposed sovereigns, and other persons of rank, residing at Benares as state prisoners. Among these I would particularize Bajee Row, the late Peishwah, who, after many changes of fortune, surrendered to the English, in 1818. He agreed to abdicate the throne, and to abandon the Deccan, on condition of his retaining all his treasures, and receiving an annual pension from the British government of eight lakhs of rupees, or £80,000 sterling. I visited his palace, and found that the ex-Peishwah still retained some semblance of royalty, in the person of one or two

Sepoys, who were on duty at his gate. He died at Benares, in 1851.

In February 1836, the deposed Rajah of Coorg came to Benares. He had been attacked, in 1834, by a division of the Madras army, and his capital, Mercara, taken. In March 1840, his Highness the ex-Rajah of Sattarah was sent to Benares, on the plea of having attempted to tamper with the loyalty of the British Sepoys. He has since died. Therefore, though Benares is not "a refuge for the destitute," unless he be a high caste Brahmin, it may nevertheless be called the "Asylum of deposed Rajahs." Nor must I omit the name of the Maharannee, the mother of the ex-Maharajah Dhuleep Singh, of Lahore, who in 1848 was sent from the Punjaub to Benares, for causing a disaffection towards the British. After residing here for a short time, her Highness was conveyed to the more secure fort, as the officials thought, of Chunar, but from whence she effected her escape, early in 1849, in the disguise of one of her attendants, not being recognised by the sentries at the gates. She is supposed to have reached Nepaul; but how she was received by the Goorkhas—how she likes the country—where her Highness intends to live—and by what funds supported—must be left to the imagination of the reader. Certain it is, that the East India Government ought not to regret the absence of so expensive a pensioner. She exerted too powerful a control over the Maharajah, her son, to be allowed to remain at Lahore with impunity. Her Highness, like many clever women, is somewhat dangerous, particularly as being the mother of the King of Lahore. But there is now no King of Lahore. The revenues of the Punjaub belong to the East India Company, the territorial supremacy, however, is vested in the crown; the Company being only the Trustees.

The life and adventures of this Queen-mother would form a most extraordinary and amusing volume. So varied have been her vicissitudes, that, while her intrigues and romantic amours might be the subject of a novel, the history of the cruelties and murders which have marked her steps since the death of her husband, Runjeet Singh, would furnish matter for a tragedy.

CHAPTER XV.

Ghazepore—The Opium Trade—Marquis Cornwallis's Mausoleum—Sand-banks—Buxar—Cossim-Ali-Khan—Sir Hector Munro—Battle of Buxar—Nawab of Oude—Emperor of Delhi—Revelgunge—The Sonus—The Ganges and Jumna—The Indus—The Berhampooter—Arrian—Dr. Alexander Adam—Dinapore—Captain Strachan—Bankipore—H.M. 16th Lancers—Deegah—Grain Golah—Earl of Munster—Patna—Buildings of Patna—Population of Benares—Magistrates—E. I. Company's Charter—Products of Patna—Walter Reinhard—Snowy Mountains—Tirhoot—Juggernauth—Gyah Proper—Cave of Nugur-jenee—Sir Charles Wilkins—Futwa—Phoolbarea—Bar—Beggars.

On the 25th of May we left Benares for Ghazepore. After steaming rapidly along the low banks we came to Saidpore, which is distinguished for a temple crowded with sacred monkeys; and lower down, also on the left bank, passed Chochukpore, where there are two handsome temples.

At seven o'clock in the evening, we anchored off Ghazepore, the "Rose Garden of India." It is a large and populous city, celebrated for its fragrant rose-water, the cultivation of the poppy, and the manufacture of opium. The commercial agent and his deputy reside here. At this season of the year the people were employed in collecting the juice which exudes from the poppy; it is kept in vessels, and when dry and solid, is cut into cakes, a process which requires great care. The Bahar or Patna opium sells at a higher price than that of Benares; the value of each chest being about 300 rupees or £30 sterling. The opium trade is an important monopoly in the hands of the government. It meets with a ready sale in China, although by the laws of the Empire it is a contraband article, and its importation stringently prohibited. In the autumn of 1836 it was generally, and confidently believed that the opium trade was about to be legalized in China; and advices to that effect reached Calcutta prior to the commencement of the sales for the season of 1837. This caused much higher prices to be paid by the usual purchasers than formerly, indeed, much above the sum which the capitalists, both of China and Calcutta, considered prudent, even had the legalization been certain. To the great dismay of the merchants, it was afterwards ascertained that so far from authorizing, the Chinese government had determined to put a total stop to the importation of opium; meanwhile the stock in Calcutta had been accumulating. What was to be done? The above report had been circulated and credited, and the opium growers had got rid of their stock. The sales of 1837 were expected to yield 25,851,386 rupees;

but certain influential merchants represented that the higher prices could not be realized without great loss and distress. The mode of payment was a deposit, a certain sum in so many days, and the remainder in some given days after; but several buyers had not even paid their deposits. After considerable demur it was agreed that rather more than three lakhs should be taken off, so that the total sales only yielded 22,789,986 Company's rupees (or at the exchange of two shillings the rupee, £2,278,998) which was the largest sum ever known to be realized. Soon after this the war broke out in China, when the amount of sales decreased, both in the prices and in the number of chests; but in 1841 it again rose, even during the war.

Much has been mooted about the monopoly of the opium trade; but when it is recollected that the land revenue is only about two-thirds of the revenue of India, and that it is by the sole privilege of the sale of this article, and that of salt, aided by that of the abkarry, or sale of spirits, that the expenses of the country can be paid, we should pause before we judge too harshly. If the people of England denounce the opium trade, let them shut up their gin-palaces before they condemn the growth and sale of opium. The people in China drink shamshoo, which is even more deleterious. It is said that if the trade in opium were thrown open, there would be an unlimited quantity manufactured, which is prevented by its being in the hands of the Government. Opium is eaten by many of the natives of Hindoostan, both Mahomedans and Hindoos; and I may add, that lawyers and other professional men, nay, even ladies, indulge in it. In China they smoke it, and it is whispered that even the Emperor is addicted to it. Now, supposing the population of China to be 360,000,000 souls, of which 125,000,000 are male adults, there would not be above half an ounce yearly to each. In 1837-38, there were 17,244 chests exported from Calcutta; if to this we add the Malwa opium, of which 40,000 chests are now yearly sent to China, still only half an ounce would be the maximum of each person. Many, no doubt, commit excesses; but is not the same done in gin-palaces?

Most of the troops formerly stationed in the cantonments of Ghazepore have been withdrawn to Benares. In 1805, on the raising of the 7th and 8th Regiments of Light Cavalry, they were quartered in these cantonments; but when the disturbances broke out at Benares, in 1809, in consequence of the house-tax, a royal regiment of Infantry was stationed at Ghazepore, which is about forty miles from Benares; indeed, so late as the year 1838, the 44th Foot were located here, the cavalry lines having been converted into barracks for the Europeans. The East India Company have a branch stud at Ghazepore, for the breed of horses, the head-quarters being at Buxar, lower down the river.

There is a magnificent mausoleum erected to the memory of the late Marquis Cornwallis, K.G., who died here October 5th, 1805, whilst on a visit to the Upper Provinces, a few months after his second arrival in India. He had been Governor-General of India from the year 1786 to the end of 1792. In 1805, his Lordship returned in his original capacity of Governor-General and Commander-in-Chief, bent upon changing most of the measures adopted by his predecessor, the Marquis Wellesley, when his own plans were frustrated, by the mighty conqueror, Death, who shows us how futile and insignificant are the vastest designs of man.

L'homme propose, et Dieu dispose.

The mausoleum is a most costly building; and Bishop Heber laments that so much money should have been lavished upon such an unmeaning structure; indeed, he is very severe upon the subject, arguing that a church might have been erected at but a little more cost, with a monument to Lord Cornwallis placed within its walls.

The commander of our steamer having taken in three hundred maunds, or nearly eleven tons, of coal, we got under weigh at half-past six on the morning of the 26th of May. At two o'clock in the afternoon our progress was arrested by the boat sticking fast on a sand-bank. We remained in this awkward position till nine the following morning. During that day and the 27th we were constantly on and off sand-banks, making very little progress. About six hours after leaving Ghazepore we were off Buxar, one of the Government stud stations, having passed the palace of Cossim Ali Khan, once a fine building, as its ruins indicate, lying on the very verge of the village.

Buxar is a small town, in the province of Bahar, in the district of Shahabad, and is built on the south-east side of the Ganges. The fort of Buxar, though of inconsiderable size, commands the river; but no attention is now paid to keep it in repair.

On the 22nd of October, 1764, a celebrated victory was gained here by the British forces, under Major (afterwards General Sir Hector) Munro, over the united armies of Sujah-ud-Dowlah, of Oude, and Cossim Ali Khan, of Moorshedabad. Major Munro had no cavalry, but taking up a strong position with his right, close to the river, he allowed the enemy, who had crossed over to Buxar by a bridge of boats, from the Oude side of the river, to commence the attack. A native historian says, "It was not an army, but rather a nation." The battle was of short continuance; the allies were defeated; the power of the Nawab of Oude destroyed; and the Emperor thrown on the protection of the English.

The British army consisted of 856 Europeans, and 6,215 Sepoys, making a total of 7,071, of whom eighty-seven Europeans, and 712 Sepoys were killed and wounded. The combined troops were computed at 40,000, of whom 2,000 are supposed to have been slain in the battle. Their flight was so rapid, that hurrying to cross a small but deep river beyond Buxar, many were drowned, or slaughtered in the attempt. The plunder in the enemy's camp was very great, as they left their tents standing; and their whole train of artillery, consisting of 133 pieces of various sizes, fell into the hands of the English. Cossim made his escape to the Rohillas, and the Emperor of Delhi signed a treaty of peace, highly advantageous to the British government, which became henceforth supreme in Bengal.

The Fort now comprises a station for several detachments of European Artillery and Infantry Invalids; as also a portion of a Native Infantry corps. The superintendent of the stud department has his head-quarters on the other side of the river, at a village called Kurruntadhee; there are several hundred horses and colts in the stables here. At Ghazepore, as I have already remarked, there is a branch, and another at Poosah, at the junction of the little Gundruk with the Ganges, which was formerly the only stud in the central Provinces.

After passing Revelgunge, a very long town, extending for more than a mile along the left bank of the river, and at a distance of twenty-eight miles above Dinapore, we came to the spot where the river Sone flows into the Ganges, seventeen miles from Revelgunge.

The Sone river, called by the Greeks "Sonus," has, with the Nerbudda, its source in the table-land of Omerkuntuc (Omercote), in the Province of Gundwana, 22° 53′ N. Lat. and 82° 15′ E. Long. It rises on the east side, and flows through Pindarah, when, being joined by numerous other streams from the north-eastern side of this mountain domain, it proceeds in a northerly direction through Sohajepore and Bogulkund, whence, turning eastward, it pursues its course to the Ganges, which it joins in the Province of Bahar, after having performed a winding course of about 500 miles. Near its source, this river is said to be designated by the natives "the Sonabudda," to distinguish it from the Nerbudda, by which, conjointly with the Ganges, the southern point of Hindoostan is insulated.[102]

Under the head of Omerkuntuc, we find it styled "a celebrated place of Hindoo pilgrimage, in the Province of Gundwana." There is no peculiar sanctity attached to this river; the sanctity, such as it is, belongs to Omerkuntuc. In Hindoo mythology, Gunga, or the Ganges, is described as the eldest daughter of the great mountain, Himavata, and is called "Gunga," on account of her flowing through "Gung," the earth. In the Hindoo Pantheon, Himalaya is deified, and described as the father of the Ganges. The Jumna and the Ganges have their sources in the Himalaya mountains, at Jumnoutrie and Gangoutrie peaks; at no great distance from each other. The Jumna enters Hindoostan Proper, in the Province of Delhi, and proceeds south, nearly in a line with the Ganges, at a distance of from fifty to seventy miles apart from each other, until they gradually join at Allahabad. Its length, including its windings, may be estimated at 780 miles. The Ganges and the Jumna may be designated "Sister Rivers."

The Indus, too, takes its rise in the Himalayas, as do all the five rivers of the Punjaub, and likewise all the rivers that enter the Ganges on the left bank. The Berhampooter also rises in the same mountains, and after a course of several hundred miles, enters the Ganges near the sea. There are other rivers coming from the Himalayas; but they are, comparatively speaking, insignificant. The three greatest rivers are—

1. The Ganges, having a course of 1,500 miles.
2. The Indus, having a course of about 1,000 miles.
3. The Jumna, having a course of 780 miles.

It is believed that the Berhampooter was not known in the time of Arrian. To return, *en passant*, to the subject of Palibothra, Arrian says the Erannoboas was the *third* river of India, which will be the present Jumna. It has been shown that the length of the Sone is only 500 miles. I think that those learned gentlemen who advocate the Sone, as being the Erannoboas of the Greeks, are in error, first, because Arrian distinctly mentions the Erannoboas and the Sonus as two of the six rivers which flow into the Ganges. Now the Sone cannot be the Erannoboas by any

[102] Vide Major Rennel.

ingenuity whatever; for it is clearly called the Sonus. Secondly, it is said that the ancient name of Patna was Pataliputra, making an approach to the word Palibothra, which, however, proves nothing. Thirdly, it is more probable that the Jumna is the Erannoboas, because, having found the Sone to be the Sonus, we require the third river in India to meet the Ganges; whereas the Sone, not being so large as the Jumna, cannot be admitted even as the fourth river of Hindoostan; besides, we expect to find a sacred stream to represent such a river as the Erannoboas. Dr. Alexander Adam, in his "Summary of Ancient and Modern Geography," says, "The Sone (Sone-budda) joins the Ganges twenty-two miles above Patna." Patna is seven miles from Dinapore, and Dinapore is now five miles from the Sone; consequently, the Sone is about twelve miles from Patna, and not twenty-two. But to proceed—

On the 29th of May, we anchored off Dinapore, at five o'clock in the afternoon, having experienced rather stormy weather for the three preceding nights. Dinapore is a considerable town, on the right bank of the Ganges, and is situated in a kind of bay, formed by the river. The cantonments are large, and the area comprised by the barracks and lines of both Queen's and Company's troops, is unusually extensive and imposing. The European barracks face the river, upon the immediate bank of which are the wards or quarters for the officers, opposite to those of the men. At right angles with these two ranges, are two others, likewise for the officers, the four ranges forming a large oblong. Beyond these, higher up the river, and close adjoining, is a smaller oblong, formed of three ranges (one being the back of the large oblong), and the fourth range, the bungalows facing the river. The lines for the two corps of Native Infantry are on the left, looking from the river front. The main guard is on the right of the cantonments, near the town. There are also some bungalows for the officers, in rear of the right, and nigh to these is a bridge over a nullah.

Dinapore has long been a considerable cantonment, a large force having been stationed here in 1786. The extension of the British dominion northwards, gradually diminished the importance of this military station; and under the rule of the Marquis Wellesley, it was intended to do away with the whole of the cantonments, and to erect barracks on the other side of the river. In consequence of this resolve, all the buildings, those occupied by the Europeans, as well as those belonging to the natives, were put up for sale, and purchased at a very low price by an officer named Harriott. Government, however, soon after repented of the step it had taken, and was very anxious to cancel the bargain; but the fortunate purchaser demurred. At last, however, Mr. Harriott re-sold to the Company a part of the cantonments at a higher rate than what he had originally paid for the whole. The Government were forced to rent from him whatever further accommodation was needed; and to this day, a descendant of that gentleman receives a monthly rent of no less than 2,000 rupees, or £200 sterling, for the buildings now occupied by the troops. Besides this, a considerable sum is realized from the numerous merchants and others, who rent various buildings included in the first purchase. Thus Governments, like individuals, will sometimes make mistakes.

Dinapore is the head-quarters of a Division of the army, and is capable of being put into a tolerable state of defence. At present there are a light field-battery of Artillery, a royal regiment of Foot, and three corps of Native Infantry stationed here. The church is a very neat building, and stands in the centre of the large oblong. It contains a tablet to two officers of the 62nd Foot, who were unfortunately drowned in company with a great portion of the right wing of the regiment, in a storm which capsized their boats, near Bhaugulpore, on the 10th of July, 1842.

The 39th Foot being quartered here, I called upon Captain Strachan, of this fine corps, under whom I had acted as Adjutant, in 1844, to a detachment of recruits, consisting of my own corps (the 9th Lancers), the 3rd Buffs, 29th, 50th and 62nd Regiments of Foot.

Beyond the cantonments, and half way to Bankipore are many good houses, some of them being occupied by officers, and others by merchants. The view from the river is extremely pleasing, numerous budgerows, and boats of all descriptions, constantly ply up and down the river, and give great animation to the scene. Dinapore is one of the steam stations; and the vessels coming up and down, stop here to take in coals and wood.

Dinapore is also a place of some trade, and is celebrated for its leather, linen, light hats, and paintings. I bought an excellent pair of boots here, for a couple of rupees—quite equal to some I had purchased at Calcutta for eight.

Having taken in 800 maunds of coals (one maund is 80lbs.), and 200 maunds of wood, there having been a scarcity of the former, we started at five o'clock, on the morning of the 30th of May. During the day we passed H.M. 16th Lancers, in country boats, who had been seven days accomplishing what we had done in seven hours; the poor fellows made no hesitation in complaining of the miserable manner in which they were proceeding to Calcutta. It is a pity that the government should have subjected a set of gallant men, to such unnecessary inconvenience and discomfort, when so many steamers were at the time available for their transport. It is only in the hour of need that a soldier's services are duly appreciated, and thus with the 16th: no other Aliwal was in prospect, or perhaps they would have fared better, and many a brave soldier's life might have been spared from an inglorious death on the river.

At a short distance from Dinapore is Deegah, which with Bankipore, almost unites Patna and Dinapore. Bankipore is called a suburb of Patna; and, as the opium agent for Benares resides at Ghazepore, so the agent for the Bahar opium resides at Bankipore. Here is a great grain Golah, or circular stone building something like a bee-hive. It is black from age, and the effects of the climate. This novel and somewhat absurd building was erected by Governor Hastings. In the year 1770 a terrible famine raged in Bengal and Bahar, and carried off thousands. The Bengal government, in order to secure the inhabitants of Patna and its neighbourhood from starvation, in the event of another similar visitation, built this Golah, for the purpose of containing rice, which is grown very extensively at Patna. But, large as was the building, it was discovered that it would not hold a day's consumption for the people of the extensive Province in which it is situated. For, supposing that there were only two millions of souls, each would require 2lbs. per diem, or about

1,800 tons of grain for the whole population, which was far beyond the capacity of the building. The engineer too contrived to make the entrance door to open *inwards;* and at the top, an aperture surrounded by a parapet; hence it was self-evident that when this granary was filled, or even if the grain were raised but a few feet above the floor, the door could not be opened; besides which, there was also a further danger that the contents would ferment and explode the building. This first and last attempt to build on such vague calculations, cost between £12,000 and £15,000. It is now used as a store-house for arms, and other purposes.

Outside this Golah, are two winding staircases, one of which the late Earl of Munster ascended on horseback for a wager; another gentleman, a civilian, did more, for he rode down also. The walls at the bottom of the granary are enormously thick, namely, twenty-one feet, but they have given way.

There is a large range of buildings for the manufacture of opium; making it into cakes, and packing them in boxes. The latter is a very delicate process. Thus some of the opium of the year 1848 was deteriorated, because the agent had used fresh planks, of a bad description of wood, for the cases. The price of opium has fallen much of late. In the year 1820-21, the Bahar (Patna) opium sold for 4,303 sicca rupees, or 4,589 Company's rupees; and the Benares opium for 4,276 sicca rupees, or 4,531 Company's rupees per chest. But at that time the amount and value of sales was less, and of course the quantity also. When the market returned to its usual state, Bahar opium sold for 1,960 sicca rupees, and Benares for 1,860: but the sales produced more revenue. Before the above period, in 1819-20, the Bahar opium sold for only 2,463 sicca rupees, and Benares for 2,435. At the sales, the buyers paid a deposit of ten per cent.: thirty per cent. in ten days, and the remainder in one month.

Our next station was Patna, which almost joins Bankipore. It is a large city in the Province of Bahar, of which it is the capital, in Latitude 25° 37′ N., and Longitude 85° 15′ E. It is situated on the south side of the Ganges, which is here very deep, and in the rainy season sometimes five miles across.

Patna is a city of great antiquity, and is supposed by some to be the site of the ancient Palibothra. Among them are Rennel, Lord Valentia, Colebrooke and Tennant. By the modern Mahomedans, Patna is named Azimabad, which signifies "The Great City"; by the Hindoos it is called "Sri Nugur." The town of Patna is one continued street, running along the right bank of the river, to the length of four miles by one in breadth. It is surrounded by a fortified wall, in bad condition. The citadel is small, and is now used as a store-house. The contrast between the lofty houses of Benares and this city is very striking; here they are, generally speaking, only one or two stories in height. The residences of the Europeans, chiefly of the civil service, are built of brick, and are very handsome, and extend as far as Bankipore; but the rest of the dwellings are rather mean, and for the most part constructed of mud. There are likewise a few elegant mosques and temples. There was formerly a college of Jews here, and also a Roman Catholic College. The latter was of very early date, probably as remote as the fourth or fifth century; for it is stated in the Asiatic Researches, "That there was, in the fourth century a Christian College at Sirhind, near the Sutlej." From this College, missionaries were sent to the town of Bettiah, ninety miles NNW. of Patna.

The town is very prosperous and populous. Taking the population of the city of Benares at something above 183,000, Patna can scarcely have more than 130,000 souls. Among the inhabitants are several Nawabs and native noblemen, whose income is as low as from 1,000 to 500 rupees a month. Many of them have been thus reduced in their worldly circumstances, in consequence of the British having gained the ascendancy over the former Mahomedan governments. Poor nobility are, however, by no means confined to Patna or to any part of India, but may be found in Poland and Germany; nay, on the Continent generally, and even in favoured England.

There are two Nawabs at Bareilly and at Meerut, holding the offices of Sudder Ameens or magistrates, on salaries of from 700 to 1,000 rupees monthly; and in the Bengal Presidency, there are five Pundits, and several Baboos in the same position, besides forty-two Baboos, one Pundit, and several learned Mahomedans (Moolvees), who are deputy collectors. These are uncovenanted appointments, and are, in addition to the civil servants on the establishment. From the printed lists, it would appear that they are almost as numerous as the covenanted appointments, for there are no less than 402 of the former, and 476 of the latter. The uncovenanted appointments are divided as follows:—

	Europeans.	Mahom.	Hindoos.	Total.
The Deputy Magistrates are	67	6	8	81
Sudder Ameens	20	89	37	146
Deputy Collectors	61	45	69	175
	148	140	114	402

In the North-Western Provinces, the Mahomedans are less than one-sixth, or 3,747,022, out of a population of 23,199,668 souls, so that the Hindoos have not their share of the loaves and fishes. The Chairman of the East India Company animadverted upon this subject a few years since. The Hindoos are usually the most studious, and have often been employed in some of the most responsible and critical posts. Chundoo Lall, a Brahmin, was Prime Minister at the Court of Hyderabad, the Nizam's capital, for many years; and a Hindoo was Prime Minister to the Emperor Akbar. Possibly the Government of India may be desirous of conciliating the Mahomedans, who were for so many years the rulers of Hindoostan. The vacancies in the above appointments are most eagerly sought for; and innumerable are the expectants for preferment. This spirit of emulation has certainly improved the minds of the higher classes, who now study English and the Company's regulations to good purpose. In Calcutta a native has been a Commissioner in the Court of Requests for many years. The subject of the extension of the system of employing natives in high civil offices of responsibility, will very probably be discussed at the end of the East India Company's Charter in 1854; for the question is one of great importance, and immediately connected with the scheme of native education.

Patna is not a large manufacturing town; but there are many cotton and linen factories in the neighbourhood, where chintzes, and various kinds of cotton diaper and damask, are made. There are also manufactories of flannels, and a sort of canvas for sails and other purposes. Linen can be procured in the neighbourhood, and is sent to the metropolis. In fact, almost every article, whether Asiatic or European, may be purchased in the bazaars.

The finest saltpetre and opium are produced in the vicinity; and immense quantities of wheat, sugar, and indigo, are grown here. Provisions are very cheap in Bahar, for instance, gram, a kind of vetch for horses, used to sell at 100 seers, or 200 lbs. for a rupee; but from 1805 to a late period, one or more native cavalry corps have been stationed at Ghazepore, which has raised the market, and the same quantity now costs three rupees. The establishment of the stud, and its branches at Kurruntadhee, Ghazepore, and Buxar, has likewise had an influence upon the price of grain. The opium and saltpetre trade is here, as elsewhere, monopolized by the Government, and exported in immense quantities to Calcutta. But a very considerable trade in all other articles is carried on by merchants from every country. It has always been a place of much commercial importance; and, at a very early period, there were English, French, Dutch, and Danish factories. Patna is the first station at which the East India Company established a factory. This was in the year 1620.

We still see the remains of the old British factory, where the fearful massacre of two hundred prisoners was perpetrated, in 1763, by the German adventurer Summer, pronounced by the natives Somroo, but whose real name was Walter Reinhard, then in the service of Mir Cossim. Much as this atrocious event must be condemned, the English had themselves to blame in the first instance; for the soldiers, who had been stationed at the factory for its protection, scaled the walls of the town, wantonly attacked the inhabitants, and plundered their houses. The native garrison immediately turned out, and succeeded in taking the English soldiers prisoners of war. They were confined in the factory; but the Nawab Cossim, incensed at the various indignities which he had received from the British Government, commissioned Somroo to kill all his prisoners, two hundred in number. This charge the German executed with the greatest barbarity. The prisoners were just seated at dinner, in the hall of the factory, when the myrmidons of Somroo fired upon them from the doors and windows, and butchered them all in cold blood. In revenge for this atrocity, Major Adams stormed the city and captured it. Since that period, Patna has owned the British sway; and it is now the residence of the Provincial Court of Appeal and other civil establishments. A monument to the memory of these wretched victims was erected in the European burial ground, but without any inscription.

The road from Patna to Dinapore is excellent, and marked by mile-stones. The snowy mountains are visible on a clear evening, during the rainy season. I am told that the Himalayas, too, command the most extensive view of the plains during the same period of the year, when the rains prevent the dust from rising into the air.

Nearly opposite Patna, is the district of Tirhoot, famous for the cultivation of indigo and sugar-cane; but the latter suffers greatly from the destructive rats which abound there. Tirhoot is near the Nepaul frontier.

About fifty-five miles south of Patna, in Lat. 24° 49′ N., and Long. 85° 5′ E., in the Province of Bahar, lies the city of Gaya, or Gyah. This ancient city is one of the most holy places of Hindoo pilgrimage, being held by tradition to have been the residence of Buddha, the great prophet and legislator of the nations east of the Ganges; and it is usually termed "Buddha Gyah." The temple is of course had in great veneration. The following extract from an inscription on one of the stones, will shew the estimation in which it was held: "This place is renowned, and it is celebrated by the name of Bhood Gaya. The forefathers of him who shall perform the ceremony of the Sraddha at this place, shall obtain salvation. A crime of a hundred-fold shall undoubtedly be expiated from a sight thereof; of a thousand-fold from a touch thereof; and of a hundred thousand-fold from worshipping thereof." The frightful image of the idol is placed in the temple, and is open to the worship of all pilgrims. A vow of sanctity is often taken here by women, and especially by widows, not unlike the Roman Catholic vow of celibacy; for they shave their heads, and promise to renounce the world. The Bengal government was wont to derive a net annual revenue of £15,000, collected from the pilgrims, a sum even exceeding that gathered from the pilgrims at the famous Juggernauth, being levied at a fixed ratio according to the magnitude of the sins which the individual had come to expiate, and, therefore, of the ceremonies which he was to perform.

The town is divided into two parts, one of which, more holy than the other, is the residence of the Brahmins and their families, called "Gyah Proper"; the other inhabited by the merchants and tradesmen, is called "Sahibgunge." The town lies inland at some distance from the river.

About fourteen miles to the north of Gyah, is a hill, or rather rock, in which a remarkable cavern has been excavated, called "Nugur-jenee" ("Nugur" a town, and "Jenee" the Jains). Being unable to visit it, I will give the account of it as communicated to me by our Captain. The cave, it seems, is about two-thirds distant from the summit of the hill; and the entrance, which is about six feet and a half high, by two and a half wide, leads to a chamber of an oval form, having a vaulted roof: this room is forty-four feet in length, eighteen in breadth, and ten in height in the centre. The whole cavity is dug out of the solid granite rock; altogether the excavation extends full a hundred feet. It was probably made for the purposes of worship by the Buddhists, whose religion differs from that of the Brahmins, and who were subjected to great persecutions on account of their tenets. We know that this was the case with the early Christians, who, in consequence of the ruthless tyranny of their heathen oppressors, were compelled to take refuge in the caves of the earth. The cavern at Gyah has two inscriptions, which have been translated by the late Sir Charles Wilkins, and published in the first volume of the "Asiatic Researches." From these inscriptions, it would appear that it is a place of great antiquity, but no dates are given.

Passing Futwa, which lies near the confluence of the Pompon and the Ganges, and is noted for the manufacture of its table linen, and for the remains of an extensive saltpetre manufactory, we reached Phoolbarea, and sometime after the little town of Bar. The whole place swarms with beggars, many of whom afforded no little amusement to our passengers, by their anxiety to pick up the coppers, which they threw from the steamer to the water's edge.

CHAPTER XVI.

Monghyr—Wells of Seetacoond—The Fort of Monghyr—Storms on the Ganges—Cossim Ali Khan—Monghyr the Birmingham of India—Employment of Women—The Gaol—A Sacred Bathing-place—Bhaugulpore—Its Population—Hill Rangers—The Bheels—Mr. Cleveland—Lieut.-Colonel Tod—Colonel Francklin—Colgong—The Jungheera Rocks—The Fakeers—The Rajmahal Hills—Sickreegullee—Boatmen of the Ganges—Rajmahal—Ruins of Gour—The Bhauguretty—Soottee—The Sunderbunds—Bogwangola—Jungepore.

AFTER a very stormy night, we reached Monghyr, and at eight on the morning of the 31st of May, cast anchor before this once celebrated fortress. It is about fifty-seven miles from Bar, and 436 from Calcutta. Monghyr is a town in the Province of Bahar, beautifully situated on the south bank of the Ganges. It was formerly a place of great importance, and is still celebrated for the cultivation of grain, and the manufacture of opium. A large portion of the district around, is hilly and unproductive, but the cultivated lands are extremely fertile, and yield rich returns. Some fifty years ago, the government tried the plan of granting certain waste lands, to the invalid officers and native Sepoys, and the experiment has succeeded beyond all expectation, some of the reclaimed lands being the best in the place. In the immediate vicinity, and about a mile from the fort, are some famous wells; they are called by the natives, "Seetacoond," and are highly venerated by the Hindoos. Seetacoond is a common appellation for hot springs among them: Koond in Sanscrit means a spring, hence the meaning would be the "spring of Seeta," which Seeta was the wife of Ram. Only one of these wells, however, is really a hot spring, for in the second well, the water is cold, and in the third chalybeate. They are all situated about half-a-mile from the Ganges, twenty paces apart from each other, in a plain backed by hills, and in the midst of rocks. The hot spring is considerable, and the air-bubbles rise in great quantities, the temperature varying from 90° to 140°. The water is much used on voyages to Europe, or on the sea, on account of its extreme purity; indeed it is asserted that it keeps for ever without becoming putrid. The renowned goddess Seeta pledges herself for its eternal purity. It certainly is very good, and people going to England, viâ the Cape, would do well to provide themselves with a few dozen large bottles, and fill them at this spring, for the water on board a ship is often extremely bad.

The Fort of Monghyr is very large and situated on a rising ground. The fortifications were formerly quite in the Indian style, encompassed with a lofty wall flanked with towers and surrounded by a dry ditch, except on the river side. But the government found it too expensive to keep these fortifications in repair, and have suffered them to fall almost into complete decay; and at present, the fort alone would be able to stand a siege. The view from the fort is one of the finest in India. The river, in the rainy season, forms quite a large expanse of water, and the Ganges becomes a rapid stream. Sometimes the violence of the torrent is so impetuous, that it undermines the banks of the river and uproots the largest trees. During the hurricanes, which are frequent here at certain seasons, the Ganges assumes the appearance of the sea; and the water dashes over the boats with such violence, that the men are frequently washed overboard; numerous boats are capsized in an instant, and men and goods swept down the engulphing stream. These storms are always accompanied by thunder, lightning, and fierce winds, against which it is impossible to make head. There is a protruding rock here, which juts out boldly into the stream, and withstands the whole force of the water. This morning the river presented a melancholy spectacle, from the numerous wrecks of vessels which had perished during last night's storm.

From a brass plate that was discovered in the immediate vicinity of the fort, in 1781, it would seem to have been a place of importance before the Christian era, and to have been subject to the Hindoo kings of Bengal, who resided at Gour. There is, however, no mention made of Monghyr by the Mahomedan historians, till the beginning of the sixteenth century, when the kings of Bahar disputed its possession with the kings of Bengal. Cossim Ali Khan, whom the British raised to the throne of Moorshedabad, in supercession of Mir Jaffier, having previously created him Nawab, on dethroning Suraj-ud-Dowlah (ludicrously called Sir Roger Dowler), in 1757, after throwing off all allegiance to the British government, repaired to Monghyr to take up his residence there. He added considerably to the strength of the fortifications, and endeavoured to discipline the natives for its defence. But the English took it after a siege of nine days, and made it a military station. At the time that the government of Bengal raised Cossim Ali Khan to the throne, it recommended him to keep troops like the British Sepoys; to drill and arm them after the English fashion, and to make them wear red coats, in fact, entirely to doff the Oriental costume and training. Cossim took this advice, but turned the weapons against those who had placed them in his hands; and for several years he fought many battles against his quondam counsellors. Had Cossim Ali Khan's plan, to lay siege to Kathmandoo (Kath, *wood*, the wooden city), succeeded, the British would have been spared the trouble of the Nepaul war of 1814-16; but at that time, there was no shadow of coming events in that direction.

In 1766, a strong brigade of six battalions, and some artillery, used to be in quarters at Monghyr; in short, one-third of the Bengal army was stationed here, while at Patna and Allahabad there were other brigades. It is now a station only for invalids, being a very healthy spot. The Commandant occupies the old palace, the former residence of the Sultan Soojah. It is extremely handsome, and is surrounded by fine gardens, tanks and plantations. The houses of the staff-officers are also convenient.

Monghyr is the Birmingham of India, for the natives excel in the manufacture of guns, pistols and rifles; many of them marked with the names of Manton, Egg, and other celebrated gun-makers. I have seen one or two of them fired off, and perhaps safely with light charges. A sporting engineer belonging to our steamer, bought a Manton for £1 4*s*., and fired several times successively. These guns are very cleverly made; and a novice could not possibly detect that they had not been manufactured by those whose names they bear. Forks and knives, cork-screws, hammers, and other articles of hardware of very good descriptions, are also made here. Fans, table-mats, straw hats and bonnets, necklaces and bracelets, made of a wood resembling jet, etc.; everything in fact may be purchased, very good, and at reasonable cost. In our visit to the bazaars, indeed all over the place, we were beset by beggars, who are excessively numerous, and in the most piteous and abject condition. All the hard work, it seems, is done by the women. I am told that they work much better than the men, and get but badly paid. About twenty brought the fuel required for our steamer, and put it on board, while the men were looking idly on.

The consumption of coals daily, on board our steamer, averages 400 maunds; but when the current is strong, 500 maunds are expended. Three maunds of wood are only equal to one maund of coals.

I really felt quite mortified at seeing the gentler sex engaged in such masculine work; one of them especially looked quite incapable of undergoing the toil. It is the custom for the men to sit lounging at home, or roaming about begging alms of strangers, while the women work in the open air—a strange perversity of our nature, and one which tends to shew the barbarous state of these people; wherever heathenism or infidelity prevails, woman is degraded. Christianity alone, restores her to her proper sphere.

I visited the gaol, which is a large building, and contains, as one of the chained men informed me, "a hundred as good as himself." I likewise went to the burying-ground, which is crowded with monuments, but they cannot last long—a few more monsoons will assuredly destroy them. There is a chaplain at Monghyr and two missionaries, besides several civilians.

Monghyr is considered a sacred bathing-place; and during the season the throng is immense. There the pilgrims, men, women and children, meet to unite in the worship of the Ganges, by bathing in its hallowed stream, and by pouring out water as libations to the sun and moon, or to the spirits of their departed friends. Sir J. Chardin observed a similar custom in Mingrelia and Georgia, as also in other Eastern countries. He says: "The people, before sitting down to a feast, go out abroad, and with eyes turned up to heaven, pour out a cup of wine on the ground as a libation." This idolatrous practice we likewise find prevalent among the Jews, who, when reproved by Jeremiah, persisted in continuing, not only to burn incense to the queen of heaven, but to pour out their drink-offerings unto her.[103]

We had a fine view of the Kurruckpore hills; and at six o'clock the same day anchored off Bhaugulpore, having passed Sooltangunge, on the right bank of the river. There is an indigo factory and house at Sooltangunge, very prettily situated; the lofty rocks of Jehangeera, crowned with a Mahomedan tomb, are in a most

[103] Jer. xliv. 17.

singular position.

Bhaugulpore is a town in the Province of Bahar, situated about two miles from the main branch of the Ganges. A nullah runs past Bhaugulpore; it separates a strip of land from the Ganges, into which it afterwards flows. The Ganges is extremely broad here; and in the rainy season, when the waters are much swollen, is full eight miles across. It is pleasantly situated; and commands a distant view of Mount Mandar, an insulated conical hill, and noted place of Hindoo pilgrimage. There are two very peculiar round towers about a mile north-west of the town, which the Rajah of Jeynugur considers so holy, that he has erected a building to shelter his subjects who frequent them from the burning rays of the sun.

At the entrance of the town is a noble banyan tree, which Lord Valentia also mentions in his travels. This tree is found in most parts of India; but perhaps the largest are to be met with towards the South. Humboldt, in his Cosmos,[104] speaking of the banyan, or Indian fig-tree, says, "The Indian fig-tree, that takes root by its branches, and whose stem has a diameter of twenty-eight feet; and which, as Onesicritus remarked with much truth to nature, forms 'a leafy canopy, similar to a tent supported by numerous pillars.'"

The population of Bhaugulpore is a mixture of Mahomedans and Hindoos. The majority are Mahomedans, who had a college, which existed in 1815, though in a state of great decay.

I must remark that many cities in India, such as Delhi, Benares, Allahabad, and Bhaugulpore, exhibit a mixture of Hindoo and Mahomedan buildings. The former, as having been the seat of the Hindoo and Mahomedan governments, is easily accounted for. At Benares, as I stated, the Mussulman emperor erected the mosque, to insult its inhabitants, who were Hindoos. In the cases of Allahabad, Bhaugulpore, and other cities, we must refer the fact to different circumstances.

At Bhaugulpore there is a corps called the "Hill-rangers": it was raised in 1792, and is composed of men who reside in the hills near the District, and sends detachments to Monghyr, Purneah, Bootan frontier, and to Titalyah. Mr. Cleveland, of the Bengal Civil Service, who died in 1784, early recognised the fact, that the wild hill tribes could only be kept in subjection by a system of strict justice and moderation. He went among them, and brought over their chiefs to a sense of the necessity of promoting peace among their people. In order to create a feeling of unanimity, and to put a stop to the quarrels in which they were continually embroiled with the Lowlanders, he disciplined a party of these men, who were subsequently formed into a corps, denominated the Paharees, or "Hill-rangers." In their mountain homes, these men are not far removed from the savage; they live by the chase, and never go unarmed. They are extremely hospitable and honest, and are remarkable for their probity, as servants. With this naturally good foundation, it will readily be conceived that they make good soldiers. They are kept in a state of admirable discipline; and in place of devastating the country, and plundering their neighbours, they now protect the district from the marauders, and both person and property are secure. The character of these tribes bears a close resemblance

[104] Vol. ii. p. 524.

to that of the Bheels and Nairs, the latter being peculiar to the Madras Presidency.

The Bheels are considered to be the Aborigines of central India; a bold, daring set of banditti, possessing nevertheless, many virtues. Truth, honesty, and fidelity are their distinguishing features. They are born warriors and despise the tillers of the soil. In 1817, Lieut.-Colonel James Tod offered some of these Bheels four rupees, or eight shillings, a month, if they would cultivate the soil; but they indignantly refused, "because their forefathers had never done so before them." In 1840, two Bheel corps were formed; one at Malwa, and the other at Mewar. The Bheels are a decidedly distinct race, and are divided into numerous tribes: they are Hindoos by religion, but some few of them have become followers of the prophet. They have been deprived of the fairest portions of their land by the Rajahs, and are now confined to the uncultivated tracts of their mountains.

Thus Mr. Cleveland's laudable efforts have been more successful than might have been expected, and the people in the neighbourhood of Bhaugulpore, instead of being in a state of continual strife, are now living very peaceably. Mr. Cleveland's former residence, a large handsome building, is situated immediately on the banks of the Ganges, and a monument to his memory has been erected in the burial-ground. There are several other very good houses, this being a civil station. A Branch of the Agricultural and Horticultural Society has been flourishing for the last ten years, and the Botanical Gardens are worth visiting. There is a resident chaplain who divides his duties between this place and Monghyr. I may remark, by the way, that all the chaplains are military; and, as in the Navy, are entitled to prize money in war time.

The late Colonel Francklin endeavoured to make Bhaugulpore the site of the ancient Palibothra, because he supposed the Chundun to be the Erannoboas of the Greeks. This subject has, however, been so fully discussed, that it is to be hoped that the mind of the reader has been duly impressed with the conviction that Allahabad is the veritable site, as being the spot where the junction of those two mighty rivers, the Ganges and the Jumna, occurs.

Bhaugulpore is noted for its silk manufacture, particularly for a very light material much used in dishabille, as well as for screens, punkahs, etc. The trade has latterly been much promoted by the facility of exportation by the Calcutta steamers, for this is one of the Company's stations.

On the 1st of June, we started at daybreak, and arrived at Colgong at half-past-seven A.M., having passed three singular and romantic looking rocks, rising to a height of about sixty feet from the bed of the river, and covered with verdure, among which some fanatics have built a few sheds.

We left Colgong at eight, A.M. on the same day. Seven miles below Colgong, the river takes a singular turn, round a hill covered with wood, and where some rocks, with carvings of Hindoo deities, jut out boldly into the stream. These rocks are very dangerous, because in descending the river, you must hug the right bank, so as to keep them on your left hand, for just below the rocks, which rise in the middle of the river, there is a strong back-water. The captain's object is to prevent his boat from getting into this back-water, and thus being carried and lost upon, these rocks. There is moreover a kind of whirlpool near the spot, so that we may call it the "Scylla and Charybdis" of the Ganges. Boats ascending the river keep to the left, where the stream is not rapid; but in descending, the boatmen, in order to meet and overcome this back-water, must pull very hard, and for a sixteen-oared boat at least twelve or fourteen of the crew must row. The back-water is probably caused by the tendency of the water to run to the rocks, in consequence of the turn in the river to the right, the rocks being on the left.

The Jungheera rocks, lower down the river, are very picturesque. A Fakeer resides in a small dwelling, on one of these rocks. The natives furnish him with food; but he sometimes makes an excursion on shore, and supplies himself. The Fakeer pleasantly sleeps in the midst of the howling storm, none the worse for the wind and rain; neither has he any fear of being blown out of his cabin, or of his house being washed down the stream; a few monkeys keep him company, and possibly some fairy queen may visit this presiding deity of the stream, and soothe, what to a stranger, would appear a wretched existence.

Just before passing Peerpointee, on the right bank, the river Koosee flows into the Ganges, and above Sickreegullee, or the dangerous pass, so called from the difficulty I have named, which the steamers and boats have in rounding it, we reached the place where the Teryagullee hills end, and those of Rajmahal commence. They are crowded with fine forest trees, shrubs, and other verdure, most pleasing for the eye to rest upon, after the tameness of the first part of our voyage. The hills abound in game; and the sportsman would be rewarded with a variety not frequently met with.

The Rajmahal hills, are intersected by a line which runs as far south as Balasore, traversing the districts of Nagore and Bishunpore, and the mountain chain between Kimore and the Ganges. Extensive coal-beds have recently been discovered along this line of demarcation, and have greatly enhanced the value and importance of the whole district. This mountain-chain is broken by numerous valleys, defiles, and wide-spreading plains, many of which are very fertile, and well cultivated, especially those which lie at the base of the mountains. The highest part of these ridges may be estimated at 4,000 feet, and some of the plains run along at an elevation of more than 2,000 feet above the level of the Ganges.

This chain is for the most part covered with lofty timber trees, and various kinds of woods, which are much used by the natives in building and in cabinet manufactures. These hills are clothed from the base to the summit, and the trees grow in tiers or terraces, down into the plain of the Ganges. In the northern rear of this chain, run the Rajmahal hills, which are divided from the Kimore range by the narrow valley of the Sone. The mountain-chain runs so close to the Ganges, between Bhaugulpore and the Rajmahal hills, as scarcely to admit of a causeway along the banks of the river. The government has wisely met this difficulty, by constructing a good road between Rajmahal and Colgong, which crosses the narrow defile of Sickreegullee.

We anchored off Rajmahal at a quarter to six in the evening of the 1st of June; and having to take in coal, we waited for the night. As usual, whenever an opportunity occurred, I hastened on shore for a stroll. Rajmahal is in the Province of Bengal, and about seventy miles from Berhampore. The Province of Bengal terminates a little below Sickreegullee, a village cultivated by invalided Sepoys, who have redeemed the land from the wilderness of former times. At Teryagullee, on the borders of the district, is the pass of Sickreegullee, which, during the Hindoo and Mahomedan dynasties, was the commanding entrance from Bahar into Bengal, and was strongly fortified. It runs up a narrow winding road, where the traveller will see a ruined gateway and fort, to tell of days gone by. He will also find a great deal of waste land, and mountainous tracts of country. The people are a wild race, quite distinct from those of the plains. They are low in stature, but stout and well proportioned, many being under four feet ten inches high, and many more under five feet three inches, than above that standard. The women are small indeed. They have flat noses, and lips thicker than those of the Lowlanders. They do not venerate the cow like the Hindoos, and have no knowledge of letters, or of any kind of written characters. They subsist principally on maize—the Indian corn. Nearly all the laborious work is done by the women; and a man is rich in proportion to the number of his wives, and who are indeed so many labourers, or, I may say, domestic slaves. These mountaineers have a great regard for the truth, and an utter abhorrence of lying, which ranks them far above their brothers of the plains, where lying is joined to the other vices.

Their traffic is in bedsteads, wood, planks, charcoal, cotton, honey, plantains, and sweet potatoes, which they barter for tobacco, rice, salt, cloth, iron arrow-heads, hatchets, crooks, and iron implements. Their weapons are the bow and arrow; but some few among them possess swords and matchlocks. Their domestic animals are hogs, goats, fowls, dogs, and cats.

It was among these wild races that Mr. Augustus Cleveland, the judge and magistrate of the district, made a permanent settlement about the year 1780. Unfortunately he died at the early age of twenty-nine, in the year 1784, as I have before observed. A monument, in the form of a pagoda, was erected by the Zumindars, or landholders of the neighbourhood, to commemorate his exemplary conduct, and another was put up at the expense of the Government, in honour of a man, who, though young, had done so much to benefit his fellow-creatures.

The Ganges flows close under the ruins of an old palace, on the brink of its right bank. Previous to the year 1638, it was the residence of Sultan Soojah, the brother of Aurungzebe, but scarcely any vestiges of the building now remain. The Ganges, about 1639, wholly quitted the vicinity of Gour, and approached the rocky bank of Rajmahal, where it still holds its course. The force of the current, on the right or Rajmahal side, is so great in the rainy season, that I am told an officer, who was sailing in a twelve-oared budgerow against the stream, which came rushing down like a torrent, actually had the sides of his boat split. The Dandees (not fops, but the boatmen of the Ganges), in sailing up the river used to call out, "Allah! Allah!" *i.e.* "God! God!" on entering that strong water, just as the native boatmen are wont to do in crossing the surf at Madras. On the left bank the river is smooth and always safe. The ruins of the palace still extend over a large space of ground. Close to the margin of the river are three arches supported by pillars of the colour of black marble. No doubt the Ganges has washed away much; and, probably, many slabs of beautiful marble, like that with which the ball-room of Government House, in Calcutta, is paved, now lie submerged under the stream. It is supposed that the Ganges, in rushing over these ruins, causes the sound of water running over rocks, which is the effect produced in this place.

The ruins of the palace are quite overspread with low jungle, abounding, as I was informed, with snakes and other reptiles. Broken gateways of beautiful architecture, mosques, and a large hall of audience—as it is reported to have been—still indicate the former importance and grandeur of this place.

In the absence of Hindoo historical dates, we must content ourselves with traditions, till we come to the Mahomedan writers. We are told that Rajmahal was anciently the seat of the Hindoo sovereigns, in whose time it bore the name of Raj Ghur. Its first mention by Mussulman historians, is in 1576; and again in 1592, when, in the reign of the Emperor Akbar, Rajah Maun Singh, governor of Bengal and Bahar, made it his capital, gave it the name of Rajmahal, and fortified it with walls and bulwarks. In 1608, Islam Khan, the Mogul governor, transferred the seat of government to Dacca, in consequence of the invasion of the Portuguese. In 1639, Sultan Soojah, the brother of Aurungzebe, again made it the royal residence, and lavished vast treasures in restoring the fortifications, and erecting the palace, of which I have just spoken.

On the expulsion of this sovereign from his dominions, the Mogul governor again moved the seat of government to Dacca. Since this period the ancient capital of Bengal has rapidly declined, not only from the withdrawal of the government; but in consequence, also, of the frequent ravages committed by those two irresistible elements, fire and water.

In recent times, Rajmahal was sought as a place of refuge by the unhappy Suraj-ud-Dowlah, who concealed himself in an out-building in a lone garden; but he was discovered, and betrayed to his enemies by a wretched Fakeer, whom he had treated with great barbarity on a former occasion, having ordered his ears and nose to be cut off. Suraj-ud-Dowlah was seized, and carried to Moorshedabad, where he was murdered with wanton cruelty.

Not many years ago, Rajmahal was a military station; but now no European resides here. There is a small Christian burial-ground, which has been walled in by some liberal and kind-hearted persons. In it is the last resting-place of many an unfortunate European, who has died near the town in his way up or down the river.

On the 2nd of June, we again proceeded at daybreak, and about noon cast anchor nearly opposite to the ancient city of Gour, and close to a village called Lall Dobree. Gour was built about 2,000 years ago, and is the ancient name of the capital of Bengal Proper: it is a few miles to the south of the town of Malda. The name of Gour is said to be derived from Gur or Goor, which, in the Sanscrit and modern languages of India, signifies raw sugar; and, from the Sanscrit term for manufactured sugar (sarcara) are derived the Persian, Greek, Latin, and many of the European names for the same article.

The ruins of Gour extend fifteen miles along the old banks of the Ganges, and are from two to three miles in breadth, which would give a circuit of thirty-four or thirty-five miles. Several villages now occupy part of the ground on which the ancient Gour stood; the remainder is either covered with thick forests, the resort of tigers and beasts of prey, or else has been converted into arable land, the soil of which contains much brick-dust. The city of Gour is nearly central to the populous parts of Bengal and Bahar, and not far from the junction of the principal rivers which form the excellent inland navigation. It is now about four miles from the Ganges; and this river, with a slip of land of a few miles in width, separates it from Rajmahal. The freak of the Ganges, in 1639, in parting from its old bed and rushing over to Rajmahal, proves that very strong shields, or river-bank defences, will be required to protect the banks of the Ganges.

The ruins of this city of former days have supplied the materials for building the more recent towns of Rajmahal, Moorshedabad, Dacca, and Malda. Enough, however, still remains to prove its former magnificence—broken palaces, mosques, mausolea, and temples, testify to its ancient splendour. Major Rennel says, that Gour is supposed to be the Gangia Regia of Ptolemy.

On re-visiting Gour, in September, 1849, I called at one of Lord Glenelg's indigo factories, the superintendent of which, Mr. R.B. M'Intosh, showed me some old coins, which had been found by his workmen at different periods; some slabs of marble, too, taken from a large Mahomedan temple, had been converted by the same gentleman into a handsome outer doorway to his house.

At a little before sunset, we changed the Ganges for the Bhauguretty river.

On the 3rd of June we were early off Sootee, on the right bank, and 210 miles from Calcutta. In 1757, when Suraj-ud-Dowlah, the Subahdar of Bengal, apprehended an attack from the English, and believed that their ships of war could proceed up the eastern branch of the Ganges to the northern point of the Cossimbazar island, and thence down the Bhauguretty to Moorshedabad, he commanded immense piles to be driven into the river at Sootee. By this act, the river has been rendered unnavigable for any vessels beyond boats, and even for these it is navigable only during the rainy season. The Subahdar remembered that Chandernagore, a French settlement, had been attacked on the 14th of March of the same year, and captured, by Admiral Watson and Colonel Clive, with line of battle ships, which cast anchor before it.

The river at times is not less than six miles broad at Sootee; during the rains, the steamers proceed down the Hoogly to Calcutta. At other seasons they go *viâ* the Bhauguretty and the Sunderbunds, or "the beautiful wilderness," where sportsmen may enjoy themselves by killing "a royal Bengal tiger," ten or twelve feet in length, from the head to the tip of the tail. The Sunderbunds consist of that part of the Delta of the Ganges, which is near the sea, and are in extent equal to the Principality of Wales. Salt is made here; and here also is found a boundless stock of timber, for boat building and other purposes.

About forty miles to the south of Mohungunge, at the head of the Bhauguretty, stands Bogwangola, a large inland trading town, eight miles N.E. of Moorshedabad. It is a great mart for grain. The town has a very poor appearance, being constructed entirely of bamboos, mats, and thatch; it has often been removed on account of the encroachment of the Ganges. It has more resemblance to a temporary fair, or an encampment, than to a town. The designation of town in Hindoostan, does not so much depend upon the nature of the buildings (for villages contain brick houses), as upon the rank of the public officer who superintends the general duties of the place, his rank depending on the extent of his charge. Bogwangola is a very stirring town; and the landing-place is always crowded with country boats of all sizes, and even with budgerows.

At about ten o'clock in the morning, we passed Jungepore, the site of one of the Company's principal silk factories, a portion of which is now conducted by private individuals; for since the loss of the Company's trading charter, their factories here and at other places, have been dismantled. Up to 1833, the East India Company, as is well known, held the monopoly of the trade in India and China; but the Government at home considering such a constitution of affairs incompatible with the position of a supreme legislative body, as well as injurious to the commercial and manufacturing interests, passed an act for the abolition of this monopoly, on the removal of what is commonly termed "the last charter of the East India Company, on the 25th of August, 1833." This act, as was expected, has already produced a vast change in the commercial relations of India. By throwing open the trade to private merchants, a greater stimulus has been given to individual enterprise and energy; and the market prices have been considerably lowered.

CHAPTER XVII.

Moorshedabad—Cossimbazar—"Eina Mahal"—The Nawab Cowar Krishnath Roy—"Snake-boats"—Population of Moorshedabad—Berhampore—Ivory and Silk Manufactures—Kulna—The Tidal-bore—English Factory at Kulna—Hoogly—Chinsurah—Chandernagore—Ishapore—Barrackpore —Serampore—Dum-Dum—Garden Reach—Calcutta.

At four o'clock on the afternoon of the 4th of June, we lay off Moorshedabad, a large, unwalled town, in the Province of Bengal, of which it was the capital from 1704 until our conquests transferred that distinction to Calcutta, in 1757.

In 1704, when Moorshed Coole Khan transferred the seat of government to this place, he changed its name of Mukhsooabad to Moorshedabad. It extends for eight miles along both sides of the most sacred branch of the Ganges, called Bhauguretty, or Cossimbazar, at a distance of about 120 miles above Calcutta. It is an excessively shabby-looking town; the houses are ill built, and have a mean appearance, most of them being only one story high. Some are of brick with tile roofs, others of mud; others again mere straw huts, all jumbled together without the slightest attention to regularity. The streets, too, like most of those in the East, are narrow and crooked, and seem to bid defiance to cleanliness and order. A redeeming point is the number of fine trees, which impart a picturesque character to this heterogeneous mass of buildings. Close to the brink of the river, however, there are some tolerable houses, mosques and temples, but these, too, are inferior to those of other cities.

The most conspicuous and handsome building in the city, is the palace of the Nawab. It is quite a magnificent place, and is called "Eina Mahal." It was planned and built under the superintendence of Lieutenant-General Duncan M'Leod, of the Bengal Engineers. It is a most chaste and elegant structure, built in the European style, of pure white marble of dazzling brightness. It almost rivals the Government House, at Calcutta. The General took a correct model of it to England for the inspection of the public, who must have admired it greatly, and commended the taste and ingenuity of the architect.

There are also some fine remains of the old palace, built by Aliverdi Khan, about 1750, constructed in the Hindoo style, with the rich black marbles and pillars that once graced the city of Gour.

Cossimbazar, a little town about one mile south of the city, and which, properly speaking, is the port of Moorshedabad, is a place of immense traffic, and great inland trade. Until the days of free trade, there was a silk factory at Cossimbazar, and the late Hon. Andrew Ramsay, uncle of the Marquis of Dalhousie, was the commercial Resident for many years.

Moorshedabad is still the residence of the Nawab of Bengal, who inhabits the Palace which I have described above. The present Nawab, Cowar Krishnath Roy, has been instructed in the English language. He is about thirty years of age; an English education has greatly improved him, and though he has not altogether divested himself of his Mahomedan habits, still those who are personally acquainted with him, inform me, that his manners are those of a well-bred European, and that he is intelligent, and very fond of reading. He sometimes goes to Calcutta, and may be seen there on the course, in his barouche and four, driven by an English coachman. My gentle readers must not be surprised to learn that the young prince has more than one wife; but they may be forgiven for being astonished at being told that European ladies have married Nawabs.

The Prince has many boats, built on the Burmese model, of great length, with short paddles. They are called "snake boats," and shoot along with the rapidity of an arrow. I have seen one of them keep pace with a steamer for several miles. They are generally rowed by twenty men. The Nawab's state barge is very handsome, it is richly painted and gilded, and draped with canopies and carpets of the richest combination of colours, which produce a gorgeous and pleasing effect. It is only used on grand occasions, and is attended by a band of music which follows in another boat.

Moorshedabad is now the residence of the British Civil Establishment, and the head-quarters of a Circuit Court, comprising six of the neighbouring districts. The mint is now under the control of the British.

The population of Moorshedabad has been given at 600,000, nay even at 700,000 persons; but taking Delhi and its suburbs, by the returns, to be 160,279 persons, and recollecting that Benares contains only 183,491, we can scarcely allow more than 200,000 inhabitants. The number of houses, of every kind, was returned, in 1814, at about 30,000; and, according to the computation usual in Bengal, of eleven individuals to every two houses, the population at that time was 165,000. The trade, and especially the inland traffic is very brisk; the staple commodities are silk and indigo; the former is manufactured in the vicinity of the city, into the most beautiful silks and taffetas. The silk goods manufactured here are considered to be of very superior quality. The trade is greatly promoted by facilities of steam and river navigation. This is especially the case during the rainy season, when the river is crowded with boats, bringing and fetching the merchandise. From October to May, the trade is very slack, for at that season the Bhauguretty is almost dry. At its junction with the Jellinghee further down, these two branches of the Ganges form the Hoogly, which runs to Calcutta.

The indigo trade is extremely lucrative; large supplies are sent to Calcutta, whence they are shipped to England, and thence to other parts of Europe. It has long formed an important branch in the East Indian trade, as the Indian indigo is highly prized on account of its superior colour. This beautiful dye, which was not known in Europe till the beginning of the 17th century, when it was first introduced by the Dutch, seems to have been in use more than 2,000 years ago, as we infer from a passage in Pliny.

Six miles from Moorshedabad is Berhampore, on the east bank of the Bhauguretty. It contains very fine barracks for European troops, with an upper story, at the extremities of a magnificent parade ground. The quarters of the officers are much like those at Dinapore, of which I have made mention. Berhampore was formerly the head-quarters of a Division of the army: the commandant's house, pleasantly situated on the bank of the river, is now occupied by an indigo planter. There is a chaplain here and two missionaries, one of whom, however, is a Roman Catholic. A few civilians also reside here; but the place is generally very dull, and much disliked.

Formerly, there used to be a European regiment, a corps of Native Infantry, and a brigade of guns: also recruits, recently arrived from England, were generally stationed here, although a sad mortality was the invariable result, on account of the numerous marshes and superabundant foliage which surround the place; its situation being scarcely above the level of the river at certain periods of the year.

At present the only troops stationed here are—a detachment of Native Foot Artillery, and the 14th Regiment Native Infantry; for owing to the demand for Europeans in our extended North-Western frontier, a regiment of our countrymen can hardly be expected to remain here, except as a temporary measure. When I revisited Berhampore, in August, 1849, I was informed, that the authorities had given orders that a portion of the barracks should be put in readiness, for one of the three regiments which had recently landed at Calcutta from England, the European barracks having been unoccupied for the last seven or eight years. The arrival of three regiments at Calcutta, in addition to those already stationed there, called for some little ingenuity in their disposal; the monsoon not being over, so as to allow of a march, and some hundred recruits in addition, being daily expected to land.

Provisions are very cheap here. Berhampore is noted for its ivory and silk manufactures, specimens of which were brought on board for sale. It is likewise one of the coal depôts for the river steamers, as well as one of the principal stations for embarking goods. The coal depôts are Mirzapore, Benares, Ghazepore, Dinapore, Bar, Monghyr, Colgong, Rajmahal, Berhampore, and Kutwa. There is a great deal of communication between this place and Calcutta, which is only 161 miles distant by the river route, the intercourse being now carried on with great regularity and speed.

Leaving Berhampore we reached Kulna, which is situated on the right bank, sixty-four miles from Calcutta. It is a very inconsiderable place.

The native boatmen, on reaching Kulna on their downward course, "rig out anchors," as it is called; that is to say, they have a frame-work, which they fill with stones, the weight of which chiefly acts as an anchor. These primitive anchors are used by the budgerows, and all the native boats, with the exception of the pinnace, which has its regular iron anchor. On nearing the Hoogly, the boatmen meet the bore, or tide, coming up with great violence against the stream. The banks being extremely narrow here, cause such a swell, that as it crosses from bank to bank, or dashes alongside, it upsets all the boats that come within its influence. By keeping in the middle of the stream, with the prow straight to the bore, a boat may remain safe from an upset.

We made but a short stay at Kulna, and were soon on our way to Hoogly, which is situated on the west side of the river of the same name, or more properly speaking, the Bhauguretty. It is twenty-eight miles from Fort William. Hoogly, like several of the large towns on the Ganges, was for a time the capital of Bengal. It is supposed to have been founded by the Portuguese, about the year 1538. They fortified and greatly improved the city, which soon became so important a mart of commerce, as to excite the jealousy of Shah Jehan, who took it after a siege of three months. During this siege, it is said that more than 5,000 of the Portuguese were killed or taken prisoners, and the most beautiful of the girls were sent to Agra, to grace the imperial harem. Shah Jehan now made it the principal port, and gave permission to the Dutch and English to build some factories, which soon became very prosperous.

The English, whose factory was situated in the town, had a body of about twenty soldiers to protect their property; but some disputes having arisen with the imperial government, the British quietly procured a detachment of 400 soldiers, who were landed from some men-of-war which came from Madras. The Nawab was alarmed at these proceedings, and brought up a large military reinforcement. A conflict ensued, in which Admiral Nicholson opened a cannonade from his men-of-war, fired the city, and, unfortunately, burnt not only 500 native houses, but destroyed the factory, which contained goods to the amount of about £300,000 sterling. The governor was terrified, and offered to indemnify the English for all the damage which they had sustained; but the Nawab not only refused to give his assent to this, but was so incensed that he issued orders for the confiscation of all the English factories and property. He was at that time at Dacca, and dispatched a body of men to expel the British from Hoogly. Just before their arrival, however, the English had withdrawn to Calcutta with all their property. The Nawab soon after relented, and requested their return, which they refused, but obtained permission to establish the factory at Calcutta.

After continued intestine disputes and constant jarring with the English, the latter took possession of Hoogly in 1757. Since that time various political changes were effected in the local government; but, in 1765, the East India Company were appointed, by the Emperor of Delhi, to be his dewans or collectors of revenues for Bengal, Bahar, and Orissa, on the condition of his receiving from them an indemnity of nine lakhs of rupees, or £90,000 per annum.

Ever since that time the importance of Hoogly has declined. The British government made Calcutta the chief port; in consequence of which all the trade has been concentrated there.

The French, Dutch, Portuguese and Danes, had formerly each a factory here.

In going down the river the tide and the bore are first felt. A mile beyond

Hoogly, is Chinsurah, once the principal Dutch settlement in the East Indies; it is also on the right bank of the river, about twenty-four miles above Calcutta. The Dutch had a factory here as early as 1656. More wary than the English, the Dutch, on receiving permission from Shah Jehan to establish a factory, built it at Chinsurah, about a couple of miles from Hoogly; and, as they employed natives as well as Dutch, they soon formed a considerable settlement. In consequence of the rebellion which broke out in Bengal in 1696, the various European factories sought and obtained permission from the Nawab to fortify their several establishments. The fortifications constructed by the Dutch were of a very superior character; and, being on the most amicable terms with the government, they quietly aided the authorities in re-capturing Hoogly, which had fallen into the hands of the rebels. This procured them great favour from the government, which granted them fresh privileges. In 1769, however, Chinsurah was blockaded by the Nawab's forces, to compel payment of arrears of duties. It was subsequently taken by the British, to whom it now belongs.

The appearance of the town, as might be expected from the national character of the Dutch, is extremely neat. The houses, generally speaking, are white, and have Venetians and pretty green verandahs running round them. Some barracks have been erected of late years for European troops. In August, 1849, the 87th Royal Irish Fusiliers were sent here, as there was no room for them at the time, either at Fort William or at Dum-Dum.

Proceeding three miles further, we came to Chandernagore, the principal French settlement in Bengal, on the right bank of the river. Its situation is far preferable to Calcutta in every respect. Like the old Dutch settlement, it forms a striking contrast to the Hindoo and Mahomedan cities. The houses look beautifully clean and white, with green Venetians, and a sort of colonnade in front. The roofs are flat, and the inmates frequently resort there in the cool of the day. The town is surrounded by gardens, and groves of trees. The factory was established a few years later than that of the Dutch, and like it was fortified. It was extremely flourishing; and the fort contained a garrison of about 300 soldiers, and a good train of artillery. At this time, 1757, Admiral Watson and Colonel Clive took it from the French by force of arms, having brought three or four sixty-four and sixty gunships before the place, though nothing beyond a large gun-boat can now approach the town.

The French are allowed to have a certain number of chests of opium, at the average of the sales. Should the opium afterwards fall in price, they may return it; but should it advance the profit is theirs. The French Consul does not reside here, but at Calcutta. The local government is carried on by nineteen functionaries; and the stranger generally meets with much hospitality and courtesy.

Three miles further down the river is Ishapore, the site of the government gunpowder works; and about five miles lower still, is Barrackpore, a military station, fifteen miles from Calcutta, with a good road between them. It is the head-quarters of the Presidency Division. At present it contains five regiments of Native Infantry; having formerly six quartered here. The cantonments are on the left bank of the Hoogly, and directly opposite to Serampore. The artillery belonging to this division is stationed at Dum-Dum, about seven miles from Calcutta.

The Governor-General has a country residence here, in the midst of a park and grounds, which are laid out, with much taste, in walks, drives, and gardens. The view from the park is very beautiful, as it comprises a most magnificent reach in the river. It formerly contained a menagerie, abounding in tigers and wild animals of all kinds, snakes, birds, etc.; but this is no longer kept up. There is a fine mausoleum in the park, erected by Lord Minto, while Governor-General, in memory of the officers who fell in Java and the Mauritius. The Marquis Wellesley intended to build a palace at Barrackpore, which was to rival his splendid residence at Calcutta; but he was deterred by the home-government. Lord Auckland established a Native school here, and left funds for its endowment. There is also a neat church.

In 1824, Barrackpore was the scene of a mutiny in the Native Infantry corps stationed there, who refused to march to the Burmese territory, in consequence of a deficiency of draught cattle. At the hour of parade, the 47th Regt. Native Infantry refused to turn out. The European officers tried every art and stratagem to overcome the mutiny, which spread to two other corps. Two regiments which were stationed at Calcutta were instantly summoned. The mutineers were drawn up on parade, and some guns placed in their rear. The officers again made every attempt to reduce them to obedience; but the men remaining obdurate, the guns were opened, and made a sad havoc among them. The ringleaders were put to death; others too were killed; and not a few were drowned in trying to escape by swimming across the river.

Serampore, which lies opposite to Barrackpore, was for many years a Danish settlement; the Danes having established a factory here, about the same time when the English, French and Dutch founded theirs, higher up the river. During the war between England and Denmark, in 1807, Serampore was taken by the Company, who subsequently restored it to its former possessors. On the 22nd of February, 1845, a treaty or deed of sale was signed between the Danish and British East India Company's governments, by which Serampore was conveyed to the latter power for the sum of £125,000; the returns for many years previously had not met the expenses, and it was merely held for commercial purposes. It still carries on an unimportant trade both with Europe and China.

Serampore was long celebrated as a missionary station, when the Danish colony flourished here; for no missionaries were allowed to reside in any part of the Bengal Presidency, except at Serampore. At that time no missionary dared venture to open his lips, or even to shew his face in Calcutta; whereas now there are above fifty missionaries, including those at Bishop's college, Howrah and Dum-Dum; whilst at Serampore there are only three, and one of these is a Roman Catholic. In the whole of the Bengal Presidency, there are one hundred and sixty-three, whose mission it is to teach the Christian religion. Of this number, however, including the Bishop, only seventy belong to the Ecclesiastical establishment, the other ninety-three being Roman Catholics, Armenians, and Greeks. The period of which I am speaking, is January, 1853. Forty-six years earlier, there were only ten missionaries in Bengal.

Serampore presents a similar appearance to Chandernagore, in regard to the extreme neatness and simplicity of the buildings. In both, the houses are white, with flat roofs, and furnished with verandahs and Venetian blinds. The church is very handsome. The town is not fortified; but a battery is drawn up near the flagstaff.

Midway between Barrackpore and Calcutta, we passed Dum-Dum. The mess-house belonging to the artillery, is considered the finest and largest in India. At present there is only one company of European and three companies of Native Artillery quartered here; this scientific and most efficient branch of the service being much needed on our lately extended frontier. There is here a remarkably fine cannon-foundery, where twelve brass guns may be bored at the same time. The iron guns are brought from Europe. All the arrangements, machinery and works, are of the first order. The Elephant Battery is most ingenious, and these noble animals perform their work with admirable precision and effect.

The young officer, on his arrival from England, receives here a course of instruction not exceeding a twelvemonth in duration, before he joins his regiment. The apartments of the officers are very handsome and comfortable.

There is a monument at Dum-Dum, to the memory of the late Colonel T.D. Pearse, who died here in 1789.

After quitting Dum-Dum, we passed the cannon foundery, which is at Cossipore, about half a mile from the town. It is pleasantly situated on the banks; and there are many fine houses belonging to the merchants of the city, who come here to enjoy some little relaxation, after the fatigues and anxieties inseparable from money-getting.

On the 8th of June, 1846, at ten o'clock in the morning, we anchored off Garden Reach, Calcutta, where I bade adieu to the accommodation-boat, "Soorma," and its civil commander and officers, and by noon was domiciled in Spence's hotel.

During my short stay at Calcutta, I received much kindness and hospitality from the arch-deacon (now Bishop of Madras), and Mrs. Dealtry, Professor and Mrs. Weidemann, Mr. and Mrs. Murray Gladstone, and Mr. William Abbott. I must reserve till the next chapter the fruits of my four several visits to this city, on my passage to and from Europe.

CHAPTER XVIII.

Project of a Railway to Calcutta—Calcutta, a Six Months' Trip from England—The Strand Road—The Mint—Professor Weidemann—The Strand Mills—The General Post Office—Custom House—Auditor General's Office—Military Board—The Commissariat—The Ice House—Metcalfe Hall—The Public Library—Bank of Bengal—The Oriental Bank—Indian Failures—Chandpaul Ghât—Baboo Ghât—Docks of Howrah—Prinsep's Ghât—Kidderpore Ghât—Fort William—Mir Jaffier—Arsenal—Chowringhee Road—Ochterlony Monument—Government House—Entertainments at Government House—Policy of Marquis Wellesley—Hotels at Calcutta—Theatricals—The Town Hall—Concerts—Fancy Fairs—The Mayor's Court—Newspapers—Merchants—Agency Business—Railways—Asiatic Society—Martinière Charity—College of Fort William—Haileybury College—Military Seminary at Addiscombe—Colleges—Schools—Mesmeric Hospital—Chloroform—Sailors' Home—Alms Houses—Masonic Lodges—Botanical Garden—Charter of 1834—Lunatic Asylums—Law Courts—Police Office—Provident Funds.

THE stupendous project of bringing Calcutta within seven or eight days of London, by means of the Euphrates valley railway route, will probably not take place in our days; but, incredible as it may seem, we yet hope we may look forward to its being carried out in those of our children. Some persons may possibly smile, and say, "It is the scheme of a visionary;" but who, let me ask, in the days of Job Charnock,—only 120 years ago, when he founded Calcutta—would have dreamt that that wretched, swampy village would have been converted into a city of palaces, and still less, that instead of a tedious sea-voyage of six or seven months from the mother country, it would be brought within the brief limits of forty-five or fifty days! Again let me ask, who only a few years ago would have conceived the possibility of a mode of communication whereby intelligence may be transmitted, not only by land but by sea, with the rapidity of lightning. Nay, that 4,000 miles of electric wire have already reached Calcutta, soon to connect every large town in India with the port of Bombay; while at the same time the submarine telegraph is in progress from Suez to Trieste, and before the expiration of 1855, will enable us to hear from our friends in any part of India in eleven or twelve days.

Calcutta is so well worth a visit, that notwithstanding the numerous and able descriptions which have been given of it by various writers, I would strongly advise all who have it in their power, to become personally acquainted with it. This can now be done in so brief a space of time, and with so much ease and comfort, that many persons will be glad to avail themselves of the opportunities now offered, and desire to know the readiest way to accomplish this object. I shall therefore note down a few data, as to the best mode of spending a pleasant and profitable six months in visiting the chief cities of India.

Persons who do not like the long sea-voyage of ninety or a hundred days, round by the Cape of Good Hope, in the ordinary sailing vessels, may reach Calcutta from England by the overland route in fifty days or under; and in two months may see the great city, as well as a part of the interior. Thus, suppose the traveller arrives at Calcutta on the 6th of November, he may leave it again by the steamer on the 8th of February. Let him leave London on the 20th of September of any year, and he may reach it again on the 25th of March following. Say that he arrives at Calcutta on the 6th of November, in fourteen days he can see all that is worth visiting in Calcutta, and as a river steamer leaves about the 20th of every month, he may go up the country on that day, and in twenty days more he will reach Allahabad, which will be the 10th of December. If he prefer it, he may travel Dâk to Bombay. Arriving at the Western Presidency about the middle of January, he may take another steamer and visit part of Scinde. Again, suppose a traveller proceeds north-west, let him leave Allahabad on the 15th or 16th of November for Lucknow, Agra, and Delhi, and even for Simla.

My calculation would be about as follows:—

To Lucknow (Dâk),	128	miles, requiring	3	days.
To Lucknow stay at			2	days.
To Agra	200	miles, requiring	4	days.
To Agra stay at			4	days.
To Delhi	112	miles,	2	days.
To Delhi stay at			6	days.
To Kurnaul	78	miles,requiring	1	days.
To Kurnaul stay at			1	days.
To Umballa	50	miles, requiring	1	days.
To Foot of hills			1	days.
To Subathoo			1	days.
To Subathoo stay at			1	days.
To Simla	23	miles, requiring	1	days.
To Simla stay at			3	days.
To Kotgurh on the Sutlej			5	days.
To Kotgurh stay at			2	days.
Back to foot of hills			7	days.
To Ferozepore			2	days.

To Lahore	1	days.
To Lahore stay at	3	days.
To Ferozepore	1	days.
To Kurnaul	3	days.
To Meerut	1	days.
To Cawnpore	4	days.
To Allahabad	2	days.
To Calcutta by steam	11	days.
January 28th.	73	days.

Thus the traveller may return on the 8th of February, and reach London on the 25th of March; a trip of six months. The longer journey would cost him about £500, and the shorter one from £280 to £300. In this manner he would see two Presidencies, and the best part of the North-Western Provinces, including Lahore.

Calcutta lies on the left or east bank of the Hoogly, or as the natives call it, Bhauguretty, or the "True Ganges," as being the chief of the ten branches which empty themselves into the sea, through their several estuaries in the Sunderbunds. It is distant about 100 miles from the Indian Ocean, in Long. 84° 22′ E., Lat. 22° 23′ N.

A magnificent line of buildings extends for six miles along the bank of the river, from Fort William on the south point, to Chitpore at the northern extremity. The princely residence of the Governor-General stands in the verdant square of the Esplanade, and is flanked on either side by the Chowringhee road, which is two miles in length.

The city is divided into two districts, the north-eastern part being inhabited by the Europeans, and the eastern by the natives. The streets are, for the most part, narrow, and the houses lofty; the lower part is appropriated to the bazaars, and the upper to the dwellings.

I propose describing Calcutta as viewed from the river. Beginning from the right, the spectator will run a line down all the way to the left of what is called the "Strand Road," or "Course," though Calcutta extends beyond the Strand Road. On the extreme right of this line is the Mint, which was planned and erected by Lieutenant-Colonel W.N. Forbes, Bengal Engineers, the present Mint-master. It is a very handsome building, one story high, supported on pillars, and was completed in the year 1830. The Mint is divided into five offices, viz., the Bullion, English, Mechanical, Assay, and Mint Committees, each of which departments gives employment to many persons. Deducting Sundays and holidays, 95 days, there will remain 270 working days.

The standard of the Bengal money is silver. Gold is sometimes coined, but the most considerable part of the currency is silver. The silver is first melted, and then run through a mould and made into long bars; next it is passed under rollers, and flattened, until it is of the thickness of the coin required, say a rupee; it is then cut into round pieces of the size of a rupee, and afterwards stamped and milled by one and the same machine. All these processes are effected by the steam engine. Next comes the weighing of the rupees, when if any be found light, they are re-melted and re-formed into bars.

Old rupees defaced, or those of native coinage, are sent down by the steamers from the Upper Provinces to Calcutta, to be re-coined. Accounts are carried on with their sub-divisions in rupees, annas, and pies; twelve pies make one anna, and sixteen annas make one rupee. The silver coins made at the Mint are rupees, half-rupees, and quarter-rupees, the copper are pice, double pice, and pies.

In the beginning of 1848, Lieutenant-Colonel Forbes, at the request of Her Majesty's Government, was ordered by the Court of Directors to proceed to England, and form part of a Royal Commission to inquire into the working of the London Mint. The Colonel was allowed to draw his Indian salary during his absence, and the expenses of his passage, home and back, were defrayed by Her Majesty's Government. The late Right Honourable R.L. Sheil, the Master of the Mint, on behalf of the Government, paid his acknowledgments for the valuable assistance which the Colonel had rendered, previous to his return to India, in June, 1849.

The Calcutta Mint is said to be more extensive than the Royal Mint. Madras has a mint, and so has Bombay; the former, however, does not appear to be much needed, as the circulation does not extend very far, and Calcutta could supply the demand.

On the occasion of my visit to the Mint, on the 27th of June, 1846, I was accompanied by my friend, the late Professor Weidemann, and his accomplished lady; and had the benefit of being conducted by some of the *employés*, who were desired to explain such parts as were new to me. In the smelting-room, the crucible is capable of containing at one time, silver enough to make 13,000 rupees; and when necessary, 250,000 can be coined in one day. Between 300 and 400 natives, and about twenty-five Europeans are attached to this scientific building, the machinery and fittings-up of which are admirable, more so, I am told, than the Mint in the Metropolis of Great Britain.

On the left of the Mint, is a large five-storied building, called the Strand Mills, belonging to Muttyloll Seal, a rich native. Here any person may have his wheat, or other corn, converted into flour on moderate terms. These mills are worked by steam. The Cossipore mills, situated near the foundry, of which I have made some mention, are similar to these.

To the left of the Strand Mills is another large building, called the Bonded Warehouse. The association was incorporated by act, of March, 1837, and consists of six Directors and a Secretary. The warehouse occupies a large oblong, the smallest front being towards the river. Some merchants at the time objected to the scheme, because having warehouses ("godowns," from the Malay word "gadong") of their own, which were usually rented on lease, they would suffer a pecuniary loss by joining the association until their leases had expired. Moreover it was an advantage to them to have their godowns near their offices.

Next to the Bonded Warehouse, stands the Marine Board Office. The river, or west front, is not very conspicuous, but it runs far back eastward. The marine superintendent is a Captain in the Indian navy. The other departments under its roof, are the master-attendant's and pilots' courts. The members of the latter court are merchants and branch pilots, usually two of each, who discuss such matters as the loss of a ship, the stranding of a vessel, etc.

The General Post Office is the next building. The post is a very important office all over India, particularly during a war, for it is then that every one looks to the arrival of news, and the post-office is literally besieged. Though India does not yet boast of railways, still the post usually travels between five and six miles an hour. An "express" to Bombay has been sent in the dry season from Calcutta in seven days, a distance of 1,300 miles. Besides the Postmaster-General, and Deputy Post-master-General, there are twenty-seven European clerks, and a very great number of native writers.

The office of the Board of Customs, salt and opium, is of great moment, for as it includes the Abkarry or spirit department, it has the control over a revenue yielding five or six crores (£5,000,000 or £6,000,000) yearly. The Board consists of three members, a secretary, deputy-secretary, thirty-four European clerks, and a large number of natives. The Custom-house, though not on a line with the last-named building, may as well be introduced here. The establishment consists of a collector, deputy-collector, and 136 European clerks, etc., independent of a vast multitude of native writers. No ships can leave Calcutta to go to sea, without first procuring a Custom-house clearance; nor can a vessel discharge her cargo without the custom-house "permit." The importance of this establishment is obvious in a city like Calcutta, not only as regards the merchants, European and native, but thousands of private individuals; for a person cannot even ship or unship a parcel, by the monthly steamer, without a pass from the Custom-house, as I can very well testify.

To the right of the Marine Board is situated the Military Auditor-General's office, though not seen from the river front. When it is stated that the pay of the Army, Ordnance, Commissariat, and Pensioners is audited and checked here to an annual amount of several crores,[105] or millions of money, the importance of this office will be understood; and such is the opinion of the Court of Directors, for the appointment of Military Auditor-General must be confirmed by them. There is a Military Auditor-General, Deputy Military Auditor-General, and first and second Assistants holding commissions in the Company's army, besides twenty-six un-covenanted clerks, and a great many native writers.

With regard to an officer's pay and allowances, if he be retrenched, it is thus effected. The Paymaster of his regiment or Circle receives the retrenchment from the Military Auditor-General's Office, signed by the chief or his deputy. If the officer thinks his charge is not according to the regulations, he writes down his reasons on the back of the paper—if the objection be lengthy, the officer appends a sheet of paper—and sends it back through the Paymaster to the Military Auditor-General's office: who, should he agree, will write in red ink "Passed." If the drawer still demurs, he requests that it may be laid before the Governor-General in council, when

[105] A Crore is 100 lakhs, or 10,000,000 rupees.

the Military Auditor-General is usually called upon to explain. An appeal lies to the Court of Directors; but this is a step which is very rarely resorted to.

The Military Board is near the river side. It is composed of a paid Member, the Commandant of Artillery (ex-officio), the Chief Engineer (ex-officio), and the Commissary-General (ex-officio). There is a secretary and two assistant secretaries, besides forty-three clerks and several native writers, who are employed in the six departments—General and Miscellaneous; Public Works, Roads and Canals; Draftsmen's; Ordnance; Commissariat; and Stud. The arms and accoutrements of a corps which are indented for by the commanding officer, are checked by this board. All Ordnance stores for practice, or service ammunition of the Artillery, or for corps; all estimates and charges for fortifications or military buildings, for civil buildings, roads and canals; in fact every item entering into the operations of war, or required in time of peace, is indented for and checked at this office. Indents are annually forwarded to the Court of Directors so as to keep the arsenals and magazines filled. Sometimes the Court clip the indents. During the Affghan war the Board sent up twelve 9-pounders instead of six 18-pounders, because it is said 9 × 12 = 108 and 18 × 6 = 108, being the ratio as to calibre, however 18-pounders will breach when 9-pounders will not. The paid member is an exception to Virgil's adage: *non omnia possumus omnes*.

The new plan which has lately been very judiciously introduced into her Majesty's army, for the education of the officers, which requires them to have some knowledge of mathematics and "that symbolical language, by which alone the laws can be fully decyphered by which God has thought good to govern the universe,"[106] leads me to remark how necessary and important it is that the officers should possess some amount of scientific learning. Thus, the member of this Military board, for instance, has an estimate sent him for erecting a building. The amount of pressure on the foundation, its superficial extent, etc., call for a considerable amount of scientific knowledge.

The Commissariat Department embraces the supplies for armies in the field; for instance, to find 25,000 or 30,000 camels for a campaign, etc. It is said that when the Commander-in-Chief took the field, in October, 1848, the government, not having previously given sufficiently early notice to the Commissariat, were obliged to buy grain at war prices, showing the penny-wise and pound-foolish system of a government, which spent £12,000,000 in the Burmese war, and £7,000,000 in the Affghan war. On the 1st of May, 1838, the Commissariat expenses for the year were, 3,800,000 rupees, or £380,000; before this, they had been £440,000.

The Company's Dispensary is not far from Government House. The reader may form some idea of the quantities of medicine consumed, when he is informed that £50,000 worth is annually sent out to Calcutta from England. The depôts up the country are supplied from this dispensary.

Near to the dispensary is the Ice-house. Ice was first introduced into Calcutta by a Mr. Tudor, of America, a person of enterprising spirit. Previous to this experiment, the good people of this luxurious city, used to cool their wines, beer, water,

[106] Vide "A Discourse on the Studies of the University of Cambridge," by Professor Sedgwick, M.A., F.R.S., etc., Vice-Master of Trinity College, Cambridge.

etc., by the application of saltpetre, but which practice is now discontinued. There was a person called an *abdar,* whose sole business it was to cool such drink as was required, and who conducted the process in a room built for the purpose; a bottle of wine could be cooled in ten or twelve minutes; but the consumption of saltpetre was great and expensive; the best white, costing three and a half, to four rupees for eighty-two pounds. Most persons still keep an *abdar,* who now cools the wine with ice. At its first introduction into India, ice was sold at four annas (sixpence) for a seer (two pounds), but now it is to be had for threepence.

Most of the steamers plying between Calcutta and Suez, take in a supply of ice for the outward and return passengers. At Madras—called the Benighted City—the benefit of Mr. Tudor's exertions have also been felt, for it, too, has now an ice-house. This invaluable article may likewise be procured at Bombay.

The Public Library, or Metcalfe Hall, is in a line beyond the ice-house, and separated from it by a street. It is a very handsome building, and has received its name in honour of the late able and talented Lord Metcalfe. The foundation-stone was laid by Brother J. Grant, the Provincial Grand Master of Bengal, assisted by Brother James Burnes, K.H., Provincial Grand Master of Western India, those masons holding office, and by a convocation of the craft, with masonic honours, on the 19th of December, 1840, in presence of the late Earl of Auckland, G.C.B., Governor-General of India, and a large assemblage of visitors.

The late Lord Metcalfe (then Sir Charles) had, as acting Governor-General, given liberty to the press of India, on the 15th of September, 1835; and there is a metal plate in the Hall, with an inscription to this effect. The funds for the erection of the building were raised chiefly by public subscription, and the valuable piece of ground on which it stands, was the munificent grant of Lord Auckland, as Governor of Bengal. The building was designed by the late Mr. C.K. Robinson, a magistrate of Calcutta, and a gentleman of great architectural taste and judgment. It was built by Messrs. Burn and Co., and cost about 68,000 Company's rupees, of which sum 16,390 rupees were contributed for the Library, and the balance by the Agricultural and Horticultural Society, and other bodies, who had originally intended to do honour to Sir Charles for the emancipation of the press, and for his public and private virtues. Owing to the alterations, the expenses exceeded the estimate, upon which Sir E. Ryan, the Chief Justice of the Supreme Court of Calcutta, liberally gave upwards of £400 sterling towards paying the balance.

The Public Library owes its origin to Mr. J.H. Stocqueler, at one time editor of the "Englishman" newspaper, who, in August, 1835, circulated an address among the principal inhabitants of Calcutta, urging the necessity of this establishment. The nucleus of the Library was formed by donations from private individuals, and by the transfer, from the library of the College of Fort William, of a valuable collection of books, consisting of 4,675 volumes. This transfer was made by the Governor-General, Lord Metcalfe (then Sir Charles), on certain conditions, one of which was, that an establishment should be provided for the reception and care of the books, subject to the approbation of the Honourable Court of Directors, who sanctioned the measure in their letter of the 14th of August, 1839.

It appears, that in 1846 there were 6,821 sets of works, and 15,408 volumes, of which 423 volumes were on East India affairs, and 362 Oriental and Hebrew. There are works in Greek, Latin, French, German, Italian, Spanish, and Portuguese. In fact there are books upon the arts and sciences, and upon almost every subject, in all languages. There are more than ninety proprietors. The subscribers are divided into three classes, enjoying different privileges, as to the number of books to be taken away at any one time. There are three curators, a librarian, two sub-librarians, and an establishment of about ten native servants.

The Agricultural and Horticultural Society here hold their meetings. The building is a great ornament to the city, and is very conspicuous, both in coming up and going down the river. The reading-room is most convenient; newspapers and periodicals are, of course, always found on the table. There are fresh arrivals of books by every steamer; and of some works, more than one copy. The public who are non-subscribers, are permitted to go there and read; but unfortunately books are occasionally lost.

The Bank of Bengal is the next building in order. It has a capital of £1,000,000 sterling; and the Government has many shares in the Bank.

At the time of its formation, there was no Bank; the houses of agents and merchants being *quasi* bankers: *i.e.,* persons for the convenience of procuring money when wanted, lodged with their agents, sums varying from £300 or £400, to the amount of even £10,000. The insolvency of the great house of Messrs. Palmer and Co., in January, 1830, the first of a series of failures of the leading houses, to the extent of many millions sterling, induced many persons to seek for a more sure plan of deposit.

In the Bank of Bengal, persons can have shares, and obtain a fair annual per centage; or they may have money in deposit for a year, or even a less period; or, if they like, they may have it in deposit with interest. No account is opened for a less sum than 500 rupees; nor are ordinary depositors allowed to draw out less sums than fifty rupees at a time. There are three directors, who are civil servants of the Government.

On the failure of the Agency houses, it was thought necessary to establish another Bank, called the "Union Bank." This establishment was not conducted on banking principles. Loans were made to carry on indigo factories. To recover these advances, the factories became mortgaged. Still the persons who had them, thought that it was necessary to work these factories, instead of adopting the wise course of a favourable sale. The directors also made advances to the Agency houses, which led to the negotiation of bank post-bills, at ten months' sight. The ruin of the Bank became inevitable, if both the factories were unprofitable, and the houses failed. The upshot was that indigo fell to low prices, and as a consequence, the houses found their sales of produce decline below par. The failure took place in the year 1848, and all the Indian world, and the merchants in Great Britain, well know the result. The insolvency of this Bank pulled down, in the crash, all the shareholders, and ruined many widows and orphans, who were living on the interest of their money, which was lodged there, and which was their only income and source of maintenance.

There was another ruinous system, which had lasted for several years. It was thought desirable to give the usual dividends, and having no profits, they actually took from their capital to pay these dividends. A case of this description was brought before the Privy Council, in July, 1849, when Lords Brougham and Campbell declared the practice to be illegal.

Of late years, several branch Banks have been formed, namely, the Agra and United Service, having a capital of 63,64,500 rupees; the North-Western Bank of India, the Delhi, and the Simla, having a capital of 22,05,600 rupees.

The Oriental Bank Corporation has a capital of £2,000,000 sterling: it was incorporated by Royal Charter in 1851. This bank does an immense deal of business, and is more liberal in its transactions than any other bank in India. It has its head office at Bombay. Now the capital of the Bengal Bank is, as I have already remarked, £1,000,000; and it has a charter, so that in case of failure, no one is liable to any loss, beyond the amount of his share. The Union Bank had no charter. The failure of the Union has caused the shareholders not to pay (besides the loss of their capital) *pro rata*; but a list of the wealthiest shareholders having been made out, one person was assessed £20,000, another £10,000, another £5,000, and others £1,000, and so on, even though the unlucky wight had only one unfortunate share. Thus, under these circumstances, the Bishop of Calcutta, as trustee of the Cathedral, for which his Lordship had subscribed a large sum, was compelled to pay a very considerable amount.

Some of the minor Banks are desirous to procure charters, and to be only liable for double the amount of their shares. These repositories advance money to officers in the civil and military services, on the security of two persons, or other satisfactory pledge. Suppose an officer borrows 4,000 rupees at ten per cent., to be paid in two years, by instalments of so much per month. If he fail to do this, the Bank immediately calls upon the Securities. Thus the Securities sign a paper, to pay so much per month, should the borrower fail to do so! They generally agree, however, that the sum in question shall be deducted by the Paymaster; but in the event of the death of the borrower, before he has refunded the loan, and without having any property, the Securities are liable for the remaining balance, and have to pay the Bank.

To return to the subject of the Houses of Agency. Of the forty-five houses which failed in Great Britain in 1847 and 1848[107] eighteen exhibited balance-sheets, which either actually exceeded, or nearly approached the aggregate of their liabilities, of which only six houses have either paid, or made arrangements to pay, twenty shillings in the pound. Of another house, a bill broker proved, that it had assets nearly triple the amount of its liabilities, the suspension being caused by temporary difficulties, which produced a complete panic. One London house connected with India, showed a schedule of assets amounting to £200,000 beyond their liabilities, still nothing had been paid in July, 1849. Another house has paid 2*s*. 6*d*. in the pound; a third, 2*s*.; a fourth, 1*s*. 6*d*.; a fifth, 1*s*.; and a sixth expects to

[107] Atlas for India, July, 1849.

pay 4*d*. in the pound!

We next arrive at the Chandpaul Ghât, which is nearly in a line with the Bank of Bengal. It is very old, and is the usual landing-place of the Governor-General.

In succession come the Steam-engine House and the Baboo Ghât, the latter having been built in the time of Lord William Bentinck, Governor-General, by a wealthy native.

We have now described the buildings which run from the extreme right, beginning with the Mint. The Strand extends beyond the Mint, and is not used as a drive, for, strictly speaking, the drive, or Course, begins a little beyond Baboo Ghât, and reaches as far as the Water gate of Fort William. This road may be three-fourths of a mile in length, and a hundred feet in width. From the Course, there is a fine view of the river and shipping, all the way down to Garden Reach. There is generally a breeze in the hot weather, and during the rains it is pretty considerable. The plan usually adopted is to drive gently down the road to the south, and then to return quickly, as the wind is at your back. Thus you best enjoy "the eating of the air," as it is called by the natives.

Besides the view of the river and the shipping, the docks and mills of Howrah give an appearance of great activity, both in ship-building and in commerce. Some years ago, it was proposed to have a steam ferry bridge thrown over the Hoogly at this place; and the plan was so far acted upon, that the bridge was actually sent out from England; but it was sold, and proved to be one of the many abortive schemes for the improvement of Calcutta, which fall to the ground for the want of public spirit. It was said, and perhaps truly, that the plan was opposed by the Dingee-walas, or native boatmen.

Opposite the Water gate at Fort William is a cenotaph, with a dome in the Oriental style, erected by Lord Ellenborough to the memory of the British soldiers who were killed in action at Maharajpore and Punniar, in December, 1843. The drive extends down to Hastings' Bridge, so named after Warren Hastings, the first and once celebrated Governor-General of India. This would extend the drive to the distance of about a mile and a half. Between the two bridges is Prinsep's Ghât, built in honour of James Prinsep, the talented Oriental scholar, of whom I have before made mention.

Beyond the second bridge, are the Kidderpore Docks, and lower still is Garden Reach, a road of about a mile and a half in length. There are some handsome houses at Garden Reach, arranged something in the character of country-seats in the suburbs of London. Here the Peninsular and Oriental Steam Navigation Company have a yard, containing marine stores, coals, and other requisites. The superintendent resides close by, in a very neat and classic building.

Fort William, which next demands our attention, was projected by Lord Clive soon after the Battle of Plassey, in 1757; but it was not finished till the year 1773. It mounts 619 guns, and is said to have cost, from first to last, £2,000,000 sterling, half of which sum was paid by Mir Jaffier, whom the British seated on the throne of Moorshedabad, after the Battle of Plassey. No doubt he was prompted to this generous act, by his gratitude to his benefactors.

Mir Jaffier was a General, in the service of the former Nawab Suraj-ud-Dowlah, who in the preceding year, 1756, took Calcutta and put 146 Europeans into the English prison, since designated by every schoolboy, "the black hole of Calcutta," where 123 were found to have died the next morning from suffocation. Lord Clive played a deep game, but the cruelty of Suraj-ud-Dowlah merited dethronement. He was killed by the son of Mir Jaffier, when taken prisoner, and although it is not proved that the father was implicated, still we know that in Eastern countries, dethronement and death are often contemporaneous.

A Queen's Regiment of Infantry has barracks in the fort. At one time the Artillery, now quartered at Dum-Dum, used to be stationed here, except during the cold, or practice season. The Church is an octagonal building in the centre of the Fort near the Government house. The Fort has several gateways, the principal of which is the Water gate. The quarters for the Staff officers of the Fort are in two ranges, where reside, the principal Commissary of Ordnance, the chief Engineer, the Fort and Town Majors, and the officer commanding the Queen's Corps. Facing the river, on the west side, is a three-storied barrack; a range called the South Barracks, and opposite, or towards the north,—being part of the Staff Row,—is another range, which together form three sides of a square. To the south of this square is the Rampart Range, running south and east, with bomb-proofs. The Arsenal is in front of the North or Staff range.

Some writers have asserted that the Fort would contain 15,000 men; it is surrounded by a dry ditch, but is furnished with two sluices, so that it can be laid under water, if needful, in a few minutes, as it is not many yards from the river. No batteries could effect anything from the other side of the water. A bombardment might destroy the Royal Barracks; but the Fort could only be attacked from the land-side. During the Burmese war, or rather before the British troops landed at Rangoon in 1824, the Burmese threatened to march to Calcutta; upon which the merchants took the alarm, and sent a memorial to government to have their cash and papers lodged in the Fort; certain it is that some of the built-up embrasures were opened. Though the Fort was safe, it is possible that 20,000 Burmese troops might have done some mischief to the lieges of Calcutta.

The Arsenal of Fort William contains a large supply of arms, and vast quantities of stores and ammunition. It is now more of a receiving depôt than formerly. During the second Sikh war of 1848-49, the Fort of Allahabad was the grand depôt, as explained under the head of Allahabad. There are hundreds of iron and brass guns in the Fort, the former garnishing the sides of the roads as if to prove to the natives, "these are the guns taken at Plassey and Seringapatam; these from the Maharattas and Sikhs." Constant exposure to the rain, and all weathers, has caused many of the guns to become "honey-combed," which renders a gun quite unfit for service.

At a short distance from the river, in the back ground to the east, is the Chowringhee Road running north and south; to begin north, or from the right: it is nearly on a line with Cossitollah Street, the northern part of the city, which I will describe afterwards. The best houses are those in the centre and left. Before reaching the Racket-court, the visitor comes to Theatre-street, where, on the north-west angle, stood "Old Drury," which, I am told, was in its glory from 1807 to 1814. The Earl of Minto, father of the present Earl, was then Governor-General, and so great a patron of the drama, that he allowed the performers, who were in the services, to wear his ambassadorial and other dresses on the stage; and Mr. H.H. Wilson, M.A., F.R.S., Sanscrit Professor of Oxford, found time, amid his duties of Assay-master of the Mint, to take part in the performances, and was, it is said, a good actor.

Between the river and the Chowringhee Road, is the Ochterlony Monument, which was raised by subscription, among the officers and admirers of Major-General Sir David Ochterlony, of whose services I have spoken, when treating of Delhi. Sir David arrived in India in the year 1775, and died in 1825. Doorjun Lall, the uncle of the present Rajah, who was a mere boy at his father's death, in the year 1825, usurped the Guddee[108] from his nephew; upon which Sir David, who was then Governor-General's Agent, and as such had the power of putting the troops in motion, assembled an army in the neighbourhood of Muttra. The Government in Calcutta, however, hearing of this, ordered the troops to be countermanded. Sir David (called the "Hero of Malown," for his gallant service in the Nepaul war, in 1814-16, when he accepted from the Government of that country the ratified treaty, which he had taken the field to obtain), was therefore constrained to order the troops back to their several stations. He conceived, as there were two parties in the city of Bhurtpore, that if a force suddenly marched to the place, the party in favour of the injured young Rajah would join the British, and open the city gates. The Government of India, however, did not, for various reasons, approve of the measure. The season of the year was certainly an objection against the marching of troops. They[109] were at that time also "greatly embarrassed by the continual difficulties and heavy disbursements of the war with Ava," which had lasted sixteen months, from April, 1824, to August, 1825; and, "influenced also by the spirit of the injunctions from home, which so decidedly deprecated interference with the internal affairs of the native principalities, the Governor-General was averse to take part in the adjustment of the succession to Bhurtpore, and disallowed the existence of any obligation to uphold the claims of the minor Rajah." However, the majority of the members of Council were of opinion,[110] "that interference might become indispensable for the protection of tranquillity in Hindoostan." The Governor-General's sentiments prevailed: the force was countermanded, and an order sent to Sir David "to retract the hostile declarations which had been published by him."

The consequence of this expressed disapprobation of his conduct, was Sir David's resignation. He was at that time sixty-eight years of age, fifty of which he had passed in the uncongenial climate of India. The mortification, caused by reversing of his arrangements, doubtless accelerated his death, for he died almost immediately after, on the 15th of July, 1825. When his decease was reported to Government, a General Order was issued on the 28th of July, in the Political department, of which the following are extracts:—

[108] "Guddee" means a "cushion." Let the reader place a cushion for the back, and one on each side, and he will have the Hindoo "Guddee" or throne.

[109] Wilson's Mill's History of India, vol. ix. p. 185.

[110] Ibid, vol. ix. p. 186.

"The Right Hon. the Governor-General has learnt, with great sorrow, the demise of Major-General Sir David Ochterlony, Resident in Malwa and Rajputana.... On the eminent military services of Major-General Sir David Ochterlony it would be superfluous to dilate.... With the name of Ochterlony, are associated many of the proudest recollections of the Bengal army.... The Governor-General is pleased to direct, that minute-guns, to the number of sixty-eight, corresponding with his age, be fired this evening, at sunset, from the ramparts of Fort William."

Sir David was the first Indian officer who obtained the Grand Cross of the Bath; an honour so highly prized, that Sir John Malcolm accepted it in preference to a baronetcy, which Lady Malcolm coveted for her son. The following remark, made by Sir John at a party at Mhow, in 1819, on returning thanks, was communicated to me by a friend who was present:—

"Gentlemen,—I preferred the military to the civil honour; and you will agree with me that I studied the honour of my profession."

Sir David, moreover, was made a baronet. He was, it is believed, an American.

The monument erected to his memory is situated to the east of Government House. Mr. C. K. Robinson, the same who built Metcalfe Hall, and well known for his great taste in civil architecture, was requested to draw a design for the column. He sketched two plans; and the one, which now forms such a conspicuous ornament among the public erections of Calcutta, was selected, as being in the Moslem style, to indicate the preference which Sir David always shewed to the followers of the prophet, over the other native population. Subscriptions were received from all classes in the Bengal Presidency—civil, military, and mercantile—amounting to nearly 40,000 rupees or £4,000. A wealthy Calcutta firm, as it was then considered, were appointed the treasurers; but the building had made only a very little progress when the firm failed, and £2,700 was lost. The committee requested the subscribers to repair the deficiency; but many refused, alleging that the committee were the responsible party, as they might have deposited the money in the Bank of Bengal. The committee excused themselves on the plea that their object was to get as much interest as possible; for, had they vested it in the Bank, they must have deposited a part for a fixed time, while the remainder would have been a floating capital without interest.

The builder had contracted to erect the monument for £3,300, without the platform or the rail around it. A fresh subscription was opened, and £1,000 collected; but the committee had not benefited by their recent experience. They placed this £1,000 with another Calcutta firm, and lost a portion of it by a second failure! Mr. Parker, the public-spirited contractor, however, agreed to finish the column on receiving an assignment of the dividend of both houses.

The monument has a pedestal and a railing. In ascending, I counted 190 steps to the first projecting balcony, and twenty-five steps further led me to the summit. The best view from the top is about sunrise; and especially in the rainy season, when the dust has been laid by the previous rain, and the whole city lies before you, with the Hoogly stretching out right and left.

On the occasion of Her Majesty's birthday, in May 1840, the Court of Directors ordered fireworks, to the amount of £2,000, when the Ochterlony monument was illuminated with variegated lamps, to keep in countenance the Government house, where all the *élite* of Calcutta were assembled. The pyrotechnist, on the occasion, was Colonel Richard Powney, the Commissary of Ordnance in Fort William, whose subsequent fêtes, in honour of many other events, are well known.

Government house was built during the vice-royalty of the Marquis Wellesley, at a cost of £130,000 sterling. It is a fine palace, but the basement is too low, to be in keeping with the superstructure. It has a centre, and four extending wings; so that, looking at it north, south, east, or west, you see the centre flanked by two wings. Above the centre, is a dome, with Britannia standing on a pedestal, armed with the trident. There are two entrances, one towards the north, and another towards the south, the grand entrance to the north, being by a magnificent flight of stone steps. Below, is a covered way for carriages, and an ingress, through the lower hall, to the stairs leading to the second floor, in the centre of which is the dining-room. The wings are appropriated to the private apartments and bedrooms. The third story is likewise used on state occasions, the centre part containing the magnificent ball-room. All the staircases are of stone. The rooms below comprise the military secretaries' offices, and the official apartments of the aides-de-camp. It is here that the visitor goes to enter his name and residence in a book, and this is denominated a call.

There are three gateways to Government House; that to the south is small and private. In front of the palace is a large verdant square, which in this hot climate is peculiarly refreshing to the eye, especially just after the grass has been cut and rolled. The front rooms of Spence's Hotel command a view of this square, and their occupants experience much pleasure in looking upon this green spot.

With regard to parties at Government House, the Governor-General has, what is called, a general list of all persons eligible to the *entrée,* not to the Queen's Palace *entrée,* but to the ball and supper, given in honour of Her Majesty's birthday, or other state occasions. Those in the two services are invited by public notice in the following manner:—

"The Governor-General requests the honour of the company of the officers of the Civil Service, and of Her Majesty's and the Honourable Company's army and navy, at a ball and supper in honour of Her Majesty's birthday."

A dinner was given in 1848, by Lord Dalhousie, on the 24th of May, and a ball on the 26th. At the former were invited all the heads of departments. At the ordinary dinners, which generally take place once a week, gentlemen and ladies are invited according to a list, and dine in turn. Merchants receive the honour of an invitation, and others of a certain class. The οἱ πολλοι only attend the great balls and suppers, when it is possible for an officer to be seated at supper next to his own coach-maker. Not that any of this class are poor, for many have realized ample fortunes. During the government of Lord Auckland, the Misses Eden, his lordship's sisters, introduced weekly *soirées* at which from 150 to 200 persons were present. His lordship was Governor-General from 1836 to 1842. These parties, I am told, were the most agreeable ever known in Calcutta; for once a week a person met not only his Calcutta friends, but many also from Europe and Upper India. People of all shades of colour were collected here, from the fair blonde of the North, to the Armenian, and even Mahomedan. At first there was a *soirée* without dancing every alternate week, but the introduction of music, and the presence of fair maidens and young bachelors soon led to the tripping of the light fantastic toe. If not a dancer, the visitor could sit down and converse with some lady, or he might cut in for a game of whist with Lord Auckland. On these occasions the Governor's band was always present, to infuse an equal harmonious temper into men's minds. At dinner parties, a guest might, if so disposed, play at billiards; or he might ask one of the Misses Eden to entreat Mrs. A. or Miss B. to sing; "such a charming creature, and the finest vocalist ever heard!"—always excepting Jenny Lind.

While Lord Metcalfe was Governor-General, he gave splendid concerts in the dancing-room, which is eighty feet long, at which all the professional talent of Calcutta was employed. Lord Auckland, who was decidedly popular as Governor-General, had, occasionally, private theatricals and concerts, his parties were numerous, and without any ostentation or show.

Ideas of grandeur only befit lofty minds. When the Marquis Wellesley sent home an account of the project of a building fit for the residence of the Governor-General of British India, his honourable masters were alarmed at the expense. The reader must look back to that period, when those gigantic measures of the Marquis had not yet prostrated the Maharattas; and he must suppose, as was the case, the Bengal Presidency to have had its northern limit at Futtyghur. If he will now take the map, and look for Peshawur, and cast his eye south-east towards Calcutta, he will find Futtyghur nearly central. He must also recollect that Bundelkund did not then belong to the Company, and that both the Madras and Bombay Presidencies were much smaller than they are at present. Besides, the East India Directors, having determined on not making any territorial acquisitions, could not understand the object of this immense palace. It was a mystery and a political device. But now the East India Company hold a greater extent of country than did Aurungzebe, the emperor, on his death, in 1707; for his successor had certainly very little power in the Deccan or south of India, nor was the Punjaub in a settled state.

We next come to the Racket Court, which is situated nearly at the end of the left of the Chowringhee Road. There are two courts, a wall dividing the north from the south court. The entrance fee is 100 rupees, with a monthly subscription of eight rupees.

I must next mention the Hotels, of which Spence's is decidedly the best. It is situated to the west of Government House, and close to the west gate. It is a long range of buildings, running north and south, having another range inside, running east and west. The latter rooms are preferable, having northern and southern aspects. The hotel can accommodate about 100 persons. A lady and gentleman, occupying a sitting and bed-room, with a separate table, pay 250 rupees, or £25 per month; for each additional room, 100 rupees, or £10. Single gentlemen, who chiefly occupy the range running north and south, having an aspect east and west, pay 100 rupees for board and lodging; that is to say, they have only one room each, and must take their meals at the *table d'hôte*. In both cases, married or single persons, pay separately for their wines, beer, spirits, soda-water, etc. The proprietors are very civil persons. The only improvement which suggested itself to me, during my frequent stay there, was the appointment of Europeans to superintend the native servants.

The Auckland Hotel, kept by Messrs. Wilson, is opposite the north-east angle of Government House. This, also, is much frequented. Indeed, I was assured that the *table d'hôte* excels Spence's in its *cuisine*. The terms are similar to Spence's.

There are other hotels on a smaller scale, and of less repute. Spence's Hotel was the first ever established in Calcutta, and is an immense concern; for the rent of the buildings alone swallows up £300 a month. Adjoining, and belonging to the hotel, is a large shop, containing ices, creams, and confectionary of all sorts, which is generally a great and favourite lounge for fresh arrivals. In the evening, numbers of carriages may be seen there at the door, waiting to take up their owners, who have gone in to quench their thirst, and recruit their strength, after the heat of the day.

About the year 1812, a theatre was built by some amateurs. Towards the end of 1813, a society of gentlemen bought the theatre, which stood on the south side of the street, near the Racket Court, called Theatre Street, the name it now bears. The manager was Mr. H.H. Wilson, whom I have had occasion to mention; and the secretary, Mr. W. Linton, organist of the old Cathedral, now St. John's Church.

Lord Minto took great pleasure in theatricals, and, as I have observed, gave his diplomatic wardrobe for the use of the performers. Sometimes the officers acted at Barrackpore, where there was a small theatre, and at which Lord Minto was generally present. The Marquis of Hastings, who came out in October, 1813, as Lord Minto's successor, also patronised theatricals.

When the theatre was burnt, in 1835, the Sans Souci, under the management of Mr. Stocqueler, was got up near Wilson's Hotel. A theatre was afterwards built in Park Street, which continued for some time; but within the last few years, a play can only be got up now and then. The Roman Catholic Archbishop has since purchased it for a College, or Seminary for students. This put a termination to the theatricals in Calcutta.

The Town Hall was raised out of the surplus of a lottery; the undertaking originated in a resolution of the British inhabitants of Calcutta, in 1804. The object of the lotteries was the improvement of the city; and twelve per cent. being deducted from all prizes, gave a surplus of about £7,000 per annum. From this fund the Town Hall was built, and is therefore public, *i.e.* government property. It is situated in Esplanade Row, in a line west from the West gate of Government house. It was built under the superintendence of the late Major-General Garstin, of the Engineers, and was finished about the year 1809, at an expense of £70,000. The members of the Lottery Committee formed the Town Hall Committee, and all applications for its use were sent to the secretary. Public meetings were held here and the lottery drawn, until about the year 1841, when Lord Auckland put a stop to these gambling concerns, in distinct compliance with the act of Parliament, which had long before been passed in England.

The length of the Town Hall, from north to south is, inside, 120 feet, its breadth 50 feet, and the height of the lower rooms about twenty-four feet, and the upper thirty-six feet. It is said to exceed the Government House in height. Large dinner-parties are frequently given here in the long room, which is also appropriated to public meetings.

There are also lesser rooms, where smaller parties and meetings are convened. The long upper room is used for balls, concerts, etc. When it was first resolved, in 1812, to have a ball in the upper rooms of the Town Hall, doubts were entertained, as to whether the beams were so situated, to render dancing safe; as the walls rested upon the beams; arches were therefore introduced to support the ceiling, and about 200 coolies were ludicrously made to jump up and down, in imitation of dancing, to test the capabilities of the beams and walls. The report being favourable, dancing was decided on, and as this pastime has now been going on for forty years, it is pretty evident, that the ladies may safely rely on the proof of long experience, that no danger need be apprehended from this quarter. Meetings of every kind are held here; at one time, before regular actresses came out to India, the ladies of the civil and military services, used to act private theatricals at the Town Hall; these are among the things that were.

In 1844 a magnificent public dinner was given here to Lord Ellenborough, prior to his return to England. Meetings have likewise been held here to decide upon testimonials of public approbation, in honour of Lords Auckland, Ellenborough, and Hardinge, of Sir Harry Smith, the hero of Aliwal, and Sir John H. Littler, late Deputy-Governor of Bengal, on his arrival in Calcutta as member of Council.

Local and charitable meetings also take place here; concerts too used to be given at the Town Hall, for many years, but latterly they have not been on the same scale as heretofore; in former times a concert used to yield £200 and even £300 a night; single tickets sold at 16*s.*, double at 24*s.*, and family tickets at 32*s.* each, whereas now, owing perhaps in some measure to the absence of musical talent in Calcutta, the same tickets fetch respectively 8*s.* or 10*s.*, 14*s.* or 16*s.*, 22*s.* or 24*s.* In August, 1848, a club was formed, called the "Calcutta Glee Club," and which in October following gave its first concert at the Town Hall, to about 250 friends, all the tickets being free. In January, 1849, the club gave a grand concert in the great room, when 800 tickets are said to have been distributed. During the season of 1849-50 the members had four grand concerts. This club is a great addition to the amusements of Calcutta society. Mr. S. Harraden, the organist of the old church, a gentleman of great talent, is the musical conductor of this Glee Club.

Mr. George Thompson, alias "Grievance Thompson," on his arrival from England with the late Dwarkanath Tagore, used to make speeches in the Town Hall, recommending to the natives of India "steam navigation." He was considered an eloquent and amusing speaker.

The upper part of the Hall, on ascending the long staircases, is ornamented with large pictures, of Lord Lake and his son, Lord Metcalfe, Mr. W.W. Bird, and Dwarkanath Tagore. In the room to the south, are the portraits of Her Majesty

Queen Victoria, and of her Royal Consort, the Prince Albert. In the Hall below, is a very fine marble statue of the late Marquis Cornwallis, and in the vestibule, a marble statue of Warren Hastings; on a raised pedestal, facing Warren Hastings, within the distance of about 100 feet, is a bronze statue of Lord William C. Bentinck.

Fancy Fairs are also frequently held in the Town Hall, on which occasions ladies occupy stalls, for the sale of articles made by themselves and other kind persons, for the benefit of different charities and schools.

The Town Hall is certainly a very handsome building; but it is of the Doric order, which looks too heavy a style for the purposes for which it is intended.

The long building called the Supreme Court is in a line with the Town Hall, and about 150 yards from it, in the direction of the river. The Court was established in 1773, with judges appointed by the Crown. It is a dark and dreary-looking building, in which much money is lost and gained. Originally, there was a chief judge and three puisne judges; but now there is only a chief judge and two puisnes, from which it is to be inferred, that litigation was more prevalent in those days than it is at present. The celebrated Sir Elijah Impey was the first Chief Justice. He was also, in 1781, appointed by Warren Hastings judge of the "Sudder Dewanny Adawlut," or the Company's Chief Native Court of Appeal, with a salary of £6,000 per annum; a step which put an end to the disputes between the Supreme Court and the East India Company. Sir Elijah, however, was recalled by the House of Commons in the following year. At present, there are nineteen barristers admitted to the Supreme Court.

When the Company had merely a factory at Calcutta, and lived under the sufferance of the Nawab, this Court was called "the Mayor's Court"; for in the year 1726 a charter was granted, enabling the Company to establish a Mayor's Court in each of the three Presidencies, Calcutta, Madras, and Bombay; also to hold Courts of Quarter Session, to determine all penal causes, save those of high treason.

An Advocate-General and a Standing Counsel are appointed by the Company. Owing to a defect in not having a jury in civil causes, the Judges are both judge and jury. In commercial cases, I am told, they often lament that there are not juries composed of commercial men; just as if the remedy were not in their own hands! There are 254 grand jurors; but including the civilians, there would be at least 270, of whom forty-three are natives. The petty jury list contains 1,586 names, and of these 533 are natives. It is to be presumed that civil juries could be easily formed. The next charter will very probably alter the present law, which is so contrary to the British constitution.

There are fifty-five attorneys; formerly there were only forty, when they were facetiously called "the forty thieves." The Supreme Court includes a "Common Law Court," an "Ecclesiastical Court," a "Court of Equity" (Chancery), and a "Vice-Admiralty Court."

When, in 1835, the Government cancelled the Sicca rupee, and coined a new one, called the "Company's rupee," which is six and two-thirds per cent. of less value than the Sicca rupee, and above two per cent. below the value of the old Sonaut; the Chamber of Commerce addressed a memorial on this subject, setting forth the fact that, while all merchants, shopkeepers, and traders, made their charges in Company's rupees, the attorneys and barristers of the Supreme Court adhered to the Sicca rupee charge. To this memorial no answer was given; but it is to be hoped, that the time is near at hand when this outrageous custom will be put a stop to, and when lawyers will be content to receive the same reductions that others have agreed to.

There are four daily Newspapers published at Calcutta; viz., the "Bengal Hurkaru," the "Englishman," the "Morning Chronicle," and the "Citizen;" the two former take the lead. There is also a talented weekly paper, called the "Friend of India," published at Serampore, sixteen miles distant. When Sir Charles (afterwards Lord) Metcalfe, on the 15th of September, 1835, emancipated the press from the old censorship, many persons thought it a bold measure. The step might have been dangerous thirty years ago; but it is now proved to be extremely useful that measures and systems should be discussed.

About 1821, the "Calcutta Journal," ably conducted by Mr. J.S. Buckingham, was prosecuted by the Civil and Military Secretaries to Government, when the learned editor was obliged to withdraw from India. For many years there was a meeting at the Town Hall, on the anniversary of the 15th of September, to commemorate the "freedom of the press," at which one of the judges usually presided. The remedy for an abuse of privilege is simple; for if an editor publishes a libellous paragraph, an action with all its consequences follows. It must be admitted, that during the commercial distress in 1847-48, and the failure of many mercantile houses, the press was of important service. Likewise during the Affghan war, in 1841-42, when, in consequence of the great distance—more than 1,000 miles from the seat of war—and the serious interruption to all commercial intercourse under the Bengal Presidency, the newspapers published many private communications of much interest from officers, whereas the Government only received intelligence from official sources.

In the Upper Provinces, the "Delhi Gazette," and the "Mofussilite," enjoy about an equal share of patronage. At Lahore, the "Chronicle" has been established, under the auspices of Mr. Cope, for many years the able editor of the "Delhi Gazette," and which bids fair to rival the other two. One of the Subalterns of the army (now Major H.B. Edwardes, C.B.), attracted notice a few years since, by some excellent letters written in the Delhi paper, called "Brahminee Bull." In fact the letters from civilians, officers in the army, merchants, indigo planters, and others, often constitute the life and soul of the Metropolitan papers. There is a great deal of talent in the services, and it is well that it should be called forth, and find a legitimate field for its exercise. The merits of a trial in the Supreme Court are sometimes discussed; and in 1849, the press certainly was in a great measure the cause of the appointment of the commission to inquire into the misconduct of the Calcutta police; and which at once led to the removal of a magistrate, who was proved to be indebted £40,000 to an influential native.

In these public journals, various improvements in the civil administration of the Provinces are often suggested; the best means for the safe navigation of the Ganges, etc. Then there are cases of cure from cholera, or the bites of snakes; letters on the state of Great Britain and our colonies; dissertations on the native languages; poetical effusions, etc. In short, many articles in these papers have led, as it would seem at the East India House, to the formation of an office for the collection of Indian statistics, so long a desideratum, and without which the Court of Directors could not state the number of acres in the North-western Provinces out of cultivation, which is now known to be 9,816,749.

In Calcutta, there are twelve printing presses; besides the daily papers, there are six weekly; also two daily, two tri-weekly, two bi-weekly, four weekly, and five monthly native newspapers. Besides, the presses publish periodicals, Army Lists, the Calcutta Review, etc., so that the lieges of Calcutta have ample means of reading, and becoming acquainted with the state of affairs in the political and social world.

The liberty of the press in India has not been abused. In a case, for instance, which occurred in October, 1849, when a barrister stated,—that if the evidence of a certain examination as to the conduct of a civil servant were published, it would prejudice the case,—the press refrained from the publication. In fact, as regards publication, it is cried down only by those whose conduct is bad; for such shun the light of truth, as a bat does the light of day.

At present there are about seventy European merchants in Calcutta, if we deduct the fallen houses. Forty years ago there were only six or seven. Large fortunes were made in what are called "the good old days;" but the merchant traded, for the most part, with borrowed capital. It will be obvious to any person, that if a merchant gave 8, 10, and at times of pressure 12 per cent., he must have made immense profits to repay the money borrowed, and realize, besides, what a merchant considers a fair profit, namely, 12 per cent. per annum. It was a ruinous system; for, when it was found prudent to speculate, it was evident that the profit, say upon half the usual outlay, would do little more than pay the borrower; whereas, by trading with your own capital, you would acquire smaller profit, but it would be all your own. When the Houses failed, in the years 1829-33, for eight or ten crores of rupees, or, in English money, for eight or ten millions sterling, the shock was dreadful. Though the smaller Houses were left in possession of the field, they could not take up the business of the bankrupt firms without pecuniary aid, and that would be by borrowing. The result would appear to have been this: the small Houses could not raise the necessary funds, but some old firms sent out a merchant to form a new House. Thus the late Capt. Cockerell, R.N. (a connexion of Cockerell and Co., London), established a business on the ruins of Palmer and Co.

It was the Agency business which destroyed many Houses; because, while there were a few wealthy servants of government who had lent money, there were a great many civilians and officers in debt, who had borrowed money from the Agents. In fact, it might happen that a House had advanced more money than it had borrowed. The system was mischievous in another way; for the Agents, to make certain that the lives of the borrowers were insured, paid the insurance themselves, and charged it as an item of account with interest: but, *cui bono!* they failed, and could not come upon the insurance office till the death of the persons so insured.

Now in the army we reckon the deaths, except in time of war, at three per cent. in Bengal, and at Madras and Bombay nearly four per cent. per annum. Now, if they had a hundred of such constituents, as they were erroneously called, they would not soon recover their advances.

Again, there was another system devised in Calcutta, namely, that of compromise. One civilian, for instance, who owed 300,000 rupees, or £30,000, compromised for £7,000, which he borrowed from a friend. Some made three and four lakhs of rupees, £30,000 or £40,000, in three or four years. Some have wound up in fifteen or twenty years; that is, on the last dividend being paid; say one anna in a hundred rupees, or three half-pence in £10! or the infinitesimal least portion. Those who had lent the Houses money, were losers, minus these dividends; *i.e.* some Houses paid 8, 10, 15, 25, and even 33 per cent.

Now, those who lent money, got, say 8 per cent., at a time when the Company's paper yielded only 4 or 5 per cent., and the Bengal bank 10 (6 per cent. was the last dividend paid in 1849). Many a man risked his whole fortune in the effort to obtain 3 or 4 per cent., with the chance of losing all; and he not only lost his all, and ruined himself and his family, but, in many cases, took refuge in drink, to drown care.

The failure of the great Houses produced a host of small ones; nearly ten times the number there were forty years ago. On the 1st of January, 1849, there were, deducting defuncts (forty insolvent firms in liquidation), about seventy European merchants, thirteen Armenian merchants and agents, and four Greek firms. Forty years since there were only six English houses, namely, Alexander and Co., Colvin and Co., Downie, Cruttenden, and Co., Fairlie and Co., Mackintosh and Co., and Palmer and Co. There are now above sixty commercial brokers, the system of brokers or middlemen being of modern date.

The Chamber of Commerce, consisting of a President, Vice-President, nineteen members, and a Secretary, was established in April, 1834. The duty of this chamber is to discuss any subject connected with commerce. Thus, in the year 1842, the merchants sent in a memorial to Sir Lawrence Peel, chief justice, complaining that the barristers and attorneys still charged sicca rupees while all the rest of the community were taking Company's rupees, or six and two-thirds per cent. less. Any matter connected with port-dues and pilots, is also considered by this committee, which is a very useful board.

The Calcutta Trade Association, established in July, 1830, is for the purpose of regulating matters of trade, and to represent to Government any grievance injurious to it.

The Indian establishment of the East India Railway Company arrived in Calcutta in November, 1847. The act for the formation of the Company guaranteeing 5 per cent., has been passed by Parliament, and a Staff of Engineers are at work in laying down the projected line of railway.

The great undertaking of a railroad from Calcutta to Delhi, a distance of more than 900 miles, and afterwards to the Sutlej will require some years for its completion. The government will thus be able to move troops, with great rapidity, to any desired spot, at any moment, and incalculable will be the advantages which India must reap on its accomplishment. I must refer the reader to a very sensible letter, written by Lieut.-Colonel Pitt Kennedy, military secretary to the late Sir Charles Napier, at that time Commander-in-Chief, in which he briefly points out the comparatively slow progress which Sir Charles made daily *en route* from Calcutta to the Upper Provinces, although, as he says, every facility practicable was afforded. He distinctly shows what a saving a railroad would effect, in the cost of the transport of goods from one station to another, and as clearly determines how the traveller may accomplish in weeks, what he now does in months, and in hours, what now occupies days.

The Asiatic Society was instituted in the year 1784. It comprises five scientific sections, as follow:

Section I., Oriental Literature and Philology;

Section II., Natural History;

Section III., Geology and Mineralogy;

Section IV., Meteorology and Physics;

Section V., Geography and Indian Statistics.

The Society meet on the first Wednesday evening in every month, to discuss the various subjects and papers submitted to their notice. The rooms are at the corner of Park-street, Chowringhee. Each member pays sixteen rupees a quarter, or sixty-four rupees a year.

The late Major-General Claud Martine, who was born at Lyons, in France, and died at Lucknow in September, 1800, left by will the sum of 350,000 Sicca rupees, or about £35,000 sterling, to the town of Calcutta, to put out at interest in government paper, on the best security; and the principal and interest to be placed under the protection of Government, or the supreme Court, in order that they might devise an Institution the most necessary for the public good of the town of Calcutta, or establish a school to educate a certain number of children of either sex, to a certain age, after which the boys were to be apprenticed to some profession, and the girls married when of proper age; "and," as the will runs, "every year a premium of a few rupees, or other thing, and a medal be given to the most deserving or virtuous boy and girl."

This was to be done on the anniversary of the General's death, when a sermon was to be preached, the prizes distributed, and a dinner given to the children. This money was most improperly allowed to remain in the hands of a House of Agency; but at length, after a lapse of more than thirty years, on the 22nd of October, 1832, the Advocate-General, having moved the Court against the Agents, the Supreme Court at Calcutta passed a decree, and directed a school to be established, to be called "La Martinière," (agreeably to the twenty-fourth clause of the General's will), and appointed 165,293 Sicca rupees, or about £16,530, for the cost of the building.

The Court nominated Mr. J.P. Parker to be the builder, and Captain George Hutchinson, of the Bengal Engineers, to superintend its erection, receiving six per cent. for his trouble. This arrangement left a large residue, invested in Government Securities. The children were to be selected from amongst the poor Christian population of Calcutta. The girls were to be not under four, nor above twelve years of age, so that there should be twenty girls at the least: well-conducted girls, moreover, were to be permitted to remain until they were sixteen years old, if not before apprenticed or married. The boys were to be not under four, nor above ten years of age, so that there should be at least thirty boys.

The Governors of the Martinière Charity met at the Government House in August, 1835, when it was decided that the religious instruction given to the children of the school should be in conformity with the principles held in common by the English, Scotch, Roman, Greek, and Armenian Churches; but the School was not to be placed under any particular denomination of Christians! There is a library attached, consisting of 4,142 volumes, and a large collection of philosophical instruments, etc.

The Principal of the College is Mr. Henry Woodrow, M.A., Fellow of Caius College, Cambridge.

On the 31st of August, 1848, the Institution contained 100 foundation scholars, 32 boarders, 42 day scholars, and 1 day boarder, making a total of 175 boys; which, with the 70 girls, made a total of 245 children. There were in December, 1849, 270 children on the books of the School. The funds of the Institution now amount to 1,575,000 Company's rupees, or £157,500, which is more than four times the sum originally left by General Martine.

The College of Fort William was established by the late Marquis Wellesley in the year 1802, with various Professors appointed for Arabic, Persian, Hindoostanee, Sanscrit, and Bengalee. The Writers intended for the Civil Service used to reside in the long range called "Writers' Buildings," situated in Tank Square, not far from the north of Government House.

Examinations were formerly held half-yearly, in the presence of the Governor-General. The Professors read their report on the number of terms kept by each student, and their individual proficiency; the students of each class being severally numbered 1, 2, 3, etc., according to the report. The Governor-General then addressed the students, particularly noticing those who had distinguished themselves in the various classes; after which the medals and prizes were distributed.

Among the eminent men who passed at these examinations were the late Lord Metcalfe, Sir Richard Jenkins, G.C.B., Director of the East India Company, and W.B. Bayley, Esq., also a Director. At that time all the Writers for the Bengal, Madras, and Bombay Presidencies passed at this College; but this system was afterwards given up, and only the Bengal Writers enter the Calcutta College.[111]

On the establishment of the Haileybury College, in England, about the year 1805, for the education of Writers, the Calcutta College became nothing more than a school for the study of the Oriental languages, for the Bengal Writers, on their

[111] Whilst correcting the press this College has been abolished, and is replaced by a Board of Examiners at Calcutta, consisting of a president, and as many members as the Government may think fit to appoint.

arrival in Calcutta. The Marquis Wellesley had proposed to the Court of Directors that there should be a Provost; in fact, that it should be placed on the footing of a college in England, with Professors for all languages. The Court of Directors and the Board of Control appear to have thought, and with good judgment, as to general education, that a college in England would be preferable. As far as the Oriental languages are concerned, the young student may learn the rudiments in England; and, in a few cases, bright examples have occurred in the persons of some Writers, who, in a very few months after their arrival, have passed in three languages. These exceptions are the cases of young men of considerable talent. It is said by the natives, that it requires seven years, to master the Arabic language, and twelve to acquire a perfect knowledge of the Sanscrit. Admitting that a profound acquaintance with the Sanscrit, or Arabic, may not be requisite, though the latter is so intimately connected with the Persian, and the former with the Hindoo languages of Hindee and Bengalee, still, great advantages result in those cases where students desire to possess a perfect knowledge of the minor languages.

At present the system in Bengal is this:—The Writers are divided into two classes; one for the Bengal Presidency, and the other for the North-west provinces. For the former, Bengalee and Hindee are the languages studied; and for the latter, Persian and Oordoo. Each Writer must pass in two languages before he can be reported "qualified for the public service." There are now two examiners; one of whom is a subaltern in the 42nd Regiment Bengal Native Infantry. The examinations are held in the College rooms, at Writers' Buildings; but, unlike the examinations of our English universities, they are private and not public. There are at times from twenty to twenty-five, or even more students, in Calcutta, some of whom are allowed, if they have relations or friends in the civil service, in the Mofussil (country), to go into the interior to study.

The usual course is to examine the students monthly; and a report of their proficiency is made quarterly, and published in the "Gazette." The "Gazette" also gives the names of those young men who have obtained prizes; for several read for "honours." It will be evident that the expenses of a college, which is to embrace the European and other languages, as well as other studies, such as general history, mathematics, and geography, would be very considerable. In England, besides, professors can easily be procured; whereas, in India, it is impossible to obtain them without great trouble and expense. The latter consideration weighed with the Court of Directors; and, while they acknowledged the validity of the Marquis's arguments on the necessity of giving a superior education to young men, who, in their progressive rise in the service, would have hundreds, or thousands under them; who would become heads of great departments in the government, and, possibly, members of the Council, still acted wisely in giving that education in England; and this, among other, for the following reasons:—

Because the young men are brought up in a more congenial climate, and do not leave England before they are nineteen or twenty years of age, when they are better able to endure the change of climate; they arrive in India when they have acquired a certain amount of practical knowledge of the world; at a period when young men begin to see the folly of indulging in the expensive habits of youth;

and, moreover, have before them the sad warning of Writers getting into debt, who might have quitted the service on a pension of £1,000 a-year, had they not involved themselves in debt in their early career. In fact, they arrive as young men, and not as boys.

It is evident, therefore, that Haileybury is far superior to any College which could be established in India.

Except in a few cases of very talented Writers, it is all lost time to study the Oriental languages in England, beyond the mere grammar and ground-work. To teach a civilian a few words and phrases, in order to enable him to ask some necessary questions and give a few orders, is all that is requisite. It is far better to devote their minds to the study of the history and political economy of the country, in which they are to reside, and to assist in governing. Let them study the laws of England as to crimes, and the civil laws as to obedience and allegiance; the law of contracts; the mode of recovering debts due to the Government, and to individuals. Let them well digest the principal regulations of the government under which they are to serve; and the customs, manners, prejudices and religion of the natives, both Hindoos and Mahomedans. These are ample subjects for the employment of the Writer's mind whilst in England; for as to the Oriental languages, there is great danger of acquiring a bad pronunciation, a point which is of the utmost importance in the colloquial languages, such as Oordoo and Persian.

At the East India Military Seminary, at Addiscombe, the students are taught mathematics and classics, fortification and artillery, military drawing and surveying, landscape drawing, geology and mineralogy, chemistry and French.

It is an important consideration, whether cadets who can now, as in the Royal Army, enter the service at sixteen years of age, should not rather leave England at the age of eighteen; for it is a well-known fact, that recruits for the army are more healthy, and bear the climate of India better, when they arrive at the age of eighteen, nineteen or twenty years. Formerly, indeed, direct cadets were sent out to India at the early age of fifteen years, and Marlow cadets at fifteen and a half.

Bishop's College was founded in 1820, by "The Incorporated Society for the Propagation of the Gospel in Foreign Parts," at the instance of Bishop Middleton. This institution is essentially a religious foundation, and is under the management of a Principal, the Rev. W. Kay, B.D., Lincoln College, Oxford, and three Professors.

Bishop's College is open for the admission of all students of moderate qualifications, who shall conform to its religious ordinances, and its academical instruction and discipline. It has a library of about 6,000 volumes, besides a large and varied collection of manuscripts, chiefly Oriental; namely, Syriac, Zend, Pehlevi, Arabic, Persian, Tibetan and Sanscrit. Among the latter are parts of the first two Vedas, and several Puranas. The Universities of Oxford and Cambridge send copies of all works printed at their presses, to Bishop's College.

The students are required to attend divine service twice daily, after the form of the Common Prayer of the United Church of England and Ireland, in the beautiful little chapel of the College. They have their meals in common, in the hall, which is a spacious and elegant room, adorned with the portraits of the Founder, Bishop Middleton, and of a former distinguished Principal, the late Rev. W.H. Mill, D.D., Trinity College, Cambridge, a man for whom I entertained the greatest respect, as well for his varied and gigantic literary attainments, as for his quiet and unassuming manners.

The students, with the exception of the natives, wear an academical dress; and, with the sanction of their parents or guardians, are expected to embrace the profession of schoolmasters, catechists or missionaries. The usual period of study is five years, after which they are employed at a fixed stipend as catechists, until of age for ordination, when they become missionaries.

There are native teachers for Arabic and Persian, Sanscrit and Bengalee, Cingalese and Tamul. At the College press, translations are made into the Oriental languages of the Holy Scriptures and of the Liturgy, under a revision of the College Syndicate, which consists of seven members. There were, in 1849, seventeen persons studying at the College, who, as soon as they become qualified, will be sent as catechists or missionaries to different parts of India. Two of the chaplains of the Bengal establishment have been ordained from this College.

The Madrissa, or Mahomedan College, is situated in Wellesley Square, Cullinga. Natives are here instructed in the Arabic, the language in which the laws of the Mahomedan Government are written; and the object is to preserve a correct knowledge of that language.

There is another Mahomedan College at Hoogly, about twenty miles from Calcutta, called the College of Mahomed Mohsin, established in August, 1836.

The Hindoo College was established in 1816. It consists of a Principal, a Lecturer on Mathematics, a Professor of Natural and Experimental Philosophy and Civil Engineering, a Surveying Master, and an Assistant Professor of Literature, besides several assistants in the respective departments.

The Sanscrit College consists of eleven Pundits, three English teachers, who are natives, two secretaries, and a librarian. The object of this Institution is to preserve a correct acquaintance with this original and learned Hindoo language, in which the Hindoo sacred books and laws are written.

The Schools in Calcutta are numerous. The Free School is a charitable institution, and its object is not only to educate, but also to apprentice the children, when they have arrived at a suitable age. Parents, whose children are not eligible on the score of poverty, may have them educated in this School, on the monthly payment of a sum, not exceeding ten rupees, or £1 sterling. On the 1st of January, 1849, there were 400 children in this Institution.

The Lower Orphan School, Alipore, is divided into two departments, a boys' and a girls'.

St. Paul's School, Chowringhee, was established in 1845. It is under a Committee of Management, of which the Right Rev. the Lord Bishop of Calcutta is the President.

St. James' School, was established by the Society for Promoting Christian

Knowledge. This benevolent Institution, founded in 1809, admits children of both sexes, and is under the control of three Trustees. The Parental Academic Institution was founded in March, 1823.

The Free Church Institution, originally established in August, 1830, under the name of "the General Assembly's Institution," and now supported by the Free Church of Scotland, consists of a College, a Normal and Preparatory School. The number of pupils is about 1,100. In immediate connexion with the Free Church Institution are three Branch Schools, mustering 550 pupils. The General Assembly's Institution, situated in Cornwallis Square, has about 500 pupils.

The Bhowanipore Christian Institution was established by the Church Missionary Society, and contains 475 scholars.

The Indian Free School, situated in Cornwallis Street, was instituted in 1839. Each scholar pays a fee of two rupees, or 4*s.* a month.

The Anglo-Indian School was established in 1829; the boys pay one and two rupees, or 2*s.* and 4*s.* per mensem.

The Patriotic College was established in 1846. The terms are from one and a half to three rupees monthly, and the course of education is the same as that adopted in the Hindoo college, with slight modifications. The Normal Institution has two schools, the one Normal and the other Model. In the former the students are divided into two classes, stipendiary and free, the first of whom receive from Government 12 rupees or £1. 4*s.* per month.

There is a Baptist Mission School, a European Female Orphan Asylum, and a Ladies' Baptist Missionary Society. In all, there are seventeen Public Seminaries for the instruction of boys, exclusive of the military Upper and Lower Orphan Schools at Kidderpore, and ten private schools for girls, besides two public schools. The military Upper and Lower Orphan Schools at Kidderpore are supported, partly by Government, but chiefly by the subscriptions of the officers of the Bengal army; the Upper Schools are for the children of officers, and the Lower for those of the non-commissioned officers and privates. There are 114 boys and 116 girls, or a total of 230 children. Fifteen of the boys are at St. Paul's school and fifty-seven of the girls at Kidderpore House. Some of the boys are sent to the regimental bands, and others are apprenticed to trades. Each girl, on her marriage, receives 1,500 rupees, or £150, as a marriage portion.

There is a Roman Catholic Cathedral Free School for boys and girls, and a Roman Catholic Seminary, established about the year 1829, for young ladies and boys under ten years of age.

The Armenian Philanthropic School, founded by the Armenian community in April, 1821, numbers sixty-seven pupils.

The Medical College comprises two classes of students, namely, one class who are taught in English, and another in Hindoostanee; the number of the former is 109, and of the latter 128. A few years since four of the students of the college were taken to England by Dr. Goodeve, one of the Professors, where they all passed the London examination with great credit; one of them took the degree of M.D. and was made F.R.C.S., a second became M.R.C.S. and is now Assistant Demonstrator of Anatomy in the college. The object is to furnish a superior class, in room of the former unscientific, native surgeons. When they have passed the usual course, the students are called Sub-Assistant Surgeons, and are sent to corps and to civil stations.

The General Hospital, situated to the south of the race-course, is for the admission of European soldiers, whose case requires more detailed treatment than they can have in Fort William. European seamen of merchant vessels requiring amputations, and patients from the native troops at Barrackpore, doing duty in Calcutta, are eligible for this hospital.

The Native Hospital is a most useful institution; besides which there is also a good Native Hospital at Howrah, and a Seaman's Hospital, supported by the mercantile community of Calcutta.

In the year 1847 the Government formed an Experimental Mesmeric Hospital, which was to be tried for a year; Dr. J. Esdaile was appointed surgeon in charge. There is no doubt that some of the medical profession at Calcutta did not like the new hospital, for it was utterly foreign to the ideas of most people in India. At the end of the year a Report was given in, and a committee appointed to determine upon its merits; but their decision being unfavourable to the renewal of the hospital for a further term, the experiment was given up. Upon this the natives of rank and influence sent a memorial to Government, who replied, that as the Hospital was chiefly for the benefit of the natives, the Government would allow Dr. Esdaile's services for the institution, on condition that the natives should subscribe to it.

In June, 1848, a meeting took place to consider the matter; when several European and native gentlemen gave donations, and offered monthly subscriptions, for the formation of the hospital. At the request of the Committee, the Government furnished the necessary instruments for operations.

Dr. Esdaile had previously published a work on the subject of Mesmerism; and had, while civil surgeon of Hoogly, privately, and at his own expense, formed a ward in his hospital for mesmeric operations. A report was published of his cases; and the result was highly satisfactory.

The new hospital was opened in August, 1848, since which time people have come from great distances to undergo a "painless operation." If Dr. Elliotson, who is considered, by many, to be one of the most accomplished medical men in Europe, and, luckily, a man of property, lost many of his patients in consequence of his advocacy of the new theory, Dr. Esdaile surely was a bold man to propose Mesmerism in Calcutta, where there are so many "ditch" jobs carried on. Had a Governor-General undergone an operation, under its mild influence, Mesmerism would have been the order of the day; for then all the members of council and secretaries of government would have become converts, as a matter of course.

The objections of the medical members who drew up the unfavourable report, were most singular. Some thought Mesmerism would affect the nervous system; others said that as it had only been tried on natives, they doubted whether Europeans could be influenced by it. Latterly, however, there has been a reaction. It is known that ether and chloroform have been extensively used in England, France, and America; indeed, in one large hospital in London, all surgical operations are effected under the influence of chloroform. Both ether and chloroform may become safe means in process of time; but as yet it cannot be denied that many fatal results have occurred. With a large army on active service, one or the other of the remedies will, doubtless, often be resorted to, after an action. But the mesmeric process would not always answer in such cases, as it frequently requires time. Some patients are altogether incapable of being affected in one day.

As to Europeans, the answer is simply this; if one manipulator be not sufficient, two, three, or more operators must be called in. At Madras, a short time ago, it was proposed to place a lady about to be confined, under the influence of ether, when her husband objected, because it is written in the Bible (Gen. iii. 16) "I will greatly multiply thy sorrow and thy conception; in sorrow thou shalt bring forth children." Upon the same principle a man ought to object to another person's taking medicine to alleviate pain. Such an unchristian perversion of doctrine was never before resorted to; as if it could be displeasing to God, that his creatures should use any means to mitigate the sufferings of humanity.

The Eye Infirmary was established about thirty years since. It is a very useful hospital, for many of the natives suffer from cataract. About twenty years ago it was proposed to establish an Eye infirmary at Meerut, and there certainly appears to be an opening for a second. About two-thirds of the Bengal army is now stationed in the Upper Provinces; and, if one such infirmary be required for the city of Calcutta, it is to be presumed that another would be necessary in a position so distant as 900 miles. The population of the North-Western provinces is, as I have stated, 23,199,668, not including some 60,000 soldiers.

The Sailors' Home was instituted in 1837. Captain T.E. Rogers, I.N., Superintendent of Marine, is President, and the American, Danish, and French Consuls, are Vice-Presidents. The object is to suppress the system of crimping. Before this "Home" was established, seamen, when ill, were obliged to go where they could, and thus they fell into the hands of crimps, who cheated them out of their money, and injured their health and morals. Now both officers and men can go to the "Home," and obtain comfortable board and lodging at reasonable rates. By another admirable rule of the institution, they may deposit their earnings with the Superintendent, during their stay in Calcutta. The Superintendent is also at liberty to provide dinners for parties coming on shore on leave, at fixed rates, on a day's notice being given. "Drunkenness, profane swearing, and inordinate conduct, will be in every way discountenanced; and orderly, sober, and industrious habits encouraged. Medical attendance when required."

The Government make an allowance of 1,100 rupees (£110) yearly for house-rent. On the 31st of January, 1849, it appears from the Report, that "the 'Home' had clothed and maintained, free of expense to the men themselves, eighty shipwrecked and distressed seamen, who, but for the 'Sailors' Home,' would have been destitute."

In the year 1848, the number of inmates was 687. The men on the whole behaved well.

The Calcutta Alms Houses, were erected by the munificence of Lady William Bentinck, about the year 1835.

There are eight Masonic Lodges in Calcutta, and about 1,700 free and accepted Masons. As a Master Mason (Scientific Lodge, No. 105), adhering to the obligations I have entered into, never to reveal any masonic secrets, which have been entrusted to my keeping, I would cautiously shun the present occasion of doing so. Although as a soldier I might be led to expatiate, still I will pass over the allegorical and symbolical science of masonry, only remarking that I never knew a mason who was a bad or troublesome soldier: but, on the contrary, the more perfect the mason, the more noble the soldier.

The Botanical Garden was established about sixty years since, under the superintendence of the late General Kyd, of the Bengal Engineers. In 1794, the late Dr. Roxburgh, of the Madras Medical Establishment, was nominated Superintendent; since that gentleman's retirement, it has been under a Bengal medical officer. The object is to collect trees, plants, and flowers from the different parts of India and adjacent countries, from the Malayan Archipelago, China, Mauritius, Africa, Europe and America. The Garden is situated on the other, or right bank of the river, opposite Garden Reach, and not far from Bishop's College. It is a very favourite resort in the cold season, when parties are made up to visit the Garden, and spend the day there. There is a branch garden at Saharunpore near the hills, under the Himalaya Mountains.

With the renewal of the charter, in 1834, it was thought necessary to appoint a Law Commission, and the President, a legal gentleman who was sent out from England, has a seat in the Council of India. Two members were at the same time appointed, one from Madras, and another from Bombay; together with a secretary. The present President is Mr. Peacock, who appears to be left alone to work out acts for India, the two members having gone. How long this office may continue, it is impossible to say: the next charter will probably introduce a new system. The members were gentlemen of the Civil Service; and if the system of law education at Haileybury should be improved, it may become possible to find one, out of eight or nine hundred civilians, competent to be President.

The Council of Education consists of a President and nine members, three of whom are natives. All Colleges and schools, supported or assisted by the Government with any allowance, are under the superintendence of the Council of Education. This Council directs the course of education for all colleges and schools where English is taught, excepting Bishop's College, and the Medical (strictly so called) College, and selects the works or books to be read. This supervision or control extends to the out-stations, and indeed to all the schools under the Bengal Presidency.

The European Lunatic Asylum, is near the General Hospital. At Benares, there is a similar one for unfortunate natives.

The Small Cause Court, is a Court for the recovery of debts due by Europeans to natives, or by natives to Europeans; in fact any person may be a plaintiff.

The maximum amount of claim or debt, sued for in this court, is 500 rupees or £50 sterling. The amount of decrees probably extends to five or six lakhs of rupees (£50,000 or £60,000) per annum. Poor people can sue in *forma pauperis,* when the judges dispense with the cost of fees. The Act is somewhat similar to the English Small Cause, or County Courts.

Military Courts of Request, are held at every station in the army. All European as well as Native Officers, Non-commissioned Officers and Sepoys are subject to them, except such European and non-commissioned officers as are holding staff appointments away from their regiments.

There is a European Court and a Native Court, in which sums of 400 and 200 rupees (£40 and £20) or under, can be respectively sued for. In certain cases, however, in the Native Courts, sums to any amount may be investigated.

The Police Office, is presided over by a Chief Magistrate and two other Magistrates, one of whom is a Native. The Chief Magistrate superintends the River Police; the Senior Magistrate, the Second or Southern Division; and the Junior Magistrate, the First or Northern Division of Calcutta. There is also a Superintendent of Police. The Native Policemen amount to about 1,900, besides a body of Mounted Police who patrol at night. On my second arrival at Calcutta, in August, 1849, I found the police in a much more efficient state than when I left for England, in July, 1846, both as regards number and general usefulness.

The Bengal Civil Fund, entitles the civil servants of the Government to obtain their pension of £1,000 per annum, by paying 4 per cent. out of their salaries. To become entitled to this pension, a civilian must pay up 50,000 rupees (£5,000); it is taken by seniority.

The Bengal Civil Service Annuity Fund, is to grant pensions to the widows and orphans of deceased civil servants, securing to the widow £300 a year, and so much for each child; if she marries, she forfeits the pension for herself, but the children are kept on the Fund. If the widow has a private income of less than £100 a year, she gets the £300; but if above £100 and under £400, the sum is made up to £400 per annum.

The object of the Bengal Military Fund, is to grant pensions to the widows of officers, after the following scale:

	If in India, per mensen.			In England per annum.		
	Rupees	Annas	Pies.	£.	*s.*	*d.*
A Colonel's widow draws	238	6	5	342	3	9
A Lieut.-Colonel's	190	11	6	273	15	0
A Major's	143	0	7	205	6	3
A Captain's	95	5	9	136	17	6
A Lieutenant's	71	3	1	102	3	9
An Ensign's	56	9	8	81	5	0

Children are allowed so much a year; boys up to a certain age, but girls may be kept on the Fund till they are married. A sick officer, provided he does not possess 5,000 rupees (£500), will obtain 1,200 rupees (£120) passage money. Subalterns when sick, if they do not possess £50 per annum above their pay, will be allowed £50 passage money.

Lord Clive's Fund, established in 1776, is now paid by the Court of Directors, and amounts to half an officer's pay, if not possessing as follow:

A Colonel	£4,000
A Lieut.-Colonel	3,000
A Major	2,500
A Captain	2,000
A Lieutenant	1,000
A Surgeon	2,000
An Ensign	750

The object of the Queen's Military Fund, which was raised in 1820, and revised in 1827, is to pay the passage home of widows and children of the Royal Service:

A Field Officer's Widow is allowed	2,000 rupees, or	£200
A Captain's and Subaltern's	1,500 rupees, or	£150

The allowance for each child

Not exceeding three, is	500 rupees, or	£50
Exceeding three	300 rupees, or	£30

A certain sum is also granted to enable widows and children, on landing, to reach their homes, which is called "travelling expenses." Officers, if so disposed, may pay so much monthly: that is to say,

	Rupees		£	s.
Commander-in-Chief	30	or	3	0
General Officer	20	or	2	0
Adjutant-General	12	or	1	4
Deputy General	10	or	1	0
Deputy Assistant General	8	or		16
Brigade-Major	6	or		12
Lieutenant-Colonel, if commanding	10	or	1	0
Lieutenant-Colonel, if not	8	or		16
Major, if commanding	8	or		16
Major, if not	6	or		12
Captain, Paymaster, or Surgeon	4	or		8

Lieutenant, or Assistant Surgeon	2	or	4
Cornet, Second Lieutenant, or Ensign	1	or	2

APPENDIX.

APPENDIX.

I.

[Page 17.]

THE TREATY WITH LAHORE OF 1809.

Treaty between the British Government and the Rajah of Lahore, (25th of April, 1809.)

Whereas certain differences which had arisen between the British Government and the Rajah of Lahore have been happily and amicably adjusted; and both parties being anxious to maintain relations of perfect amity and concord, the following articles of treaty, which shall be binding on the heirs and successors of the two parties, have been concluded by the Rajah Runjeet Singh in person, and by the agency of C.T. Metcalfe, Esquire, on the part of the British Government.

Article 1.—Perpetual friendship shall subsist between the British Government and the State of Lahore: the latter shall be considered, with respect to the former, to be on the footing of the most favoured powers, and the British Government will have no concern with the territories and subjects of the Rajah to the northward of the river Sutlej.

Article 2.—The Rajah will never maintain in the territory which he occupies on the left bank of the river Sutlej, more troops than are necessary for the internal duties of that territory, nor commit or suffer any incroachments on the possessions or rights of the Chiefs in its vicinity.

Article 3.—In the event of a violation of any of the preceding articles, or of a departure from the rules of friendship, this treaty shall be considered null and void.

Article 4.—This treaty, consisting of four articles, having been settled and concluded at Umritsur, on the 25th day of April, 1809, Mr. C.T. Metcalfe has delivered to the Rajah of Lahore a copy of the same in English and Persian, under his seal and signature; and the Rajah has delivered another copy of the same under his seal and signature, and Mr. C.T. Metcalfe engages to procure within the space of two months, a copy of the same duly ratified by the Right Honourable the Governor-General in Council, on the receipt of which by the Rajah, the present treaty shall be considered complete and binding on both parties, and the copy of it now delivered to the Rajah shall be returned.

II.

[Page 17.]

SIR DAVID OCHTERLONY'S PROCLAMATION OF 1809.

Precept or "Ittillah Nameh," under the Seal of General St. Leger, and under the Seal and Signature of Colonel Ochterlony; written on the 9th of February, 1809, corresponding to the 23d Zee Hijeh, 1223, Hijree.

The British army having encamped near the frontiers of the Maharajah Runjeet Singh, it has been thought proper to signify the pleasure of the British Government, by means of this precept, in order to make all the Chiefs of the Maharajah acquainted with the sentiments of the British Government, which have solely for their object and aim to confirm the friendship with the Maharajah, and to prevent any injury to his country, the preservation of friendship between the two States, depending on particular conditions which are hereby detailed.

The Thânnahs in the fortress of Khur'r, Khanpore, and other places on this side of the river Sutlej, which have been placed in the hands of the dependents of the Maharajah, shall be razed, and the same places restored to their ancient possessors.

The force of cavalry and infantry which may have crossed to this side of the Sutlej must be recalled to the other side, to the country of the Maharajah.

The troops stationed at the Ghât of Philour must march thence, and depart to the other side of the river as described, and in future the troops of the Maharajah shall never advance into the country of the Chiefs situated on this side of the river, who have called in for their security and protection Thânnahs of the British Government; but if in the manner that the British have placed Thânnahs of moderate number on this side of the Sutlej, if in like manner a small force by way of Thânnah be stationed at the Ghât of Philour, it will not be objected to.

If the Maharajah persevere in the fulfilment of the above stipulations, which he so repeatedly professed to do in the presence of Mr. Metcalfe, such fulfilment will confirm the mutual friendship. In case of non-compliance with these stipulations, then shall it be plain that the Maharajah has no regard for the friendship of the British, but, on the contrary, resolves on enmity. In such case the victorious British army shall commence every mode of defence.

The communication of this precept is solely with the view of publishing the sentiments of the British, and to know those of the Maharajah. The British are confident that the Maharajah will consider the contents of this precept as abounding to his real advantage, and as affording a conspicuous proof of their friendship; that with their capacity for war they are also intent on peace.

III.

[Page 25.]

GENERAL THOMAS'S OPINION OF ARTILLERY.

I MUST here observe, that in having so very large an Artillery, General Thomas proved his appreciation of powerful batteries, an experience which he had probably acquired on board a man-of-war, as everything, in a naval action, depends upon the quick application of a powerful broadside of, say thirty, forty, or sixty guns. General Thomas had twelve guns to every thousand men. In Europe, the largest number ever used, was by the Russians, in 1807, namely seven guns to every thousand men. Hyder Ali Khan and Tippoo Sultan always used a great number of guns of a large calibre; in like manner the Maharatta chiefs, Sindiah and Holcar brought eighty and a hundred guns into the field of battle. Except very recently, we have had fewer guns than the Sikhs; the battle of Goojerat (Feb. 21, 1849) being the only one in which we appear to have been superior to the enemy in this respect.

IV.

[PAGE 25.]

THE TREATY WITH LAHORE OF 1806.

Treaty of Friendship and Unity between the Honourable East India Company and the Sirdars Runjeet Singh and Futteh Singh. (1st of January, 1806.)

SIRDAR Runjeet Singh and Sirdar Futteh Singh have consented to the following articles of agreement concluded by Lieutenant-Colonel John Malcolm, under the special authority of the Right Honourable Lord Lake, himself duly authorized by the Honourable Sir George Hilaro Barlow, Bart., Governor-General, and Sirdar Futteh Singh, as principal on the part of himself, and plenipotentiary on the part of Runjeet Singh:—

Article 1.—Sirdar Runjeet Singh and Sirdar Futteh Singh Aloowalla, hereby agree that they will cause Jeswunt Rao Holcar to remove with his army to the distance of thirty coss from Umritsur immediately, and will never hereafter hold any further connection with him, or aid or assist him with troops, or in any other manner whatever; and they further agree that they will not in any way molest such of Jeswunt Rao Holcar's followers or troops as are desirous of returning to their homes in the Deccan, but, on the contrary, will render them every assistance in their power for carrying such intention into execution.

Article 2.—The British Government hereby agrees, that in case a pacification should not be effected between that Government and Jeswunt Rao Holcar, the British army shall move from its present encampment, on the banks of the river Beeah, as soon as Jeswunt Rao Holcar aforesaid shall have marched his army to the distance of thirty coss from Umritsur; and that in any treaty which may hereafter be concluded between the British Government and Jeswunt Rao Holcar, it shall be stipulated that, immediately after the conclusion of the said treaty, Holcar shall evacuate the territories of the Sikhs, and march towards his own, and that he shall in no way whatever injure or destroy such parts of the Sikh country as may lie in his route. The British Government further agrees that, as long as the said Chieftains, Runjeet Singh and Futteh Singh, abstain from holding any friendly connection with the enemies of that Government, or from committing any act of hostility on their own parts against the said Government, the British armies shall never enter the territories of the said Chieftains, nor will the British Government form any plans for the seizure or sequestration of their possessions or property.

Dated 1st of January, 1806.

V.

[PAGE 26.]

PROCLAMATION OF PROTECTION TO CIS SUTLEJ STATES AGAINST LAHORE OF 1809.

Translation of an "Ittilah Nameh," addressed to the Chiefs of the Country of Malwa and Sirhind, on this side of the river Sutlej. (3rd of May, 1809.)

IT is clearer than the sun and better proved than the existence of yesterday, that the marching of a detachment of British troops to this side of the river Sutlej was entirely at the application and earnest entreaty of the several Chiefs, and originated solely from friendly considerations in the British Government, to preserve them in their possessions and independence. A treaty having been concluded, on the 25th of April, 1809, between Mr. Metcalfe on the part of the British Government, and Maharajah Runjeet Singh, agreeably to the orders of the Right Honourable the Governor-General in Council, I have the pleasure of publishing, for the satisfaction of the Chiefs of the country of Malwa and Sirhind, the pleasure and resolution of the British Government, as contained in the seven following articles:—

Article 1.—The country of the Chiefs of Malwa and Sirhind having entered under the British protection, they shall in future be secured from the authority and influence of Maharajah Runjeet Singh, conformably to the terms of the treaty.

Article 2.—All the country of the Chiefs thus taken under protection shall be exempted from all pecuniary tribute to the British Government.

Article 3.—The Chiefs shall remain in the full exercise of the same rights and authority in their own possessions which they enjoyed before they were received under the British protection.

Article 4.—Should a British force, on purposes of general welfare, be required to march through the country of the said Chiefs, it is necessary and incumbent that every Chief shall, within his own possessions, assist and furnish, to the full of his power, such force with supplies of Grain and other necessaries which may be demanded.

Article 5.—Should an enemy approach from any quarter, for the purpose of conquering this country, friendship and mutual interest require that the Chiefs join the British army with all their force, and, exerting themselves in expelling the enemy, act under discipline and proper obedience.

Article 6.—All European articles brought by merchants from the eastern districts, for the use of the army, shall be allowed to pass, by the Thânnahdars and Sayerdars of the several Chiefs, without molestation and the demand of duty.

Article 7.—All horses purchased for the use of cavalry regiments, whether in the district of Sirhind or elsewhere, the bringers of which being provided with sealed "Rahdaries" from the Resident at Delhi, or officer commanding at Sirhind, shall be allowed to pass through the country of the said Chiefs without molestation or the demand of duty.

VI.

[Page 27.]

PROCLAMATION OF PROTECTION TO CIS SUTLEJ STATES AGAINST ONE ANOTHER OF 1811.

For the Information and Assurance of the Protected Chiefs of the Plains between the Sutlej and the Jumna. (22nd of August, 1811.)

On the 3rd of May, 1809, an "Ittilah Nameh," comprised of seven articles, was issued by the orders of the British Government, purporting that the country of the Sirdars of Sirhind and Malwa having come under their protection, Rajah Runjeet Singh, agreeably to treaty, had no concern with the possessions of the above Sirdars: That the British Government had no intention of claiming Peishkushs or Nuzerana, and that they should continue in the full control and enjoyment of their respective possessions. The publication of the above "Ittilah Nameh" was intended to afford every confidence to the Sirdars, that the protection of the country was the sole object, that they had no intention of control, and that those having possessions should remain in full and complete enjoyment thereof.

Whereas several Zumindars and other subjects of the Chiefs of this country have preferred complaints to the officers of the British Government, who, having in view the tenor of the above "Ittilah Nameh," have not attended, and will not in future pay attention to them;—for instance, on the 15th of June, 1811, Delawur Ali Khan of Samana complained to the Resident of Delhi against the officers of Rajah Sahib Singh, for jewels and other property said to have been seized by them, who, in reply, observed, that the "Cusba of Samana being in the Ameeldary of Rajah Sahib Singh, his complaint should be made to him;" and also, on the 12th of July, 1811, Dussowndha Singh and Goormook Singh complained to Colonel Ochterlony, Agent to the Governor-General, against Sirdar Churrut Singh, for their shares of property, etc.; and in reply it was written on the back of their urzee, "that since during the period of three years, no claim was preferred against Churrut Singh by any of his brothers, nor even the name of any co-partner mentioned; and since it was advertised in the 'Ittilah Nameh' delivered to the Sirdars, that every Chief should remain in the quiet and full enjoyment of his domains, the petition could not be attended to,"—the insertion of these answers to complaints is intended as examples, and also that it may be impressed on the minds of every Zumindar and other subject, that the attainment of justice is to be expected from their respective Chiefs only, that they may not, in the smallest degree swerve from the observance of subordination.—It is, therefore, highly incumbent upon the Rajahs and other Sirdars of this side of the river Sutlej, that they explain this to their respective subjects, and court their confidence, that it may be clear to them, that complaints to the officers of the British Government will be of no avail, and that they consider their respective Sirdars as the source of justice, and that, of their free will and accord, they observe uniform obedience.

And whereas, according to the first Proclamation, it is not the intention of the British Government to interfere in the possessions of the Sirdars of this country, it is nevertheless, for the purpose of ameliorating the condition of the community, particularly necessary to give general information, that several Sirdars have, since the incursion of Rajah Runjeet Singh, wrested the estates of others, and deprived them of their lawful possessions, and that in the restoration they have used delays, until detachments of the British army have been sent to effect restitution, as in the case of the Rannee of Terah, the Sikhs of Cholian, the Talookas of Carowley and Chehloundy, and the village of Cheeba; and the reason of such delays and evasions can only be attributed to the temporary enjoyment of the revenues, and subjecting the owners to irremediable losses:—It is, therefore, by order of the British Government, hereby proclaimed, that if any one of the Sirdars or others has forcibly taken possession of the estates of others, or otherwise injured the lawful owners, it is necessary that, before the occurrence of any complaint, the proprietor should be satisfied, and by no means to defer the restoration of the property,—in which, however, should delays be made, and the interference of the British authority become requisite, the revenues of the estate from the date of ejection of the lawful proprietor, together with whatever other losses the inhabitants of that place may sustain from the march of troops, shall without scruple be demanded from the offending party; and for disobedience of the present orders, a penalty, according to the circumstances of the case and of the offender, shall be levied, agreeably to the decision of the British Government.

VII.

[Page 28.]

INDUS NAVIGATION TREATY OF 1832.

Articles of Convention established between the Honourable the East India Company, and his Highness the Maharajah Runjeet Singh, the Ruler of the Punjaub, for the opening of the Navigation of the rivers Indus and Sutlej. (Originally drafted 26th of December, 1832.)

By the grace of God, the relations of firm alliance and indissoluble ties of friendship existing between the Honourable the East India Company and his Highness the Maharajah Runjeet Singh, founded on the auspicious treaty formerly concluded by Sir T.C. Metcalfe, Bart., and since confirmed in the written pledge of sincere amity presented by the Right Honourable Lord W.C. Bentinck, G.C.B. and G.C.H., Governor-General of British India, at the meeting at Rooper, are, like the sun, clear and manifest to the whole world, and will continue unimpaired, and increase in strength from generation to generation:—By virtue of these firmly established bonds of friendship, since the opening of the navigation of the rivers Indus proper (*i.e.* Indus below the confluence of the Punjaub) and Sutlej, (a measure deemed expedient by both States, with a view to promote the general interests of commerce),—has lately been effected through the agency of Captain C.M. Wade, Political Agent at Loodianna, deputed by the Right Honourable the Governor-General for that purpose. The following Articles, explanatory of the conditions by which the said navigation is to be regulated, as concerns the nomination of officers, the mode of collecting the duties, and the protection of the trade by that route, have been framed, in order that the officers of the two States employed in their execution may act accordingly:—

Article 1.—The provisions of the existing treaty relative to the right bank of the river Sutlej and all its stipulations, together with the contents of the friendly pledge already mentioned, shall remain binding, and a strict regard to preserve the relations of friendship between the two States shall be the ruling principle of action. In accordance with that treaty, the Honourable Company has not, nor will have any concern with the right bank of the river Sutlej.

Article 2.—The tariff which is to be established for the line of navigation in question is intended to apply exclusively to the passage of merchandise by that route, and not to interfere with the transit duties levied on goods proceeding from one hank of the river to the other, nor with the places fixed for their collection: they are to remain as heretofore.

Article 3.—Merchants frequenting the same route, while within the limits of the Maharajah's Government, are required to show a due regard to his authority, as is done by merchants generally, and not to commit any acts offensive to the civil and religious institutions of the Sikhs.

Article 4.—Any one purposing to go the said route will intimate his intention to the Agent of either State, and apply for a passport, agreeably to a form to be laid down; having obtained which, he may proceed on his journey. The merchants coming from Umritsur, and other parts on the right bank of the river Sutlej, are to intimate their intentions to the agent of the Maharajah, at Hurrekee, or other appointed places, and obtain a passport through him; and merchants coming from Hindoostan, or other parts on the left bank of the river Sutlej, will intimate their intentions to the Honourable Company's Agent and obtain a passport through him. As foreigners, and Hindoostanees, and Sirdars of the protected Sikh States and elsewhere, are not in the habit of crossing the Sutlej without a passport from the Maharajah's officers, it is expected that such persons will hereafter also conform to the same rule, and not cross without the usual passports.

Article 5.—A tariff shall be established exhibiting the rate of duties leviable on each description of merchandise, which, after having been approved by both Governments, is to be the standard by which the superintendents and collectors of customs are to be guided.

Article 6.—Merchants are invited to adopt the new route with perfect confidence: no one shall be suffered to molest them or unnecessarily impede their progress, care being taken that they are only detained for the collection of the duties, in the manner stipulated, at the established stations.

Article 7.—The officers who are to be entrusted with the collection of the duties, and examination of the goods on the right bank of the river shall be stationed at Mithenkote and Hurrekee; at no other places but these two, shall boats in transit on the river be liable to examination or stoppage. When the persons in charge of boats stop of their own accord to take in or give out cargo, the goods will be liable to the local transit duty of the Maharajah's Government, previously to their being landed, as provided in Article 2. The superintendent stationed at Mithenkote having examined the cargo, will levy the established duty, and grant a passport, with a written account of the cargo and freight. On the arrival of the boat at Hurrekee, the superintendent of that station will compare the passport with the cargo; and whatever goods are found in excess will be liable to the payment of the established duty, while the rest, having already paid duty at Mithenkote, will pass on free. The same rule shall be observed in respect to merchandise conveyed from Hurrekee by the way of the rivers towards Scinde, that whatever may be fixed as the share of duties on the right bank of the river Sutlej, in right of the Maharajah's own dominions and of those in allegiance to him, the Maharajah's officers will collect it at the places appointed. With regard to the security and safety of merchants who may adopt this route, the Maharajah's officers shall afford them every protection in their power; and merchants, on halting for the night on either bank of the Sutlej, are required, with reference to the treaty of friendship which exists between the two States, to give notice, and to show their passports to the Thânnahdar, or officers in authority at the place, and request protection for themselves: if, notwithstanding this precaution, loss should at any time occur, a strict enquiry will be made, and reclamation sought from those who are blamable. The Articles of the present treaty for opening the navigation of the rivers above mentioned having, agreeably to subsisting relations, been approved by the Right Honourable the Governor-General, shall be carried into execution accordingly.

Dated Lahore the 26th of December, 1832.

* * * * *

[PAGE 28.]

SUPPLEMENTARY INDUS NAVIGATION TREATY OF 1834.

Draft of a Supplementary Treaty between the British Government and Maharajah Runjeet Singh for establishing a Toll on the Indus. (29th of November, 1834.)

IN conformity with the subsisting relations of friendship, as established and confirmed by former treaties, between the Honourable the East India Company and his Highness Maharajah Runjeet Singh; and whereas in the 5th Article of the treaty concluded at Lahore on the 26th day of December, 1832, it was stipulated that a moderate scale of duties should be fixed by the two Governments in concert, to be levied on all merchandise on transit up and down the rivers Indus and Sutlej; the said Governments being now of opinion that, owing to the inexperience of the people of these countries in such matters, the mode of levying duties then proposed (*viz.* on the value and quantity of goods) could not fail to give rise to mutual misunderstandings and reclamations, have, with a view to prevent these results, determined to substitute a toll, which shall be levied on all boats, with whatever merchandise laden. The following articles have therefore been adopted as supplementary to the former treaty; and in conformity with them, each Government engages that the toll shall be levied, and its amount neither be increased nor diminished except by mutual consent.

Article 1.—A toll of 570 Rupees shall be levied on all boats laden with merchandise in transit on the rivers Indus and Sutlej, between the sea and Rooper, without reference to their size, or to the weight or value of their cargo; the above toll to be divided among the different States in proportion to the extent of territory which they possess on the banks of these rivers.

Article 2.—The portion of the above toll appertaining to the Lahore Chief in right of his territory on both banks of these rivers, as determined in the subjoined scale shall be levied opposite to Mithenkote on boats coming from the sea towards Rooper, and in the vicinity of Hurrekee Puttun on boats going from Rooper towards the sea, and at no other place:—

In right of territory on the right bank of the rivers Indus and Sutlej, 155 Rupees 4 annas.

In right of territory on the left bank of the rivers Indus and Sutlej, the Maharajah's share, of 67 Rupees 15 annas. 9 pies.

Article 3.—In order to facilitate the realization of the toll due to the different States, as well as for the speedy and satisfactory adjustment of any disputes which may arise connected with the safety of the navigation and the welfare of the trade by the new route, a British officer will reside opposite to Mithenkote, and a native agent on the part of the British Government, opposite to Hurrekee Puttun. These officers will be subject to the orders of the British Agent at Loodianna; and the Agents who may be appointed to reside at those places on the part of the other States concerned in the navigation, *viz.* Bhawulpore and Scinde, together with those of Lahore, will co-operate with them in the execution of their duties.

Article 4.—In order to guard against imposition on the part of merchants in making false complaints of being plundered of their property which formed no part of their cargoes, they are required, when taking out their passports, to produce an invoice of their cargo, which, being duly authenticated, a copy of it will be annexed to their passports; and wherever their boats may be brought to for the night, they are required to give immediate notice to the Thânnahdars or officers of the place, and to request protection for themselves, at the same time showing the passports they may have received at Mithenkote or Hurrekee, as the case may be.

Article 5.—Such parts of the 5th, 7th, 9th, and 10th Articles of the Treaty of the 26th of December, 1832, as have reference to the fixing a duty on the value and quantity of merchandise, and to the mode of its collection are hereby rescinded, and the foregoing articles substituted in their place, agreeably to which, and the conditions of the preamble, the toll will be levied.

N.B.—A distribution of the shares due to the British protected States and the feudatories of the Maharajah on the left bank of the Sutlej will be determined hereafter.

VIII.

[Page 32.]

DECLARATION OF WAR OF 1845.

Proclamation by the Governor-General of India.

Camp Lushkuree Khan ke Serai,
December 13th, 1845.

The British Government has ever been on terms of friendship with that of the Punjaub.

In the year 1809, a treaty of amity and concord was concluded between the British Government, and the late Maharajah Runjeet Singh, the conditions of which have always been faithfully observed by the British Government, and were scrupulously fulfilled by the late Maharajah.

The same friendly relations have been maintained with the successors of Maharajah Runjeet Singh by the British Government up to the present time.

Since the death of the late Maharajah Shere Singh, the disorganized state of the Lahore Government has made it incumbent on the Governor-General in Council to adopt precautionary measures for the protection of the British frontier: the nature of these measures and the cause of their adoption, were, at the time, fully explained to the Lahore Durbar.

Notwithstanding the disorganized state of the Lahore Government during the last two years, and many most unfriendly proceedings on the part of the Durbar, the Governor-General in Council has continued to evince his desire to maintain the relations of amity and concord which had so long existed between the two States, for the mutual interests and happiness of both. He has shown, on every occasion, the utmost forbearance, from consideration to the helpless state of the infant Maharajah, Dhuleep Singh, whom the British Government had recognised as the successor to the late Maharajah Shere Singh.

The Governor-General in Council sincerely desired to see a strong Sikh Government re-established in the Punjaub, able to control its army, and to protect its subjects; he had not, up to the present moment, abandoned the hope of seeing that important object effected by the patriotic efforts of the Chiefs and people of that country.

The Sikh army recently marched from Lahore towards the British frontier, as it was alleged, by the orders of the Durbar, for the purpose of invading the British territory.

The Governor-General's Agent, by direction of the Governor-General, demanded an explanation of this movement, and no reply being returned within a reasonable time, the demand was repeated. The Governor-General, unwilling to believe in the hostile intentions of the Sikh Government, to which no provocation had been given, refrained from taking any measures which might have a tendency to embarrass the Government of the Maharajah, or to induce collision between the two States.

When no reply was given to the repeated demand for explanation, while active military preparations were continued at Lahore, the Governor-General considered it necessary to order the advance of troops towards the frontier, to reinforce the frontier posts.

The Sikh army has now, without a shadow of provocation, invaded the British territories.

The Governor-General must therefore take measures for effectually protecting the British provinces, for vindicating the authority of the British Government, and for punishing the violators of treaties and the disturbers of the public peace.

The Governor-General hereby declares the possessions of Maharajah Dhuleep Singh, on the left or British bank of the Sutlej, confiscated and annexed to the British territories.

The Governor-General will respect the existing rights of all Jaghirdars, Zumindars, and tenants in the said possessions, who, by the course they now pursue, evince their fidelity to the British Government.

The Governor-General hereby calls upon all the Chiefs and Sirdars in the protected territories to co-operate cordially with the British Government for the punishment of the common enemy, and for the maintenance of order in these States. Those of the Chiefs who show alacrity and fidelity in the discharge of this duty, which they owe to the protecting power, will find their interests promoted thereby; and those who take a contrary course will be treated as enemies to the British Government, and will be punished accordingly.

The inhabitants of all the territories on the left bank of the Sutlej are hereby directed to abide peaceably in their respective villages, where they will receive efficient protection by the British Government. All parties of men found in armed bands, who can give no satisfactory account of their proceedings, will be treated as disturbers of the public peace.

All subjects of the British Government, and those who possess estates on both sides of the river Sutlej, who by their faithful adherence to the British Government, may be liable to sustain loss, shall be indemnified and secured in all their just rights and privileges.

On the other hand, all subjects of the British Government who shall continue in the service of the Lahore State, and who disobey the Proclamation by not immediately returning to their allegiance, will be liable to have their property on this side the Sutlej confiscated, and themselves declared to be aliens and enemies of the British Government.

IX.

[Page 42.]

SERVICES OF CAPTAIN HUMBLEY, RIFLE BRIGADE.

Captain Humbley served with the 95th (Rifle Brigade) at the siege of Copenhagen, in 1807, and was engaged in some skirmishes near that city, and in the action of

Kioge; he was also present at the surrender of Copenhagen, and of the whole of the Danish navy. In 1808, he landed with a detachment in Portugal, and was present at the battles of Roleia and Vimiera, the advance from Lisbon into Spain, the subsequent retreat from Salamanca, the action of Calcavellas, and the battle of Corunna. He served on the Walcheren expedition, in 1809, commanded an advanced outpost before Flushing, on the night of the 31st of July, when he surprised, and took prisoners, an outlying picquet of the enemy; on the following day, while under the fortifications of Flushing, he was severely wounded in the forehead by a musket-ball, which lodged and was extracted, and the head trepanned.

Captain Humbley joined the army in the Peninsula in March, 1810, and served there until the end of that war in 1814, with the exception of four months in 1812.

On the passage to Spain, December the 5th, 1812, he was present at the capture, after a running fight of several miles, of a large, well-armed, American merchant ship.

Captain Humbley was present at the defence of Cadiz and Fort Matagorda, debarked at Tarifa, and was present at the battles of Barrosa, Salamanca, and Vittoria, and, in the last engagement, was severely wounded in the left arm. He took part in the action at Vera Bridge, storming the heights of Vera, and in the battles of the Pyrenees, where he was wounded near the left eye. He was present at the crossing of the Bidassoa, at the battles of Nivelle, Nive, and Orthes, in which last he was severely wounded in the right thigh; he was also in the action of Tarbes, and the battle of Toulouse, besides several minor engagements, skirmishes, and affairs of outposts.

Captain Humbley served also in the campaign of 1815, and was severely wounded at the battle of Waterloo, by a musket-ball in each shoulder. The two balls having lodged, one was extracted two days afterwards, but the other still remains lodged under the scapula in the left shoulder.

Captain Humbley has received the War Medal and Twelve Clasps.

X.

[Page 45.]

INSCRIPTION ON COLONEL CURETON'S MONUMENT.

A monument, by R. Westmacott, Junr., R.A., F.R.S., is about to be erected at Shrewsbury, to the memory of Colonel Cureton. The gallant Colonel will be represented at full length, lying on his back, with his hands clasped. The following is the inscription:

SACRED TO THE MEMORY
OF
COLONEL G.R. CURETON,
C.B., AND A.D.C., TO THE QUEEN,
ADJUTANT-GENERAL OF H.M. FORCES IN INDIA,
AND LATE LIEUT.-COLONEL COMMANDING THE 16TH LANCERS WHO
FELL IN AN ENGAGEMENT WITH THE SIKH TROOPS AT

RAMNUGGUR, ON THE 22ND OF NOVEMBER, 1848,
WHEN COMMANDING THE CAVALRY OF THE BRITISH ARMY
UNDER GENERAL LORD GOUGH, G.C.B.,
THIS MONUMENT IS ERECTED BY HIS COMRADES AND BROTHER
OFFICERS IN INDIA. BY WHOM HE WAS HELD, AS A
SOLDIER, IN UNIVERSAL ADMIRATION AND
RESPECT; AND IN LOVE AND ESTEEM
AS A FRIEND.

XI.

[Page 71.]

OFFICIAL DESPATCHES.

From the Governor-General of India to the Secret Committee of the East India Company, dated Camp, Ferozepore, Dec. 31st, 1845.

The Sikh army, in large numbers, commenced crossing the Sutlej on the 11th, and, after investing Ferozepore on one side, took up an entrenched position at the village of Ferozeshah, about ten miles in advance of Ferozepore, and about the same distance from the village of Moodkee.

In this camp the enemy had placed 108 pieces of cannon, some of large calibre, with a force exceeding 50,000 men, for the purpose of intercepting the approach of the British force moving up from Umballa, to the relief of Ferozepore, which had been thus treacherously attacked, without provocation or declaration of hostilities.

I had ordered, on the 8th inst., that portion of our army posted at Umballa for defensive purposes, to move up on the 11th; and, after a rapid march of 150 miles, it reached Moodkee on the 18th, where, on the evening of the same day, it repulsed an attack of the Sikh army, and captured seventeen guns. On the following day the army was concentrated at Moodkee, and, on the 21st, moved by its left on Ferozepore; and having, on the march, formed its junction, at half-past one o'clock, with 5,000 men and twenty-one guns, under Major-Gen. Sir John Littler, which had moved from Ferozepore that morning, the Commander-in-Chief formed the army in order of battle, and attacked the enemy's entrenched camp, and, on that evening and the following morning, captured severity pieces of artillery, taking possession of the enemy's camp, with a large quantity of ammunition and warlike stores.

These successful and energetic operations have been followed by the retreat of the Sikh army to the other side of the Sutlej; the British army being now encamped between Ferozepore and the fords of the Sutlej.

You will not fail to observe that these important and brilliant successes have been achieved by that portion of our army posted at and in advance of Umballa for defensive purposes, and that our forces from Meerut and other stations from the rear, ordered to move up at the same time, are in reserve, and will reach this neighbourhood between the 5th and the 9th of January.

I have the honour to inclose two reports from the Commander-in-Chief, detailing the admirable manner in which these important duties have been performed.

The Commander-in-Chief has successfully accomplished every object I had directed him to effect for the relief of Ferozepore, and the protection of the British States. No accident or failure has occurred during: the complicated operations of a combined movement; and our army, whether for defence or attack, has shewn, as heretofore, that its power is irresistible.

From General Sir Hugh Gough, Bart., G.C.B., the Commander-in-Chief of the Army in India, to the Governor-General of India.

Head Quarters, Army of the Sutlej,
Camp, Moodkee, Dec. 19th, 1845.

Right Hon. Sir,

It would be a superfluous form in me to address to you a narrative of the campaign which has opened against the Sikhs, and the successful action of yesterday, since you have in person shared the fatigues and dangers of our army, and witnessed its efforts and privations, but that my position at its head renders this my duty; and it is necessary, from that position, I should place these events on record, for the information of all Europe, as well as of all India.

You, Sir, know, but others have to be told, that the sudden and unprovoked aggression of the Sikhs, by crossing the Sutlej with the great proportion of their army, with the avowed intention of attacking Ferozepore in time of profound peace, rendered indispensable, on our side, a series of difficult combinations for the protection of our frontier station, so unjustifiably and so unexpectedly menaced.

From the advanced and salient situation of Ferozepore, and its vicinity to the Sikh capital, its defence against a sudden attack became a difficult operation. It was always possible for the Sikh government to throw a formidable force upon it before one sufficiently numerous could on our side be collected to support it; but when, upon the 11th instant, it became known at Umballa, where I had established my head-quarters, that this invasion had actually taken place, the efforts to repel it followed each other in rapid succession; notwithstanding I had the fullest confidence in Major-General Sir John Littler, commanding at Ferozepore, and in the devotedness and gallantry of the troops occupying it.

The troops from the different stations in the Sirhind division were directed to move by forced marches upon Bussean, where, by a most judicious arrangement, you had directed supplies to be collected, within a wonderfully short space of time.

The main portion of the force at Loodianna was withdrawn, and a garrison thrown into the little fortress there. From this central position, already alluded to, both Loodianna and Ferozepore could be supported, and the safety of both places might be considered to be brought, in some measure, within the scope of the contingencies of a general action to be fought for their relief. All this is soon related; but most harassing have been the marches of the troops in completing this concentration. When their march had been further prolonged to this place, they had moved over a distance of upward of 150 miles in six days, along roads of heavy sand; their perpetual labour allowing them scarcely time to cook their food, even when they received it, and hardly an hour for repose, before they were called upon for renewed exertions.

When our leading corps reached Wudnee, a small jaghire of the late Maharajah Shere Singh, its garrison shut the gates of the fort against them; and, as our battering guns were far in the rear, it was determined to reserve it for future chastisement, and we remained content with compelling the village to furnish supplies (it could, however, provide little, except for our overworked cattle), under pain of enduring a cannonade and assault; this it did, without the necessity of firing a shot.

When we reached Wudnee, it was evident that the force before Ferozepore felt the influence of our movements, as we heard that a very large portion of that force had been detached to oppose our further advance; their feeling parties retired on the morning of the 18th before our Cavalry picquets, near the village and fort of Moodkee.

Soon after mid-day, the division under Major-General Sir Harry Smith, a brigade of that under Major-General Sir J. M'Caskill, and another of that under Major-General Gilbert, with five troops of Horse artillery, and two light field batteries, under Lieutenant Colonel Brooke, of the Horse Artillery (brigadier in command of the Artillery force), and the Cavalry division, consisting of H.M. 3rd Light Dragoons, the body-guard, 4th and 5th Light Cavalry, and 9th Irregular Cavalry, took up their encamping ground in front of Moodkee.

The troops were in a state of great exhaustion, principally from the want of water, which was not procurable on the road, when, about three P.M., information was received that the Sikh army was advancing; and the troops had scarcely time to get under arms, and move to their positions, when the fact was ascertained.

I immediately pushed forward the Horse Artillery and Cavalry, directing the Infantry, accompanied by the field batteries, to move forward in support. We had not proceeded beyond two miles when we found the enemy in position. They were said to consist of 15,000 to 20,000 Infantry, about the same force of Cavalry, and forty guns. They evidently had either just taken up this position, or were advancing in order of battle against us.

To resist their attack, and to cover the formation of the Infantry, I advanced the Cavalry under Brigadiers White, Gough, and Mactier, rapidly to the front, in columns of squadrons, and occupied the plain. They were speedily followed by the five troops of Horse Artillery, under Brigadier Brooke who took up a forward position, having the Cavalry then on his flanks.

The country is a dead flat, covered at short intervals with a low, but in some places, thick jhow jungle, and dotted with sandy hillocks. The enemy screened their Infantry and Artillery behind this jungle, and such undulations as the ground afforded; and whilst our twelve battalions formed from echelon of brigade into line, opened a very severe cannonade upon our advancing troops, which was vigorously replied to by the battery of Horse Artillery under Brigadier Brooke, which was soon joined by the two light field batteries. The rapid and well-directed fire of our artillery appeared soon to paralyse that of the enemy; and as it was necessary to complete our infantry dispositions without advancing the Artillery too near to the jungle, I directed the Cavalry under Brigadiers White and Gough, to make a flank movement on the enemy's left, with a view of threatening and turning that flank if possible. With praiseworthy gallantry, the 3rd Light Dragoons, with the 2nd brigade of Cavalry, consisting of the body guard and 5th Light Cavalry, with a portion of the 4th Lancers, turned the left of the Sikh army, and, sweeping along the whole rear of its Infantry and guns, silenced for a time the latter, and put their numerous cavalry to flight. Whilst this movement was taking place on the enemy's left, I directed the remainder of the 4th Lancers, the 9th Irregular Cavalry, under Brigadier Mactier, with a light field battery, to threaten their right. This manœuvre was also successful. Had not the Infantry and guns of the enemy been screened by the jungle, these brilliant charges of the Cavalry would have been productive of greater effect.

When the Infantry advanced to the attack, Brigadier Brooke rapidly pushed on his Horse Artillery close to the jungle, and the cannonade was resumed on both sides. The Infantry under Major-Generals Sir Harry Smith, Gilbert, and Sir John M'Caskill, attacked in echelon of lines the enemy's Infantry, almost invisible amongst wood and the approaching darkness of night. The opposition of the enemy was such as might have been expected from troops who had everything at stake, and who had long vaunted of being irresistible. Their ample and extended line, from their great superiority of numbers, far outflanked ours; but this was counter-acted by the flank movements of our Cavalry. The attack of the Infantry now commenced, and the roll of fire from this powerful arm soon convinced the Sikh army that they had met with a foe they little expected; and their whole force was driven from position after position with great slaughter, and the loss of seventeen pieces of artillery, some of them of heavy calibre; our infantry using that never failing weapon, the bayonet, whenever the enemy stood. Night only saved them from worse disaster; for this stout conflict was maintained during an hour and a half of dim starlight, amidst a cloud of dust from the sandy plain, which yet more obscured every object.

I regret to say, this gallant and successful attack was attended with considerable loss; the force bivouacked upon the field for some hours, and only returned to its encampment after ascertaining that it had no enemy before it, and that night prevented the possibility of a regular advance in pursuit.

H. Gough, General,
Commander-in-Chief.

From His Excellency the Commander-in-Chief to the Right Hon. the Governor-General of India, dated Camp, Ferozeshah, December 22nd, 1845.

Right Honourable Sir,

I have again to congratulate you on the success of our arms. A grand battle has been fought against the Sikh army at this place, and, by the blessing of Divine providence, victory has been won, by the valour of our troops, against odds and under circumstances which will render this action one of the most memorable in the page of Indian history.

After the combat of the 18th at Moodkee, information was received the following day, that the enemy, increased in numbers, were moving on to attack us. A line of defence was taken up in advance of our encampment, and dispositions made to repel assault; but the day wore away without their appearing, and at night we had the satisfaction of being reinforced by H.M. 29th Foot, and the East India Company's 1st European Light Infantry, with our small division of heavy guns.

I must here allude to a circumstance most favourable to our efforts in the field. On this evening, in addition to the valuable counsel with which you had in every emergency before favoured me, you were pleased yet further to strengthen my hands, by kindly offering your services as second in command in my army. I need hardly say with how much pleasure the offer was accepted.

On the morning of the 21st, the offensive was resumed; our columns of all arms debouched four miles on the road to Ferozeshah, where it was known that the enemy, posted in great force, and with a most formidable artillery, had remained since the action of the 18th, incessantly employed in entrenching his position. Instead of advancing to the direct attack of their formidable works, our force manœuvred to their right: the second and fourth divisions of infantry, in front, supported by the first division and cavalry in second line, continued to defile for some time out of cannon-shot between the Sikhs and Ferozepore. The desired effect was not long delayed, a cloud of dust was seen on the left, and according to the instructions sent him on the preceding evening, Major-General Sir John Littler, with his division, availing himself of the offered opportunity, was discovered in full march to unite his force with mine. The junction was soon effected; and thus was accomplished one of the great objects of all our harassing marches and privations, in the relief of this division of our army from the blockade of the numerous forces by which it was surrounded.

Dispositions were now made for a united attack on the enemy's entrenched camp. We found it to be a parallelogram, of about a mile in length, and half a mile in breadth, including within its area the strong village of Ferozeshah; the shorter sides looking towards the Sutlej and Moodkee, and the longer towards Ferozepore and the open country. We moved against the last-named face, the ground in front of which was like the Sikh position in Moodkee, covered with low jungle.

The divisions of Major-general Sir John Littler, Brigadier Wallace (who had succeeded Major-general Sir John M'Caskill), and Major-general Gilbert, deployed into line, having in the centre our whole force of artillery, with the exception of three troops of horse artillery, one on either flank and one in support, to be moved as occasion required. Major-general Sir Harry Smith's division, and our small cavalry force, moved in second line, having a brigade in reserve to cover each wing.

I should here observe, that I committed the charge and direction of the left wing to Lieutenant-general Sir Henry Hardinge, while I personally conducted the right.

A very heavy cannonade was opened by the enemy, who had dispersed over their position upwards of one hundred guns, more than forty of which were of battering calibre; these kept up a heavy and well-directed fire, which the practice of our far less numerous artillery, of much lighter metal, checked in some degree, but could not silence; finally, in the face of a storm of shot and shell, our infantry advanced and carried these formidable intrenchments; they threw themselves upon their guns, and with matchless gallantry wrested them from the enemy; but, when the batteries were partially within our grasp, our soldiery had to face such a fire of musketry from the Sikh infantry, arrayed behind their guns, that, in spite of the most heroic efforts, a portion only of the entrenchment could be carried. Night fell while the conflict was everywhere raging.

Although I now brought up Major-general Sir Harry Smith's division, and he captured and long retained another point of the position, and her Majesty's 3rd Light Dragoons charged and took some of the most formidable batteries, yet the enemy remained in possession of a considerable portion of the great quadrangle, whilst our troops, intermingled with theirs, kept possession of the remainder, and finally bivouacked upon it, exhausted by their gallant efforts, greatly reduced in numbers, and suffering extremely from thirst, yet animated by an indomitable spirit. In this state of things the long night wore away.

Near the middle of it, one of their heavy guns was advanced and played with deadly effect upon our troops. Lieut.-general Sir Henry Hardinge immediately formed H.M. 80th Foot and the 1st European Light Infantry. They were led to the attack by their commanding officers, and animated in their exertions by Lieut.-col. Wood (aide-de-camp to the Lieut.-general), who was wounded in the outset. The 80th captured the gun, and the enemy, dismayed by this counter-check, did not venture to press on further. During the whole night, however, they continued to harass our troops by fire of artillery, wherever moonlight discovered our position.

But with daylight of the 22nd came retribution. Our infantry formed line, supported on both flanks by horse artillery, whilst a fire was opened from our centre by such of our heavy guns as remained effective, aided by a flight of rockets. A masked battery played with great effect upon this point, dismounting our pieces and blowing up our tumbrils. At this moment Lieutenant-general Sir Henry Hardinge placed himself at the head of the left, whilst I rode at the head of the right wing.

Our line advanced, and, unchecked by the enemy's fire, drove them rapidly out of the village of Ferozeshah and their encampment; then, changing front to its left, on its centre, our force continued to sweep the camp, bearing down all opposition, and dislodged the enemy from their whole position. The line then halted, as if on a day of manœuvre, receiving its two leaders, as they rode along its front, with a gratifying cheer, and displaying the captured standards of the Khalsa army. We had taken upwards of seventy-three pieces of cannon, and were masters of the whole field.

The force assumed a position on the ground which it had won, but even here its labours were not to cease. In the course of two hours, Sirdar Tej Singh, who had commanded in the last great battle, brought up from the vicinity of Ferozepore fresh battalions and a large field of artillery, supported by 30,000 Ghorepurras, hitherto encamped near the river. He drove in our cavalry parties, and made strenuous efforts to regain the position at Ferozeshah; this attempt was defeated; but its failure had scarcely become manifest, when the Sirdar renewed the contest with more troops and a large artillery. He commenced by a combination against our left flank; and when this was frustrated, made such a demonstration against the captured village, as compelled us to change our whole front to the right. His guns during this manœuvre, maintained an incessant fire, whilst our artillery ammunition being completely expended in these protracted combats, we were unable to answer him with a single shot.

I now directed our almost exhausted cavalry to threaten both flanks at once, preparing the infantry to advance in support, which apparently caused him suddenly to cease his fire, and to abandon the field.

For twenty-four hours not a Sikh has appeared in our front. The remains of the Khalsa army are said to be in full retreat across the Sutlej, at Nuggurputhur and Tella, or marching up its left bank towards Hurrekeeputhur, in the greatest confusion and dismay. Of their chiefs, Bahadur Singh is killed; Lall Singh said to be wounded; Mehtab Singh, Adjoodhia Pershad, and Tej Singh, the late governor of Peshawur, have fled with precipitation. Their camp is the scene of the most awful carnage, and they have abandoned large stores of grain, camp equipage, and ammunition.

Thus has apparently terminated this unprovoked and criminal invasion of the peaceful provinces under British protection.

On the conclusion of such a narrative as I have given, it is surely superfluous in me to say that I am, and shall be to the last moment of my existence, proud of the army which I had the honour to command on the 21st and 22nd instant. To their gallant exertions I owe the satisfaction of seeing such a victory achieved, and the glory of having my own name associated with it.

The loss of this army has been heavy; how could a hope be formed that it should be otherwise? Within thirty hours this force stormed an intrenched camp, fought a general action, and sustained two considerable combats with the enemy. Within four days it has dislodged from their positions, on the left bank of the Sutlej, 60,000 Sikh soldiers, supported by upwards of 150 pieces of cannon, 108 of which the enemy acknowledge to have lost, and ninety-one of which are in our possession.

In addition to our losses in the battle, the captured camp was found to be everywhere protected by charged mines, by the successive springing of which many brave officers and men have been destroyed.

I have the honour to be, etc.,
H. Gough, General,
Commander-in-Chief, East Indies.

Extract from a Despatch of His Excellency the Commander-in-Chief to the Right Hon. the Governor-General, dated Feb. 1, 1846.

Head Quarters, Army of the Sutlej.

Meanwhile the Upper Sutlej has become the scene of very interesting operations.

It is a strange feature of this war, that the enemy, pressed for supplies on his own bank, has been striving to draw them from his jaghire estates on this side of the river. In the town and fort of Dhurmkote, which were filled with grain, he had in the second week of January a small garrison of mercenaries—Rohillas, Eusufzies, and Affghans. Major-General Sir Harry Smith was on the 18th sent against this place with a single brigade of his division and a light field battery. He easily effected its reduction, the troops within surrendering at discretion after a few cannon shots. But whilst he was yet in march, I received information of a more serious character. There remained little cause to doubt that Sirdar Runjoor Sing Mujetheea had crossed from Philour, at the head of a numerous force of all arms, and established himself in a position at Baran Hara, between the old and the new courses of the Sutlej: not only threatening the city of Loodianna with plunder and devastation, but indicating a determination to intersect the line of our communications at Bussean and Rackote.

The safety of the rich and populous town of Loodianna had been, in some measure, provided for by the presence of three battalions of Native Infantry, under Brigadier Godby, and the gradual advance of our reinforcements, amongst which was included her Majesty's 53rd regiment, and the position of the Shekawattee brigade, near Bussean, gave breathing time to us in that direction.

But on receipt of intelligence which could be relied on, of the movements of Runjoor Singh and his apparent views, Major-general Sir Harry Smith, with the brigade at Dhurmkote, and Brigadier Cureton's cavalry, was directed to advance by Jugraon towards Loodianna, and his second brigade, under Brigadier Wheeler, moved on to support him.

Then commenced a series of very delicate combinations, the momentous character of which can only be comprehended by reflecting on the task which had devolved on this army of guarding the frontier from Rooper down to Mundote.

The Major-General, breaking up from Jugraon, moved towards Loodianna, when the Sirdar, relying on the vast superiority of his forces, assumed the initiative, and endeavoured to intercept his progress by marching in a line parallel to him, and opening upon his troops a furious cannonade. The Major-General continued coolly to manœuvre; and when the Sikh Sirdar, bending round one wing of his army, enveloped his flank, he extricated himself by retiring with the steadiness of a field-day by echelon of battalions, and effected his communication with Loodianna, but not without severe loss.

Reinforced by Brigadier Godby, he felt himself to be strong; but his manœuvres had thrown him out of communication with Brigadier Wheeler; and a portion of his baggage had fallen into the hands of the enemy. The Sikh Sirdar took up an entrenched position at Buddiwal, supporting himself on its fort, but, threatened on either flank by General Smith and Brigadier Wheeler, finally decamped and moved down to the Sutlej. The British troops made good their junction, and occupied the abandoned position of Buddiwal; the Shekawattee brigade and her Majesty's 53rd regiment also added to the strength of the Major-General, and he prepared to attack the Sikh Sirdar on his new ground. But on the 26th, Runjoor Singh was reinforced from the right bank with 4,000 regular troops, 12 pieces of artillery, and a large force of cavalry.

Emboldened by this accession of strength, he ventured on the measure of advancing towards Jugraon apparently with the view of intercepting our communications by that route.

It is my gratifying duty to announce, that this presumption has been rebuked by a splendid victory obtained over him. He has not only been repulsed by the Major-General, but his camp at Aliwal carried by storm, the whole of his cannons and munitions of war captured, and his army driven headlong across the Sutlej, even on the right bank of which he found no refuge from the fire of our artillery.

I have now the honour to forward the Major-General's report, which has just reached me. It is so ample and luminous, that I might perhaps have spared some of the details into which admiration of the General's conduct, and of the brave army confided to him in these operations, has led me.

* * * * *

Camp, Field of the Battle of Aliwal,
January 30, 1846.

To the Adjutant-General of the Army.

Sir,

My despatch to his Excellency the Commander-in-Chief, of the 23rd instant, will have put his Excellency in possession of the position of the force under my command after having formed a junction with the troops at Loodianna, hemmed in by a formidable body of the Sikh army under Runjoor Sing and the Rajah of Ladwa. The enemy strongly entrenched himself around the little fort of Buddiwal by breastworks and "abattis," which he precipitately abandoned on the night of the 22nd instant (retiring, as it were, upon the ford of Tulwun), having ordered all the boats which were opposite Philour, to that ghât. This movement he effected during the night, and, by a considerable détour, placed himself at a distance of ten miles, and consequently out of my reach. I could, therefore, only push forward my cavalry so soon as I had ascertained he had marched during the night, and I occupied immediately his vacated position. It appeared subsequently he had no intention of re-crossing the Sutlej, but moved down to the Ghât of Tulwun (being cut off from that of Philour by the position my force occupied after its relief of Loodianna), for the purpose of protecting the passage of a very considerable reinforcement of twelve guns and 4,000 of the Regular or Aicen troops, called Avitabile's battalion, entrenching himself strongly in a semi-circle, his flanks resting on the river, his position covered with from forty to fifty guns (generally of large calibre), howitzers, and mortars. The reinforcement crossed during the night of the 27th instant, and encamped to the right of the main army.

Meanwhile his Excellency the Commander-in-Chief, with that foresight and judgment which marks the able general, had reinforced me by a considerable addition to my cavalry, some guns, and the 2nd brigade of my own division under Brigadier Wheeler, C.B. This reinforcement reached me on the 26th, and I had intended the next morning to move upon the enemy in his entrenchments; but the troops required one day's rest after the long marches Brigadier Wheeler had made.

I have now the honour to lay before you the operations of my united forces on the morning of the eventful 28th of January, for his Excellency's information. The body of troops under my command having been increased, it became necessary so to organize and brigade them as to render them manageable in action. The cavalry under the command of Brigadier Cureton, and horse artillery under Major Lawrenson, were put into two brigades; the one under Brigadier Mac Dowell, C.B., and the other under Brigadier Stedman. The 1st division as it stood, two brigades; her Majesty's 53rd and 30th Native Infantry, under Brigadier Wilson of the latter corps; the 36th Native Infantry and Nusseree battalion, under Brigadier Godby; and the Shekawattee brigade, under Major Forster. The Sirmoor battalion I attached to Brigadier Wheeler's brigade of the 1st division, the 42nd Native Infantry having been left at head-quarters.

At daylight on the 28th my order of advance was, the Cavalry in front, in contiguous columns of squadrons of regiments; two troops of Horse Artillery in the interval of brigades; the Infantry in contiguous columns of brigades at intervals of deploying distance; Artillery in the intervals, followed by two eight-inch howitzers on travelling carriages, brought into the field from the fort of Loodianna by the indefatigable exertions of Lieutenant-Colonel Lane, Horse Artillery; Brigadier Godby's brigade, which I had marched out from Loodianna the previous evening, on the right; the Shekawattee Infantry on the left; the 4th Irregular Cavalry and the Shekawattee Cavalry considerably to the right, for the purpose of sweeping the banks of the wet nullah on my right, and preventing any of the enemy's horse attempting an inroad towards Loodianna, or any attempt upon the baggage assembled round the Fort of Buddiwal.

In this order the troops moved forward towards the enemy, a distance of six miles, the advance conducted by Captain Waugh, 16th Lancers, the Deputy Assistant Quartermaster of Cavalry; Major Bradford of the 1st Cavalry, and Lieutenant Strachey, of the Engineers, who had been jointly employed in the conduct of patrols up to the enemy's position, and for the purpose of reporting upon the facility and points of approach. Previously to the march of the troops, it had been intimated to me by Major Mackeson, that the information by spies led to the belief that the enemy would move somewhere at daylight, either on Jugraon, my position of Buddiwal, or Loodianna. On a near approach to his outposts this rumour was confirmed by a spy, who had just left his camp, saying the Sikh army was actually in march towards Jugraon. My advance was steady, my troops well in hand, and if he had anticipated me on the Jugraon road, I could have fallen upon his centre with advantage.

From the tops of the houses of the village of Poorcin, I had a distant view of the enemy. He was in motion, and appeared directly opposite my front on a ridge, of which the village of Aliwal may be regarded as the centre. His left appeared still to occupy its ground in the circular entrenchment; his right was brought forward and occupied the ridge. I immediately deployed the cavalry into line, and moved on. As I neared the enemy, the ground became most favourable for the troops to manœuvre, being open and hard grass land. I ordered the Cavalry to take ground to the right and left by brigades, thus displaying the heads of the Infantry columns, and as they reached the hard ground I directed them to deploy into line. Brigadier Godby's brigade was in direct echellon to the rear of the right; the Shekawattee Infantry in like manner to the rear of my left; the cavalry in direct echelon on, and well to the rear of both flanks of the Infantry; the Artillery massed on the right, and centre, and left. After deployment I observed the enemy's left to out-flank me, I therefore broke into open columns and took ground to my right: when I had gained sufficient ground, the troops wheeled into line; there was no dust, the sun shone brightly. The manœuvres were performed with the celerity and precision of the most correct field-day. The glistening of the bayonets and swords of this order of battle was most imposing, and the line advanced. Scarcely had it moved forward 150 yards, when at ten o'clock the enemy opened a fierce cannonade from his whole line. At first his balls fell short, but quickly reached us. Thus upon him, and capable of better ascertaining his position, I was compelled to halt the line, though under fire, for a few moments, until I ascertained that by bringing up my right and carrying the village of Aliwal, I could with great effect precipitate myself upon his left and centre. I therefore quickly brought up Brigadier Godby's brigade, and with it and the 1st brigade under Brigadier Hicks, made a rapid and noble charge, carried the village, and two guns of large calibre. The line I ordered to advance,—her Majesty's 31st Foot and the Native regiments contending for the front, and the battle became general. The enemy had a numerous body of Cavalry on the heights to his left, and I ordered Brigadier Cureton to bring up the right brigade of cavalry, who, in the most gallant manner, dashed in among them, and drove them back upon their Infantry. Meanwhile a second gallant charge to my right was made by the Light Cavalry and the body-guard. The Shekawattee brigade was moved well to the right, in support of Brigadier Cureton. When I observed the enemy's encampment, and saw it was full of Infantry, I immediately brought upon it Brigadier Godby's brigade, by changing front, and taking the enemy's Infantry *en reverse*. They drove them before them, and took some guns without a check.

Whilst these operations were going on upon the right, and the enemy's left flank was thus driven back. I occasionally observed the brigade under Brigadier Wheeler, an officer in whom I have the greatest confidence, charging and carrying guns and everything before it, again connecting his line and moving on in a manner which ably displayed the coolness of the Brigadier and the gallantry of his irresistible brigade—her Majesty's 50th Foot, the 48th Native Infantry, and the Sirmoor battalion, although the loss was, I regret to say, severe in the 50th. Upon the left, Brigadier Wilson, with her Majesty's 53rd and 30th Native Infantry, equalled in celerity and regularity their comrades on the right; and this brigade was opposed to the "Aieen" troops, called Avitabile's, when the fight was fiercely raging.

The enemy, well driven back on his left and centre, endeavoured to hold his right to cover the passage of the river, and he strongly occupied the village of Bhoondee. I directed a squadron of the 16th Lancers, under Major Smith and Captain Pearson, to charge a body to the right of the village, which they did in the most gallant and determined style, bearing everything before them, as a squadron under Captain Bere had previously done, going through a square of infantry, wheeling about and re-entering the square in the most intrepid manner with the deadly lance. This charge was accompanied by the 3rd Light Cavalry, under Major Angelo, and as gallantly sustained. The largest gun upon the field and seven others were then captured, while the 53rd regiment carried the village by the bayonet, and the 30th Native Infantry wheeled round to the rear in a most spirited manner. Lieutenant-Colonel Alexander's and Captain Turton's troops of Horse Artillery, under Major Lawrenson, almost dashed among the flying infantry, committing great havoc, until about 800 or 1,000 men rallied under the high bank of a nullah, and opened a heavy, but ineffectual fire from below the bank. I immediately directed the 30th Native Infantry to charge them, which they were able to do upon their left flank, while in a line in rear of the village. This native corps nobly obeyed my orders, and rushed among the Avitabile troops, driving them from under the bank, and exposing them once more to the deadly fire of twelve guns within three hundred yards. The destruction was very great, as may be supposed, by guns served as these were. Her Majesty's 53rd Regiment moved forward in support of the 30th Native Infantry, by the right of the village. The battle was won, our troops advancing with the most perfect order to the common focus, the passage of the river. The enemy, completely hemmed in, were flying from our fire, and precipitating themselves in disordered masses into the ford and boats, in the utmost confusion and consternation. Our 8-inch howitzers soon began to play upon their boats, when the "debris" of the Sikh army appeared upon the opposite and high bank of the river, flying in every direction, although a sort of line was attempted to countenance their retreat, until all our guns commenced a furious cannonade, when they quickly receded. Nine guns were on the verge of the river by the ford. It appears as if they had been unlimbered to cover the ford. These, being loaded, were fired once upon our advance. Two others were sticking in the river; one of them we got out. Two were seen to sink in the quick-sands; two were dragged to the opposite bank and abandoned. These, and the one in the middle of the river, were gallantly spiked by Lieutenant Holmes, of the 11th Irregular Cavalry, and Gunner Scott, of the 1st Troop 2nd Brigade Horse Artillery, who rode into the stream, and crossed for the purpose, covered by our guns and light infantry.

Thus ended the battle of Aliwal, one of the most glorious victories ever achieved in India. By the united efforts of her Majesty's and the Hon. Company's troops, every gun the enemy had fell into our hands, as I infer from his never opening one upon us from the opposite bank of the river, which is high and favourable for the purpose: fifty-two guns are now in the Ordnance Park, two sunk in the bed of the Sutlej, and two were spiked on the opposite bank—making a total of fifty-six pieces of cannon captured or destroyed.[112] Many jinjalls which were attached to

[112] Eleven guns since ascertained to be sunk in the river, total sixty-seven; thirty odd jinjalls fell into our hands.

Avitabile's corps, and which aided in the defence of the village of Bhoondee, have also been taken. The whole army of the enemy has been driven headlong over the difficult ford of a broad river; his camp, baggage, stores of ammunition, and of grain—his all, in fact—wrested from him by the repeated charges of cavalry and infantry, aided by the guns of Alexander, Turton, Lane, Mill, Boileau, and of the Shekawattee brigade, and by the eight-inch howitzers, our guns literally being constantly ahead of everything. The determined bravery of all was as conspicuous as noble. I am unwont to praise when praise is not merited; and I here most avowedly express my firm opinion and conviction, that no troops in any battle on record ever behaved more nobly. British and native (no distinction) cavalry all vying with her Majesty's 16th Lancers, and striving to head in the repeated charges. Our guns and gunners, officers and men, may be equalled, but cannot be excelled, by any artillery in the world. Throughout the day no hesitation, a bold and intrepid advance; and thus it is that our loss is comparatively small, though I deeply regret to say severe. The enemy fought with much resolution; they maintained frequent rencontres with our cavalry hand to hand. In one charge of infantry upon her Majesty's 16th Lancers, they threw away their muskets, and came on with their swords and targets against the lance.

Having thus done justice, and justice alone, to the gallant troops his Excellency entrusted to my command, I would gladly, if the limits of a despatch (already too much lengthened, I fear), permitted me, do that justice to individuals all deserve. This cannot be....

The Fort of Goongrana has, subsequently to the battle, been evacuated, and I yesterday evening blew up the fort of Buddiwal. I shall now blow up that of Noorpore. A portion of the peasantry, viz., the Sikhs, appear less friendly to us, while the Mussulmans rejoice in being under our government.

I have, etc.,
(Signed) H.G. Smith,
Maj.-Gen. commanding.
Camp, Field of Battle of Aliwal, 30th January, 1846.
True copy (Signed) P. Grant, Major,
Dep. Adj.-Gen. of the army.

* * * * *

TO THE RIGHT HON. THE GOVERNOR-GENERAL OF INDIA.

Head-quarters, Army of the Sutlej,
Camp Kussoor, Feb. 13.

Right Hon. Sir,

This is the fourth despatch which I have had the honour of addressing to you since the opening of the campaign. Thanks to Almighty God, whose hand I desire to acknowledge in all our successes, the occasion of my writing now is to announce a fourth and most glorious and decisive victory!

My last communication detailed the movements of the Sikhs, and our counter-manœuvres, since the great day of Ferozeshah. Defeated on the Upper Sutlej, the enemy continued to occupy his position on the right bank, and formidable *tête de pont* and entrenchments on the left bank of the river, in front of the main body of our army. But on the 10th instant, all that he held of British territory, which was comprised in the ground on which one of his camps stood, was stormed from his grasp, and his audacity was again signally punished by a blow, sudden, heavy, and overwhelming. It is my gratifying duty to detail the measures which have led to this glorious result.

The enemy's works had been repeatedly reconnoitred during the time of my head-quarters being fixed at Nihalkee, by myself, by my departmental staff, and my engineer and artillery officers. Our observations, coupled with the reports of spies, convinced us that there had devolved on us the arduous task of attacking, in a position covered with formidable entrenchments, not fewer than 30,000 men, the best of the Khalsa troops, with seventy pieces of cannon, united by a good bridge to a reserve on the opposite bank, on which the enemy had a considerable camp and some artillery, commanding and flanking his field-works on our side. Major-General Sir Harry Smith's division having rejoined me on the evening of the 8th, and part of my siege-train having come up with me, I resolved, on the morning of the 10th, to dispose our mortars and battering guns on the alluvial land, within good range of the enemy's works. To enable us to do this, it was necessary first to drive in the enemy's pickets at the post of observation in front of Koodeewalla, and at the little Sobraon. It was directed that this should be done during the night of the 9th; but the execution of this part of the plan was deferred, owing to misconceptions and casual circumstances, until near daybreak. The delay was of little importance, as the event showed that the Sikhs had followed our example in occupying the two posts in force by day only. Of both, therefore, possession was taken without opposition. The battering and disposed field-artillery was then put in position in an extended semi-circle, embracing within its fire the works of the Sikhs. It had been intended that the cannonade should have commenced at daybreak; but so heavy a mist hung over the plain and river, that it became necessary to wait until the rays of the sun had penetrated it, and cleared the atmosphere. Meanwhile, on the margin of the Sutlej, on our left, two brigades of Major-General Sir R. Dick's division, under his personal command, stood ready to commence the assault against the enemy's extreme right. His 7th brigade, in which was the 10th Foot, reinforced by the 53rd Foot, and led by Brigadier Stacey, was to head the attack, supported, at 200 yards' distance, by the 6th brigade, under Brigadier Wilkinson. In reserve, was the 5th brigade, under Brigadier the Hon. T. Ashburnham, which was to move forward from the entrenched village of Koodeewalla, leaving, if necessary, a regiment for its defence. In the centre, Major-General Gilbert's division was deployed for support or attack; its right wing resting on, and in the village of the little Sobraon. Major-General Sir Harry Smith's was formed near the village of Guttah, with its right thrown up towards the Sutlej. Brigadier Cureton's cavalry, threatened, by feigned attacks, the ford of Hurrekee and the enemy's horse, under Rajah Lall Singh Misr, on the opposite bank. Brigadier Campbell, taking an intermediate position in the rear, between Major-General Gilbert's right and Major-General Sir Harry Smith's left, protected both. Major-General Sir Joseph Thackwell, under whom was Brigadier Scott, held in reserve on our left, ready to act as circumstances might demand, the rest of the Cavalry.

Our batteries of 9-pounders, enlarged into twelves, opened near the little Sobraon, with a brigade of howitzers, formed from the light field-batteries and troops of Horse-artillery, shortly after daybreak. But it was half-past six before the whole of our artillery fire was developed. It was the most spirited and well-directed. I cannot speak in terms too high of the judicious disposition of the guns, their admirable practice, or the activity with which the cannonade was sustained; but notwithstanding the formidable calibre of our iron guns, mortars, and howitzers, and the admirable way in which they were served, and aided by a rocket-battery, it would have been visionary to expect that they could, within any limited time, silence the fire of seventy pieces, behind well constructed batteries of earth, plank, and fascines; or dislodge troops covered either by redoubts or epaulements, or within a treble-line of trenches. The effect of the cannonade was, as has since proved by an inspection of the camp, most severely felt by the enemy; but it soon became evident that the issue of this struggle must be brought to the arbitrament of musketry and the bayonet.

At nine o'clock, Brigadier Stacey's brigade, supported on either flank by Captains Horsford's and Fordyce's batteries, and Lieut.-Colonel Lane's troop of Horse-artillery, moved to the attack in admirable order. The Infantry and guns aided each other correlatively. The former marched steadily on in line, which they halted only to correct when necessary. The latter took up successive positions at the gallop, until at length they were within three hundred yards of the heavy batteries of the Sikhs; but, notwithstanding the regularity and coolness, and scientific character of this assault, which Brigadier Wilkinson well supported, so hot was the fire of cannon, musketry, and zumbooruks kept up by the Khalsa troops, that it seemed for some moments impossible that the entrenchments could be won under it; but soon, persevering gallantly, we triumphed; and the whole army had the satisfaction to see the gallant Brigadier Stacey's soldiers driving the Sikhs in confusion within the area of their encampment. The 10th Foot, under Lieutenant-Colonel Franks, now for the first time brought into serious contact with the enemy, greatly distinguished themselves. This regiment never fired a shot till it got within the works of the enemy. The onset of her Majesty's 53rd Foot was as gallant and effective. The 43rd and 59th N.I. brigaded with them, emulated both in cool determination.

At the moment of this first success, I directed Brigadier the Hon. T. Ashburnham's brigade to move on in support; and Major-General Gilbert's and Sir Harry Smith's divisions to throw out their light troops to threaten their works, aided by artillery. As these attacks of the centre and right commenced, the fire of our heavy guns had first to be directed to the right, and then gradually to cease; but at one time the thunder of 120 pieces of ordnance reverberated in this mighty combat through the valley of the Sutlej; and as it was soon seen that the weight of the whole force within the Sikh camp was likely to be thrown upon the two brigades that had passed its trenches, it became necessary to convert into close and serious attacks the demonstrations with skirmishers and artillery of the centre and right; and the battle raged with inconceivable fury from right to left. The Sikhs, even when at particular points their entrenchments were mastered with the bayonet, strove to regain them by the fiercest conflict, sword in hand. Nor was it until the cavalry of the left, under Major-General Sir Joseph Thackwell, had moved forward, and ridden through the openings of the entrenchments made by our sappers, in single file, and re-formed as they passed them; and the 3rd Dragoons, whom no obstacle usually held formidable by horse appears to check, had on this day, as at Ferozeshah, galloped over and cut down the obstinate defenders of batteries and field-works, and until the full weight of three divisions of Infantry, with every Field-artillery gun which could be sent to their aid, had been cast into the scale, that victory finally declared for the British. The fire of the Sikhs first slackened and then nearly ceased; and the victors then pressing them on every side, precipitated them in masses over the bridge, and into the Sutlej, which a sudden rise of seven inches had rendered hardly fordable. In their efforts to reach the right bank, through the deepened water, they suffered from our Horse-artillery a terrible carnage. Hundreds fell under this cannonade; hundreds upon hundreds were drowned in attempting the perilous passage. Their awful slaughter, confusion, and dismay, were such as would have excited compassion in the hearts of their generous conquerors, if the Khalsa troops had not, in the early part of the action, sullied their gallantry by slaughtering and barbarously mangling every wounded soldier whom, in the vicissitudes of attack, the fortune of war left at their mercy. I must pause in this narrative, especially to notice the determined hardihood and bravery with which our battalions of Ghoorkhas, the Sirmoor and Nusseree, met the Sikhs wherever they were opposed to them. Soldiers of small stature, but indomitable spirit, they vied in ardent courage in the charge with the Grenadiers of our own nation; and armed with the short weapon of their mountains, were a terror to the Sikhs throughout this great combat.

Sixty-seven pieces of cannon, upwards of two hundred camel-swivels (zumbooruks), numerous standards, and vast munitions of war, captured by our troops, are the pledges and trophies of our victory. The battle was over by eleven in the morning, and in the forenoon I caused our engineers to burn a part and to sink a part of the vaunted bridge of the Khalsa army, across which they had boastfully come once more to defy us, and to threaten India with ruin and devastation.

The loss of the enemy has been immense; an estimate of it must be formed with a due allowance for the spirit of exaggeration which pervades all statements of Asiatics, where their interest leads them to magnify numbers; but our own observation on the river banks and in the enemy's camp combine, with the reports brought to our intelligence department, to convince me that the Khalsa casualties were between 8,000 and 10,000 men killed and wounded in action, and drowned in the passage of the river. Amongst the slain, are Sirdars Sham Singh, Attareewalla, Generals Gholab Singh, Koopta, and Heera Singh, Topee, Sirdar Kishen Singh, son of the late Jemadar Kooshall Singh, Generals Mobaruck Ally, and Illahee Buksh, and Shah Newaz Khan, son of Futteh-ood-deen Khan, of Kussoor. The body of Sham Singh was sought for in the captured camp by his followers; and, respecting the gallantry with which he is reported to have devoted himself to death rather than accompany the army in its flight, I forbade his people being molested in their search, which was finally successful.

The consequences of this great action have yet to be fully developed. It has at least, in God's providence, once more expelled the Sikhs from our territory, and planted our standards on the soil of the Punjaub. After occupying their entrenched position for nearly a month, the Khalsa army had, perhaps, mistaken the caution which had induced us to wait for the necessary material, for timidity. But they must now deeply feel, that the blow which has fallen on them from the British arm, has only been the heavier for being long delayed.

I have, etc.,
(Signed) H. Gough, General,
Commander-in-Chief, East Indies.

XII.

[Page 73.]

THE LATE MAJOR-GENERAL SIR ROBERT HENRY DICK.

The monument erected to the memory of Sir Robert Dick, at the church of Tullymet, Perthshire, by his brother officers, is of white marble; the main features being a sculptured representation of the veteran soldier, who has just received the deadly shot, whilst animating, by his dauntless example, Her Majesty's 80th Regiment. In the upper portion of the monument is a group of war trophies; and, surrounded by laurel, are inscribed the names of the several battles in which this gallant officer had participated.

SACRED TO THE MEMORY
OF
MAJOR-GENERAL SIR ROBERT HENRY DICK,
K.C.B., K.C.H.,
WHO, AFTER DISTINGUISHED SERVICES IN THE PENINSULA,
IN THE COMMAND OF A LIGHT BATTALION
AT WATERLOO, WITH THE 42ND ROYAL HIGHLAND REGIMENT, FELL
MORTALLY WOUNDED, WHILST LEADING THE THIRD DIVISION OF
THE ARMY OF THE SUTLEJ TO THE ATTACK ON THE
SIKH ENTRENCHED CAMP, AT SOBRAON,
ON THE
10TH OF FEBRUARY, 1846.

* * * * *

THE OFFICERS WHO HAD THE HONOUR OF SERVING UNDER HIM IN
HIS LAST BATTLE, AND OTHERS, HIS FRIENDS, IN HER
MAJESTY'S AND THE HONOURABLE EAST INDIA
COMPANY'S SERVICE, IN BENGAL,
HAVE CAUSED THIS MONUMENT TO BE PLACED IN
HIS PARISH CHURCH
IN TESTIMONY OF THEIR RESPECT AND AFFECTION FOR A
GENEROUS, COURTEOUS, AND CONSIDERATE

COMMANDER,
A GALLANT AND DEVOTED SOLDIER.

XIII.

[Page 76.]

PROCLAMATION OF PEACE.

Foreign Department, Camp, Lahore, Feb. 22nd, 1846.

The British Army has this day occupied the gateway of the citadel of Lahore the Badshahee Mosque, and the Hazuree Bagh. The remaining part of the citadel is the residence of his highness, the Maharajah, and also that of the families of the late Maharajah Runjeet Singh, for so many years the faithful ally of the British Government. In consideration of these circumstances, no troops will be posted within the precincts of the palace-gate.

The army of the Sutlej has now brought its operations in the field to a close, by the dispersion of the Sikh army, and the military occupation of Lahore, preceded by a series of the most triumphant successes ever recorded in the military history of India. The British Government, trusting to the faith of treaties, and to long subsisting friendship between the two states, had limited military preparations to the defence of its own frontier.

Compelled suddenly to assume the offensive, by the unprovoked invasion of its territories, the British army, under the command of its distinguished leader, has, in sixty days, defeated the Sikh forces in four general actions; has captured 220 pieces of field artillery; and is now at the capital, dictating to the Lahore Durbar the terms of a treaty, the conditions of which will tend to secure the British provinces from the repetition of a similar outrage. The Governor-General being determined, however, to mark with reprobation the perfidious character of the war, has required and will exact, that every remaining piece of Sikh artillery which has been pointed against the British army during the campaign shall be surrendered. The Sikh army, whose insubordinate conduct is one of the chief causes of the anarchy and misrule which have brought the Sikh state to the brink of destruction, is about to be disbanded.

The soldiers of the army of the Sutlej have not only proved their superior prowess in battle, but have, on every occasion, with subordination and patience, endured the fatigues and privations inseparable from a state of active operations in the field. The native troops of this army have also proved that a faithful attachment to their colours, and to the Company's service, is an honourable feature in the character of the British sepoy. The Governor-General has repeatedly expressed, on his own part and on that of the Government of India, admiration and gratitude for the important services which the army has rendered. The Governor-General is now pleased to resolve, as a testimony of the approbation of the Government of India of the bravery, discipline, and soldier-like bearing of the army of the Sutlej, that all the generals, officers, non-commissioned officers, and privates, shall receive a gratuity of twelve months' batta.

Every regiment which, in obedience to its orders, may have remained in posts and forts between Loodianna and Ferozepore, and was not present in action—as in the case of the troops ordered to remain at Moodkee to protect the wounded, and those left in the forts of Ferozepore and Loodianna—shall receive the gratuity of twelve months' batta. Obedience to orders is the first duty of a soldier; and the Governor-General, in affirming the principle, can never admit that absence caused by the performance of indispensable duties, on which the success of the operations in the field greatly depended, ought to disqualify any soldier placed in these circumstances, from participating in the gratuity given for the general good conduct of the army in the field. All regiments and individuals ordered to the frontier, and forming part of the army of the Sutlej, which may have reached Loodianna or Bussean before the date of this order, will be included as entitled to the gratuity.

By order of the Right Hon. the Governor-General of India,

F. Currie,
Secretary to the Government of India
with the Governor-General.

XIV.

[Page 76.]

FIRST TREATY WITH LAHORE OF 1846.

Treaty between the British Government and the State of Lahore, concluded at Lahore, on the 9th of March, 1846.

Whereas the treaty of amity and concord, which was concluded between the British Government and the late Maharajah Runjeet Singh, the Ruler of Lahore, in 1809, was broken by the unprovoked aggression on the British provinces, of the Sikh army, in December last: And whereas, on that occasion, by the Proclamation dated the 13th of December, the territories then in the occupation of the Maharajah of Lahore, on the left or British bank of the river Sutlej, were confiscated and annexed to the British provinces; and, since that time, hostile operations have been prosecuted by the two Governments, the one against the other, which have resulted in the occupation of Lahore by the British troops: And whereas it has been determined that, upon certain conditions, peace shall be re-established between the two Governments, the following treaty of peace between the Honourable English East India Company, and Maharajah Dhuleep Singh Bahadoor, and his children, heirs and successors, has been concluded, on the part of the Honourable Company, by Frederick Currie, Esq., and Brevet Major Henry Montgomery Lawrence, by virtue of full powers to that effect vested in them by the Right Honourable Sir Henry Hardinge, G.C.B., one of Her Britannic Majesty's most Honourable Privy Council, Governor-General, appointed by the Honourable Company to direct and control all their affairs in the East Indies; and, on the part of his Highness the Maharajah Dhuleep Singh, by Bhaee Ram Singh, Rajah Lall Singh, Sirdar Tej Singh, Sirdar Chutter Singh Attareewalla, Sirdar Runjoor Singh Mujetheea, Dewan Deena Nath, and Fakeer Noor-ood-deen, vested with full power and authority on the part of his Highness.

Article 1.—There shall be perpetual peace and friendship between the British Government, on the one part, and Maharajah Dhuleep Singh, his heirs and successors, on the other.

Article 2.—The Maharajah of Lahore renounces for himself, his heirs and successors, all claim to, or connection with, the territories lying to the south of the river Sutlej, and engages never to have any concern with those territories, or the inhabitants thereof.

Article 3.—The Maharajah cedes to the Honourable Company, in perpetual sovereignty, all his forts, territories, and rights, in the Doab, or country, hill and plain, situate between the rivers Beas and Sutlej.

Article 4.—The British Government having demanded from the Lahore State as indemnification for the expenses of the war, in addition to the cession of territory described in Article 3, payment of one and a half crores of rupees; and the Lahore Government being unable to pay the whole of this sum at this time, or to give security satisfactory to the British Government for its eventual payment; the Maharajah cedes to the Honourable Company, in perpetual sovereignty, as equivalent for one crore of rupees, all his forts, territories, rights, and interests, in the hill countries which are situate between the rivers Beas and Indus, including the provinces of Cashmere and Hazarah.

Article 5.—The Maharajah will pay to the British Government the sum of fifty lacs of rupees on or before the ratification of this treaty.

Article 6.—The Maharajah engages to disband the mutinous troops of the Lahore army, taking from them their arms; and his Highness agrees to reorganize the regular, or Aieen, or regiments of infantry, upon the system, and according to the regulations as to pay and allowances, observed in the time of the late Maharajah Runjeet Singh. The Maharajah further engages to pay up all arrears to the soldiers that are discharged under the provisions of this article.

Article 7.—The regular army of the Lahore State shall henceforth be limited to 25 battalions of infantry, consisting of 800 bayonets each, with 12,000 cavalry: this number at no time to be exceeded without the concurrence of the British Government. Should it be necessary at any time, for any special cause, that this force should be increased, the cause shall be fully explained to the British Government; and when the special necessity shall have passed, the regular troops shall be again reduced to the standard specified in the former clause of this article.

Article 8.—The Maharajah will surrender to the British Government all the guns, thirty-six in number, which have been pointed against the British troops, and which, having been placed on the right bank of the river Sutlej, were not captured at the battle of Sobraon.

Article 9.—The control of the rivers Beas and Sutlej, with the continuations of the latter river, commonly called the Garrah and Punjnud, to the confluence of the Indus at Mithenkote, and the control of the Indus from Mithenkote to the borders of Beloochistan, shall, in respect to tolls and ferries, rest with the British Government. The provisions of this article shall not interfere with the passage of boats belonging to the Lahore Government on the said rivers, for the purposes of traffic, or the conveyance of passengers up and down their course. Regarding the ferries between the two countries respectively, at the several ghâts of the said rivers, it is agreed that the British Government, after defraying all the expenses of management and establishments, shall account to the Lahore Government for one half of the net profits of the ferry collections. The provisions of this article have no reference to the ferries on that part of the river Sutlej which forms the boundary of Bhawulpore and Lahore respectively.

Article 10.—If the British Government should, at any time, desire to pass troops through the territories of his Highness the Maharajah, for the protection of the British territories, or those of their allies, the British troops shall, on such special occasions, due notice being given, be allowed to pass through the Lahore territories. In such case the officers of the Lahore State will afford facilities in providing supplies, and boats for the passage of rivers; and the British Government will pay the full price of all such provisions and boats, and will make fair compensation for all private property that may be endamaged. The British Government will more over observe all due consideration to the religious feelings of the inhabitants of those tracts through which the army may pass.

Article 11.—The Maharajah engages never to take, or retain, in his service, any British subject, nor the subject of any European or American State without the consent of the British Government.

Article 12.—In consideration of the services rendered by Rajah Goolab Singh of Jummoo to the Lahore State, towards procuring the restoration of the relations of amity between the Lahore and British Governments, the Maharajah hereby agrees to recognise the independent sovereignty of Rajah Goolab Singh, in such territories and districts in the hills as may be made over to the said Rajah Goolab Singh by separate agreement between himself and the British Government, with the dependencies thereof, which may have been in the Rajah's possession since the time of the late Maharajah Khurruk Singh: and the British Government, in consideration of the good conduct of Rajah Goolab Singh, also agrees to recognise his independence in such territories, and to admit him to the privileges of a separate treaty with the British Government.

Article 13.—In the event of any dispute or difference arising between the Lahore State and Rajah Goolab Singh, the same shall be referred to the arbitration of the British Government; and by its decision the Maharajah engages to abide.

Article 14.—The limits of the Lahore territories shall not be, at any time changed, without the concurrence of the British Government.

Article 15.—The British Government will not exercise any interference in the internal administration of the Lahore State; but in all cases or questions which may be referred to the British Government, the Governor-General will give the aid of his advice and good offices for the furtherance of the interests of the Lahore Government.

Article 16.—The subjects of either State shall, on visiting the territories of the other, be on the footing of the subjects of the most favoured nation.

This treaty, consisting of sixteen articles, has been this day settled by Frederick Currie, Esq., and Brevet Major Henry Montgomery Lawrence, acting under the directions of the Right Honourable Sir Henry Hardinge, G.C.B., Governor-General, on the part of the British Government; and by Bhaee Bam Singh, Rajah Lall Singh, Sirdar Tej Singh, Sirdar Chutter Singh Attareewalla, Sirdar Runjoor Singh Mujetheea, Dewan Deena Nath, and Fakeer Noor-ood-deen, on the part of Maharajah Dhuleep Singh; and the said treaty has been this day ratified by the seal of the Right Honourable Sir Henry Hardinge, G.C.B., Governor-General, and by that of his Highness Dhuleep Singh.

Done at Lahore, this 9th day of March, in the year of our Lord 1846, corresponding with the 10th day of Rubbeeool-awul, 1262, Hijree, and ratified on the same day.

[Page 76.]

SUPPLEMENTARY ARTICLES TO THE FIRST TREATY WITH LAHORE OF 1846.

Articles of Agreement concluded between the British Government and the Lahore Durbar, on the 11th of March, 1846.

Whereas the Lahore Government has solicited the Governor-General to leave a British force at Lahore for the protection of the Maharajah's person and of the capital, till the reorganization of the Lahore army, according to the provisions of Article 6 of the Treaty of Lahore, dated the 9th instant: And whereas the Governor-General has, on certain conditions, consented to the measure: And whereas it is expedient that certain matters concerning the territories ceded by articles 3 and 4 of the aforesaid treaty should be specifically determined; the following eight articles of agreement have this day been concluded between the afore-mentioned contracting parties.

Article 1.—The British Government shall leave at Lahore, till the close of the current year, A.D. 1846, such force as shall seem to the Governor-General adequate for the purpose of protecting the person of the Maharajah, and the inhabitants of the city of Lahore, during the reorganization of the Sikh army, in accordance with the provisions of article 6 of the treaty of Lahore; that force to be withdrawn at any convenient time before the expiration of the year, if the object to be fulfilled shall, in the opinion of the Durbar, have been obtained; but the force shall not be detained at Lahore beyond the expiration of the current year.

Article 2.—The Lahore Government agrees that the force left at Lahore for the purpose specified in the foregoing article, shall be placed in full possession of the fort and the city of Lahore, and that the Lahore troops shall be removed from within the city. The Lahore Government engages to furnish convenient quarters for the officers and men of the said force, and to pay to the British Government all the extra expenses in regard to the said force, which may be incurred by the British Government, in consequence of them troops being employed away from their own cantonments, and in a foreign territory.

Article 3.—The Lahore Government engages to apply itself immediately and earnestly to the reorganization of its army, according to the prescribed conditions, and to communicate fully with the British authorities left at Lahore, as to the progress of such reorganization, and as to the location of the troops.

Article 4.—If the Lahore Government fails in the performance of the conditions of the foregoing article, the British government shall be at liberty to withdraw the force from Lahore, at any time before the expiration of the period specified in Article 1.

Article 5.—The British Government agrees to respect the *bonâ fide* rights of those Jaghirdars within the territories ceded by Articles 3 and 4 of the Treaty of Lahore, dated the 9th instant, who were attached to the families of the late Maharajah Runjeet Singh, Khurruk Singh and Shere Singh; and the British Government wall maintain these Jaghirdars in their *bonâ fide* possessions, during their lives.

Article 6.—The Lahore Government shall receive the assistance of the British local authorities in recovering the arrears of revenue justly due to the Lahore Government from their Kardars and managers in the territories ceded by the provisions of Articles 3 and 4 of the Treaty of Lahore, to the close of the Khureef harvest of the current year, viz. 1902, of the Sumbut Bikramajeet.

Article 7.—The Lahore Government shall be at liberty to remove from the forts in the territories specified in the foregoing article, all treasures and state property with the exception of guns. Should, however, the British Government desire to retain any part of the said property, they shall be at liberty to do so, paying for the same at a fair valuation; and the British officers shall give their assistance to the Lahore Government in disposing on the spot of such part of the aforesaid property as the Lahore Government may not wish to remove, and the British officers may not desire to retain.

Article 8.—Commissioners shall be immediately appointed by the two Governments, to settle and lay down the boundary between the two States, as defined by Article 4 of the Treaty of Lahore, dated March the 9th, 1846.

XV.

[Page 78.]

PUNCHEES OR PUNCHAYETS.

Puncheess or Punchayets were a jury or assembly of five persons. These assemblies, which were of very ancient origin, obtained, both in the military and civil services of the Sikhs. In the former, five men who had distinguished themselves by their valour, were selected from every battalion or company, and to them were referred for decision, all affairs which brought the army into contact with the Government. In the latter, every tribe had its Punt. The system was also generally adopted in every trade and calling. The decision of the Punchees was definitive.

XVI.

[Page 79.]

TREATY WITH GOOLAB SINGH OF 1846.

Treaty between the British Government and Maharajah Goolab Singh, concluded at Umritsur on March 16th, 1846.

Treaty between the British Government on the one part, and Maharajah Goolab Singh of Jummoo on the other, concluded on the part of the British Government, by Frederick Currie, Esq., and Brevet Major Henry Montgomery Lawrence, acting under the orders of the Right Honourable Sir Henry Hardinge, G.C.B., one of Her Britannic Majesty's most Honourable Privy Council, Governor-General, appointed by the Honourable Company to direct and control all their affairs in the East Indies, and by Maharajah Goolab Singh in person.

Article 1.—The British Government transfers and makes over, for ever, in independent possession, to Maharajah Goolab Singh, and the heirs male of his body, all the hilly or mountainous country, with its dependencies, situated to the eastward of the river Indus, and westward of the river Ravee, including Chumba and excluding Lahool, being part of the territory ceded to the British Government by the Lahore State, according to the provisions of Article 4 of the Treaty of Lahore, dated March the 9th, 1846.

Article 2.—The eastern boundary of the tract transferred by the foregoing Article to Maharajah Goolab Singh shall be laid down by commissioners appointed by the British Government and Maharajah Goolab Singh respectively, for that purpose, and shall be defined in a separate engagement, after survey.

Article 3.—In consideration of the transfer made to him and his heirs by the provisions of the foregoing Articles, Maharajah Goolab Singh will pay to the British Government the sum of seventy-five lakhs of rupees (Nanukshahee), fifty lakhs to be paid on ratification of this treaty, and twenty-five lakhs on or before the 1st of October of the current year, A.D. 1846.

Article 4.—The limits of the territories of Maharajah Goolab Singh shall not be at any time changed without the concurrence of the British Government.

Article 5.—Maharajah Goolab Singh will refer to the arbitration of the British Government any disputes or questions that may arise between himself and the Government of Lahore, or any other neighbouring State, and will abide by the decision of the British Government.

Article 6.—Maharajah Goolab Singh engages for himself and heirs, to join, with the whole of his military force, the British troops, when employed within the hills, or in the territories adjoining his possessions. Article 7.—Maharajah Goolab Singh engages never to take, or retain, in his service any British subject, nor the subject of any European or American State, without the consent of the British Government.

Article 8.—Maharajah Goolab Singh engages to respect, in regard to the territory transferred to him, the provisions of Articles 5, 6, and 7, of the separate engagement between the British Government and the Lahore Durbar, dated March the 11th, 1846.

Article 9.—The British Government will give its aid to Maharajah Goolab Singh, in protecting his territories from external enemies.

Article 10.—Maharajah Goolab Singh acknowledges the supremacy of the British Government, and will, in token of such supremacy, present annually to the British Government one horse, twelve perfect shawl goats of approved breed (six male and six female), and three pairs of Cashmere shawls.

This treaty, consisting of ten articles, has been this day settled by Frederick Currie, Esq., and Brevet Major Henry Montgomery Lawrence, acting under the directions of the Right Honourable Sir Henry Hardinge, G.C.B., Governor-General, on the part of the British Government, and by Maharajah Goolab Singh in person; and the said treaty has been this day ratified by the seal of the Right Honourable Sir Henry Hardinge, G.C.B., Governor-General.

Done at Umritsur, this 16th day of March, in the year of our Lord 1846, corresponding with the 17th day of Rubbeeool-awul, 1262, Hijree.

XVII.

[Page 79.]

SECOND TREATY WITH LAHORE OF 1846.

Foreign Department, Camp, Bhyrowal Ghât, on the left Bank of the Beas, the 22nd of December, 1846.

The late Governor of Cashmere on the part of the Lahore State, Sheik Imam Ooddeen, having resisted by force of arms the occupation of the province of Cashmere by Maharajah Goolab Singh, the Lahore Government was called upon to coerce their subject, and to make over the province to the representative of the British Government, in fulfilment of the conditions of the treaty of Lahore, dated the 9th of March, 1846.

A British force was employed to support and aid, if necessary, the combined forces of the Lahore State and Maharajah Goolab Singh in the above operations.

Sheik Imam Ooddeen intimated to the British Government that he was acting under orders received from the Lahore Durbar in the course he was pursuing; and stated that the insurrection was instigated by written instructions received by him from the Vizier Rajah Lall Singh.

Sheik Imam Ooddeen surrendered to the British Agent on a guarantee from that officer, that if the Sheik could, as he asserted, prove that his acts were in accordance with his instructions, and that the opposition was instigated by the Lahore minister, the Durbar should not be permitted to inflict upon him, either in his person or his property, any penalty on account of his conduct on this occasion. The British Agent pledged his Government to a full and impartial investigation of the matter.

A public inquiry was instituted into the facts adduced by Sheik Imam Ood-deen, and it was fully established that Rajah Lall Singh did secretly instigate the Sheik to oppose the occupation by Maharajah Goolab Singh of the province of Cashmere.

The Governor-General immediately demanded that the ministers and Chiefs of the Lahore State should depose and exile to the British provinces the Vizier Rajah Lall Singh.

* * * * *

His Lordship consented to accept the deposition of Rajah Lall Singh as an atonement for the attempt to infringe the treaty by the secret intrigues and machinations of the Vizier. It was not proved that the other members of the Durbar had cognizance of the Vizier's proceedings; and the conduct of the Sirdars, and of the Sikh army in the late operations for quelling the Cashmere insurrection, and removing the obstacles to the fulfilment of the treaty, proved that the criminality of the Vizier was not participated in by the Sikh nation.

The Ministers and Chiefs unanimously decreed, and carried into immediate effect, the deposition of the Vizier.

After a few days' deliberations, relative to the means of forming a Government at Lahore, the remaining members of the Durbar, in concert with all the Sirdars and Chiefs of the State, solicited the interference and aid of the British Government for the maintenance of an administration, and the protection of the Maharajah Dhuleep Singh during the minority of his Highness.

This solicitation by the Durbar and Chiefs has led to the temporary modification of the relations between the British Government and that of Lahore, established by the treaty of the 9th of March of the present year.

The terms and conditions of this modification are set forth in the following Articles of Agreement.

Articles of Agreement concluded between the British Government and the Lahore Durbar, on 16th of December, 1846.

Whereas the Lahore Durbar and the principal Chiefs and Sirdars of the State have, in express terms, communicated to the British Government their anxious desire that the Governor-General should give his aid and his assistance to maintain the administration of the Lahore State during the minority of Maharajah Dhuleep Singh, and have declared this measure to be indispensable for the maintenance of the government: And whereas the Governor-General has, under certain conditions, consented to give the aid and assistance solicited, the following articles of agreement, in modification of the articles of agreement executed at Lahore on the 11th of March last, have been concluded, on the part of the British Government, by Frederick Currie, Esq., Secretary to the Government of India, and Lieutenant-Colonel Henry Montgomery Lawrence, C.B., Agent to the Governor-General, North-West Frontier, by virtue of full power to that effect vested in them by the Right Honourable Viscount Hardinge, G.C.B., Governor-General, and on the part of his Highness Maharajah Dhuleep Singh, by Sirdar Tej Singh, Sirdar Shere Singh, Dewan Deena Nath, Fakeer Noor-ood-deen, Raee Kishen Chund, Sirdar Runjoor Singh Mujetheea, Sirdar Utter Singh Kaleewalla, Bhaee Nidhan Singh, Sirdar Kan Singh Mujetheea, Sirdar Shumshere Singh, Sirdar Lall Singh Morarea, Sirdar Kher Singh Sindhanwalla, Sirdar Urjun Singh Rungmungleea, acting with the unanimous consent and concurrence of the Chiefs and Sirdars of the State assembled at Lahore.

Article 1.—All and every part of the treaty of peace between the British Government and the state of Lahore, bearing date the 9th day of March, 1846, except in so far as it may be temporarily modified in respect to clause 15 of the said treaty by this engagement, shall remain binding upon the two Governments.

Article 2.—A British officer, with an efficient establishment of assistants, shall be appointed by the Governor-General to remain at Lahore, which officer shall have full authority to direct and control all matters in every department of the State.

Article 3.—Every attention shall be paid in conducting the Administration to the feelings of the people, to preserving the national institutions and customs, and to maintain the just rights of all classes.

Article 4.—Changes in the mode and details of administration shall not be made, except when found necessary for effecting the objects set forth in the foregoing clause, and for securing the just dues of the Lahore Government. These details shall be conducted by native officers, as at present, who shall be appointed and superintended by a Council of Regency, composed of leading Chiefs and Sirdars, acting under the control and guidance of the British Resident.

Article 5.—The following persons shall in the first instance constitute the Council of Regency, *viz.*—Sirdar Tej Singh, Sirdar Shere Singh Attareewalla, Dewan Deena Nath, Fakeer Noor-ood-deen, Sirdar Runjoor Singh Mujetheea, Bhaee Nidhan Singh, Sirdar Utter Singh Kaleewalla, Sirdar Shumshere Singh Sindhanwalla; and no change shall be made in the persons thus nominated, without the consent of the British Resident, acting under the orders of the Governor-General.

Article 6.—The administration of the country shall be conducted by this Council of Regency in such manner as may be determined on by themselves in consultation with the British Resident, who shall have full authority to direct and control the duties of every department.

Article 7.—A British force, of such strength and numbers, and in such positions, as the Governor-General may think fit, shall remain at Lahore for the protection of the Maharajah, and the preservation of the peace of the country.

Article 8.—The Governor-General shall be at liberty to occupy with British soldiers any fort or military post in the Lahore territories, the occupation of which may be deemed necessary by the British Government for the security of the capital, or for maintaining the peace of the country.

Article 9.—The Lahore State shall pay to the British Government twenty-two lakhs of new Nanukshahee rupees, of full tale and weight, per annum, for the maintenance of this force, and to meet the expenses incurred by the British Government, such sum to be paid by two instalments, or 13 lakhs and 20,000 in May or June, and 8 lakhs and 80,000 in November or December of each year.

Article 10.—Inasmuch as it is fitting that her Highness the Maharannee, the mother of Maharajah Dhuleep Singh, should have a proper provision made for the maintenance of herself and dependents, the sum of one lakh and 50,000 rupees shall be set apart annually for that purpose, and shall be at her Highness's disposal.

Article 11.—The provisions of this engagement shall have effect during the minority of his Highness Maharajah Dhuleep Singh, and shall cease and terminate on his Highness attaining the full age of 16 years, or on the 4th September of the year 1854; but it shall be competent to the Governor-General to cause the arrangement to cease, at any period prior to the coming of age of his Highness, at which the Governor-General and the Lahore Durbar may be satisfied that the interposition of the British Government is no longer necessary for maintaining the government of his Highness the Maharajah.

This agreement, consisting of eleven articles, was settled and executed at Lahore, by the officers and Chiefs and Sirdars above named, on the 16th day of December, 1846.

XVIII.

[Page 79.]

NOTIFICATION.

Foreign Department, Camp, Ferozepore.
March, 30.

The Governor-General is pleased to direct, that the accompanying Proclamation, by which the Punjaub is declared to be a portion of the British Empire in India, be published for general information, and that a royal salute be fired at every principal station of the army, on the receipt thereof.

By order of the Right Honourable,
the Governor-General of India.
P. Melvill,
Under Secretary to the Government of India,
with the Governor-General.

* * * * *

PROCLAMATION OF THE GOVERNOR GENERAL.

Head Quarters, Ferozepore,
March 29, 1849.

For many years, in the time of Maharajah Runjeet Singh, peace and friendship prevailed between the British nation and the Sikhs. When Runjeet Singh was dead, and his wisdom no longer guided the counsels of the state, the Sirdars and Khalsa army, without provocation and without cause, suddenly invaded the British territories. Their army was again and again defeated. They were driven with slaughter and in shame from the country they had invaded, and, at the gates of Lahore, the Maharajah, Dhuleep Singh, tendered to the Governor-General the submission of himself and his chiefs, and solicited the clemency of the British Government. The Governor-General extended the clemency of his Government to the State of Lahore, he generously spared the kingdom which he had acquired a just right to subvert; and the Maharajah having been replaced on the throne, treaties of friendship were formed between the States.

The British have faithfully kept their word, and have scrupulously observed every obligation which the treaties imposed upon them. But the Sikh people and their chiefs have, on their part, grossly and faithlessly violated the promises by which they were bound. Of their annual tribute no portion whatever has at any time been paid, and large loans advanced to them by the Government of India have never been repaid. The control of the British Government, to which they voluntarily submitted themselves, has been resisted by arms. Peace has been cast aside. British officers have been murdered when acting for the State; others engaged in the like employment have treacherously been thrown into captivity. Finally, the whole of the State and the whole Sikh people, joined by many of the Sirdars in the Punjaub who signed the treaties, and led by a member of the Regency itself, have risen in arms against us, and have waged a fierce and bloody war for the proclaimed purpose of destroying the British and their power.

The Government of India formerly declared that it required no further conquest and it proved by its acts the sincerity of its professions. The Government of India has no desire for conquest now; but it is bound in its duty to provide fully for its own security, and to guard the interests of those committed to its charge. To that end, and as the only sure mode of protecting the State from the perpetual recurrence of unprovoked and wasting wars, the Governor-General is compelled to resolve upon the entire subjection of a people whom their own Government has long been unable to control, and whom (as events have now shown) no punishment can deter from violence, no act of friendship can conciliate to peace. Wherefore the Governor-General of India has declared, and hereby proclaims, that the kingdom of the Punjaub is at an end; and that all the territories of Maharajah Dhuleep Singh, are now and henceforth a portion of the British empire in India. His Highness the Maharajah shall be treated with consideration and with honour.

The few chiefs who have not engaged in hostilities against the British shall retain their property and their rank. The British Government shall leave to all the people, whether Mussulman, Hindoo or Sikh, the free exercise of their own religions, but it will not permit any man to interfere with others in the observance of such forms and customs as their respective religions may either enjoin or permit.

The jaghires and all the property of Sirdars, and others who have been in arms against the British, shall be confiscated to the State. The defences of every fortified place in the Punjaub which is not occupied by British troops shall be totally destroyed, and effectual measures shall be taken to deprive the people of the means of renewing either tumult or war.

The Governor-General calls upon all the inhabitants of the Punjaub, Sirdars, and people, to submit themselves peaceably to the authority of the British Government, which has hereby been proclaimed.

Over those who shall live as obedient and peaceful subjects of the State, the British Government will rule with mildness and beneficence. But if resistance to constituted authority shall again be attempted, if violence and turbulence be renewed, the Governor-General warns the people of the Punjaub that the time for leniency will then have passed away, and that their offence will be punished with prompt and most rigorous severity.

By order of the Right Honourable the
Governor-General of India.
H.M. Elliott,
Secretary to the Government of India,
with the Governor-General.

XIX.

[Page 95.]

SUPPLY OF HORSES IN INDIA.

After Shah Soojah of Cabool had lost his throne, the number of Northern horses formerly sent to India became greatly reduced. Hence studs were formed by the East India Company in Bengal. Some of the stud horses have English, some Arab blood. The losses in the Sikh campaign of 1845-46 were 1,300 horses killed and wounded. Now the animal re-mount is equal to about one twentieth of the full complement of Horse Artillery, Dragoons, Light Cavalry, and Field Batteries; so, supposing the complement to be 10,000 horses, the re-mounts yearly are 500. Some time since an officer was sent to Sydney, New South Wales, to procure horses. Many of these horses have heavy shoulders; but it is certain that good and serviceable ones may be bred in New South Wales. A mixture of English and Arab blood is required; and the stud should be there and not in India. Some persons, however, are of opinion that it is best to breed them in the climate in which they are to live. Lord William Bentinck nearly destroyed the central stud at Buxar and Kurruntadhee. The Cape has been tried; but the horses though strong are under size.

XX.

[Page 114.]

REVENUE OF THE EMPEROR OF DELHI.

One hundred and twenty thousand pounds seems to be a large sum even as the annual revenue of an Emperor of Delhi, but it must be borne in mind that the Emperor's family, including his seraglio, suite, and dependents, amounted, at least, to 4,000 persons. Just now there is a political difficulty respecting the succession to the throne of Delhi. When Shah Allum died in 1806, he was succeeded by his eldest son, Akbar, although he endeavoured to secure the throne for his third son, Wulli Ahud; but this was refused by the British Government. The present Emperor (1854), desires that his younger son, Prince Jewan Bukht, should succeed him, and has actually invested him with the imperial dignity without waiting for the sanction of the East India Company. Generally speaking, younger sons are more obedient to their fathers; for the eldest often sticks upon his rights, and this doubtless is the case in the family of the Emperor of Delhi.

XXI.

[Page 132.]

NOTICE OF DR. JAMES, BISHOP OF CALCUTTA.

This extract is from the pen of my lamented friend the late Right Reverend Dr. James, Lord Bishop of Calcutta, in his most interesting work, entitled "Journal of a Tour through Germany, Sweden, Russia, and Poland," 1813-1814, third edition 1819, vol. i., pp. 5-6. Poor Dr. James was for some years, and up to the period of his leaving England for India, Vicar of Silsoe, in Bedfordshire, where I resided with my father during my holidays—for I am speaking now of more than twenty years ago, at a period when I was at the school of my most esteemed friend and much valued correspondent, the Rev. John Fell, M.A., Huntingdon—I can remember distinctly Dr. James's kind and excellent advice to me, and the undissembled pleasure which shone in his countenance every time I met him. How very brief was his term of usefulness in his far distant diocese, for he only reached it to die there!

XXII.

[Page 136.]

ANCIENT SCRIPTURAL CUSTOMS.

There are many customs observed in India which are mentioned in the Old and New Testaments, to wit:—the custom above named of *drawing water,* "Behold, I stand here by the well of water; and the daughters of the men of the city come out to draw water." Gen. xxiv. 13. "And the damsel was very fair to look upon; and she went down to the well, and filled her pitcher, and came up," verse 16; and in verse 15 we read, "with her pitcher upon her shoulder."—Again "*trough for watering cattle.*" In India there are troughs made of brick and mortar, and sometimes also of earth, whither the camels and horses are taken to drink water.—*Cakes,* "And make cakes upon the hearth" Gen. xviii. 6. These cakes are placed upon an iron plate and turned often.—*Milch Camels,* "Thirty milch camels with their colts," Gen. xxxii. 15. The milk of camels is drunk by the natives of India when in a weak state of health; it is more nutritious than asses' milk, and is very fattening.—*Earrings,* "And all their ear-rings which were in their ears," Gen. xxxv. 4. Men as well as women in India wear ear-rings, nay even many of the native officers of the Sepoy corps.—*Wheat in a mortar,* "Though thou shouldest bray a fool in a mortar among wheat with a pestle," Prov. xxvii. 22. Wheat is frequently brayed in a mortar to clear it from the chaff.—*Not new wine into old bottles,* Our Saviour said, "Neither do men put new wine into old bottles; else the bottles break, and the wine runneth out, and the bottles perish: but they put new wine into new bottles: and both are preserved," Matt. ix. 17. Sir J. Chardin, a well-known traveller in India says; compare Joshua ix. 4. "The Arabs and all those who live a wandering life, still keep their milk, water, and other liquors in leathern bottles (*mashks*) which are generally made of goats' skins." In India water is put into sheeps' skins. "These natives never go a journey without a small leathern bottle of water hanging by their side like a scrip; when these bottles are old, and much used, they mend them, either by sewing on a piece, or by gathering up the broken place, in the manner of a purse." The Bombay Column which went to Affghanistan and Cabool, in 1839, had each man a little keg of wood, painted white, large enough to contain a quart of water; and it is to be regretted that the troops in the Sikh campaign of 1845-6 were not similarly supplied, for they suffered much from want of water. Surgeon Taylor in his report of killed and wounded, in H.M. 29th regiment, with the army of the Sutlej, in 1845-46, says; "during the three days they remained exposed to the powerful heat of the sun by day, and the very disproportionately cold air of the night, many of them suffered from the most agonizing thirst; only a very small quantity of water could be got, and that was very putrid. The excessive thirst of the men, and the impossibility of obtaining water may be judged of by the fact, that on the morning of the 22nd, men of this and other regiments were literally seen to drink their own urine."

Grinding grain, "Two women shall be grinding at the mill; the one shall be taken and the other left," Matt. xxiv. 41. Dr. E. Clarke says; "The two women, seated on the ground, held between them two round flat stones. In the centre of the upper stone was a cavity for pouring in the corn, and by the side of this, an upright wooden handle, for moving the stone. As the operation began, one of the women, with her right hand, pushed this handle to the woman opposite, who again sent it to her companion; thus communicating a rotary and very rapid motion to the upper stone, the left hand being all the while employed in supplying fresh corn, as fast as the bran and flour escaped from the sides of the machine."

The above are large stones, called in India chakkis, sometimes a smaller kind is used by one woman who turns the chakki round with her right hand, from left to right, in the same rotary motion; the women may be heard at this work in the villages before daybreak, singing their monotonous songs to while away the time. They also form an important appendage to a cavalry corps, having to grind all the corn required for the horses.

THE END.

Printed by Libri Plureos GmbH in Hamburg,
Germany